A SPINOZA READER

A Spinoza Reader

THE *ETHICS* AND
OTHER WORKS

Benedict de Spinoza

EDITED AND
TRANSLATED BY

Edwin Curley

PRINCETON UNIVERSITY
PRESS

Copyright © 1994 by Princeton University Press
Published by Princeton University Press, 41 William Street,
Princeton, New Jersey 08540
In the United Kingdom: Princeton University Press,
Chichester, West Sussex

Libraby of Congress Cataloging-in-Publication Data

Spinoza, Benedictus de, 1632–1677.
[Selections. English. 1994]
A Spinoza reader : the Ethics and other works / Benedict de
Spinoza ; edited and translated by Edwin Curley.
p. cm.
Includes index
ISBN 0-691-03363-3 (alk. paper) — ISBN 0-691-00067-0 (pbk. : alk. paper)
1. Philosophy—Early works to 1800. 2. Ethics—Early works to 1800
I. Spinoza, Benedictus de, 1632–1677. Ethica. English. 1994.
II. Curley, E. M. (Edwin M.), 1937– . III. Title.
B3958.C87 1994
199'.492—dc20   93-1628

This book has been composed in Adobe Janson

Princeton University Press books are printed on
acid-free paper and meet the guidelines for permanence
and durability of the Committee on Production
Guidelines for Book Longevity of the
Council on Library Resources

Printed in the United States of America

6   8   10   9   7

For Richard

CONTENTS

CONTENTS

INTRODUCTION

I. Spinoza's Life and Philosophy

Most philosophers lead lives of quiet contemplation, and for the most part Spinoza's life was no exception. He read, he thought, he wrote, and the only moments of high drama in his life occurred when what he thought and wrote brought him into conflict with the society in which he lived. In the early years his radical ideas about religion led to his expulsion from the Dutch Jewish community in which he had been brought up, and (according to his early biographers) led one of its members to make an attempt on his life. The widespread perception that his work was atheistic made it impossible, in his lifetime, to publish the definitive expression of his religious ideas, his *Ethics*. Later his commitment to the tolerant, republican politics of the De Witt brothers led him to write and speak out on behalf of their program, again at some danger to his life. This volume will try to tell the first half of that story, focusing on Spinoza the revolutionary religious thinker, and leaving the story of Spinoza the political thinker for another day.

Benedict[1] de Spinoza was born on 24 November 1632 to Michael de Spinoza, a prosperous member of the Amsterdam Jewish community, and to Deborah, his second wife. Like many Jews of the time, the Spinozas had originally come to Holland as a refuge from religious persecution in Spain and Portugal. Toward the end of the fifteenth century Ferdinand and Isabella had given Spanish Jews an unpleasant choice: either convert to Christianity or go into exile (leaving their gold and silver behind, to become the crown's). Since most of the major European countries of the time either barred the Jews completely or imposed severe restrictions on them, many chose to make at least a nominal conversion.

But life as a *converso* (or "new Christian" or "Marrano") was not easy. Quite apart from the internal conflicts generated by having to practice a religion in which they did not believe, and by being false to the religion in which they did believe, they had to live under the surveillance of an Inquisition suspicious of the sincerity of these conversions. It was

---

[1] Before his excommunication Spinoza was known either as "Baruch" (which means *blessed* in Hebrew) or as "Bento" (the Portuguese equivalent). After his excommunication he adopted the Latin version of that name.

difficult to maintain, even in secret, the traditions and faith so important to their conception of themselves as Jews. When it seemed safe to do so, they began to emigrate. Many went first to Portugal, where they found conditions little better. Most ultimately wound up in the Netherlands, which had been under the political control of Spain, but which was, by the end of the sixteenth century, engaged in a war of independence against its former master, and had a tradition of relative religious toleration. There the Jews were allowed, at least informally, to practice their religion.[2]

Spinoza's mother died just before he turned six. When he was nine, his father married again, this time to a spinster of forty. This stepmother died when Spinoza was nineteen and his father followed a year and a half later when Spinoza was twenty-one. In addition, his childhood saw the deaths of a half-brother, when he was sixteen, and a sister, when he was eighteen. Later Spinoza was to write that the "free man thinks of nothing less than of death, and his wisdom is a meditation on life, not on death" (E IVP67). If Spinoza attained such freedom, it was not without having had considerable experience with death.

All indications are that he had the kind of education normal for a young Jew of that time and place. He would have begun attending the Talmud Torah school at about age seven, learning first to read the traditional prayers, then the Hebrew Bible. At about age thirteen or fourteen he would have been introduced to the study of the Talmud and of medieval Jewish philosophy. Entrance into these higher studies did not imply an intention to become a rabbi; most were there simply to learn more of the Holy Law. This religious education was all the more precious to the members of the community because it had been denied them during their years as *conversos* in the Iberian peninsula. It was this kind of education the editor of Spinoza's *Opera posthuma* was referring to when he wrote that

> from his childhood on the author was trained in letters, and in his youth for many years he was occupied principally with theology; but when he reached the age at which the intellect is mature and capable of investigating the nature of things, he gave himself up entirely to philosophy. He was driven by a burning desire for knowledge; but because he did not get full satisfaction either from his teachers or from those writing about these sciences, he decided

[2] Official permission for public worship did not come until 1619, and full citizenship was granted only in 1657, by which time Spinoza was no longer a member of the community.

to see what he himself could do in these areas. For that purpose he found the writings of the famous René Descartes, which he came upon at that time, very useful.[3]

This passage is as interesting for the questions it raises as for those it answers. Why, for instance, did the young Spinoza find the instruction he received from his teachers unsatisfactory? And what was it about the writings of Descartes which attracted him?

The answer to the first of these questions seems to be that the close study of Scripture, and of the traditional commentaries on Scripture, is apt to raise many doubts in a mind as acute as Spinoza's. How are we to take the anthropomorphic conception of God we often find in Scripture? How are we to reconcile the conception of a God subject to human limitations, a God often presented as having a corporeal form, a God apt to be angry with his creatures, and to repent of having created them, with the philosophic conception of God as a perfect being? Can we reconcile the philosophic conception of God with the Scriptural conception of him as intervening miraculously in natural processes which seem to be thought of as manifesting a power distinct from God's? Is there any basis in Scripture (i.e., in what Christians would call the Old Testament) for the belief in an afterlife in which the soul survives the body, the good are rewarded, and the evil punished? How are we to understand the traditional belief that the Jews are God's chosen people? Why would God not communicate knowledge of his existence, nature, and commandments to all men? And if the Jews are God's chosen people, how could he permit their terrible suffering at the hands of the Inquisition and other persecutors? What attitude should a reasonable man take to a system of law whose complexity is matched only by the apparent arbitrariness of many of its requirements? How are we to reconcile the chronology of the world implied in Scripture with the existence of civilizations which go back many thousands of years before the supposed date of the creation? Or the traditional view that Scripture is God's revelation of himself to man with the internal evidence which shows it to be "full of faults, mutilated, tampered with, and inconsistent," the work of many fallible human hands over many generations, often writing many years after the events they recorded? To judge from what Spinoza later wrote,[4] and from the ideas circulating among the

---

[3] From Jarig Jelles' preface to Spinoza's *Nagelate Schriften* (*Posthumous Works*), given in F. Akkerman, *Studies in the Posthumous Works of Spinoza* (Krips Repro Meppel, 1980), pp. 216–217.

[4] See, for example, the selections from the *Theological-Political Treatise*, in §II of the Preliminaries.

more heterodox members of the Amsterdam Jewish community, free thinkers with whom Spinoza is known to have associated, doubts like these must have been among those which led the young Spinoza to be dissatisfied with the education he had received from the rabbis.

By the time he was in his early twenties he was working in his father's import business, and learning Latin from an ex-Jesuit, Francis van den Enden. One of Spinoza's earliest biographers, a Lutheran minister in the Hague named Colerus, claimed that Van den Enden had taught his students more than Latin, that he sowed the seeds of atheism in their minds. Perhaps. But this much seems reasonably certain: through his instruction Van den Enden did enlarge Spinoza's cultural horizons, giving him not only a good acquaintance with classical authors like Terence, Ovid, Tacitus, Cicero, and Seneca, but also some familiarity with modern philosophers like Descartes and Hobbes. In both these authors Spinoza would have found much to encourage him to distrust tradition and authority, and to rely on his own intellectual abilities. He would also have found a method for investigating the truth which, to judge from the *Ethics*, he came to think provided the proper model: the mathematical method of beginning with simple, evident truths, axioms and definitions, and proceeding from them by careful deductive steps.

At some point during this process of doubt and discovery, the Jewish community excommunicated him. We know the date of this event (27 July 1656), but we do not know much, with any certainty, about the reasons for it. The sentence of excommunication refers vaguely to Spinoza's "evil opinions and acts," and it has been suggested that his acts (and omissions) weighed more heavily in the proceedings against him than his opinions did. Excommunication was a common method of discipline in the community, often imposed for comparatively trivial offenses and lifted after the offender mended his ways. Because the rabbis and elders of the community were engaged in a constant struggle to reintroduce the ex-Marranos into the religious traditions of Judaism, and to restore a pattern of Jewish life which had been disrupted by the period of Christian practice and education, "the issue of unity was . . . more crucial than any other . . . acts like Spinoza's, which challenged tradition in the name of freedom of thought and sabotaged the endeavor to repair the torn fabric of Jewish life, could not be tolerated."[5] If Spinoza had been content to keep his opinions to himself, and to maintain an external adherence to the requirements of Jewish law, he

[5] Yirmiahu Yovel, "Why Spinoza Was Excommunicated," *Commentary*, November 1977, p. 50.

might have escaped excommunication. There are credible reports that he was offered a pension if he would keep up his attendance at the synagogue. Whether we believe those reports or not, it is evident that by this time in his life Spinoza was unwilling to do what would have been necessary to remain in the community.

This was no light matter. The sentence of excommunication forbade members of the community to have anything to do with him: "None may communicate with him by word of mouth or writing, nor show him any charity whatsoever, nor stay with him under one roof, nor come into his company, nor read any composition made or written by him." This would have made it impossible for him to continue to run the family business, as he and a younger brother had been doing since their father's death. Faced with similar pressure, his friend Juan de Prado recanted and did everything he could to remain within the community (though in the end his efforts were unsuccessful). Spinoza, on the other hand, composed a defense of his opinions and acts, addressed to the elders of the synagogue, and resigned himself to a life outside the Jewish community.

The years immediately following Spinoza's excommunication have always been something of a mystery to Spinoza scholars, since the early biographies shed little light on them. But recently some intriguing evidence of Spinoza's activities and opinions during that period has turned up in a surprising place: the files of the Inquisition. In 1659 a South American monk, Tomas Solano, who had spent some time in Amsterdam during the preceding year, made a report to Madrid about some of the people of Iberian origin whom he had met during his stay there. Among them were Spinoza and Juan de Prado. According to Solano, Spinoza and Prado said they had been expelled from the synagogue because they believed that the Jewish law was not the true law, that the soul dies with the body, and that God only exists philosophically. He also reported that Spinoza had been a student at the University of Leiden and that he was a good philosopher.

It is difficult to know quite what to make of this report. What precisely does it mean to say that God only exists philosophically? Solano equates this with atheism. Is this fair? Again, in one of the earliest writings we have from Spinoza we find him arguing *for* the immortality of the soul, not against it. But the account given by one early biographer suggests that Spinoza did indeed have doubts on this score. Jean Lucas reports that shortly before Spinoza's excommunication two young men from the synagogue, professing to be his friends, came to quiz him about the Biblical teaching on three issues: the corporeality of God, the existence of angels, and the immortality of the soul. According to Lucas, Spinoza replied that "wherever Scripture speaks of it, the word 'soul' is used simply to express life, or anything that is living. It would be useless to search for any passage in support of its immortality. As for the contrary view, it may be seen in a hundred places, and nothing is so easy as to prove it."[6] These early reports should be kept in mind when we try to decide what the teaching of Spinoza's writings actually is on the issue of the immortality of the soul.

However we ultimately resolve these matters, Solano's report that Spinoza had studied at the University of Leiden seems credible. That university was a center of Dutch Cartesianism, so a period of studying philosophy there would fit in well with what we know independently of Spinoza's interests. In the earliest correspondence we have from Spinoza, we find him living in Rijnsburg, a small town near Leiden. And among his closest friends were men who we know studied there during that period.

The first selection presented in this volume, under the heading "A Portrait of the Philosopher as a Young Man," consists of the opening passages of a work on method, the *Treatise on the Emendation of the Intellect*, which probably dates from the period between 1656 and 1661. Spinoza was never able to finish this work in a way which satisfied him, and it was published only posthumously, in the fragmentary state in which he left it when he died. But readers have always been moved by Spinoza's description of the spiritual quest which led him to philosophy, his dissatisfaction with the things people ordinarily strive for— wealth, honor, and sensual pleasure—and his hope that the pursuit of knowledge would lead him to discover the true good: "the knowledge of the union that the mind has with the whole of nature." Exactly what this union consists in Spinoza does not say. This passage is one which encourages the interpretation of Spinoza as a mystic, but I would suggest

---

[6] *The Oldest Biography of Spinoza*, pp. 45–46. In 1632 Spinoza's teacher, Manasseh ben Israel, published his *Conciliator*, a systematic attempt to identify and resolve every apparent contradiction in Scripture. Among the passages he is anxious to explain are those apparently denying immortality. See, for example, his comments on Job 7:9, Eccl. 3:19, or Eccl. 9:10 (vol. II, pp. 40–41 and 309–315 of the English translation of this work, published by E. H. Lindo, London, 1842).

With respect to the corporeality of God, Lucas reports Spinoza as saying that "since nothing is to be found in the Bible about the non-material or incorporeal, there is nothing objectionable in believing that God is a body. All the more so since, as the Prophet says, God is great, and it is impossible to comprehend greatness without extension and, therefore, without body." The problem of Scriptural evidence for the corporeality of God and the angels is a major issue in Maimonides' *Guide of the Perplexed*, I, i–xlix. In the *Theological-Political Treatise* (vii, 75–87) Spinoza is highly critical of Maimonides for his rejection of this evidence, which Spinoza thinks violates the proper principles of textual interpretation.

that we understand him to be referring, not to a special experience of the kind which seems to be central to philosophers like Plotinus, but to the fact that the human mind is a part of nature, subject to the same universal laws which govern the rest of nature. This would contrast with the Cartesian view of man's relation to nature, which conceives man (to use a phrase of Spinoza's from the preface to Part III of the *Ethics*) as a dominion within a dominion, that is, as insulated from the causal processes to which other things in nature are subject.

Following that short first selection, I present, under the heading "A Critique of Traditional Religion," selections from a work Spinoza published in 1670, the *Theological-Political Treatise*, which became a seminal work in the developing science of Biblical criticism. By the time Spinoza began this work in 1665, he was already well-advanced in the composition of his best-known work, the *Ethics*, a systematic attempt to work out, in geometric fashion, his views on the nature of God, the relation between mind and body, human psychology, and the best way to live. But he interrupted work on the *Ethics* to write the *Theological-Political Treatise*, whose main purpose is to provide a defense of freedom of thought and expression. Why did he do this? One reason, clearly, was that the project of defending freedom of thought gave him an ideal opportunity to deal with those theological issues which had led to his expulsion from the Jewish community, problems about prophecy, the divine law, miracles, and the interpretation and historicity of Scripture. Contemporaries who knew the now-lost defense of his opinions, written on leaving the synagogue, say that much of its content resurfaced in the *Theological-Political Treatise*. So some of the ideas of the TPT were ones Spinoza had been working out in the earliest stages of his development as a philosopher. Another motive, I think, was that he felt he needed to attack the claim of revelation to provide a basis for religious knowledge, and to criticize the usual conception of God in a nongeometric argument, before he could expect to find a receptive audience for his own austere, geometric defense of a radically different conception. He wanted, I suggest, to prepare readers for the positive ideas of the *Ethics* by presenting some of them in a nontechnical form, for example, the idea that everything which occurs in nature is an instance of an eternal and immutable law, or that God cannot coherently be conceived as a giver of laws which men can break.

The next section presents excerpts from the *Treatise on the Emendation of the Intellect* which illuminate his theory of knowledge, focusing on his account of the four kinds of knowledge and the theory of definition. According to Spinoza, the right method of discovery is "to form thoughts from some given definition," and the better the definition from which we proceed the greater will be our success. So it is very important to understand what the requirements for a good definition are.

This passage is also important for the hints it gives toward the interpretation of Spinoza's metaphysics, in those sections which contrast the fixed and eternal things with the singular changeable things which depend on them and are to be understood through them. The fixed and eternal things are characterized as being present everywhere and as having laws "inscribed in them, as in their true codes." If we may identify these fixed and eternal things with the attributes and infinite modes of the *Ethics*, and the singular changeable things with the finite modes of that work, then we have a clue to the nature of the dependence of the finite on the infinite: we understand how a finite thing depends on the infinite when we understand how to deduce its existence from the eternal laws of nature. This interpretation is encouraged by the emphasis in the *Theological-Political Treatise* on the immutability of the laws of nature and its notion that God's action in the world consists in the operation of those laws.

The *Treatise on the Intellect* was clearly written as an introduction to a systematic presentation of Spinoza's philosophy, probably the work which has come down to us under the title of the *Short Treatise on God, Man and his Well-Being*, a first draft of the *Ethics*, not written in geometric style, and composed in the first instance for private circulation among Spinoza's friends, not for publication. (For nearly two centuries after Spinoza's death it was not known that a manuscript of this work had survived; it was first published only in the mid-nineteenth century.) In a letter probably written early in 1662 Spinoza gives a brief description of this work, and of his reasons for hesitating to publish it:

> As for your . . . question how things have begun to be, and by what connection they depend on the first cause, I have composed a whole short work devoted to this matter. . . . I am engaged in transcribing and emending it, but sometimes I put it to one side because I do not yet have any definite plan regarding its publication. I fear, of course, that the theologians of our time may be offended and with their usual hatred attack me, who absolutely dread quarrels.
>
> I shall look for your advice regarding this matter, and to let you know what is contained in this work of mine which might offend the preachers, I say that I regard as creatures many 'attributes' which they (and everyone, so far as I know) attribute to God. Conversely, other things, which they, because of their prejudices, re-

gard as creatures, I contend are attributes of God, which they have misunderstood. Also, I do not separate God from nature, as everyone known to me has done. (Letter 6, IV/36)

In making selections from this work I have been guided by this description of its contents and problems, choosing three chapters from the first part of the work, dealing with the problem of identifying the attributes which in Spinoza's view really do pertain to God, and explaining what the infinite modes are which Spinoza contends depend immediately on the attributes (a matter the *Ethics* leaves very obscure). These chapters also amplify the discussion of definition begun in the *Treatise on the Intellect* and shed light on the sense in which it is true that Spinoza does not separate God from nature: he identifies God with what he calls *natura naturans*, which is another name for the attributes, those self-existing beings which he had called (in §75 of the *Treatise on the Intellect*) "the first elements of the whole of nature." The selections from the *Short Treatise* include also passages dealing with the nature of the soul and its immortality, interesting (among other things) for their recognition of the existence of souls corresponding to the modes of the unknown attributes. These selections conclude with a dialogue on various problems about God's causality, such as how an eternal being can be the cause of things which perish.

Spinoza may have hesitated to publish the *Short Treatise*, not merely because of the hostile reaction he thought it would generate, but also because, by the time he finished the rough draft of the work which has come down to us, he had become dissatisfied with the form in which it was written. The earliest correspondence we have from him, written at a time when he was still working on the *Short Treatise*, shows him experimenting with the geometrical method. Though he had not yet published anything, by the latter half of 1661 Spinoza had acquired sufficient reputation as a philosopher that Henry Oldenburg, soon to become the first secretary of the Royal Society, sought him out in Rijnsburg. After Oldenburg's return to England, Spinoza sent him a paper in which he tried to prove geometrically (i.e., by demonstration from definitions and axioms) a number of propositions which would later be central to Part I of the *Ethics*, for example, that it is of the essence of a substance to exist, or that every substance must be infinite. This paper has been lost, but we can reconstruct some of its content from the correspondence (see the letters in §V of the Preliminaries). Part of the interest of this early geometrical sketch of Part I of the *Ethics* lies in what it tells us about Spinoza's undogmatic attitude toward his axioms. Oldenburg asks whether Spinoza regards them as principles which neither need nor are capable of demonstration. Spinoza replies that he does not insist that they have that status. But he does insist that they are true. Later, in the *Ethics*, a number of these axioms will be treated as propositions, that is, as truths capable of being demonstrated from even more fundamental assumptions. Spinoza adopts a flexible attitude toward his axioms. If he puts a principle forward as an axiom and it meets with opposition, then he may later try to find an argument for it. Also of interest here is Spinoza's tendency to define "attribute" in the same terms he would later use for "substance."

By 1663 Spinoza seems to have committed himself to the project of developing his philosophy geometrically. An interesting exchange of letters between him and his friend Simon de Vries (presented in §VII) not only sheds further light on his view of definitions, but also shows that a draft of (the greater part, at least, of) Part I of the *Ethics* was by then circulating among Spinoza's friends, who had formed a study group in Amsterdam in which they debated its meaning. They would then write to Spinoza in Rijnsburg about any difficulties they had. It was these friends who in the same year encouraged Spinoza to publish his first work, a geometric exposition of Descartes' *Principles of Philosophy*. Spinoza had originally developed a portion of this exposition while tutoring a young student in theology from the University of Leiden. His friends found it so valuable that they requested him to expand what he had previously done and assisted him in getting it published. This work shows Spinoza to have a thorough grasp of the Cartesian philosophy. I have excerpted two brief passages from it here: one in which Spinoza criticizes Descartes' solution to the problem of the Cartesian circle (and offers his own alternative solution), and a second in which he criticizes a Cartesian argument for the existence of God in the Third Meditation. The latter selection is particularly important for its criticism of the apparent distinction Descartes makes in that argument between a substance and its principal attribute. Spinoza maintains that there is no real distinction between them, a view Descartes himself sometimes subscribed to (cf. his *Principles of Philosophy* I, 62). The identification of substance with its principal attribute is crucial to a central argument of Part I of the *Ethics*.

The preface to this work, written by Lodewijk Meyer at Spinoza's request, is also worth our attention here. Meyer calls Descartes "the brightest star of our age" for having introduced the mathematical method into philosophy and for having uncovered "firm foundations" for philosophy. The scholastic philosophy which preceded Descartes (and was still dominant in most universities at that time) had been futile, and had led only to strife and disagreement, because it relied on merely probable arguments. But having praised Descartes generously for his innovations, Meyer goes on to acknowledge that Spinoza himself rejected many of Descartes' specific positions:

> Descartes only assumes, but does not prove, that the human mind is a substance thinking absolutely [i.e., unconditionally]. Though our author [i.e., Spinoza] admits, of course, that there is a thinking substance in nature, he nevertheless denies that it constitutes the essence of the human mind. Instead he believes that just as extension is determined by no limits, so also thought is determined by no limits. Therefore, just as the human body is not extension absolutely, but only an extension determined in a certain way, according to the laws of extended nature, by motion and rest, so also the human mind, or soul, is not thought absolutely, but only a thought determined in a certain way, according to the laws of thinking nature, by ideas, a thought which, one infers, must exist when the human body begins to exist. From this definition, he thinks, it is not difficult to demonstrate that the will is not distinct from the intellect, much less endowed with that liberty which Descartes ascribes to it. (I/132)

This brief passage foreshadows some of the central claims of the metaphysic Spinoza was in the process of developing in the *Ethics*: neither the human mind nor the human body is a substance, because each of these entities lacks the independence of other minds or bodies which would be required for it to be a substance; the mind's determination by other ideas parallels the body's determination by other bodies, each in accordance with unalterable laws. There is even a slight suggestion of the mind's ontological dependence on the body, in the observation that it begins to exist when the body does.

But Spinoza is not content to declare (through Meyer) his disagreement with Cartesian metaphysics. He also registers some reservations about Cartesian methodology. When faced with certain problems (such as the apparent contradiction between God's preordination of all things and human freedom), Descartes was willing to say that their solution surpassed the human understanding. Spinoza will have none of this. If rationalism consists in the conviction that everything is fundamentally intelligible, then Spinoza was a much more consistent rationalist than Descartes. So he had Meyer report his view that

> all those things, and even many others more sublime and subtle, can not only be conceived clearly and distinctly, but also explained very satisfactorily—provided that the human intellect is guided in

the search for truth and knowledge of things along a different path from that which Descartes opened up and made smooth. The foundations of the sciences brought to light by Descartes, and the things he built on them, do not suffice to disentangle and solve all the very difficult problems which occur in metaphysics. Different foundations are required, if we wish our intellect to rise to that pinnacle of knowledge. (ibid.)

Much as Spinoza admired Descartes' use of the mathematical method, he did not think Descartes had started in the right place. To begin with a radical doubt about the existence of the external world and about the truth of those simple propositions whose evidence forces our assent is a mistake. As his critique of Descartes' answer to the accusation of circular reasoning had argued, if we start from a clear and distinct idea of God, we will not be able to coherently state the hypothesis which grounds such a doubt. So it is legitimate for us to take certain general propositions of metaphysics as axiomatic without needing first to establish the reliability of our reason. Using those axioms (and appropriate definitions) we can establish the existence and nature of God. And if we follow the proper order, we should establish these truths about God before we discuss the existence and nature of the human mind and its relationship to the body. That is why the *Ethics* begins in the way that it does.

The *Ethics* is not only Spinoza's masterwork, it is also his life's work. We know from the correspondence that he began writing it early in the 1660s, that a substantial draft of the work was in existence by 1665, and that he then put it aside to write his *Theological-Political Treatise*, which appeared in 1670. He had published his exposition of Descartes' philosophy to pave the way for his *Ethics*. His hope was that by demonstrating his mastery of the new philosophy of Descartes, and by giving hints of his advances on Descartes, he would generate sufficient interest in his own writings that the leaders of his country would want to see them published, and would protect him against any adverse consequences of publication. I have suggested that the *Theological-Political Treatise* had a similar motivation. But if Spinoza did think of the TPT as preparing the way for the *Ethics*, he could not have been more mistaken. For his challenge to the theologians generated a storm of protest which made it impossible for him to publish the latter work during his lifetime. He continued to work on it during the years immediately following the publication of the TPT and no doubt made many changes, particularly in the latter part of the *Ethics*, which shows quite strongly the influence on him of the philosophy of Hobbes, whom he had studied closely in writing the *Theological-Political Treatise*.

In the fall of 1675 he evidently had the *Ethics* ready to go to the publishers, for he writes to his friend Oldenburg that he was about to leave for Amsterdam to see to its printing when

> a rumor was spread everywhere that a book of mine about God was in the press, and that in it I strove to show that there is no God. Many people believed this rumor. So certain theologians—who had, perhaps, started the rumor themselves—seized this opportunity to complain about me to the Prince and the magistrates. Moreover, the stupid Cartesians, who are thought to favor me, would not stop trying to remove this suspicion from themselves by denouncing my opinions and writings everywhere. When I learned this from certain trustworthy men, who also told me the theologians were everywhere plotting against me, I decided to put off the publication I was planning until I saw how the matter would turn out. (Letter 68, IV/299)

In the end Spinoza had to settle for posthumous publication. He died only about a year and a half after this, on 21 February 1677, of a lung disease probably aggravated by the dust of the lenses he had been grinding in order to support himself. A few months later his friends arranged for the publication of the *Ethics*, along with his correspondence and three other unfinished works: the *Treatise on the Emendation of the Intellect*, the *Political Treatise*, and a *Hebrew Grammar*.

What is the nature of the work to which Spinoza devoted so much of his adult life, the work on which his fame as a philosopher now primarily rests?[7] We have seen that his contemporaries frequently accused him of atheism, and that he had to defer publication of the *Ethics* because it was alleged to be an atheistic work. Spinoza deeply resented this accusation.[8] It is easy to see why he might think it unfair: the *Ethics* begins by constructing a geometric demonstration of the existence of God (IP11) and ends by claiming that our salvation consists in the intellectual love of God (VP36S). But the God whom Spinoza celebrates in this work has not always seemed to other men to be recognizable as God. Spinoza's contemporary, Pascal, wrote that "the God of the philosophers is not

---

[7] In what follows I sketch an interpretation of the *Ethics* developed at greater length in *Behind the Geometrical Method*. Readers should be aware that the account I offer here is a controversial one; many students of Spinoza would view these matters in a very different light. But the risk of error is the price we pay for trying to reformulate Spinoza's ideas in more illuminating and contemporary language.

[8] See, for example, Letter 30. Part of Spinoza's objection to the accusation lay in what he felt it implied about his way of life: "For atheists usually seek honors and riches immoderately; but all those who know me, know that I have always disdained these things" (Letter 43, IV/219/16–18).

the God of Abraham, Isaac and Jacob." Spinoza's God is very much the God of the philosophers, a principle of explanation, a first cause of everything which exists, itself neither needing nor susceptible of explanation by anything external to itself, an eternal, necessary being, standing in contrast with the temporal, contingent beings we find in our daily life, but not a personal being with thoughts, desires, and emotions, not a creator of the universe, not a being who acts for the sake of any purposes, and therefore not a being whose purposes might be manifested in the world it causes. If a being must be a personal, purposeful creator to rightly be called God, if anything other than the God of Abraham, Isaac, and Jacob is not God, then Spinoza's affirmation of the God of the philosophers (and implicit denial of the God of Abraham, Isaac, and Jacob) is a form of atheism. On those assumptions, to say that God only exists philosophically, that is, that only the God of the philosophers exists, is to deny the existence of God. From his point of view Father Solano may have been right to characterize Spinoza's position as atheism. One of the questions Spinoza forces us to ask is whether it is legitimate to make those assumptions. If his argument in Part I of the *Ethics* is correct, then there is a first cause of all things, an ultimate principle of explanation, but that first cause cannot coherently be conceived as a personal creator of the universe. From Spinoza's point of view, if we cannot accept his God as God, we can have no God at all.

The argument for this conclusion is couched in the terminology and framed in the assumptions of seventeenth-century Cartesian metaphysics. It has force today just to the extent that we still find that terminology and those assumptions intelligible and plausible. Descartes had assumed a world consisting of a plurality of material and immaterial substances, most of them finite: bodies and minds, each possessing a principal attribute which constituted the essence of the substance in question. The essence of bodies consisted in their being extended things; the essence of minds, in their being thinking things. The nonessential properties of things, their modes, were particular specifications of these fundamental attributes. The whole world of finite minds and bodies, with their constantly changing modes, was created and continually sustained by the infinite mind, God, who was conceived as being both personal and supremely perfect.

One of the first controversial conclusions Spinoza tries to demonstrate in the *Ethics* is that there cannot be more than one substance having any given attribute (IP5). The argument for this proposition is difficult to grasp and has been the subject of much debate among Spinoza's commentators. But arguably it relies only on assumptions which would have been acceptable to any good Cartesian. Suppose we have two entities with the same attribute, which are alleged to be distinct substances. What is it which makes them distinct from one another? Not their attribute, since that, by hypothesis, is the same. Not their modes, since modes, by definition, are inessential, transitory states of the substance to which they belong, which cannot be used to distinguish one substance from another. (This is an implication of Descartes' famous discussion of the piece of wax at the end of the Second Meditation.) But there is nothing else by which our 'two' substances might be distinguished, since whatever is, is either an attribute or a mode. This is a consequence of Spinoza's first axiom, plus the fact that Spinoza consistently does, what Descartes does only intermittently: identify substance with its attribute(s).

If this argument is successful, important consequences follow. For example, since a substance could only be produced by another substance of the same kind, if there cannot be two substances of the same kind, substances cannot be produced, but must exist in virtue of their own nature, which is to say that they must exist eternally (IPP6, 7, 19). Again, since a finite substance would have to be limited by another substance of the same kind, if there cannot be two substances of the same kind, no substance can be finite (IP8). Most important, since God is defined as a substance consisting of infinite attributes, he must exist (Pll), and his existence must exclude the existence of any other substance, since any other substance would have to share an attribute with him (P14D). So there is only one substance, God, and everything else is only a mode of God (IPP14, 15).

From Cartesian assumptions a most uncartesian conclusion has been drawn. What exactly is the import of this conclusion? What are we saying when we say that there is just one substance, and that everything else is a mode of that substance? Given the traditional association between the concept of substance and the concept of a logical subject of predication, there is a strong temptation to suppose that Spinoza's monism implies that there is only one subject of predication, of which everything else is somehow a predicate. In his famous *Dictionary* article on Spinoza, Pierre Bayle gave in to this temptation, and concluded, reasonably enough on that supposition, that Spinoza was talking nonsense, that God would have to be the subject of contradictory predicates and constant change. Clearly this was not Spinoza's intention.

But the traditional theory of substance also tended to identify the substantial with what has independent existence. In line with that strand in the traditional theory, I suggest that Spinoza identifies his one substance with those permanent and pervasive features of the world he sometimes calls fixed and eternal things, and sometimes calls the divine attributes. The claim that the world does possess these permanent and pervasive features is, in effect, the claim that there is an ontological foundation for science, that when we organize science as a deductive system in which laws of greater generality are shown to entail laws of lesser generality, then (if we have our science right) those laws are descriptive of enduring and omnipresent features of reality. And the claim that everything else in the world is a mode of the one substance is the claim that every other feature of the world can be shown to follow from the most general of these permanent features (IP16). Some things follow from the attributes in such a way that they too are permanent and pervasive. That is to say that the most general of the permanent features of reality have less general consequences which are equally permanent and equally universal in their application. These are the infinite modes whose production Spinoza describes in PP21–23. The most general laws of science have as consequences less general laws, which, in spite of their lesser generality, are applicable at all times and places, and require their own ontological foundation. Other things follow from the attributes in such a way that they come into being and pass away at particular times and places. These are the particular events or states of affairs which follow from the laws of nature if (and only if) the appropriate antecedent conditions are present, the finite modes of P28, which Spinoza there speaks of as if they were generated solely by the infinite series of other finite modes preceding them in time, but which he surely thinks could not have been so generated were it not for the influence exerted at all times by the permanent features of reality. The world of finite changing things stretches back into the infinite past: there was no moment of creation. But the infinite series of finite things could not have produced the world we know if it had not been determined to exist and act in the way it does by a finite series of infinite causes, those permanent and pervasive features of reality described by the laws of nature. The explanation of any phenomenon in nature requires a knowledge both of its antecedent conditions and of the laws governing the operation of those conditions. The requirement that we know antecedent conditions means that no finite intellect can ever fully understand any event. But the explanation of the laws themselves is finite, and comprehensible, since lower level laws must be explained in terms of higher level, more general laws, and there is an inherent limit to the process of going from a less general to a more general law.

Spinoza's God is an ultimate principle of explanation. Itself the cause of all things other than itself, it is also its own cause in the sense that the permanent and pervasive features of reality described by the most general laws of nature have no explanation other than their own nature. Insofar as they are those features of reality described by the most general laws of nature, and insofar as explanation must always be by deduction from more general principles, there is nothing else by which they could be explained. That is why they possess the independence required of substance.

Descartes too had given the laws of nature an extremely important role to play in his account of the nature of things, but he had tried to explain them in a way compatible with Judaeo-Christian theology. As one of the pioneers of the new science, he understood full well that scientific explanation consists in uncovering the laws in accordance with which things happen in nature. And he saw certain theological advantages in treating these laws as an intermediary between God and the world of finite things. Conceiving God as a perfect being, he recognized that this must imply God's immutability. But if God cannot change, how can he be the continuous cause of a constantly changing world? Descartes' solution was to claim that God caused change in the finite world by establishing the laws according to which change took place. God causes change indirectly, by causing laws of change which are themselves unchanging.

But what is the status of these laws? Descartes thought of them as eternal, that is, necessary, truths, which would hold in any world God might have created. When some of his contemporaries objected that it seemed an infringement of God's omnipotence to talk about the essences of things as being eternal and immutable, Descartes' reply was that he did not conceive of the eternal truths as being independent of God. Rather God had established them as a king might establish the laws of his kingdom. They depend on his will, and are eternal and immutable only because his will is eternal and immutable. But if the laws of nature are the result of a divine choice, how can they be eternal and immutable? Does not the very notion of choice imply that they could have been otherwise? And if they could have been otherwise, how can it be necessary now that they not be otherwise? For Spinoza, to introduce a personal creator at this point was to give up the hope of a rational explanation of things, to betray the sciences Descartes had hoped to found. Better to identify God himself with those most general principles of order described by the fundamental laws of nature. It is in this sense that Spinoza does not separate God from nature; he does not identify God with nature where nature is conceived simply as the totality of finite things (IP29S).

If Part I of the *Ethics* explains the sense in which it is true that God (only) exists philosophically, Part II addresses the vexed question of the nature of man and the relation of the human mind to the human body. For Descartes a human being was a composite substance, whose constituent substances were a mind and a body. Part of what was implied in characterizing the mind and the body as substances was that each possessed sufficient capacity for independent existence to be capable of existing without the other. By arguing for this conclusion, Descartes was attempting to provide a metaphysical foundation for a belief in personal immortality. Though he was never able to demonstrate that in fact the mind does not die with the body, he did think he had demonstrated the possibility of the mind's separate existence, leaving it to the theologian to provide grounds from revelation for believing in the actuality of that separate existence.

Descartes, however, was not content to say merely that the mind and the body were two distinct substances. Ultimately he wanted to argue also that the human mind is not present in the body "as a sailor is present in his ship," but is very closely conjoined to it, so that together mind and body constitute one thing and are, as he put it, "substantially united." Descartes was never able to explain clearly what this substantial union consisted in, but he seems to have been led to affirm it by the very special relationship each mind has to the particular body to which it is united: it feels what happens in that body in a way it does not feel what happens in other bodies and it cares about what happens in that body in a way it does not care about what happens in other bodies.

From Spinoza's point of view, Descartes' talk of the substantial union of mind and body is an awkward way of expressing a truth more happily put by saying that the mind and body are one and the same thing, "conceived now under the attribute of Thought, now under the attribute of Extension." (IIP21S) If the talk of substantial union is meant to imply that the human mind and the human body, though each a substance in its own right, nevertheless combine to form yet a third substance, it cannot be right, of course. Part I has shown that there is only one substance. This squares with the teaching of experience, which shows that the mind cannot be a substance because of its dependence on the body (cf. E IIIP2S). Nevertheless, it is true that each human mind has a special relationship to some particular body: the essence of the human mind is to be the idea (in the attribute of thought) of the human body (in the attribute of extension) (IIPP11, 13). For Spinoza this relationship is only a special case of a parallelism existing throughout the attributes of thought and extension. For every mode of extension, there is in thought an idea of that mode, and for every mode of thought which has a mode of extension as its object, there is in extension a mode corresponding to that idea.

Spinoza's way of putting this in Part II is to say that "the order and connection of ideas is the same as the order and connection of things" (IIP7). The argument he offers for this proposition is brief and not in itself convincing, but with a little imagination (and the help of some of

Spinoza's earlier works) we can reconstruct an alternative argument for the same conclusion, drawing partly on doctrines common to Descartes and Spinoza and partly on theses Spinoza claims to have demonstrated in Part I:

1. My mind is a thinking thing, but it is finite, and thus cannot be a thinking substance, since every substance is infinite.

2. Since my mind cannot be a substance, and everything which exists must be either a substance or a mode, my mind must be a mode of thought. There is, then, at least one mode of thought.

3. If there is a mode of thought, there must be a thinking substance.

4. There must be a thinking substance, and since there is only one substance, God, God is a thinking substance.

So far what we have is only an alternate demonstration of IIP1. We can easily add a demonstration of IIP2:

5. We are aware of a certain body (viz. our own body), which is finite, and therefore cannot be a substance.

6. There is, then, at least one mode of extension.

7. But the existence of modes of extension implies the existence of an extended substance, and since God is the only substance, God is an extended substance.

These propositions being established, the parallelism follows swiftly:

8. As a thinking and extended substance, God must be infinite and perfect.

9. Since God is an infinite and perfect thinking substance, it must have an idea of each existing mode of extension. And if God is perfect, it cannot have an idea of a mode of extension, if no such mode exists.

10. Since every mode of extension or of thought must exist in a substance, and there is only one substance for them to exist in, every mode of extension or of thought is a mode of the one substance.

11. So, in God, the one substance, for every mode of extension existing in God, there is an idea of that mode, and for every idea of a mode of extension, there is a mode of extension corresponding to that idea.

Since the human mind does involve an idea of the human body, and there can be no idea of the human body other than the one which exists in God, this argument leads to an identification of the human mind with the idea existing in God of the human body, and the claim that the human mind is part of the infinite intellect of God (IIP11C). It leads also to Spinoza's famous doctrine of panpsychism. For if the human mind is just the idea existing in God of the human body, if there must be an idea in God of every other mode of extension, then every other body must have a mind in precisely the same sense that man does. Spinoza puts this by saying that all things are animate (IIP13S), but he hastens to add that they are animate in different degrees. A mind's capacity for thought is strictly correlated with its body's capacity for interaction with its environment. So the minds of very simple things, which can only act and be acted on in very limited ways, are capable of thought only to a very limited extent. We are not to imagine that stones feel pain, much less that they think of Vienna.

Given the above, we can also see, I think, why Spinoza was led to claim that the mind and the body are one and the same thing, conceived in different ways. If they were really distinct from one another, in the sense in which Descartes had understood that term, each would have to be capable of existing apart from the other. But the argument for parallelism has led to the conclusion that whenever the mode of thought which constitutes my mind exists, the mode of extension which constitutes my body must also exist in the same substance. The converse also holds: whenever my body exists, my mind must also exist in the same substance. Neither can exist without the other; they are not really distinct from one another. But they are conceptually distinct from one another. To conceive this one thing as a mind is to conceive it as a mode of the attribute of thought; to conceive it as a body is to conceive it as a mode of the attribute of extension.

Spinoza's doctrine that the mind and the body are one thing, conceived in different ways, sounds like a form of materialism, and given only that doctrine, we might well expect Spinoza to hold the view Father Solano reported to the inquisitors: the soul dies with the body. This makes it all the more puzzling that, in addition to the arguments for the immortality of the soul which we find in the *Short Treatise*, we also find in the fifth part of the *Ethics* an argument that "something of the mind" which is eternal remains when the body is destroyed (VP23). Spinoza scholars have exerted a great deal of energy trying to reconcile what has seemed to them an inconsistency in Spinoza's position here, and it would be beyond the scope of this introduction to try to resolve that debate. I make only these observations: it does appear that Spinoza is trying to find a place in his system for a popular belief which he thinks cannot be true in the way in which it is ordinarily understood, but which he thinks can be reinterpreted in a way which will express a philosophical truth (cf. VP23S, P34S); it seems clear that what 'remains' after the destruction of the body is not, for Spinoza, a person continuous with the person who existed before the destruction of the body. For Spinoza emphasizes that the capacities for imagination and memory exist only as long as the body exists (VP21), and he seems to regard continuity of memory as essential to the continued existence of the same person (IVP39S). If the soul survives the death of the body, this is so "only philosophically," that is, in the sense that an idea of the essence of the body is contained eternally in God's infinite idea, which is an infinite mode of the attribute of thought (VP23D, IIP8C). This explanation itself, of course, would require much explanation in a comprehensive exposition of Spinoza's philosophy.

To say that the Jewish law is not the true law is to imply a knowledge of what the true law is. One way of looking at the latter part of Spinoza's *Ethics* is as an attempt to specify that true law. In the *Theological-Political Treatise* Spinoza had argued that the law of Moses, with all of its ceremonial requirements, was not intended as a universal law, binding on all men, but only as a prescription for the Jewish people; that it was aimed at the preservation of the Jewish state, and was not binding even on the Jewish people after the destruction of their state. There Spinoza had summed up the true, universal law in the precept that we should love God as the supreme good, it being understood that this love of God entailed love of, and justice toward, one's neighbor. But his argument there for regarding the love of God as man's supreme good was very brief and sketchy. He left the provision of detail, the full discussion and rational defense of the way of life this end required, to the comprehensive treatise on ethics he already had under way, that is, to the work we know as his *Ethics*.

In a properly philosophical treatment of the right way of living, the true law will not be thought of as an arbitrary commandment, issued by a personal God, to a being capable either of obeying or of disobeying, and subject to extrinsic rewards and penalties, depending on whether he chooses obedience or disobedience.[9] Rather, the law will be thought of as a system of eternal truths, following from the nature of man in the same way the properties of a triangle follow from its definition, instructing us as to the necessary consequences of acting one way rather than another, and deriving whatever motivational force it has from the fact

---

[9] See the excerpt from the *Theological-Political Treatise* in Preliminaries II.D.

that, whether we are conscious of it or not, we necessarily desire certain ends. The first step toward a philosophical treatment of the true law, therefore, is to expand the theory of human nature whose metaphysical outlines were given in Part II by developing the systematic psychology of Part III.

In the seventeenth century developing a systematic psychology involved giving an account of the various passions to which man was liable. Descartes' last work, *The Passions of the Soul,* had been an attempt to define the principal human passions, with a view toward learning how to subject those passions to reason, as a means of reaching true peace of mind. Spinoza is engaged in a similar project: he will identify three primitive passions—desire, joy, and sadness—though he will prefer to call them affects, since sometimes we are active, and not passive, when we are in these states; he will attempt to explain how all other human affects—love and hate, hope and fear, self-esteem and humility, and the like—are particular complications of these basic three, usually because they involve the combination of a purely affective state (like joy) with some kind of cognitive state (such as a belief about an external object that it is the cause of the joy); and he will do all this with a view to determining which affects are good, or in accordance with reason, and which are evil, or contrary to reason. Psychology is in the service of ethics here. Ultimately we want to know how to control, as far as possible, those affects which are contrary to reason.

But Spinoza's psychology, unlike Descartes', is not primarily classificatory. Conceiving man as a part of nature, rather than as a dominion within a dominion, he is convinced that human behavior exemplifies laws as strict as any in physics, laws which can be organized into a deductive system in which the less general laws (those, say, which explain the behavior of people in the grip of some particular affect, like hate or envy or jealousy) are derived from more fundamental principles. Part of the task of psychology is to systematize those laws.[10] Chief among them is the law Spinoza enunciates in IIIP6: "Each thing, as far as it can by its own power, strives to persevere in its being." As Spinoza interprets this principle, sometimes referred to as the *conatus* doctrine (from the Latin word here translated as "striving"), it requires not merely that things strive for self-preservation, but also that they strive to increase their power of action (IIIP12). From this basic principle (together, sometimes, with assumptions from Part II about how man's cognitive powers function), Spinoza undertakes to deduce a great many principles which

---

[10] That Spinoza does conceive this to be the task of psychology seems a strong confirmation of the interpretation I advanced above of his theory of causality and explanation.

he thinks will be helpful in constructing a rational plan of life: for example, that hate is increased by being returned, but can be destroyed by love (IIIP43), or that hate is destroyed if the sadness it involves is attached to the idea of another cause (IIIP48).

The *conatus* doctrine functions not only as a foundation for psychology, but also as a foundation for ethics, insofar as it gives content to the notion of a rational plan of life. Spinoza defines the good as "what we certainly know to be useful to us" (IVD1) and evil as "what we certainly know prevents us from being masters of some good" (IVD2). We can identify what is truly useful to us with what helps us to persevere in our being and increase our power of action, for these are ends we necessarily have. Insofar as our actions can be explained by our striving for these things, we act in accordance with reason and we act virtuously (IVP18S). Insofar as our lives are dominated by affects which express this striving, we possess the good. So, for example, when the body's overall power of acting is increased (and hence the mind's overall power of thinking is increased), we experience that special kind of joy Spinoza calls cheerfulness, and this is always good (IVP42). On the other hand, when our overall power of acting and thinking is decreased, we experience melancholy, which is always evil. Other affects require more complex judgments. Sometimes we may feel a pleasure which in itself is good, but overall is evil because it interferes with the total functioning of mind and body (IVP43). And sometimes affects like pity, humility, and repentance, which in themselves involve sadness and to that extent are evil, may, because of their consequences, be more useful than harmful (IVPP50, 53, 54). But hate, and related affects, like envy, mockery, anger, and vengeance, can never be good (IVP45, 45C). The feelings and behavior which the *Ethics* recommends as good, it recommends as necessary means to a necessary end; those which it condemns as evil, it condemns as necessarily frustrating that end.

Of the various things which are useful to man, none, according to Spinoza, is more useful than his fellow man (IVP18S). So one of the first requirements of reason is that people should seek "to form associations, to bind themselves by those bonds most apt to make one people of them, and absolutely, to do those things which serve to strengthen friendships" (IVApp12). The central association which people rationally pursuing their self-interest must form is the state (IVP37S2). For only if individual human beings come together to create an entity with the power to prescribe a common rule of life, to make laws, and to enforce them with the threat of punishment for violation, will they have any reasonable level of security against the possibility of harm from their fellows. Spinoza accepts this Hobbesian conclusion, not on the

Hobbesian ground that the rational pursuit of self-interest in the state of nature would lead to preemptive violence of each individual against every other individual, but on the Spinozistic ground that people are not reliably rational. Instead they are regularly subject to passions which are capable of overpowering their rational desires. If they lived according to the guidance of reason, they would be able to possess their natural right to pursue their own interest without injury to anyone else. Because they do not, the state is necessary to prevent outbreaks of violence which would be disadvantageous to all concerned.

This difference between Hobbes and Spinoza comes partly from a difference of opinion about what is truly good, or about what would be desired by someone who was thinking clearly about her own interests. Hobbes sees people as necessarily competing for such things as honor, riches, and power over others, goods which cannot be shared without at least one of those who shares having less than she would have had otherwise. Spinoza, on the other hand, thinks that the highest good is the knowledge of God (IVP28)—understood as a knowledge of nature (VP24)—and this is a good which can be shared by many without anyone's portion being thereby diminished. In fact, I think Spinoza attaches the importance he does to friendship because he sees that as friends share their knowledge with each other, each finds that his own portion of knowledge is increased. The state is necessary not only as a device for preventing violence, but also as providing the only environment in which people will be able to cultivate their highest capacity, the capacity for knowledge.

Part III of the Ethics undertakes to explain the causes and consequences of the ways people commonly act. Part IV attempts to turn these descriptive laws into a set of prescriptions, dictates of reason, the free man's substitute for the law of Moses. Given people's fundamental desires, and given the necessary consequences of acting one way rather than another, a man of reason, a free man, would love even his enemies (IVP46), would always act honestly and not deceptively (IVP72), would strive to bind other men to him in friendship (IVAppl2), and so on. But men are not free; they do not, for the most part, act according to the dictates of reason. On the contrary, nothing is clearer than that they often see the better course and follow the worse (IVPref, P17S). One of Spinoza's purposes in Parts III and IV has been to explain why this is so, why our passions exercise such great power over us.

In Part V one of his purposes is to explain how we can, in some measure, bring those passions under the power of reason. His most promising strategies for doing this rely on the fact that many affects involve a cognitive element. Hate, for example, is defined as sadness accompanied by the idea of an external cause, that is, by a belief about some person or thing that it is the cause of my sadness. If that belief is false or ill-founded, as may often be the case, I may be able to rid myself of my hate by coming to recognize the inadequacy of the belief it involved (VP2). I may, of course, still be sad, but sadness is, in general, a less harmful emotion than hate, since it does not perpetuate a vicious cycle of attempts to harm and to retaliate for harm. Similarly, Spinoza argues that if we come to understand the actions of others as a necessary effect of the circumstances in which they were placed, this will tend to diminish the negative emotions we feel toward them, redirecting them at other, possibly less harmful targets. For example (to use the jargon of contemporary psychotherapy), if I come to understand your actions as the product of low self-esteem, caused long ago by negative lessons learned from parents and teachers, the anger I feel toward them may be less dangerous to my well-being, since I may not have to deal with them in any direct way. Spinozistic therapy may require favorable circumstances to be effective, but that, unfortunately, is true of any therapy.

Since the *Ethics* was published only after Spinoza's death, he was unable to respond to the criticisms its publication provoked. But his work did circulate in manuscript form before it was published and received some very illuminating criticism from a young German nobleman, Ehrenfried Walther von Tschirnhaus, who carried on an extended correspondence with Spinoza, sometimes through their mutual friend, George Hermann Schuller. Both Tschirnhaus and Schuller had been students at the University of Leiden. This correspondence ranged over a variety of subjects: freedom, the relation among the attributes, the nature of the infinite modes, and the deduction of bodies from the nature of extension. Our selections conclude with highlights from that correspondence.

II. Bibliographical Note

Most of the translations in this volume come from Volume I of *The Collected Works of Spinoza* (Princeton University Press, 1985), and incorporate numerous corrections suggested to me by readers of that volume. (Thanks are due to Jonathan Bennett, Peter Ghiringelli, Timothy O'Hagan, and especially Samuel Shirley.) The translations of excerpts from the *Theological-Political Treatise* and of letters with a number greater than 29 foreshadow the appearance of Volume II. Where materials in this volume appeared in Volume I of *The Collected Works of Spinoza*, the work of translation was done largely with the research support of the Australian National University. Where they foreshadow material which will appear in Volume II, I have had support from the National

Endowment for the Humanities, the Guggenheim Foundation, the National Humanities Center and the University of Illinois at Chicago.

Students at any level who want more biographical information about Spinoza might consult the two early biographies of Spinoza mentioned in the text: the one by Colerus (an English translation of which is published as an appendix to Pollock's *Spinoza, His Life and Philosophy*, London, 1899), the other by Jean Maximilian Lucas (translated by Abraham Wolf in *The Oldest Biography of Spinoza*, London, 1927). These are the source of many well-known anecdotes about Spinoza; be warned that modern scholars are skeptical of many of the stories they tell. Bayle's article on Spinoza in his *Historical and Critical Dictionary* also contains valuable biographical information, and is interesting as an example of how an intelligent contemporary could radically misread Spinoza. Of more recent biographies, Dan Levin's *Spinoza, the Young Thinker Who Destroyed the Past* (New York: Weybright and Talley, 1970) is highly readable and will make available many of the results of twentieth-century research; Lewis Feuer's *Spinoza and the Rise of Liberalism*, 2d ed. (New Brunswick, N.J.: Transaction Books, 1987) also contains valuable information and perspectives. Henry Allison's *Benedict de Spinoza: An Introduction* (Yale University Press, 1987) is an excellent general introduction to Spinoza's thought, as is Stuart Hampshire's *Spinoza* (Penguin, 1951). My own *Behind the Geometrical Method* (Princeton, 1988) is intended to provide beginning students with a guide to the *Ethics*.

More advanced students should consult the careful survey of the sources for a biography in H. G. Hubbeling's "Spinoza's Life. A Synopsis of the Sources and Some Documents," *Giornale critico della filosofia italiana* 56 (1977): 390–409; A. M. Vaz Dias and W. G. van der Tak, *Spinoza, Merchant and Autodidact*, in *Studia Rosenthaliana* 16 (1982): 103–195; I. S. Revah, *Spinoza et le Docteur Juan de Prado* (La Haye: Mouton, 1959) and "Aux origines de la rupture spinozienne," *Revue des études juives* 3 (1964): 359–431; K. O. Meinsma, *Spinoza et son Cercle* (Paris: Vrin, 1983); Yirmiahu Yovel, *Spinoza and Other Heretics* (Princeton, 1989), especially the first volume; and Richard Popkin, *The History of Skepticism from Erasmus to Spinoza* (University of California Press, 1979). The most important recent commentaries on the *Ethics* are Jonathan Bennett's *A Study of Spinoza's Ethics* (Hackett, 1984) and Alan Donagan's *Spinoza* (University of Chicago Press, 1988).

III. Abbreviations and Other Conventions

"NS" introduces a variant reading from the Dutch translation of Spinoza's works which appeared at the same time as the *Opera posthuma*. When "or" is in italics, it translates the Latin *sive* or *seu*, which normally indicates an equivalence rather than an alternative. I put scare quotes around the word "attribute" whenever Spinoza uses it to refer to items which are commonly (but in his view, wrongly) called attributes of God. Footnotes with an asterisk attached are Spinoza's. Those without are mine. Roman numerals refer to parts of the *Ethics*. Arabic numerals are used for axioms, definitions, propositions, and the like.

E = *Ethics*
A = Axiom
P = Proposition
D (following a Roman numeral) = Definition
D (following P + an arabic numeral) = the Demonstration of
    the proposition
C = Corollary
S = Scholium
Exp = Explanation
L = Lemma
Post = Postulate
Pref = Preface
App = Appendix
DefAff = the definitions of the affects at the end of Part III

So "E ID1" refers to Definition 1 of Part I of the *Ethics*. "E IIIP15C" refers to the corollary to Proposition 15 of Part III, and so on. A reference like "IV/299" refers to the volume and page numbers in the standard edition of Spinoza's works, *Opera*, 4 vols., ed. C. Gebhardt (Heidelberg: C. Winter, 1925).

A SPINOZA READER

Preliminaries

I. A Portrait of the Philosopher
as a Young Man[1]

[1] After experience had taught me that all the things which regularly II/5 occur in ordinary life are empty and futile, and I saw that all the things which were the cause or object of my fear had nothing of good or bad in themselves, except insofar as [my] mind was moved by them, I resolved at last to try to find out whether there was anything which would be the true good, capable of communicating itself, and which alone would affect the mind, all others being rejected—whether there was something which, once found and acquired, would continuously give me the greatest joy, to eternity.

[2] I say that *I resolved at last*—for at first glance it seemed ill-advised to be willing to lose something certain for something then uncertain. I saw, of course, the advantages that honor and wealth bring, and that I would be forced to abstain from seeking them, if I wished to devote myself seriously to something new and different; and if by chance the greatest happiness lay in them, I saw that I should have to do without it. But if it did not lie in them, and I devoted my energies only to acquiring them, then I would equally go without it.

[3] So I wondered whether perhaps it would be possible to reach my new goal—or at least the certainty of attaining it—without changing the conduct and plan of life which I shared with other men. Often I tried this, but in vain. For most things which present themselves in life, and which, to judge from their actions, men think to be the highest good, may be reduced to these three: wealth, honor, and sensual pleasure. The II/6 mind is so distracted by these three that it cannot give the slightest thought to any other good.

[4] For as far as sensual pleasure is concerned, the mind is so caught up in it, as if at peace in a [true] good, that it is quite prevented from thinking of anything else. But after the enjoyment of sensual pleasure is past, the greatest sadness follows. If this does not completely engross, still it thoroughly confuses and dulls the mind.

The mind is also distracted not a little by the pursuit of honors and wealth, particularly when the latter is sought only for its own sake, because it is assumed to be the highest good. [5] But the mind is far more distracted by honor. For this is always assumed to be good through itself and the ultimate end toward which everything is directed.

---

[1] From the *Treatise on the Emendation of the Intellect*, Bruder §§1–17.

Nor do honor and wealth have, as sensual pleasure does, repentance as a natural consequence. The more each of these is possessed, the more joy is increased, and hence the more we are spurred on to increase them. But if our hopes should chance to be frustrated, we experience the greatest sadness. And finally, honor has this great disadvantage: to pursue it, we must direct our lives according to other men's powers of understanding—fleeing what they commonly flee and seeking what they commonly seek.

[6] Since I saw that all of these things stood in the way of my working toward this new goal, indeed were so opposed to it that one or the other must be given up, I was forced to ask what would be more useful to me. For as I say, I seemed to be willing to lose the certain good for the uncertain one. But after I had considered the matter a little, I first found that, if I devoted myself to this new plan of life, and gave up the old, I would be giving up a good by its nature uncertain (as we can clearly infer from what has been said) for one uncertain not by its nature (for I was seeking a permanent good) but only in respect to its attainment.

[7] By persistent meditation, however, I came to the conclusion that, if only I could resolve, wholeheartedly, [to change my plan of life], I would be giving up certain evils for a certain good. For I saw that I was in the greatest danger, and that I was forced to seek a remedy with all my strength, however uncertain it might be—like a man suffering from a fatal illness, who, foreseeing certain death unless he employs a remedy, is forced to seek it, however uncertain, with all his strength. For all his hope lies there. But all those things men ordinarily strive for, not only provide no remedy to preserve our being, but in fact hinder that preservation, often cause the destruction of those who possess them, and always cause the destruction of those who are possessed by them.

[8] There are a great many examples of people who have suffered persecution to the death on account of their wealth, or have exposed themselves to so many dangers to acquire wealth that they have at last paid the penalty for their folly with their life. Nor are there fewer examples of people who, to attain or defend honor, have suffered most miserably. And there are innumerable examples of people who have hastened their death through too much sensual pleasure.

[9] Furthermore, these evils seemed to have arisen from the fact that all happiness or unhappiness is placed in the quality of the object to which we cling with love. For strife will never arise on account of what is not loved, nor will there be sadness if it perishes, nor envy if it is possessed by another, nor fear, nor hatred—in a word, no disturbances of the mind. Indeed, all these happen only in the love of those things that can perish, as all the things we have just spoken of can do.

[10] But love toward the eternal and infinite thing feeds the mind

with a joy entirely exempt from sadness. This is greatly to be desired, and to be sought with all our strength.

But not without reason did I use these words *if only I could resolve in earnest*. For though I perceived these things [NS: this evil] so clearly in my mind, I still could not, on that account, put aside all greed, desire for sensual pleasure, and love of esteem.

[11] I saw this, however: that so long as the mind was turned toward these thoughts, it was turned away from those things, and was thinking seriously about the new goal. That was a great comfort to me. For I saw that those evils would not refuse to yield to remedies. And although in the beginning these intervals were rare, and lasted a very short time, nevertheless, after the true good became more and more known to me, the intervals became more frequent and longer—especially after I saw that the acquisition of money, sensual pleasure, and esteem are only obstacles so long as they are sought for their own sakes, and not as means to other things. But if they are sought as means, then they will have a limit, and will not be obstacles at all. On the contrary, they will be of great use in attaining the end on account of which they are sought, as we shall show in its place.

II/8

[12] Here I shall only say briefly what I understand by the true good, and at the same time, what the highest good is. To understand this properly, it must be noted that good and bad are said of things only in a certain respect, so that one and the same thing can be called both good and bad according to different respects. The same applies to perfect and imperfect. For nothing, considered in its own nature, will be called perfect or imperfect, especially after we have recognized that everything that happens happens according to the eternal order, and according to certain laws of Nature.

[13] But since human weakness does not grasp that order by its own thought, and meanwhile man conceives a human nature much stronger and more enduring than his own, and at the same time sees that nothing prevents his acquiring such a nature, he is spurred to seek means that will lead him to such a perfection. Whatever can be a means to his attaining it is called a true good; but the highest good is to arrive— together with other individuals if possible—at the enjoyment of such a nature. What that nature is we shall show in its proper place: that it is the knowledge of the union that the mind has with the whole of Nature.

[14] This, then, is the end I aim at: to acquire such a nature, and to strive that many acquire it with me. That is, it is part of my happiness to take pains that many others may understand as I understand, so that their intellect and desire agree entirely with my intellect and desire. To do this it is necessary, *first*, to understand as much of Nature as suffices for acquiring such a nature; *next*, to form a society of the kind that is

II/9

desirable, so that as many as possible may attain it as easily and surely as possible.

[15] *Third*, attention must be paid to Moral Philosophy and to Instruction concerning the Education of children. Because Health is no small means to achieving this end, *fourth*, the whole of Medicine must be worked out. And because many difficult things are rendered easy by ingenuity, and by it we can gain much time and convenience in life, *fifth*, Mechanics is in no way to be despised.

[16] Before anything else we must devise a way of healing the intellect, and purifying it, as much as we can in the beginning, so that it understands things successfully, without error and as well as possible. Everyone will now be able to see that I wish to direct all the sciences toward one end and goal, namely, that we should achieve, as we have said, the highest human perfection. So anything in the sciences which does nothing to advance us toward our goal must be rejected as useless— in a word, all our activities and thoughts are to be directed to this end.

[17] But while we pursue this end, and devote ourselves to bringing the intellect back to the right path, it is necessary to live. So we are forced, before we do anything else, to assume certain rules of living as good:

1. To speak according to the power of understanding of ordinary people, and do whatever does not interfere with our attaining our purpose. For we can gain a considerable advantage from this, if we yield as much to their understanding as we can. Moreover, in this way, they will give a favorable hearing to the truth.

2. To enjoy pleasures just so far as suffices for safeguarding our health.

3. Finally, to seek money, or anything else, just so far as suffices for sustaining life and health, and conforming to those customs of the community that do not conflict with our aim.

II. A Critique of Traditional Religion

A. On Religion and Superstition[2]

[1] If men could manage all their affairs by a certain plan, or if fortune were always favorable to them, they would never be in the grip of superstition. But since they are often reduced to such straits that they can bring no plan into operation, and since they generally vacillate wretch-

III/5

---

[2] From the preface to the *Theological-Political Treatise*, Bruder §§1–4, 7–10, 14–20.

edly between hope and fear, from an immoderate desire for the uncertain goods of fortune, for the most part their hearts are ready to believe anything at all. While they are in doubt, a slight impulse drives them this way or that; and this happens all the more easily when, torn by hope and fear, they are at a loss to know what to do; at other times they are too trusting, boastful, and overconfident.

[2] Everyone, I think, knows this, though most people, I believe, do not know themselves. For no one has lived among men without seeing that, when they are prospering, even those who are quite inexperienced are generally so overflowing with wisdom that they believe themselves to be wronged if anyone wants to give them advice. In adversity, on the other hand, they do not know where to turn and humbly ask advice of everyone. They hear no advice so foolish and so absurd or groundless that they do not follow it. They hope now for better things, and then again fear worse, all for the slightest reasons. [3] For if, while they are tormented by fear, they see something happen which reminds them of some past good or evil, they think that it portends either a fortunate or an unfortunate outcome, and for that reason they call it a favorable or unfavorable omen, even though it may deceive them a hundred times. Again, if they see something unusual, and wonder greatly at it, they believe it to be a portent of disaster, which indicates the anger of the Gods or of the supreme God. Prey to superstition and contrary to religion, men consider it a sacrilege not to avert the disaster by sacrifices and votive offerings. They create countless fictions and interpret nature in amazing ways, as if the whole of nature were as insane as they are.

[4] In these circumstances, we see that it is particularly those who immoderately desire uncertain things who are thoroughly enslaved to every kind of superstition, and that they all invoke divine aid with votive offerings and unmanly tears, especially when they are in danger and cannot help themselves. Because reason cannot show a certain way to the hollow things they desire, they call it blind, and human wisdom hollow. The delusions of the imagination, on the other hand, and dreams and childish follies they believe to be divine answers. Indeed, they believe God rejects the wise, and writes his decrees not in the mind, but in the entrails of animals, or that fools, madmen, and birds foretell his decrees by divine inspiration and prompting. Thus does fear make men insane.

[7] Whatever some may say, who think that superstition arises from the fact that all mortals have a certain confused idea of divinity, from the cause of superstition I have given, it follows clearly, [first,] that all men by nature are liable to superstition; next, that, like all delusions of the mind and impulses of frenzy, it must be very fluctuating and inconstant; III/6

and finally, that it is preserved only by hope, hate, anger, and deception, because it arises, not from reason, but only from the most effective of affects.

[8] As easily, then, as men are taken in by any kind of superstition, it is just as difficult to make them stand firm in one and the same superstition. Indeed, because the common people always remain equally wretched, they are never satisfied for long, but are most pleased by what is new, and has not yet deceived them. This inconstancy, indeed, has been the cause of many outbreaks of disorder and bloody wars. For as is evident from what we have just said, and as Curtius noted very aptly, "Nothing sways the masses more effectively than superstition."[3] That is why they are easily led, under the pretext of religion, now to worship their Kings as Gods, now to curse and loathe them as the common plague of the human race.

[9] To avoid this evil [of inconstancy], immense zeal is brought to bear to embellish religion—whether true or false—with ceremony and pomp, so that it will be considered weightier than every [other] influence and always worshiped by everyone with the utmost deference. The Turks have succeeded so well at this that they consider it a sacrilege even to discuss [matters of religion] and they fill everyone's judgment with so many prejudices that they leave no room in the mind for sound reason even to suggest a doubt.

[10] But if the great secret of monarchic rule, and its whole interest, is to keep men deceived and to cloak in the specious name of religion the fear by which they must be checked, so that they will fight for slavery as they would for salvation, and will think it not shameful, but an honorable achievement, to give their life and blood that one man may have a ground for boasting, nevertheless, in a free state nothing more unfortunate can be contrived or attempted. For it is completely contrary to the common freedom to fill the free judgment of each man with prejudices, or to restrain it in any way. . . .

[14] I have often wondered that men who boast of their allegiance to the Christian religion—that is, to love, gladness, peace, continence, and honesty toward all—would contend so unfairly against one another, and indulge daily in the bitterest hate toward one another, so that each man's faith is known more easily from the latter [i.e., his hate] than from the former [i.e., his love, etc.]. For long ago things reached the point where you can hardly know what anyone is, whether Christian, Turk, Jew, or Pagan, except by the external grooming and dress of his body, or because he frequents this or that place of worship, or because he is at-

III/7

III/8

---

[3] * *History of Alexander the Great*, IV, x, 7.

tached to this or that opinion, or because he is accustomed to swear by the words of some teacher. All lead the same kind of life.

[15] What, then, is the cause of this evil? Doubtless that to ordinary people religion has consisted in regarding the ministry of a church as a position worthy of respect, its offices as sources of income, and its clergy as deserving the highest honor. For as soon as this abuse began in the church, the worst men acquired a great desire to administer the sacred offices; the love of propagating divine religion degenerated into sordid greed and ambition, and the house of worship itself into a theater, where one hears not learned ecclesiastics, but orators, each possessed by a longing, not to teach the people, but to carry them away with admiration for himself, to censure publicly those who disagree, and to teach only those new and unfamiliar doctrines which the people most admire. From this, of course, there had to come great quarrels, envy, and hate, whose violence no passage of time could lessen.

[16] It is no wonder, then, that nothing has remained of the religion that used to be, beyond its external ceremony, by which the people seem more to flatter God than to worship him, no wonder that faith is nothing now but credulity and prejudices. And what prejudices! They turn men from rational beings into beasts, since they completely prevent everyone from using his free judgment and from distinguishing the true from the false, and seem deliberately designed to put out the light of the intellect entirely. [17] Piety—good heavens!—and religion consist in absurd mysteries, and those who scorn reason completely, and reject the intellect as corrupt by nature, they are the ones who are most undeservedly thought to have the divine light. Of course if they only had even the least spark of divine light, they would not rave so proudly, but would learn to worship God more wisely, and would surpass others in love, not, as now, in hate. Instead of persecuting with such a hostile spirit those who disagree with them, they would pity them—if, indeed, they feared for the salvation of the others, and not for their own position.

[18] Moreover, if they had any divine light, it would at least be manifest from their teaching. I confess that they could never have wondered sufficiently at the most profound mysteries of Scripture. Nevertheless, I do not see that they have taught anything but Aristotelian and Platonic speculations. Not to seem to constantly follow Pagans, they have accommodated Scripture to these speculations. [19] It was not enough for them to be insane with the Greeks; they wanted the Prophets to rave with them. This clearly shows, of course, that they do not see the divinity of Scripture even through a dream. The more immoderately they wonder at these mysteries, the more they show that they do not so much

III/9

believe Scripture as give [merely verbal] assent to it. This is also evident from the fact that most of them suppose, as a foundation for understanding Scripture and unearthing its true meaning, that it is, in every passage, true and divine. So what one ought to establish by understanding Scripture, and subjecting it to a strict examination, and what we would be far better taught by Scripture itself, which needs no human inventions, they maintain at the outset as a rule for the interpretation of Scripture.

[20] When I weighed these matters in my mind—when I considered that the natural light is not only scorned, but condemned by many as a source of impiety, that human inventions are treated as divine teachings, that credulity is considered faith, that the controversies of the Philosophers are debated with the utmost passion in the Church and in the State, and that in consequence the most savage hatreds and disagreements arise, by which men are easily turned to rebellions—when I considered these and a great many other things, which it would take too long to tell here, I resolved earnestly to examine Scripture afresh, with an unimpaired and free spirit, to affirm nothing concerning it, and to admit nothing as its teaching, which it did not very clearly teach me.

B. On Revelation[4]

III/15   [1] Prophecy, *or* Revelation, is the certain knowledge of some thing, revealed by God to men. And the Prophet is he who interprets the things revealed by God to those who cannot have certain knowledge of them, and who thus can only embrace the things revealed by sheer faith. . . . [2] From the definition we have just given [of prophecy], it follows that natural knowledge can be called prophecy. For the things we know by the natural light depend on the knowledge of God and of his eternal decrees. But this natural knowledge is common to all men, since it depends on foundations common to all men. Hence, the people, who are always thirsting for things which are rare and foreign to their nature, and who spurn their natural gifts, do not put much value on it. When they speak of prophetic knowledge, they wish to exclude natural knowledge. [3] Nevertheless, it can be called divine with as much right as anything else, since God's nature, insofar as we participate in it, and his decrees, as it were, dictate it to us. Nor does [this natural knowledge] differ from that which everyone calls divine except that the latter ex-

[4] From the *Theological-Political Treatise*, ch. I ("Of Prophecy"), Bruder §§1–10, 13–19, 21–25, 40, 43, and 44, and ch. II ("Of Prophets"), §§1–4, 6, 10, 12–15, 25–27, 30–31, 35–39, 41–47, 53, and 57.

tends beyond the limits of [natural knowledge] and that the laws of human nature, considered in themselves, cannot be its cause. But in the certainty which natural knowledge involves, and in the source from which it is derived, which is God, it is in no way inferior to prophetic knowledge—unless, perhaps, someone wishes to understand, or rather to dream, that the Prophets had, indeed, a human body, but not a human mind, and thus that their sensations and awareness were of an entirely different nature than ours are. III/16

[4] But though natural knowledge is divine, nevertheless those who spread it cannot be called Prophets. For the things they teach other men can perceive and embrace with the same certainty and excellence as they do, and that not by faith alone.

[5] Simply because our mind contains objectively in itself, and partic-ipates in, the nature of God, it has the power to form certain notions which explain the nature of things and teach us how to conduct our lives. We can, therefore, rightly maintain that the nature of the mind, insofar as it is conceived in this way, is the first cause of divine revela-tion. For whatever we clearly and distinctly understand, the idea of God (as we have just indicated) and nature dictate to us, not indeed in words, but in a far more excellent way, which agrees best with the nature of the mind, so that everyone who has tasted the certainty of the intellect has doubtless experienced it in himself.

[6] Since my principal purpose is to speak only of those things which concern Scripture, it is enough to have said these few things about the natural light. So I proceed to discuss in greater detail the other causes and means by which God reveals to men those things which exceed the limits of natural knowledge—and even those which do not exceed them. (For nothing prevents God from communicating to men in other ways the same things we know by the light of nature.)

[7] But whatever can be said about these matters must be derived from Scripture alone. For what can we say about things exceeding the limits of our intellect beyond what has been passed down to us from the Prophets themselves, either orally or in writing? And because today, so far as I know, we have no Prophets, nothing is left to us but to expound the sacred books left to us by the Prophets. But with this precaution: we should maintain nothing about such things, nor attribute anything to the Prophets themselves which they did not clearly say repeatedly.

[8] Here the first thing to be noted is that the Jews never mention or heed intervening, *or* particular, causes, but for the sake of religion and of piety, *or* (as is commonly said) of devotion, they always recur to God. III/17
For example, if they have made money by trade, they say that God has

11

provided it to them; if they desire that something should happen, they say that God has [so] disposed their heart; and if they even think something, they say that God has told them this. So not everything which Scripture asserts that God has said to someone is to be regarded as prophecy and supernatural knowledge, but only those things which Scripture expressly says were prophecy *or* revelation, or [whose status as prophecy] follows from the circumstances of the narration.

[9] So if we run through the sacred books, we will see that all those things God revealed to the Prophets were revealed to them either in words, or in visible forms, or in both words and visible forms. The words and the visible forms were either true, and outside the imagination of the Prophet who heard or saw them, or else imaginary, [occurring] because the imagination of the Prophet was so disposed, even while he was awake, that he clearly seemed to himself to hear words or to see something.

[10] It was by a true voice that God revealed to Moses the laws he willed to be prescribed to the Hebrews, as is apparent from Exodus 25:22. . . . This indeed shows that God used a true voice, since Moses used to find God there, available to speak to him, whenever he wanted to. And as I shall soon show, this was the only true voice by which the law was pronounced. . . .

III/18 [13] In the opinion of certain Jews, the words of the Decalogue were not pronounced by God. They think, rather, that the Israelites only heard a sound, which did not pronounce any words, and that while it lasted, they perceived the laws of the Decalogue with a pure mind. I too have sometimes conjectured this, because I saw that the words of the Decalogue in Exodus are not the same as those of the Decalogue in Deuteronomy.[5] Since God spoke only once, it seems to follow from this [variation] that the Decalogue does not claim to teach the very words of God, but only their meaning. [14] But unless we wish to do violence to Scripture, we absolutely must grant that the Israelites heard a true voice. For Scripture says expressly, in Deuteronomy 5:4, that *face to face God spoke to you and so on*, that is, as two men usually communicate their concepts to one another, by means of their two bodies. So it seems more compatible with Scripture [to suppose] that God truly created some voice, by which he revealed the Decalogue. . . .

[15] But not every difficulty is removed in this way. For it seems quite foreign to reason to maintain that a created thing, dependent on God in the same way as any other, could express, in reality or in words, or

---

[5] Cf. Exodus 20:1–17 with Deuteronomy 5:1–21.

12

explain through his own person, the essence or existence of God, by saying in the first person, "I am your God, Yehowah, and so on." Of course, when someone says orally, "I have understood," no one thinks that the mouth of the man saying this has understood, but only that his mind has. Nevertheless, because the mouth is related to the nature of the man saying this, and also because he to whom it is said had perceived the nature of the intellect, he easily understands the mind of the man speaking by comparison with his own. [16] But if people knew nothing of God beyond his name—and desired to speak to him, in order to become certain of his Existence—I do not see how their request would be satisfied by a creature (who was no more related to God than any other creature and who did not pertain to God's nature) who said, "I am God." What if God had twisted Moses' lips to pronounce and say the same words, "I am God"? Would they have understood from that that God exists? What if they were the lips, not of Moses, but of some beast?

III/19

[17] Next, Scripture seems to indicate absolutely that God himself spoke—that was why he descended from heaven to the top of Mt. Sinai—and that the Jews not only heard him speaking, but that the Elders even saw him. See Exodus 24[:10]. Nor did the law revealed to Moses (to which nothing could be added and from which nothing could be taken away, and which was established as the legislation of the Country) ever command us to believe that God is incorporeal, or that he has no image *or* visible form, but only to believe that God exists, to trust in him, and to worship him alone.

Lest they fall away from his worship, it commanded them not to fictitiously ascribe any image to him, and not to make any image. [18] For since they had not seen the image of God, they could not make any which would resemble God, but only one which would resemble another created thing which they had seen. So when they worshiped God through that image, they would think not about God, but about the thing that image resembled, and they would bestow on that thing the honor and worship due to God. But Scripture clearly indicates that God has a visible form and that it was granted to Moses, when he heard God speaking, to look upon it, though he was permitted to see only the back parts.[6] I do not doubt but what there is some mystery concealed here. . . .

[19] That Revelation has happened by images alone is evident from 1 Chronicles 21[:16] where God shows his anger to David through an

---

[6] See Exodus 33:20–23.

Angel holding a sword in his hand. . . . Maimonides and others claim that this story, and likewise all those that tell the appearance of some angel,[7*] happened in a dream, but not really, because a person could not see an Angel with his eyes open. But they talk nonsense, of course. For their only concern is to extort from Scripture Aristotelian rubbish and their own inventions. Nothing seems more ridiculous to me.

III/20   [21] But all these things are confirmed more clearly from the text of Numbers 12:6–8, which reads: *if there is some Prophet among you, I shall reveal myself to him in a vision*, that is, through visible forms and symbols, for of the Prophecy of Moses he says that it is a vision without symbols, *I shall speak to him in a dream*, that is, not with real words and a true voice. *But to Moses* (I do) *not* (reveal myself) *in this way; to him I speak mouth to mouth, and in a vision, but not with enigmatic sayings; and he looks upon the image of God*, that is, he looks upon me as a friend and is not terrified when he speaks with me, as is maintained in Exodus 33:11. So there can be no doubt that the other Prophets did not hear a true voice. This is confirmed still further by Deuteronomy 34:10, where it is said that *there has never existed* (strictly, arisen) *in Israel a prophet like Moses, whom God knew face to face*. This, indeed, must be understood to refer to the voice alone. For not even Moses had ever seen God's face (Exodus 33[:20]).

[22] Besides these means I do not find in the Sacred Texts any others by which God communicated himself to men. So as we have shown above, no others are to be feigned or admitted. Of course, we clearly understand that God can communicate himself immediately to men, for he communicates his essence to our mind without using any corporeal means. Nevertheless, for a man to perceive by the mind alone things
III/21   which are not contained in the first foundations of our knowledge, and cannot be deduced from them, his mind would necessarily have to be far more outstanding and excellent than the human mind is.

[23] I do not believe that anyone has reached such perfection, surpassing all others, except Christ, to whom God immediately revealed— without words or visions—the conditions which lead men to salvation. So God revealed himself to the Apostles through Christ's mind, as formerly he had revealed himself to Moses by means of a heavenly voice. And therefore Christ's voice, like the one Moses heard, can be called the voice of God. And in this sense we can also say that God's Wisdom, that is, a Wisdom surpassing human wisdom, assumed a human nature in Christ, and that Christ was the way to salvation.

---

[7] * E.g., to Manoah [Judges 13:8–20], and to Abraham when he was intending to sacrifice his son [Genesis 22:11–18].

14

[24] But it is necessary to warn here that I am not speaking at all about those things which certain Churches maintain about Christ, nor do I deny them. For I freely confess that I do not grasp them.[8] I have only affirmed what I conclude from Scripture itself. For nowhere have I read that God appeared or spoke to Christ, but that God was revealed to the Apostles through Christ, that he is the way to salvation, and finally, that the old law was imparted by an Angel, but not by God immediately. So, if Moses spoke with God face to face, as a man usually does with a friend (i.e., by means of their two bodies), Christ, indeed, communicated with God mind to mind.

[25] We have asserted, therefore, that except for Christ no one received God's revelations without the aid of the imagination, that is, without the aid of words or images, and so that there is no need to have a more perfect mind in order to prophesy, but only a more vivid imagination. . . .

[40] Let us come round, finally, to the point we have been aiming at. III/27 From all these [examples] these phrases of Scripture become clear: *the Spirit of God was in the Prophet, God infused his Spirit into men, men were filled with the Spirit of God, and with the Holy Spirit*, and the like. For they mean nothing other than that the Prophets had a singular virtue, beyond what is ordinary, that they cultivated piety with exceptional constancy of heart, and that they perceived God's mind, *or*, judgment. . . .

[43] Therefore, we can now affirm, without any reservation, that the III/28 Prophets perceived God's revelations only with the aid of the imagination, that is, by the mediation of words or of images, the latter of which might be either true or imaginary. For since we find no other means in Scripture except these, we are not permitted to feign any others.

[44] If you ask by what laws of nature this [revelation] was made, I confess that I do not know. I could, indeed, say, as others do, that it was made by the power of God. But that would be idle chatter. For it would be the same thing as trying to explain the form of some singular thing by some transcendental term. All things are made through the power of God. Because the power of nature is nothing but the power of God

---

[8] Spinoza's references to Jesus in the *Theological-Political Treatise* caused concern among some of his first readers. In response to a request from Spinoza to indicate the passages in this work which had made learned men uneasy (Letter 68), Oldenburg wrote that some readers thought Spinoza might be concealing his "opinion concerning Jesus Christ, the redeemer of the world and sole mediator for mankind, and his incarnation and atonement." In subsequent correspondence with Oldenburg Spinoza explains that he thinks the doctrine of the incarnation, according to which God assumed a human nature, involves a contradiction (Letter 73), and that he accepts Christ's passion, death, and burial literally, but his resurrection only allegorically (Letter 78).

itself,[9] it is certain that insofar as we are ignorant of natural causes, we do not understand God's power. So it is foolish to fall back on that same power of God when we do not know the natural cause of some thing, that is, when we do not know God's power itself. But there is no need now for us to know the cause of prophetic knowledge. For as I have already indicated, here we are trying only to investigate the teachings of Scripture in order to draw our conclusions from them, as we would draw conclusions from the data of nature. We are not concerned in the least with the causes of those teachings.

III/29   [1] . . . [A]s we have already indicated, the prophets were endowed, not with a more perfect mind, but instead, with a power of imagining unusually vividly. The Scriptural narratives also teach this abundantly. For it is agreed that Solomon excelled all other men in wisdom, but not in the gift of prophecy. . . . This agrees also with both experience and reason. For those who have the most powerful imaginations are less able to grasp things by pure intellect. And conversely, those who are more capable in their intellect, and who cultivate it most, have a more moderate power of imagining, and have it more under their control. They keep it, as it were, in check, lest it be confused with the intellect.

     [2] So those who look in the books of the prophets for wisdom, and knowledge of natural and spiritual matters, go entirely astray. Since the time, philosophy and, finally, the matter itself demand it, I have decided to show this fully here. I care little for the protests of superstition, whose greatest hatred is directed against those who cultivate true III/30   knowledge and true life. Alas! Things have reached a state now where those who openly confess that they have no idea of God, and that they know God only through created things (of whose causes they are ignorant), do not blush to accuse philosophers of atheism.

     [3] To develop my subject in an orderly way, I shall show that prophecies varied, not only with the imagination and physical temperament of

---

[9] Another passage which caused concern among Spinoza's readers. Oldenburg complained (Letter 71) that Spinoza seemed to "speak ambiguously about God and Nature, and in the opinion of many, to confuse these two things." In reply Spinoza acknowledged that he had an opinion about the relation between God and Nature very different from the one modern Christians usually defend: "For I maintain that God is, as they say, the immanent, but not the transitive, cause of all things. That all things are in God and move in God, I affirm, I say, with Paul, and perhaps also with all the ancient philosophers, although in another way; and I would also dare to say, with all the ancient Hebrews, as far as it is permissible to conjecture from certain traditions, corrupted as they are in many ways. Nevertheless, some people think the *Theological-Political Treatise* rests on the assumption that God is one and the same as Nature (by which they understand a certain mass, or corporeal matter). This is a complete mistake." On the relation between God and Nature, see the excerpt in §IV.B. from the *Short Treatise*, I, ch. viii, and *Ethics* IP29S.

each prophet, but also with the opinions with which they were imbued, and so, that prophecy never made the prophets more learned, as I shall shortly explain more fully. But first, I must treat here of the certainty of the prophets, both because it is relevant to the argument of this chapter, and also because it will be of some use in demonstrating the conclusion we intend to establish.

[4] Unlike a clear and distinct idea, the simple imagination [of a thing] does not, of its nature, involve any certainty. Something must be added to the imagination—namely, reasoning—if we are to be able to be certain of the things we imagine. From this it follows that prophecy, through itself, cannot involve certainty, for as we have shown, it depends solely on the imagination. Therefore, the prophets were certain concerning God's revelation, not through that revelation itself, but through some sign. This is evident from Genesis 15:8, where Abraham asked for a sign after he had heard God's promise. He trusted God, of course, and did not ask for a sign in order to have faith in God. He asked for a sign in order to know that it was God who had made this promise to him. . . .

[6] In this respect, therefore, prophecy is inferior to natural knowledge, which requires no sign, but involves certainty of its own nature. And indeed, this prophetic certainty was not mathematical, but only moral, as may also be established from Scripture itself. For in Deuteronomy 13[:2] Moses warns that any prophet who wants to teach new Gods should be condemned to death, even though he confirms his teaching with signs and miracles. For as Moses himself goes on to say, God also makes signs and miracles to test the people. . . .   III/31

[10] The whole of prophetic certainty, therefore, is founded on these three things:

1) That they imagined the things revealed to them very vividly, in the way we are usually affected by objects when we are awake;

2) On a sign;

3) Finally, and mainly, that they had a heart inclined only to the right and the good.

And although Scripture does not always make mention of a sign, nevertheless we must believe that the prophets always had a sign. For as many have already noted, Scripture is not accustomed always to narrate all the conditions and circumstances, but rather to suppose them as known. . . .

[12] Since the certainty which arose in the prophets from signs was   III/32
not mathematical (i.e., did not follow from the necessity of the perception of the thing perceived or seen), but only moral, and signs were

17

given only to persuade the prophet, it follows that signs were given according to the opinions and capacity of the prophet, in such a way that a sign which would render one prophet certain of his prophecy could not convince at all another, who was imbued with different opinions. So the signs varied in each prophet.

[13] So also the revelation itself varied, as we have said, in each prophet, according to the disposition of his physical temperament and of his imagination, and according to the opinions he had previously embraced. It varied according to his temperament in this way: if the prophet was cheerful, victories, peace, and things which move men in turn to joy were revealed to him; for such men usually imagine things of that kind more frequently; on the other hand, if the prophet was sad, wars, punishments, and all evils were revealed to him; and thus, as the prophet was compassionate, calm, prone to anger, severe, and the like, to that extent he was more ready for one kind of revelation than for another.

[14] It varied also according to the disposition of his imagination, in the following way. If the prophet was refined, he perceived the mind of God in a refined style; but if he was confused, then he perceived it confusedly. It varied similarly concerning those revelations which were represented through images. If the prophet was a countryman, bulls and cows were represented to him; if he was a soldier, generals and armies; if he was a courtier, the royal throne and things of that kind.

[15] Prophecy varied, finally, according to differences in the opinions of the prophets. To the magi, who believed in the trifles of astrology, Christ's birth was revealed through the imagination of a star rising in the east (see Matthew 2). To the augurs of Nebuchadnezzar the destruction of Jerusalem was revealed in the entrails of animals (see Ezekiel 21:26). The same king also understood this from oracles and from the direction of arrows which he hurled up into the air. Again, to those prophets who believed that men act from free choice and from their own power, God was revealed as indifferent, and as unaware of future human actions. We shall demonstrate all these things separately from Scripture itself. . . .

III/33

III/35 [25] With remarkable rashness everyone has persuaded himself that the prophets knew everything the human intellect can attain to. And although certain passages of Scripture indicate to us as clearly as possible that the prophets were ignorant of certain things, they prefer to say that they do not understand Scripture in those passages, rather than to concede that the prophets were ignorant of something. Or else they strive to twist the words of Scripture so that it says what it plainly does not mean. Of course, if either of these [ways of dealing with Scripture] is permissible, then it is all up with the whole of Scripture. In vain will we strive to show something from Scripture, if it is permissible to number the clearest [passages] among those which are obscure and impenetrable or to interpret them as one pleases.

[26] For example, nothing in Scripture is clearer than that Joshua, and perhaps also the author who wrote his history, thought that the sun moves around the earth, but that the earth is at rest, and that the sun stood still for some time. Nevertheless, there are many who do not want to concede that there can be any change in the heavens, and who therefore explain this passage in such a way that it seems to say nothing like that. Others, who have learned to philosophize more correctly, since they understand that the earth moves, whereas the sun is at rest, *or* does not move around the earth, strive with all their powers to twist the same [truth] out of Scripture, though it cries out in open protest against this treatment. I wonder at them indeed.   III/36

[27] Are we, I ask, bound to believe that Joshua, a soldier, was skilled in astronomy? and that the miracle could not be revealed to him, or that the light of the sun could not remain longer than usual above the horizon unless Joshua understood the cause of this? Both of these [alternatives] seem to me ridiculous. I prefer, therefore, to say openly that Joshua did not know the true cause of the greater duration of that light, that he and the whole crowd who were present all thought that the sun moves with a daily motion around the earth, and that on that day it stood still for some time. They believed this to be the cause of the greater duration of that light and they did not attend to the fact that a refraction greater than usual could arise from the great amount of ice which was then in that part of the air (see Joshua 10:11), or from something else like that, which is not our present concern. . . .

[30] If it is permissible to feign that Scripture thought otherwise, but wished, because of some reason unknown to us, to write in this way, then this is nothing but a complete overturning of the whole of Scripture. For each [interpreter] with equal right will be able to say the same thing about every passage in Scripture. As a result, it will be permissible to defend and to put into practice whatever absurdity or evil human malice can think up, without harm to the authority of Scripture. But what we have maintained contains no impiety. For though Solomon, Isaiah, Joshua, and the rest were prophets, they were nevertheless men, and nothing human should be thought alien to them.   III/37

[31] The revelation to Noah that God was destroying the human race [Genesis 6:11–13] was also according to his power of understanding, because he thought that the earth was not inhabited outside of Palestine. The prophets could be ignorant not only of things of this kind, but

also of others of greater moment, without harm to their piety. And they really were ignorant of these things. For they taught nothing singular concerning the divine attributes, but had quite ordinary opinions about God. And their revelations were also accommodated to these opinions, as I shall now show by many testimonies from Scripture. From this you will easily see that [the prophets] are praised, and greatly commended, not so much on account of the loftiness and excellence of their understanding as on account of their piety and constancy of heart. . . .

III/38   [35] And Moses,[10] too, did not sufficiently perceive that God is omniscient and that all human actions are directed by his decree alone. For although God had told him (see Exodus 3:18) that the Israelites would obey him, he called the matter in question and replied (see Exodus 4:1): *what if they do not believe me and do not obey me.* And therefore God was revealed to him as indifferent and unaware of future human actions. For he gave him two signs and said (Exodus 4:8): *if it should happen that they do not believe the first sign, still they will believe the latter; but if they do not believe even the latter, take (then) some water from the river and so on.*

[36] And if anyone wants to assess carefully and without prejudice Moses' judgments, he will find clearly that his opinion of God was that he is a being who has always existed, exists, and always will exist. For this reason he calls him by the name *Yehowah*, which in Hebrew expresses these three times of existing. But concerning his nature he teaches nothing else than that he is compassionate, kind, and the like, and supremely jealous, as is established by a great many passages in the Pentateuch.[11] Next, he believed and taught that this being differs so from all other beings that it cannot be expressed by any image of anything seen, nor can it even be seen—not so much because the thing involves a contradiction as because of human weakness. Moreover, he also taught that by reason of his power he is singular or unique.

[37] He conceded, of course, that there are beings which—doubtless from God's order and command—perform the functions of God, that is, beings to whom God has given the authority, right, and power to direct nations, to provide for them, and to care for them. But he taught III/39   that this being, which [the Jews] were bound to worship, was the highest and supreme God, *or* (to use a Hebrew phrase) the God of Gods. And so in the song of Exodus (15:11) he said: *who among the Gods is like you, Yehowah?* And Jethro [says] (in Exodus 18:11): *now I know that Yehowah*

---

[10] Spinoza gives many examples, but focuses particularly on Moses, because, as he points out, there is Scriptural warrant for giving him a special place among the prophets. Cf. Exodus 33:11 and Deuteronomy 34:10. The superiority of Moses to the other prophets was one of the thirteen principles Maimonides identified as essential to Judaism.

[11] E.g., in Exodus 20:5 and Deuteronomy 5:9.

is greater than all the Gods, that is, at last I am forced to concede to Moses that Yehowah is greater than all the Gods and singular in power. But it can be doubted whether Moses believed that these beings which perform the functions of God were created by God, since, so far as we know, he never said anything about their creation and beginning.

[38] In addition, he taught that this being brought this visible world out of chaos into order (see Genesis 1:2), that he put seeds in nature, so that he has the highest right and the highest power over all things, and (see Deuteronomy 10:14–15) that in accordance with this highest right and highest power he chose, for himself alone, the Hebrew nation and a certain region of the world (see Deuteronomy 4:19, 32:8–9), but that he left the other nations and regions to the care of the other Gods substituted by him. For that reason [Yehowah] was called the God of Israel and of Jerusalem (see 2 Chronicles 32:19), whereas the other Gods were called the Gods of the other nations.

[39] And for this reason also the Jews believed that the region God had chosen for himself required a special worship of God, different from that of other regions, and indeed that it could not permit the worship of other Gods, which was proper to other regions. For those nations which the King of Assyria brought into the lands of the Jews were believed to be torn to pieces by lions because they did not know the worship of the Gods of that land. (See 2 Kings 17:25, 26, etc.). . . .

[41] Finally, [Moses] believed that this being, *or* God, had his dwelling place in the heavens (see Deuteronomy 33:27), an opinion which was very common among the Gentiles.

If we attend now to Moses' revelations, we shall find that they were   III/40
accommodated to these opinions. For because he believed that God's nature admits of all those conditions which we have mentioned, compassion, kindness, and the like, God was revealed to him according to this opinion of his and under these attributes. (See Exodus 34:6–7, where it is told how God appeared to Moses, and the Decalogue, [Exodus 20:]4–5.)

[42] Next, we are told in [Exodus] 33:18[–23] that Moses asked God to be allowed to see him. But since, as we have already said, Moses had formed no image of God in his brain, and since, as we have already shown, God is revealed to the Prophets only according to the disposition of their imagination, God did not appear to him by any image. I say that this happened because it was inconsistent with Moses' imagination [for him to see God]. For other Prophets testify that they saw God, namely, Isaiah, Ezekiel, Daniel, and so on. [43] And for this reason God replied to Moses, *you will not be able to see my face.* And because Moses believed that God is visible, that is, that it implies no contradiction in

21

the divine nature [for God to be seen] (for otherwise he would not have asked anything like that), [God] adds, *since no one shall see me and live.* He therefore renders to Moses a reason consistent with his own opinion. For he does not say that it involves a contradiction on the part of the divine nature [for God to be seen], as it really does, but that it cannot happen because of human weakness.

[44] Next, to reveal to Moses that because the Israelites had worshiped the calf, they had become like the other nations, God says (Exodus 33:2–3) that he will send an angel, that is, a being which would take care of the Israelites in place of the supreme being, but that he does not wish to be among them. For this left nothing to Moses which would show him that the Israelites were dearer to God than the other nations, which God also gave over to the care of other beings, *or* angels. This is shown by Exodus 33:16.

[45] Finally, because God was believed to live in the heavens, he was revealed as descending from heaven to the top of a mountain. Moses also went up the mountain to speak with God, which would not be necessary for him at all, if he could imagine God to be everywhere with equal ease.

The Israelites knew almost nothing about God, even though he was revealed to them. They showed this more than sufficiently when, after a few days, they handed over the honor and worship due him to a calf [Exodus 32], and believed that it was the Gods which had brought them out of Egypt. [46] Nor is it credible that men accustomed to the superstitions of the Egyptians, unsophisticated, and worn out by the most wretched bondage, would have understood anything sensible about God, or that Moses would have taught them anything other than a way of living—and that not as a philosopher, so that after some time they might be constrained to live well from freedom of mind, but as a legislator, so that they would be constrained by the command of the law to live well.

[47] So the way of living well, *or* true life, and the worship and love of God were to them more bondage than true freedom, and the grace and gift of God. For he ordered them to love God and to keep his law that they might acknowledge past goods received from God, such as their freedom from bondage in Egypt. He terrified them with threats, if they transgressed those precepts, and he promised them many goods if they respected them. So he taught them in the same way parents customarily do children who are lacking in all reason. Hence, it is certain that they did not know the excellence of virtue and true blessedness. . . .

[53] We conclude, therefore, that we are not bound to believe the Prophets regarding anything except what is the end and substance of

III/41

III/42

revelation. In all other things each person is free to believe as he pleases. For example, the revelation to Cain teaches us only that God warned him to lead a true life, for that was the only intent and substance of the revelation, not teach the freedom of the will or philosophic matters. So even though the freedom of the will is contained very clearly in the words and reasonings of that warning, we are permitted to think the contrary, since those words and reasonings were only accommodated to Cain's power of understanding. . . .

III/43

[57] Finally, we must say absolutely the same thing about the reasonings and signs of the Apostles. There is no need to speak more fully about these matters. For if I were to enumerate all those Passages in Scripture which are written only *ad hominem*, *or*, according to someone's power of understanding, and which cannot be defended as divine teaching without great prejudice to Philosophy, I would give up the brevity I desire. Let it suffice, therefore, to have touched on a few, universal things. The rest the inquiring reader may weigh for himself.[12]

III/44

C. On God as an Agent in History[13]

[1] The true happiness and blessedness of each person consists only in the enjoyment of the good, but not in a self-esteem founded on the fact that he alone, to the exclusion of all the others, enjoys the good. For he who thinks himself more blessed because things are well with him, but not with others, or because he is more blessed than others and more fortunate, does not know true happiness and blessedness, and the joy which he conceives from that, unless it is childish, arises only from envy and a bad heart.

[2] For example, the true happiness and blessedness of man consist only in wisdom and in knowledge of the true, but not at all in the fact that one is wiser than others, or that the others lack true knowledge. For this does not increase his wisdom at all, that is, his true happiness. So someone who is glad for that reason is glad because of someone else's evil, and therefore is envious and evil. He knows neither true wisdom nor the peace of true life.

[3] Therefore when Scripture, to exhort the Hebrews to obey the law, says that God chose them for himself before the other nations (Deuter-

---

[12] It is characteristic of the *Theological-Political Treatise* to concentrate much more heavily on the Old Testament than the New. Spinoza excuses this neglect by disclaiming adequate knowledge of Greek to deal with it properly, but perhaps an unacknowledged reason is his concern for the sensibilities of his largely Christian audience. Cf. the provisional morality of the *Treatise on the Intellect* §17.

[13] From the *Theological-Political Treatise*, ch. III ("On the Calling of the Hebrews"), Bruder §§1–15.

onomy 10:15), that he is close to them, but not to others (Deuteronomy 4:4–7), that he has prescribed just laws only for them (Deuteronomy 4:8), and finally, that he has become known to them only, the others being treated as inferior (Deuteronomy 4:32), and so on, it speaks only according to the power of understanding of those who, as we have shown in the preceding chapter, and as Moses also witnesses (Deuteronomy 9:6–7), did not know true blessedness. [4] For surely they would have been no less blessed if God had called all equally to salvation; God would have been no less favorably disposed toward them, no matter how close he had been to the others; the laws would have been no less just, if they had been prescribed to all, nor would they themselves have been less wise; miracles would have shown the power of God no less if they had been performed on account of other nations also; and finally, the Hebrews would have been no less bound to worship God if God had bestowed all these gifts equally on all people.

III/45

[5] Moreover, what God says to Solomon—that no one after him would be as wise as he was (1 Kings 3:12)—seems to be only a manner of speaking, to signify exceptional wisdom. However that may be, we must not in any way believe that God promised Solomon, for his greater happiness, that he would not afterwards bestow such great wisdom on anyone else. For this would not increase Solomon's intellect at all, nor would a prudent King give less thanks to God for such a great gift, even if God had said that he would endow all with the same wisdom.

[6] But even if we say that in the passages of the Pentateuch just cited Moses was speaking according to the Hebrews' power of understanding, we still do not wish to deny that God prescribed those laws of the Pentateuch to them alone, nor that he spoke only to them, nor, finally, that the Hebrews saw wonders the like of which happened to no other nation. We mean only that Moses wanted to warn the Hebrews in this way, and especially by these reasons, so that he might bind them more to the worship of God, in accordance with their childish power of understanding. Next, we wished to show that the Hebrews did not excel the other nations in knowledge or in piety, but in something altogether different—*or* (to speak, with Scripture, according to their power of understanding) that, though the Hebrews were frequently warned, they were not chosen by God before all others for their true life and sublime speculations, but for something entirely different. What this was, I shall show here in an orderly fashion. [7] But before I begin, I want to explain briefly what, in the following, I shall understand by God's guidance, by God's aid (both external and internal), by God's choice, and finally, by fortune.

By God's guidance I understand the fixed and immutable order of

nature, *or* the connection of natural things. [8] For we have said above, III/46
and have already shown in another place, that the universal laws of nature, according to which all things happen and are determined, are
nothing but the eternal decrees of God, which always involve eternal
truth and necessity. Therefore, whether we say that all things happen
according to the laws of nature, or whether we say that they are ordered
according to the decree and guidance of God, we say the same thing.

[9] Next, because the power of all natural things is nothing but the
power of God, through which alone all things happen and are determined, it follows that whatever man, who is also a part of nature, provides for himself, as an aid to the preservation of his being, or whatever
nature provides for him, he himself doing nothing, all that is provided
for him by the power of God alone, either insofar as it acts through
human nature or through things outside human nature. Therefore,
whatever human nature can provide, from its own power alone, for preserving its being, we can rightly call the internal aid of God, and whatever turns out for his advantage from the power of external causes, we
can rightly call God's external aid.

[10] But from these [definitions] it is easy to infer what should be
understood by God's choice. For since no one does anything except
according to the predetermined order of nature, that is, according to
God's eternal guidance and decree, it follows that no one chooses any
manner of living for himself, nor does anything, except by the special
calling of God, who has chosen him before others for this work, or for
this manner of living.

[11] Finally, by fortune I understand nothing but God's guidance,
insofar as it directs human affairs through external and unforeseen
causes. With these preliminaries, we shall return to our purpose, which
was to see why the Hebrew nation was said to have been chosen by God
before others. To show this, I proceed as follows.

[12] Whatever we can honorably desire is related above all to these
three things: [i] to understand things through their first causes; [ii] to
gain control over the passions, *or* to acquire the habit of virtue; and
finally, [iii] to live securely and healthily. The means which lead directly
to the first and second of these, and can be considered their proximate
and efficient causes, are contained in human nature itself. So acquiring
them depends chiefly on our power alone, *or* on the laws of human
nature alone. For this reason we must absolutely maintain that these III/47
gifts are not peculiar to any nation, but have always been common to the
whole human race—unless we wish to dream that formerly nature produced different kinds of men. [13] But the means which lead to living
securely and preserving the body are chiefly placed in external things,

and for that reason they are called gifts of fortune, because they depend for the most part on the course of external causes of which we are ignorant. So in this matter, the wise man and the fool are almost equally happy or unhappy.

Nevertheless, human guidance and vigilance can do much to help us to live securely and to avoid injuries from other men, and also from the beasts. [14] To this end reason and experience teach no more certain means than to form a society with definite laws, to occupy a definite area of the world, and to reduce the powers of all, as it were, into one body, the body of society. But to form and preserve a society requires no mean intelligence and vigilance. So the society which for the most part is founded and directed by prudent and vigilant men will be more secure, more stable, and less vulnerable to fortune. Conversely, if a society is established by men of untrained intelligence, it will depend for the most part on fortune and will be less stable. [15] If, in spite of this, it has lasted a long time, it will owe this to the guidance of another, not to its own guidance. Indeed, if it has overcome great dangers and matters have turned out favorably for it, it will only be able to wonder at and worship the guidance of God (i.e., insofar as God acts through hidden external causes, but not insofar as he acts through human nature and the human mind). Since nothing has happened to it except what is completely unexpected and contrary to opinion, this can even be considered to be really a miracle.

D. On Law and God as a Lawgiver[14]

III/57   [1] The word *law*, taken absolutely, means that according to which each individual, or all or some members of the same species, act in one and the same certain and determinate manner. This depends either on a necessity of nature or on a decision of men. A law which depends on a necessity of nature is one which follows necessarily from the very nature *or* definition of a thing. One which depends on a decision of men, and which is more properly called a rule of right, is one which men prescribe for themselves and others, for the sake of living more safely and conveniently, or for some other reasons.

[2] For example, that all bodies, when they strike against other lesser bodies, lose as much of their motion as they communicate to the other bodies is a universal law of all bodies, which follows from a necessity of III/58   nature. Similarly, that a man, when he recalls one thing, immediately

---

[14] *Theological-Political Treatise*, ch. IV, §§1–7, 9–21, 23–34, 37–39.

recalls another like it, or one which he had perceived together with it, is a law which necessarily follows from human nature. But that men should yield, or be compelled to yield, the right they have from nature and bind themselves to a certain manner of living depends on a human decision.

[3] And although I grant absolutely that everything is determined by the universal laws of nature to exist and produce an effect in a certain and determinate way, I still say that the latter laws depend on a decision of men:

(I) Because, insofar as man is a part of nature, he constitutes part of the power of nature. So those things which follow from the necessity of human nature, that is, from nature itself, insofar as we conceive it through a determinate human nature, still follow, even though by necessity, from human power. Hence it can very well be said that the enactment of those laws depends on a decision of men, because in this way it depends chiefly on the power of the human mind. Nevertheless the human mind, insofar as it perceives things under the aspect of the true or the false, can be conceived quite clearly without the latter laws, but not without a necessary law, as we have just defined it.

[4] (II) Because we ought to define and explain things through their proximate causes. That universal consideration concerning fate and the connection of causes cannot help us to form and order our thoughts concerning particular things. Moreover, we are completely ignorant of the very order and connection of things, that is, of how things are really ordered and connected. So for practical purposes it is better, indeed necessary, to consider things as possible. These remarks will suffice concerning law considered absolutely.

[5] But since the word *law* seems to be applied figuratively to natural things, and commonly nothing is understood by law but a command which men can either carry out or neglect, since law confines human power under certain limits, beyond which that power is extended and does not command anything beyond [human] powers—for that reason law seems to need to be defined more particularly: that it is a manner of living which man prescribes to himself and others for some end.

[6] Nevertheless, since the true end of laws is usually evident only to a few, and since for the most part men are almost incapable of perceiving it and do anything but live according to reason, legislators, to bind all men equally, have wisely set up another end, very different from that which necessarily follows from the nature of laws, by promising to the defenders of the laws what the multitude most love, and on the other hand, by threatening those who would break the laws with what they

III/59

most fear. In this way they have striven to restrain the multitude, like a horse with a harness, as far as they could.

[7] That is how it has happened that law is generally taken to be a manner of living which is prescribed to men according to the command of others, and consequently that those who obey the laws are said to live under the law, and seem to be slaves. And really, whoever gives each one his own because he fears the gallows does act according to the command of another and is compelled by evil. He cannot be called just. But the person who gives to each his own because he knows the true reason for the laws and their necessity, that person acts from a constant disposition, and by his own decision, not that of another. So he is rightly called just. . . .

[9] Since, therefore, the law is nothing but a manner of living which men prescribe to themselves or to others for some end, it seems that law must be distinguished into human and divine. By human law I understand a manner of living which serves only to protect life and the state; by a divine law, one which aims only at the greatest good, that is, the true knowledge and love of God. I call this law divine because of the nature of the greatest good, which I shall show here as briefly and clearly as I can.

[10] Since the intellect is the better part of us, it is certain that if we want to really seek our advantage, we should strive above all to perfect it as much as we can. For our greatest good must consist in the perfection of the intellect. Next, since all our knowledge, and the certainty which really removes all doubt, depend only on the knowledge of God (both because nothing can either be or be conceived without God, and because we can doubt everything so long as we have no clear and distinct idea of God), it follows that our greatest good and perfection depend only on the knowledge of God and so on.

III/60

[11] Next, since nothing can be or be conceived without God, it is certain that all things in nature involve and express the concept of God, in proportion to their essence and perfection. Hence the more we know natural things, the greater and more perfect is the knowledge of God we acquire, or (since knowledge of an effect through its cause is nothing but knowing some property of the cause) the more we know natural things, the more perfectly do we know God's essence, which is the cause of all things.

[12] So all our knowledge, that is, our greatest good, not only depends on the knowledge of God, but consists entirely in it. This also follows from the fact that a man is more perfect in proportion to the nature and perfection of the thing which he loves before all others, and

28

conversely. Therefore, the man who is necessarily the most perfect and who participates in the greatest blessedness is the one who loves above all else the intellectual knowledge of God, the most perfect being, and takes the greatest pleasure in that knowledge. Our greatest good, then, and our blessedness come back to this: the knowledge and love of God.

[13] The means, therefore, which this end of all human actions (i.e., God, insofar as his idea is in us) requires can be called the commands of God, because they are prescribed to us, as it were, by God himself, insofar as he exists in our minds. Hence the manner of living which aims at this end is very well called the divine law. But what these means are, and what manner of living this end requires, and how the foundations of the best state and the manner of living among men follow from this, these matters all pertain to a complete Ethics. Here I shall proceed to treat only of the divine law in general.

[14] Since, then, the love of God is man's highest happiness and blessedness, and the ultimate end and object of all human actions, the only one who follows the divine law is the one who undertakes to love God, not from fear of punishment, nor from love for another thing, such as pleasures or reputation, and the like, but only because he knows God, *or* because he knows that the knowledge and love of God is the highest good.

[15] So the sum-total of the divine law, and its highest precept, is to love God as the highest good, as we have said, not from fear of some punishment or penalty, nor from the love of some other thing, in which we desire to take pleasure. For the idea of God dictates this: that God is our greatest good, *or* that the knowledge and love of God is the ultimate end toward which all our actions are to be directed. III/61

[16] In spite of this, the man of the flesh cannot understand these things, and to him they seem hollow, because he has too meager a knowledge of God, and also because he finds nothing in this highest good to touch or eat, or affect the flesh which gives him his greatest pleasure, since [this good] consists only in contemplation and in a pure mind. But those who know that they have nothing more excellent than their intellect and a healthy mind will doubtless judge these things very solid.

[17] We have explained, therefore, what the divine law above all consists in, and which laws are human, namely, all those which have another aim, unless they have been enacted by revelation. For in this respect also things are referred to God (as we have shown above), and it is in this sense that the law of Moses, although it is not universal, but accommo-

dated very much to the temperament and special preservation of one people, can still be called the law of God, *or* the divine law. For we believe that it was enacted by the light of prophecy.

[18] If now we attend to the nature of natural divine law, as we have just explained it, we shall see:

I. that it is universal, *or* common to all men; for we have deduced it from universal human nature;

II. that it does not require faith in historical narratives of any kind; for since this natural divine law is understood simply by the consideration of human nature, it is certain that we can conceive it as much in Adam as in any other man, as much in a man who lives among other men as in a man who lives a solitary life. [19] Nor can faith in historical narratives, however certain, give us any knowledge of God. Hence it also cannot give us the love of God. For the love of God arises from the knowledge of God, and the knowledge of God must be drawn from common notions which, through themselves, are certain and known. So it is far from being the case that faith in historical narratives is necessary for us to attain our greatest good. Nevertheless, although faith in historical narratives cannot give us the knowledge and love of God, we do not deny that reading them is very useful in relation to civil life. For the more we have observed and the better we know the character and circumstances of men—which can best be known from their actions—the better will we be able to live more cautiously among them and accommodate our lives to their temperament, as much as reason suggests.

III/62

[20] III. We see that this natural divine law does not require ceremonies, that is, actions which in themselves are indifferent, and are called good only by institution or which represent some good necessary for salvation, or, if you prefer, actions whose reason surpasses man's power of understanding. For the natural light requires nothing which that light itself does not reach, but only that which can indicate to us very clearly the good, *or* the means to our blessedness. Those things which are good only by command and institution, or because they are representatives of some good, cannot perfect our intellect and are nothing but empty forms. They cannot be counted among the actions which are, as it were, the offspring or fruits of the intellect and of a healthy mind. But there is no need to show this more fully here.

[21] IV. Finally, we see that the highest reward of the divine law is the law itself, namely, to know God and to love him from true freedom and with a whole and constant heart. The penalty [for violating the divine law] is the privation of these things and bondage to the flesh, *or* an inconstant and vacillating heart. . . .

[23] We can easily deduce what must be maintained regarding the question [whether, by the natural light, we can conceive God as a lawgiver, or prince prescribing laws to men?] from the nature of God's will, which is distinguished from his intellect only in relation to our reason, that is, in themselves God's will and God's intellect are really one and the same. They are distinguished only in relation to the thoughts we form concerning God's intellect.

[24] For example, when we attend only to the fact that the nature of a triangle is contained in the divine nature from eternity, as an eternal truth, then we say that God has the idea of the triangle, *or* understands the nature of the triangle. But when we attend afterwards to the fact that the nature of the triangle is contained in the divine nature in this way, solely from the necessity of the divine nature, and not from the necessity of the essence and nature of the triangle, indeed, that the necessity of the essence and properties of the triangle, insofar as it is also conceived as an eternal truth, depends only on the necessity of the divine nature and intellect, and not on the nature of the triangle, then the very thing we called God's intellect we call God's will *or* decree. III/63

[25] So in relation to God we affirm one and the same thing when we say that from eternity God willed and decreed that the three angles of a triangle are equal to two right angles, or [when we say] that God understood this very thing. From this it follows that God's affirmations and negations always involve eternal necessity *or* truth.

[26] So if, for example, God said to Adam that he did not want him to eat of the tree of the knowledge of good and evil [Genesis 2:17], it would imply a contradiction for Adam to be able to eat of that tree. So it would be impossible that he should eat of it. For that divine decree would have had to involve eternal necessity and truth. But since Scripture nevertheless relates that God did order Adam not to eat, and that notwithstanding Adam ate of the tree, we must say that God revealed to Adam only the evil which would necessarily befall him if he ate of that tree, but not the necessity of the connection between that act and that evil.

[27] That is why Adam perceived that revelation, not as an eternal and necessary truth, but as a law, that is, as an institution which profit or loss follows, not from the necessity and nature of the action performed, but solely from the pleasure and absolute command of some Prince. So it is only in relation to Adam, and because of a defect in his knowledge, that that revelation was a law, and God, as it were, a lawgiver or Prince.

[28] For the same reason, namely, because of a defect in their knowledge, the Decalogue was a law only in relation to the Hebrews. For since they did not know God's existence as an eternal truth, they had to

31

perceive as a law what was revealed to them in the Decalogue: that God exists and that he alone is to be worshiped. If God had spoken to them immediately, without using any corporeal means, they would have perceived this, not as a law, but as an eternal truth.

[29] And what we say about the Israelites and Adam must also be said about all the Prophets who prescribed laws in the name of God, namely, that they did not perceive God's decrees adequately, as eternal truths. For example, it must be said even of Moses himself that by revelation, or from the foundations revealed to him, he perceived the way the people of Israel could best be united in a certain region of the world, and could form a whole society, *or* set up a State, as well as the way that people could best be compelled to obedience. But he did not perceive, nor was it revealed to him, that that way is best, nor even that the goal at which they were aiming would necessarily follow from the general obedience of the people in such a region of the world. [30] Hence he did not perceive all these things as eternal truths, but as precepts and things instituted, and he prescribed them as laws of God. That is why he imagined God as a ruler, a lawgiver, a king, as compassionate, just, and the like, when all these things are attributes only of human nature, and ought to be removed entirely from the divine nature.

But I say this only about the prophets, who prescribed laws in the name of God, and not about Christ.[15] [31] For however much Christ may seem also to have prescribed laws in the name of God, nevertheless we must hold that he perceived things truly and adequately. Christ was not so much a prophet as the mouth of God. For God revealed certain things to the human race through the mind of Christ (as we have shown in Chapter I), as previously he had revealed them through angels, that is, through a created voice, visions, and so on. So it would be as contrary to reason to maintain that God accommodated his revelations to the opinions of Christ as to maintain that, to communicate to the prophets the things to be revealed, God previously accommodated his revelations to the opinions of the angels, that is, of a created voice and of visions. No one could maintain anything more absurd than that, particularly since he was sent to teach, not only the Jews, but the whole human race. So it was not enough for him to have a mind accommodated only to the opinions of the Jews, [he required a mind accommodated] to the opin-

III/64

---

[15] Spinoza's contention that, Scriptural appearances to the contrary notwithstanding, Jesus did not conceive God inadequately, as a lawgiver, may be another example of "yielding to the understanding" of his audience wherever possible. At any rate, though Matthew 13:10ff does suggest that Jesus taught one thing to his disciples and another to the multitudes, even what he taught his disciples was a doctrine of reward and punishment (cf. Matthew 13:40–43).

ions and teachings universal to the human race, that is, to common and true notions.

[32] And of course, from the fact that God revealed himself immediately to Christ, *or* to his mind, and not, as he did to the prophets, through words and images, we can understand nothing but that Christ perceived truly, *or* understood, the things revealed. For when a thing is perceived with a pure mind, without words and images, it is understood. Christ, therefore, perceived the things revealed truly and adequately. III/65 [33] If he ever prescribed them as laws, he did this because of the people's ignorance and stubbornness. So in this respect he acted in the manner of God, because he accommodated himself to the mentality of the people. And for that reason, although he spoke somewhat more clearly than the other prophets, he still taught these revelations obscurely, and quite frequently through parables, especially when he was speaking to those to whom it was not yet given to understand the kingdom of heaven (see Matthew 13:10 etc.).

[34] But doubtless for those to whom it was given to know the mysteries of heaven, he taught things as eternal truths and did not prescribe them as laws. In this way he freed them from bondage to the law, and nevertheless, confirmed and stabilized the law more, and wrote it thoroughly in their hearts. . . .

[37] We conclude, therefore, that [i] it is only because of the multitude's power of understanding and a defect in their thinking that God is described as a lawgiver or prince, and called just, merciful, and so on, [ii] that God really acts and guides all things only from the necessity of his own nature and perfection, and finally, [iii] that his decrees and volitions are eternal truths, and always involve necessity. . . .

[38] Let us pass therefore to the second question, and survey Holy Scripture to see what it teaches concerning the natural light and this III/66 divine law. The first thing which strikes us is the story of the first man, where it is related that God commanded Adam not to eat the fruit of the tree of the knowledge of good and evil [Genesis 2:17]. This seems to mean that God commanded Adam to do and seek the good for the sake of the good, and not insofar as it is contrary to the evil, that is, that he should seek the good from love of the good, and not from fear of evil. For as we have already shown, he who does good from a true knowledge and love of the good acts freely and with a constant heart, whereas he who acts from fear of evil is compelled by evil, acts like a slave, and lives under the authority of another.

[39] And so this one thing which God commanded Adam to do contains the whole divine natural law, and agrees absolutely with the dictate

of the natural light. It would not be difficult to explain that whole story, *or* parable, of the first man from this foundation. But I prefer to put this to one side, not only because I cannot be absolutely certain that my explanation agrees with the mind of the author, but also because most people will not grant that this story is a parable, but maintain without qualification that it is a simple narrative.

E. On Miracles[16]

III/81   [1] As men are accustomed to call divine that knowledge which surpasses man's power of understanding, so they are accustomed to call divine, *or* a work of God, a work whose cause the multitude does not know. For the multitude think God's power and providence are established as clearly as possible when they see something happen in nature which is unusual and contrary to the opinion which they have of nature from custom. This is particularly so if the event has been to their profit or advantage. They judge that nothing proves the existence of God more clearly than that nature, as they think, does not maintain its order. That is why they think that those who explain things and miracles by their natural causes, or who devote themselves to understanding them, eliminate God, or at least God's providence.

[2] They judge, that is, that God does nothing so long as nature acts in its usual order, and conversely, that the power of nature and natural causes are inactive so long as God acts. Therefore, they imagine two powers numerically distinct from one another, the power of God and the power of natural things, the latter, nevertheless, determined by God in a certain way, or (as most think instead today) created [by God in a certain way].

[3] But what they understand by these two powers, and by God and nature, of course they do not know, except that they imagine God's power as the dominion of a certain royal majesty, whereas they imagine nature's power as force and impulse. The multitude therefore call unusual works of nature miracles, *or* works of God, and partly from devotion, partly from a desire to oppose those who cultivate the natural sciences, they do not want to know the natural causes of things. They want only to hear the things they are most ignorant of, and which, for that reason, they greatly wonder at. [4] They can worship God and relate all things to his dominion and will only by eliminating natural causes and imagining things outside the order of nature. They wonder most at the

---

[16] From the *Theological-Political Treatise*, ch. VI, §§1–6, 7–26, 30–32, 34.

power of God when they imagine the power of nature to be, as it were, subdued by God.

This [attitude] seems to have originated with the first Jews. The Gentiles of their time worshiped visible Gods, such as the Sun, the Moon, the Earth, Water, Air, and the like. To prove them wrong and to show them that those Gods were weak and inconstant, *or* changeable, and III/82 under the command of an invisible God, the Jews related their miracles, by which they strove in addition to show that the whole of nature was directed only for their convenience, according to the command of the God whom they worshiped. This was so pleasing to men that to this day they have not ceased to feign miracles, so that they might be believed to be dearer to God than the rest, and the final cause on account of which God has created, and continually directs, all things.

[5] What claims does the foolishness of the multitude not make for itself, because it has no sound concept either of God or of nature, because it confuses the decisions of God with those of men, and finally, because it feigns a nature so limited that it believes man to be its chief part!

[6] This will be sufficient as a description of the opinions and prejudices of the multitude concerning nature and miracles. But to present my own views in an orderly fashion, I shall show (i) that nothing happens contrary to nature, but that it preserves a fixed and immutable eternal order, and at the same time, I shall show what must be understood by a miracle [§7–15]; (ii) that we cannot know either the essence or the existence of God from miracles, and hence, that we cannot know his providence from miracles, but that all these things are far better perceived from the fixed and immutable order of nature[17] [§16–38]. . . .

[7] As for the first, this is easily shown from the things we have demonstrated in Chapter IV regarding the divine law: namely, that whatever God wills *or* determines involves eternal necessity and truth; [8] for we have shown, from the fact that God's intellect is not distinguished from his will, that we affirm the same thing when we say that God wills something as when we say that he understands it. So by the same necessity with which it follows from the divine nature and perfection that God understands some thing as it is, it follows also that God wills it as it is. [9] But since nothing is necessarily true except by the divine decree alone, it follows quite clearly from this that the universal laws of nature are nothing but decrees of God, which follow from the necessity and III/83

[17] Another claim Oldenburg regarded as troublesome: "You seem to many to take away the authority and value of miracles, which almost all Christians believe to be the sole foundation for the certainty of divine revelation" (Letter 71).

perfection of the divine nature. Therefore, if anything were to happen in nature which was contrary to its universal laws, it would also necessarily be contrary to the divine decree, intellect, and nature. Or if someone were to maintain that God does something contrary to the laws of nature, he would be compelled to maintain at the same time as well that God acts in a way contrary to his own nature. Nothing would be more absurd than that.

We could also show the same thing from the fact that the power of nature is the divine power and virtue itself. Moreover, the divine power is the very essence of God. But for the present I prefer to pass over this.

[10] Nothing, therefore, happens in nature[18*] which is contrary to its universal laws. Nor does anything happen which does not agree with those laws or does not follow from them. For whatever happens, happens by God's will and eternal decree, that is, as we have now shown, whatever happens, happens according to laws and rules which involve eternal necessity and truth.

[11] Thus nature always observes laws and rules which involve eternal necessity and truth, although they are not all known to us, and so it also observes a fixed and immutable order. Nor does any sound reason urge us to attribute a limited power and virtue to nature, or to maintain that its laws are suited for only certain things and not everything. For since nature's virtue and power is the very virtue and power of God, and its laws and rules are God's decrees themselves, we must believe without reservation that the power of nature is infinite, and that its laws are so broad that they extend to everything which is conceived by the divine intellect itself. [12] For otherwise what else is being maintained but that God has created a nature so impotent, and established laws and rules for it so sterile, that often he is compelled to come to its aid anew, if he wants it to be preserved and wants things to turn out as he wished? Of course I judge that nothing is more foreign to reason than that.

[13] From these conclusions—that nothing happens in nature which does not follow from its laws, that its laws extend to all things conceived by the divine intellect itself, and finally, that nature maintains a fixed and immutable order—it clearly follows that the term "miracle" cannot be understood except in relation to men's opinions, and means nothing but a work whose natural cause we cannot explain by the example of another customary thing, or at least which cannot be so explained by the one who writes or relates the miracle.

III/84

[14] Indeed, I could say that a miracle is that whose cause cannot be

---

[18] * NB: By Nature here I do not understand only matter and its affections, but in addition to matter, infinite other things.

explained according to the principles of natural things known to the natural light. But since miracles have been performed according to the power of understanding of the multitude, who were, in fact, completely ignorant of the principles of natural things, it is certain that the ancients took for a miracle what they could not explain in the way the multitude are accustomed to explain natural things, namely, by going back to the memory to recall some other similar thing they are accustomed to imagine without wonder. For the multitude think they understand a thing sufficiently when they do not wonder at it. [15] Hence, the ancients, and almost everyone up till now, has had no other standard for a miracle than this. So no doubt many things are related as miracles in the Sacred Texts whose causes can easily be explained according to known principles of natural things, as we have already hinted in Chapter II [§26–28] when we spoke about the sun's standing still in the time of Joshua, and its going backwards in the time of Ahaz. . . .

[16] It is time now to . . . show that from miracles we understand neither God's essence, nor his existence, nor his providence, but that on the contrary these things are far better perceived from the fixed and immutable order of nature. I proceed to demonstrate this as follows.

[17] Since God's existence is not known through itself,[19*] it must necessarily be inferred from notions whose truth is so firm and steady that no power can be or be conceived by which they could be changed. At least they must so appear to us at the time when we infer God's existence from them, if we want to infer it from them beyond any chance of doubt. For if we could conceive that the notions themselves could be changed by some power, whatever in the end it was, we would doubt their truth, and consequently also doubt our conclusion, namely, God's existence, nor would we ever be able to be certain of anything.

[18] Next, we know that nothing agrees with nature or is contrary to it except what we have shown to agree with those principles or to be contrary to them. So if we could conceive that by some power (whatever in the end it was) something could happen in nature which was contrary   III/85

[19] * We doubt God's existence, and consequently we doubt everything, so long as the idea we have of God himself is not clear and distinct, but confused. For just as one who does not rightly know the nature of a triangle does not know that its three angles are equal to two right angles, so one who conceives the divine nature confusedly does not see that existence pertains to the nature of God. But for us to be able to conceive God's nature clearly and distinctly it is necessary for us to attend to certain very simple notions which they call common, and connect with them those which pertain to the divine nature; then for the first time it becomes evident to us that God exists necessarily and is everywhere, and at the same time that all the things we conceive involve in themselves the nature of God and are conceived through it, and finally, that all those things are true which we conceive adequately. But on these matters see the preface of the book entitled *The principles of philosophy demonstrated in a geometric manner*. [See below, §VI.A.]

to nature, that would be contrary to those first notions. And so either we would have to reject it as absurd, or else we would have to doubt the first notions (as we have just shown) and consequently, doubt God and all things, however they might have been perceived.

[19] So insofar as a miracle is understood as work contrary to the order of nature, it is far from true that miracles show us the existence of God. On the contrary, they would make us doubt his existence, since without them we could be absolutely certain of his existence, that is, since we know that all things in nature follow a certain and immutable order.

[20] But suppose a miracle is something which cannot be explained by natural causes. This can be understood in either of two ways: either that it in fact has natural causes which nevertheless cannot be found by the human intellect, or that it has no cause except God, *or* God's will. [21] But because all things which happen through natural causes also happen only according to God's power and will, in the end we must arrive at this: that whether a miracle has natural causes or not, it is a work which cannot be explained by its cause, that is, a work which surpasses man's power of understanding. But from such a work, and from anything surpassing our power of understanding, we can understand nothing. For whatever we understand clearly and distinctly must become known to us either through itself or through something else which through itself is understood clearly and distinctly. [22] So from a miracle, *or* from a work surpassing our power of understanding, we can understand neither God's essence, nor his existence, nor absolutely anything concerning God and nature.

On the other hand, when we know that all things are determined and enacted by God, that the operations of nature follow from God's essence, indeed, that the laws of nature are God's eternal decrees and volitions, we must conclude absolutely that we know God and God's will better as we know natural things better, and understand more clearly how they depend on their first cause, and how they operate according to the eternal laws of nature.

[23] So in relation to our intellect we have a far better right to call those works which we clearly and distinctly understand works of God and to refer them to the will of God than we do those of which we are completely ignorant, although the latter occupy our imagination powerfully and sweep men along into wondering at them. For only those III/86 works of nature which we understand clearly and distinctly make our knowledge of God more elevated and indicate God's will and decrees as clearly as possible. Those who recur to the will of God when they have no knowledge of a thing are just trifling. It is a ridiculous way of confessing one's ignorance.

38

[24] Again, even if we could infer something from miracles, we could still not infer God's existence from them in any way. For since a miracle is a limited work, and never expresses any power except a definite and limited one, it is certain that from such an effect we cannot infer the existence of a cause whose power is infinite, but at most that of a cause whose power is greater [than that expressed by the effect]. I say *at most*, because from many causes concurring together, there can also follow a work whose force and power is indeed less than the power of all the causes together, but far greater than the power of each cause. [25] But since (as we have already shown) the laws of nature extend to infinitely many things, and we conceive them under a certain species of eternity, and nature proceeds according to them in a definite and immutable order, to that extent they indicate to us in some way the infinity, eternity, and immutability of God.

[26] We conclude, therefore, that we cannot know God, and his existence and providence, by miracles, but that we can infer these things far better from the fixed and immutable order of nature. In this conclusion I speak of a miracle only as a work which surpasses, or is believed to surpass, men's power of understanding. For insofar as it would be supposed to destroy, *or* to interrupt, the order of nature, or to be contrary to its laws, to that extent (as we have just shown) not only could it give no knowledge of God, but on the contrary it would take away the knowledge we naturally have, and make us doubt concerning God and concerning all things. . . .

[30] . . . And although Scripture nowhere teaches explicitly [that we cannot know God from miracles] nevertheless this can easily be inferred from Scripture, especially from what Moses commands (Deuteronomy 13[:1–5]), that they should condemn to death a prophet who leads them astray, even if he performs miracles. [31] For he says that (even if) *a sign and a wonder which he has foretold to you should happen and so on, do not* (nevertheless) *assent to the words of this prophet and so on because the Lord your God tests you and so on.* (Therefore) *let that prophet be condemned to death and so on.* From this it clearly follows that even false prophets can perform miracles, and that unless men are well protected by the true knowledge and love of God, miracles can lead them to embrace false Gods as easily the True God. For Moses adds *since Yehowah your God tests you in order to know whether you love him with all your heart and all your soul.* III/87

[32] Again, the Israelites, with so many miracles, were still not able to form any sound concept of God, as experience itself has testified. For when they believed that Moses had left them, they sought visible divinities from Aaron, and a calf—what shame!—was their idea of God, the one they finally formed from so many miracles [Exodus 32:1–6]. . . .

III/88   [34] Finally, it was quite obscure to almost all the prophets how the order of nature and human outcomes could agree with the concept they had formed concerning God's providence; this was always quite clear to the philosophers, who strive to understand things, not from miracles, but from clear concepts. The philosophers locate true happiness only in virtue and peace of mind and are not eager that nature should obey them, but that they should obey nature; they know certainly that God directs nature as its universal laws require, but not as the particular laws of human nature require, and that God takes account, not of the human race only, but of the whole of nature.

F. On Interpreting Scripture[20]

III/97   [1] Everyone says that Sacred Scripture is the word of God, that it teaches men true blessedness or the way to salvation. But in their conduct men reveal something very different. For the multitude seem to care nothing about living according to the teachings of Sacred Scripture; we see that almost everyone hawks his own inventions as the word of God, and is concerned only to compel others to think as he does, under the pretext of religion.

    [2] We see, I say, that the Theologians have mainly been anxious to twist their own inventions and beliefs out of the Sacred Texts and fortify them with divine authority. They have no scruple about interpreting Scriptures; they read the mind of the Holy Spirit with great recklessness. If they fear anything, it is not that they may ascribe some error to the Holy Spirit and stray from the path to salvation, but that others may convict them of error, lessening their authority and making others scorn them.

    [3] But if men were sincere in what they say about Scripture, they would have a very different manner of living. These frequent disagreements would not trouble them so; they would not display such hatred in their disputes; and they would not be in the grip of such a blind and reckless desire to interpret Scripture and think up new doctrines in religion. On the contrary, they would not dare to embrace anything as the teaching of Scripture which it does not teach as clearly as possible. And finally, those sacrilegious people who have not been afraid to corrupt Scripture in so many passages would have taken great care to avoid such a crime; they would have kept their sacrilegious hands away from those texts.

    [4] But in the end ambition and wickedness have been so powerful

---

[20] From the *Theological-Political Treatise*, ch. VII, §§1–33, 43–46, 65–69.

that religion is identified not so much with obeying the teachings of the Holy Spirit as with defending human inventions, so that religion consists not in lovingkindness, but in spreading disagreement among men, and in propagating the most bitter hatred, which they shield under the false name of divine zeal and passionate enthusiasm. To these evils we may add superstition, which teaches men to scorn reason and nature, and to admire and venerate only what is contrary to both of these.

[5] So it is no wonder that to make Scripture more admired and venerated, men have been eager to explain it in such a way that it seems to be as contrary as possible to both reason and nature. Therefore they dream that the most profound mysteries lie hidden in the Sacred Texts, and they weary themselves in investigating these absurdities, neglecting what is useful. Whatever they thus invent in their madness, they attribute to the Holy Spirit, and they strive to defend it with the utmost force and violence of the affects. For men are so constituted that what they conceive by the pure intellect, they defend only with the intellect and reason, whereas if they think something because of some affects of the heart, they also defend it with those affects.

[6] Now to free ourselves from these disorders, to liberate our minds from theological prejudices, and not to recklessly embrace men's inventions as divine teachings, we must treat and discuss the true method of interpreting Scripture; for so long as we are ignorant of this, we cannot know anything with certainty about what either Scripture or the Holy Spirit wishes to teach.

To sum it up briefly, I say that the method of interpreting Scripture does not differ from the method of interpreting nature, but agrees with it completely. [7] For just as the method of interpreting nature consists above all in putting together a history of nature, from which, as from certain data, we infer the definitions of natural things, so also to interpret Scripture it is necessary to prepare a straightforward history of Scripture and to infer the mind of the authors of Scripture from it, by legitimate reasonings, as from certain data and principles. [8] For if someone has admitted as principles or data for interpreting Scripture and discussing the things contained in it only those drawn from Scripture itself and its history, he will always proceed without any danger of error, and will be able to discuss the things which surpass our grasp as safely as those we know by the natural light.

[9] But to establish clearly that this way is not only certain, but also the only way, and that it agrees with the method of interpreting nature, we must note that Scripture very often treats of things which cannot be deduced from principles known to the natural light. For historical narratives and revelations make up the greatest part of it. [10] But the his-

III/99 torical narratives give a prominent place to miracles, that is, (as we have shown in the preceding chapter) narratives of unusual things in nature, accommodated to the opinions and judgments of the historians who have written them. Moreover, the revelations were also accommodated to the opinions of the prophets, as we have shown in the Second Chapter, and they really surpass man's power of understanding. So the knowledge of all these things, that is, of almost everything in Scripture, must be sought only from Scripture itself, just as the knowledge of nature must be sought from nature itself.

[11] As for the moral teachings also contained in the Bible, although they can be demonstrated from common notions, still it cannot be demonstrated from common notions that Scripture teaches them. This can only be established from Scripture itself. Indeed, if we wish, without prejudice, to certify the divinity of Scripture, we must establish from it alone that it teaches true moral doctrines. Only from this can we demonstrate its divinity. For we have shown that the prophets' own certainty was established principally by the fact that they had a heart inclined toward the right and the good. So to be able to have faith in them we too must establish the same thing.

[12] Moreover, we have also demonstrated already that the divinity of God cannot be proven by miracles, not to mention that miracles could also be performed by false prophets. So the divinity of Scripture must be established only by the fact that it teaches true virtue. But this can only be established by Scripture. If it could not be done, it would only be as a result of great prejudice that we would embrace it and testify to its divinity. Therefore, all knowledge of Scripture must be sought only from Scripture itself.

[13] Finally, Scripture does not give definitions of the things of which it speaks, any more than nature does. So just as the definitions of natural things are to be inferred from the different actions of nature, in the same way [the definitions of the things spoken of in Scripture] are to be drawn from the different narratives occurring in the texts concerning them.

[14] Therefore, the universal rule in interpreting Scripture is to attribute nothing to Scripture as its teaching which we have not understood as clearly as possible from its history. But now we must say here what sort of history that must be and what things it mainly relates.

[15] First, it must contain the nature and properties of the language in which the books of Scripture were written, and which their authors
III/100 were accustomed to speak. For in this way we shall be able to find out all the meanings which each utterance can admit in ordinary conversational usage. And because all the authors, both of the Old Testament

42

and the New, were Hebrews, it is certain that the history of the Hebrew language is necessary above all others, not only for understanding the books of the Old Testament, which were written in this language, but also for understanding those of the New Testament. For although they have been made common to all in other languages, nevertheless they express themselves in a Hebrew manner.

[16] Second, it must collect the sayings of each book and organize them under main headings so that we can readily find all those concerning the same subject. Next, it must note all those which are ambiguous or obscure or which seem inconsistent with one another. I call these sayings clear or obscure here, insofar as it is easy or difficult to derive their meaning from the context of the utterance, not insofar as it is easy or difficult to perceive their truth by reason. For we are concerned only with the meaning of the utterances, not with their truth. [17] Indeed, we must take great care, so long as we are looking for the meaning of Scripture, not to be preoccupied with our own reasoning, insofar as it is founded on the principles of natural knowledge (not to mention now our prejudices). But lest we confuse the true meaning with the truth of things, that meaning must be found out solely from the usage of language, or from reasoning which recognizes no other foundation than Scripture.

To make all these things clearer, I shall illustrate them with an example. [18] These sayings of Moses—that *God is a fire* and that *God is jealous*[21]—are as clear as possible, so long as we attend only to the meaning of the words. Therefore, I put them among the clear sayings, even though they are very obscure in relation to truth and reason. Indeed, although their literal meaning is contrary to the natural light, unless it is also clearly opposed to the principles and foundations derived from the history of Scripture, that literal meaning will nevertheless have to be retained. And conversely, if these sayings, according to their literal interpretation, were found to be contrary to principles derived from Scripture, even though they agreed completely with reason, they would still have to be interpreted differently (i.e., metaphorically).

[19] Therefore, to know whether or not Moses believed that God is a fire, we must not in any way infer our answer from the fact that this opinion agrees with reason or is contrary to it, but we must rely only on other sayings of Moses himself. Since Moses also teaches clearly in a great many places that God has no likeness to any of the visible things which exist in the heavens, on the earth, or in the sea, either this saying or all of those are to be explained metaphorically.

III/101

---

[21] Both claims are made in Deuteronomy 4:24.

[20] But because we must depart as little as possible from the literal meaning, we must first ask whether this one sentence, *God is a fire*, admits another meaning beyond the literal one, that is, whether the term *fire* signifies something other than natural fire. If [that term] is not found, according to linguistic usage, to signify something else, then this sentence also is not to be interpreted in any other way, however much it may be contrary to reason. On the contrary, all the others, although in agreement with reason, would still have to be accommodated to this one. [21] If this also could not be done according to linguistic usage, then these sentences would be irreconcilable, and therefore we would have to suspend judgment about them. But because the term *fire* is also taken for anger and jealousy (see Job 31:12), these sentences of Moses are easily reconciled, and we infer legitimately that these two sentences, *God is a fire* and *God is jealous*, are one and the same sentence [i.e., express one and the same opinion].

[22] Next, since Moses clearly teaches that God is jealous, and nowhere teaches that God lacks passions *or* passive states of mind, from this we must conclude without reservation that Moses believed this, or at least that he wished to teach it, however much we may believe that this opinion is contrary to reason. For as we have already shown, it is not permissible for us to twist the intent of Scripture according to the dictates of our reason and according to our preconceived opinions. The whole knowledge of the Bible must be sought from the Bible alone.

[23] Finally, this history must describe fully, with respect to all the books of the prophets, the circumstances of which a record has been preserved, namely, the life, character, and concerns of the author of each book, who he was, on what occasion he wrote, at what time, for whom, and finally, in what language. Next, it must relate the fate of each book: how it was first received, into whose hands it fell, how many different readings of it there were, by whose deliberation it was accepted among the Sacred Books, and finally, how all the books which everyone now acknowledges to be sacred came to be unified into one body.

The history of Scripture, I say, must contain all these things. [24] For in order for us to know which sayings are put forward as laws and which as moral teachings, it is important to know the life, character, and concerns of the author. Moreover, the better we know someone's spirit and temperament, the more easily we can explain his words. Next, if we are not to confuse eternal teachings with those which could be useful only for a time or only for a few people, it is important also to know on what occasion, at what time, and for which nation or age all these teachings were written. [25] Finally, it is important to know the other things I have mentioned in addition, in order to know also, beyond the authority of each book, whether or not it could have been corrupted by illicit

III/102

44

hands, and whether errors have crept in or whether they have been corrected by men sufficiently expert and worthy of trust. It is very necessary to know all these things so that we are not carried away by a blind impulse to embrace whatever has been thrust upon us, but embrace only what is certain and indubitable.

[26] Now after we have this history of Scripture and have firmly decided to maintain nothing with certainty as the teaching of the prophets which does not follow from this history, or is not derived from it as clearly as possible, then it will be time for us to get ready to investigate the mind of the prophets and of the Holy Spirit. But for this purpose we also require a method and order like the one we use for interpreting nature according to its history.

[27] In examining natural things we strive, before all else, to investigate the things which are most universal and common to the whole of nature—namely, motion and rest, and their laws and rules, which nature always observes and through which it continuously acts—and from these we proceed gradually to other less universal things. In just the same way, the first thing to be sought from the history of Scripture is what is most universal, what is the basis and foundation of the whole of Scripture, and finally, what all the prophets commend in it as an eternal teaching, most useful for all mortals. For example, that a unique and omnipotent God exists, who alone is to be worshiped, who cares for all, and who loves above all those who worship him and who love their neighbor as themselves, and so on.

[28] Scripture, I say, teaches these and similar things everywhere, so clearly and so explicitly that there has never been anyone who disputed the meaning of Scripture concerning these things. But what God is, and in what way he sees all things, and provides for them—these and similar things Scripture does not teach openly and as an eternal doctrine. On   III/103 the contrary, we have already shown above that the prophets themselves did not agree about them. So concerning such things we must maintain nothing as the doctrine of the Holy Spirit, even if it can be determined very well by the natural light.

[29] Once this universal teaching of Scripture is rightly known, we must proceed next to other, less universal things, which nevertheless concern how we ordinarily conduct our lives and which flow from this universal teaching like streams. For example, all the particular external actions of true virtue, which can only be put to work on a given occasion. Whatever is found to be obscure *or* ambiguous in the texts about these things must be explained and determined according to the universal teaching of Scripture. But if we find any things which are contrary to one another, we must see on what occasion, and at what time, and for whom they were written.

[30] For example, when Christ says *blessed are those who mourn, for they shall receive comfort* [Matthew 5:4], we do not know from this text what kind of mourners he means. But because he teaches later that we should be anxious about nothing except the kingdom of God and his justice, which he commends as the greatest good (see Matthew 6:33), from this it follows that by mourners he understands only those who mourn for the kingdom of God and the justice men have neglected. For only this can be mourned by those who love nothing but the divine kingdom *or* fairness, and who completely scorn what fortune may bring.

[31] So also, when he says *to a man who strikes you on the right cheek, turn to him the other also,* and so on [Matthew 5:39] If Christ had ordered these things as a lawgiver orders judges, he would have destroyed the law of Moses with this precept.[22] Nevertheless, he warns expressly that this is not his intention. See Matthew 5:17. So we must see who said these things, to whom, and at what time.

[32] It was Christ who spoke, who did not institute laws as a legislator, but taught doctrines as a teacher, because (as we have shown above) he did not want to correct external actions so much as the heart. Next, he said these things to oppressed men, who were living in a corrupt state, where justice was completely neglected, a state whose ruin he saw to be near at hand. But we have seen that the very same thing which Christ teaches here, when the ruin of the city is at hand, Jeremiah also taught at the first destruction of the city, that is, at a similar time (see Lamentations 3:25–30).

III/104

[33] So the prophets taught this only in a time of oppression, and nowhere put it forward as a law, whereas Moses (who did not write at a time of oppression, but—note this—worked for the institution of a good state), although he also condemned vengeance and hatred of one's neighbor, commanded that an eye be paid for an eye. From this it follows very clearly, just from the fundamental principles of Scripture themselves, that this teaching of Christ and Jeremiah that we should submit to injuries and yield to the impious in everything is appropriate only in those places where justice is neglected and in times of oppression, but not in a good state. Indeed, in a good state, where justice is defended, everyone is bound, if he wants to be thought just, to exact a penalty for injuries in the presence of a judge (see Leviticus 5:1), not for the sake of vengeance (see Leviticus 19:17–18), but with the intention of defending justice and the laws of one's native land, and so that the evil should not profit by being evil. . . .

III/106

[43] . . . Since this method of ours, which is founded on the principle that the knowledge of Scripture is to be sought only from Scripture, is

[22] Cf. Exodus 21:23–25, Leviticus 24:19–20.

the only true method [of interpreting Scripture], whatever it cannot furnish for acquiring a complete knowledge of Scripture, we must absolutely give up as hopeless. [44] But we must now say what difficulty this method involves, or what is to be desired in it, for it to be able to lead us to a complete and certain knowledge of the Sacred Texts.

To begin with, a great difficulty in this method arises from the fact that it requires a complete knowledge of the Hebrew language. But where is this now to be sought? [45] The ancient cultivators of the Hebrew language left nothing to posterity regarding its foundations and teaching. At least we have absolutely nothing from them: no dictionary, no grammar, no rhetoric. Moreover, the Hebrew nation has lost all its adornments and marks of distinction—this is no wonder, after it has suffered so many disasters and persecutions—and has retained only some few fragments of its language and of a few books. For almost all the names of fruits, birds, fish, and a great many other things have perished in the unjust treatment of the ages. Again, the meaning of many nouns and verbs which occur in the Bible is either completely unknown or is disputed.

[46] We lack, not only all these things, but also and especially, a phraseology of this language. For time, the devourer, has obliterated from the memory of men almost all the idioms and manners of speaking peculiar to the Hebrew nation. Therefore, we will not always be able, as we desire, to find out, with respect to each utterance, all the meanings it can admit according to linguistic usage. Many utterances will occur whose meaning will be very obscure, indeed, completely incomprehensible, even though they are expressed in well-known terms. . . .

[65] These are all the difficulties[23] I had undertaken to recount arising from this method of interpreting Scripture according to the history we can have of it. I judge them to be so great that I do not hesitate to affirm that in very many places we either do not know the true meaning of Scripture or are divining it without certainty. [66] On the other hand, we should note again that all these difficulties can only prevent us from grasping the intention of the prophets concerning things which are incomprehensible and which we can only imagine, but not concerning things which we can grasp with the intellect and of which we can easily form a clear concept. For those things which, by their nature, are easily perceived can never be said so obscurely that they are not easily understood, according to the proverb: to one who understands a word is enough.

[67] Euclid, who wrote only about things which were quite simple and

III/111

---

[23] The editing of the text has eliminated some of the difficulties Spinoza discusses, such as the ambiguities arising from the fact that the Biblical text is written without vowels.

most intelligible, is easily explained by anyone in any language. For to grasp his intention and to be certain of his true meaning it is not necessary to have a complete knowledge of the language in which he wrote, but only a quite common and almost childish knowledge. Nor is it necessary to know the life, concerns, and customs of the author, nor in what language, to whom, and when he wrote, nor the fate of his book, nor its various readings, nor how nor by whose deliberation it was accepted.

[68] What I have said here about Euclid must be said about everyone who has written about things by their nature comprehensible. So we conclude that concerning moral teachings we can easily grasp the intention of Scripture from the history we have of it and that in this case we can be certain of its true meaning. For the teachings of true piety are expressed in the most familiar words, since they are very ordinary and no less simple and easy to understand. And because true salvation and blessedness consists in true peace of mind, and we truly find peace only in those things which we understand very clearly, [69] it is evident that we can grasp with certainty the intention of Scripture concerning things salutary and necessary for blessedness. So there is no reason why we should be so anxious about the rest. Since for the most part we cannot embrace these other things by reason and the intellect, such concern would show more curiosity than regard for our advantage.

III. Fragments of
a Theory of Scientific Method

A. The Four Kinds of Knowledge[24]

[18] Having laid down these rules, I come now to what must be done first, before all else: emending the intellect and rendering it capable of understanding things in the way the attainment of our end requires. To do this, the order we naturally have requires me to survey here all the modes of perceiving which I have had up to now for affirming or denying something without doubt, so that I may choose the best of all, and at the same time begin to know my powers and the nature that I desire to perfect.

[19] If I consider them accurately, I can reduce them all to four main kinds:

1. There is the perception we have from report or from some conventional sign.

2. There is the perception we have from random experience, that

II/10

---

[24] From the *Treatise on the Emendation of the Intellect*, §§18–29.

is, from experience that is not determined by the intellect. But it has this name only because it comes to us by chance, and we have no other experience that opposes it. So it remains with us unshaken.

3. There is the perception that we have when the essence of a thing is inferred from another thing, but not adequately. This happens, either when we infer the cause from some effect, or when something is inferred from some universal, which some property always accompanies.

4. Finally, there is the perception we have when a thing is perceived through its essence alone, or through knowledge of its proximate cause.

[20] I shall illustrate all of these with examples. I know only from report my date of birth, and who my parents were, and similar things, which I have never doubted. By random experience I know that I shall die, for I affirm this because I have seen others like me die, even though they had not all lived the same length of time and did not all die of the same illness. Again, I also know by random experience that oil is capable of feeding fire, and that water is capable of putting it out. I know also that the dog is a barking animal, and man a rational one. And in this way I know almost all the things that are useful in life. II/11

[21] But we infer [one thing] from another in this way: after we clearly perceive that we feel such a body, and no other, then, I say, we infer clearly that the soul is united[25]* to the body, which union is the cause of such a sensation; but we cannot understand absolutely from this what that sensation and union are. Or after we have come to know the nature of vision, and that it has the property that we see one and the same thing as smaller when we look at it from a great distance than when we look at it from close up, we infer that the sun is larger than it appears to be, and other things of the same kind.

[22] Finally, a thing is perceived through its essence alone when, from the fact that I know something, I know what it is to know something, or from the fact that I know the essence of the soul, I know that it is united to the body. By the same kind of knowledge, we know that two and three are five, and that if two lines are parallel to a third line, they are also parallel to each other, and so on. But the things I have so far been able to know by this kind of knowledge have been very few.

[23] That you may understand all these things better, I shall use only

---

[25] * We see clearly from this example what I have just noted. For we understand nothing through that union except the sensation itself, that is, the effect, from which we inferred the cause, concerning which we understand nothing.

one example. Suppose there are three numbers. Someone is seeking a fourth, which is to the third as the second is to the first. Here merchants will usually say that they know what to do to find the fourth number, because they have not yet forgotten that procedure which they simply heard from their teachers, without any demonstration.

II/12   Others will construct a universal axiom from an experience with simple numbers, where the fourth number is evident through itself—as in the numbers 2, 4, 3, and 6. Here they find by trial that if the second is multiplied by the third, and the product then divided by the first, the result is 6. Since they see that this produces the same number which they knew to be the proportional number without this procedure, they infer that the procedure is always a good way to find the fourth number in the proportion.

[24] But mathematicians know, by the force of the demonstration of proposition 19 in Book VII of Euclid, which numbers are proportional to one another, from the nature of proportion, and its property, namely, that the product of the first and fourth numbers is equal to the product of the second and third. Nevertheless, they do not see the adequate proportionality of the given numbers. And if they do, they see it not by the force of that proposition, but intuitively, [NS: or] without going through any procedure.

[25] To choose the best mode of perceiving from these, we are required to enumerate briefly the means necessary to attain our end:

1. To know exactly our nature, which we desire to perfect, and at the same time,

2. [To know] as much of the nature of things as is necessary,
(a) to infer rightly from it the differences, agreements, and oppositions of things,
(b) to conceive rightly what they can undergo and what they cannot,
(c) to compare [the nature of things] with the nature and power of man.

This done, the highest perfection man can reach will easily manifest itself.

[26] Having considered these requirements, let us see which mode of perceiving we ought to choose.

As for the first, it is evident in itself that from report—apart from the fact that it is a very uncertain thing—we do not perceive any essence of a thing, as is clear from our example. And since the existence of any singular thing is not known unless its essence is known (as we shall see

50

afterwards), we can clearly infer from this that all the certainty we have from report is to be excluded from the sciences. For no one will ever be able to be affected by simple report, unless his own intellect has gone before.

[27] As for the second, again, no one should be said to have the idea of that proportion which he is seeking. Apart from the fact that it is a very uncertain thing, and without end, in this way no one will ever perceive anything in natural things except accidents. But these are never understood clearly unless their essences are known first. So that also is to be excluded. II/13

[28] Concerning the third, on the other hand, we can, in a sense, say that we have an idea of the thing, and that we can also make inferences without danger of error. But still, it will not through itself be the means of our reaching our perfection.

[29] Only the fourth mode comprehends the adequate essence of the thing and is without danger of error. For that reason, it is what we must chiefly use. So we shall take care to explain how it is to be used, that we may understand unknown things by this kind of knowledge and do so as directly as possible. . . .

B. Achieving Clear and Distinct Ideas[26]

[91] To arrive finally at the second part of this method, I shall set forth first our aim in it, and then the means to attain it. The aim, then, is to have clear and distinct ideas, that is, such as have been made from the pure mind, and not from fortuitous motions of the body. And then, so that all ideas may be led back to one, we shall strive to connect and order them so that our mind, as far as possible, reproduces objectively the formal character of nature, both as to the whole and as to the parts. II/34

[92] As for the first, our ultimate end requires (as we have already said) that the thing be conceived either through its essence alone or through its proximate cause. If the thing is in itself, *or*, as is commonly said, is the cause of itself, then it must be understood through its essence alone; but if it is not in itself, but requires a cause to exist, then it must be understood through its proximate cause. For really, knowledge[27] of the effect is nothing but acquiring a more perfect knowledge of its cause.

[93] Therefore, so long as we are dealing with the Investigation of

---

[26] *Treatise on the Emendation of the Intellect*, §§91–104.

[27] * Note that it is evident from this that we cannot [NS: legitimately or properly] understand anything of Nature without at the same time rendering our knowledge of the first cause, *or* God, more ample.

things, we must never infer anything from abstractions, and we shall take very great care not to mix up the things that are only in the intellect with those that are real. But the best conclusion will have to be drawn from some particular affirmative essence, *or*, from a true and legitimate definition. For from universal axioms alone the intellect cannot descend to singulars, since axioms extend to infinity, and do not determine the intellect to the contemplation of one singular thing rather than another.

[94] So the right way of discovery is to form thoughts from some given definition. This will proceed the more successfully and easily, the better we have defined a thing. So the chief point of this second part of the method is concerned solely with this: knowing the conditions of a good definition, and then, the way of finding good definitions. First, therefore, I shall deal with the conditions of definition.

[95] To be called perfect, a definition will have to explain the inmost essence of the thing, and to take care not to use certain *propria* in its place.[28] So as not to seem bent on uncovering the errors of others, I shall use only the example of an abstract thing to explain this. For it is the same however it is defined. If a circle, for example, is defined as a figure in which the lines drawn from the center to the circumference are equal, no one fails to see that such a definition does not at all explain the essence of the circle, but only a property of it. And though, as I have said, this does not matter much concerning figures and other beings of reason, it matters a great deal concerning physical and real beings, because the properties of things are not understood so long as their essences are not known. If we neglect them, we shall necessarily overturn the connection of the intellect, which ought to reproduce the connection of nature, and we shall completely miss our goal.

II/35

[96] These are the requirements which must be satisfied in Definition, if we are to be free of this fault:

1. If the thing is created, the definition, as we have said, will have to include the proximate cause. For example, according to this law, a circle would have to be defined as follows: it is the figure that is described by any line of which one end is fixed and the other moving. This definition clearly includes the proximate cause.

2. We require a concept, *or* definition, of the thing such that when it is considered alone, without any others conjoined, all the thing's properties can be deduced from it (as may be seen in this definition of the circle). For from it we clearly infer that all the lines drawn from the center to the circumference are equal.

---

[28] In traditional logic, *propria* are properties which, while not part of the essence of a thing, follow from its essence, so that they are universal to the species, as *capable of laughter* in the case of man.

That this is a necessary requirement of a definition is so plain through itself to the attentive that it does not seem worth taking time to demonstrate it, nor to show also, from this second requirement, that every definition must be affirmative. I mean intellectual affirmation—it matters little whether the definition is verbally affirmative; because of the poverty of language it will sometimes, perhaps, [only] be able to be expressed negatively, although it is understood affirmatively.

[97] These are the requirements for the definition of an uncreated thing:

1. That it should exclude every cause, that is, that the object should require nothing else except its own being for its explanation.

2. That, given the definition of this thing, there should remain no room for the question—does it exist?

3. That (as far as the mind is concerned) it should have no substantives that could be changed into adjectives, that is, that it should not be explained through any abstractions.

4. Finally (though it is not very necessary to note this) it is required   II/36 that all its properties be inferred from its definition.

All these things are evident to those who attend to them accurately.

[98] I have also said that the best conclusion will have to be drawn from a particular affirmative essence. For the more particular an idea is, the more distinct, and therefore the clearer it is. So we ought to seek knowledge of particulars as much as possible.

[99] As for order, to unite and order all our perceptions, it is required, and reason demands, that we ask, as soon as possible, whether there is a certain being, and at the same time, what sort of being it is, which is the cause of all things, so that its objective essence may also be the cause of all our ideas, and then our mind will (as we have said) reproduce nature as much as possible. For it will have nature's essence, order, and unity objectively.

From this we can see that above all it is necessary for us always to deduce all our ideas from physical things, *or* from the real beings, proceeding, as far as possible, according to the series of causes, from one real being to another real being, in such a way that we do not pass over to abstractions and universals, neither inferring something real from them, nor inferring them from something real. For to do either interferes with the true progress of the intellect.

[100] But note that by the series of causes and of real beings I do not here understand the series of singular, changeable things, but only the

series of fixed and eternal things. For it would be impossible for human weakness to grasp the series of singular, changeable things, not only because there are innumerably many of them, but also because of the infinite circumstances in one and the same thing, any of which can be the cause of its existence or nonexistence. For their existence has no connection with their essence, *or* (as we have already said) is not an eternal truth.

[101] But there is also no need for us to understand their series. The essences of singular, changeable things are not to be drawn from their series, *or* order of existing, since it offers us nothing but extrinsic denominations, relations, or at most, circumstances, all of which are far from the inmost essence of things. That essence is to be sought only II/37 from the fixed and eternal things, and at the same time from the laws inscribed in these things, as in their true codes, according to which all singular things come to be, and are ordered. Indeed these singular, changeable things depend so intimately, and (so to speak) essentially, on the fixed things that they can neither be nor be conceived without them. So although these fixed and eternal things are singular, nevertheless, because of their presence everywhere, and most extensive power, they will be to us like universals, *or* genera of the definitions of singular, changeable things, and the proximate causes of all things.

[102] But since this is so, there seems to be a considerable difficulty in our being able to arrive at knowledge of these singular things. For to conceive them all at once is a task far beyond the powers of the human intellect. But to understand one before the other, the order must be sought, as we have said, not from their series of existing, nor even from the eternal things. For there, by nature, all these things are at once. So other aids will have to be sought beyond those we use to understand the eternal things and their laws.

Nevertheless, this is not the place to treat them, nor is it necessary until after we have acquired a sufficient knowledge of the eternal things and their infallible laws, and the nature of our senses has become known to us. [103] Before we equip ourselves for knowledge of singular things, there will be time to treat those aids, all of which serve to help us know how to use our senses and to make, according to certain laws, and in order, the experiments that will suffice to determine the thing we are seeking, so that at last we may infer from them according to what laws of eternal things it was made, and its inmost nature may become known to us, as I shall show in its place.[29]

Here, to return to our theme, I shall only try to treat those things that

---

[29] This passage is one which should help correct the common picture of Spinoza as a philosopher whose epistemology had no room for appeals to experience.

seem necessary for us to be able to arrive at knowledge of eternal things, and for us to form their definitions according to the conditions laid down above. [104] To do this, we must recall what we said above: when the mind attends to a thought—to weigh it, and deduce from it, in good order, the things legitimately to be deduced from it—if it is false, the mind will uncover the falsity; but if it is true, the mind will continue successfully, without any interruption, to deduce true things from it. This, I say, is required for our purpose. For our thoughts cannot be determined from any other foundation.   II/38

IV. From a Non-Geometric Draft
of the *Ethics*

A. Of the 'Attributes' Which Do Not Belong to God, and on Definition[30]

[1] Here we shall begin to discuss those 'attributes'[31]* which are commonly ascribed to God, but which do not belong to him, and also those through which they try in vain to define God. We shall also speak of the rules of true definition.   I/44

[2] To do this, we shall not trouble ourselves much with the things men commonly imagine about God; we shall only investigate briefly what the philosophers can tell us about him. They have defined God as a *being existing of himself, cause of all things, omniscient, omnipotent, eternal, simple, infinite, the greatest good, of infinite compassion*, and so on. But before we enter into this investigation, let us first see what they allow us [to say about God].

[3] First, they say that no true or legitimate definition of God can be given; for they think there can be no definition except by genus and difference, and since God is not a species of any genus, he cannot be properly or legitimately defined.

[4] Next, they say again that God cannot be defined because the definition must represent the thing absolutely and affirmatively, and in their   I/45

---

[30] From the *Short Treatise on God, Man and his Well-Being*, I, vii.

[31] * Regarding the attributes of which God consists, they are nothing but infinite substances, each of which must, of itself, be infinitely perfect. Clear and distinct reason convinces us that this must necessarily be so. So far, however, only two of all these infinite attributes are known to us through their essence: thought and extension. All other things commonly ascribed to God are not attributes, but only certain modes, which may be attributed to him either in consideration of everything (i.e., all his attributes) or in consideration of one attribute. For example, that God is one, eternal, existing through himself, infinite, the cause of everything, immutable—these things are attributed to God in consideration of all his attributes. That God is omniscient and wise, and the like, are attributed to him in consideration of the attribute of thought. And that he is omnipresent and fills all, and the like, are attributed to him in consideration of the attribute of extension.

view one cannot know God affirmatively, but only negatively. So no legitimate definition of God can be given.

[5] Moreover, they also say that God can never be proven a priori (because he has no cause), but only probably, or through his effects. Because they have sufficiently conceded, by these doctrines, that they have a very slight and inconsiderable knowledge of God, we may now go on to investigate their definition.

[6] First, we do not see that they give us here any attributes through which it is known what the thing (God) is, but only *propria*, which indeed belong to a thing, but never explain what it is. For though *existing of itself, being the cause of all things, the greatest good, eternal*, and *immutable*, and so on, are proper to God alone, nevertheless through those *propria* we can know neither what the being to which these *propria* belong is, nor what attributes it has.

[7] It is time now also to look at those things which they ascribe to God, and which, nevertheless, do not belong to him,[32]* such as being *omniscient, compassionate, wise*, and the like. Because these things are only certain modes of the thinking thing, they can neither be nor be understood without that substance of which they are modes. That is why they cannot be attributed to him, who is a being existing of himself, without anything else.

[8] Finally, they call him the greatest good. But if by that they understand anything other than what they have already said, namely, that God is immutable, and a cause of all things, then they are confused in their own concept or have not been able to understand themselves. This

I/46 arises from their error regarding good and evil, since they think man himself, and not God, is the cause of his sins and evil. But according to what we have already proven, this cannot be, unless we are compelled to maintain that man is also a cause of himself. But this will be still clearer when we treat, afterwards, of man's will.

[9] Now we must untangle the sophistries by which they try to excuse their lack of knowledge of God.

First, then, they say *that a legitimate definition must be by genus and difference*. But though all the logicians admit this, I do not know where they get it from.

Certainly if this must be true, then one can know nothing. For if we can only know a thing perfectly through a definition consisting of genus and difference, then we can never know perfectly the highest genus, which has no genus above it. Now if the highest genus, which is the cause of the knowledge of all other things, is not known, the other

---

[32] * I.e., in consideration of all that he is, or all his attributes. On this, see the note to §1.

things which are explained by that genus are much less known or understood.

However, since we are free, and do not consider ourselves in any way bound to their positions, we shall produce, according to the true Logic, other laws of definition, guided by the division of nature we make.

[10] We have already seen that the attributes (or as others call them substances) are things, or, to put it better and more properly, a being existing through itself; and that this being therefore makes itself known through itself. We see that other things are only modes of those attributes, and without them can neither exist nor be understood. So definitions must be of two kinds:

1. Of attributes, which are of a self-existing being; these require no genus, or anything else through which they are better understood   I/47 or explained; for since they, as attributes of a being existing through itself, exist through themselves, they are also known through themselves.

2. Of those things which do not exist through themselves, but only through the attributes of which they are modes, and through which, as their genus, they must be understood.

And this is what we have to say about their position on definitions.

[11] Regarding their second claim, that we cannot know God with an adequate knowledge, Descartes has answered this satisfactorily, in his reply to the objections regarding this.

[12] And as for their third contention—that God cannot be proven a priori—we have already answered that previously. Since God is the cause of himself, it is enough that we prove him through himself, and such a proof is much more conclusive than an a posteriori one, which usually proceeds only by external causes.

B. On Natura naturans[33]

Here, before we proceed to anything else, we shall briefly divide the whole of Nature into *Natura naturans* and *Natura naturata*. By *Natura naturans* we understand a being that we conceive clearly and distinctly through itself, without needing anything other than itself (like all the attributes which we have so far described), that is, God. The Thomists have also understood God by this phrase, but their *Natura naturans* was a being (as they called it) beyond all substances.

We shall divide *Natura naturata* in two: a universal and a particular.

---

[33] From the *Short Treatise*, I, viii.

The universal consists in all those modes which depend on God immediately. We shall treat them in the next chapter. The particular consists
in all those singular things which are produced by the universal modes.
So *Natura naturata* requires some substances in order to be conceived
properly.

C. On Natura naturata[34]

I/48 [1] Turning now to universal *Natura naturata*, or those modes or
creatures which immediately depend on, or have been created by
God—we know only two of these: motion in matter, and intellect in the
thinking thing. We say, then, that these have been from all eternity, and
will remain to all eternity, immutable, a work truly as great as the greatness of the workman.

[2] With regard particularly to motion, it belongs more properly to a
treatise on natural science than here, [to show] that it has been from all
eternity, and will remain to all eternity, immutable, that it is infinite in
its kind, that it can neither exist nor be understood through itself, but
only through extension. So we shall not treat any of these things here,
but shall say only that it is a Son, product, or effect, created immediately
by God.

[3] As for intellect in the thinking thing, this too is a Son, product, or
immediate creature of God, also created by him from all eternity, and
remaining immutable to all eternity. Its sole property is to understand
everything clearly and distinctly at all times. From this arises immutably
a satisfaction infinite, or most perfect, since it cannot omit doing what
it does. And though what we have just said is sufficiently clear through
itself, we shall nevertheless prove it more clearly later when we treat of
the affections of the soul. So we shall say no more about it here.

D. Of the Human Soul[35]

I/117 [1] Since man is a created, finite thing, and so on, it is necessary that
what he has of thought, and what we call the soul, is a mode of that
attribute we call thought, without any thing other than this mode belonging to his essence; so much so that if this mode perishes, the soul is
also destroyed, although the preceding attribute remains immutable.

[2] Similarly, what he has of extension, which we call the body, is
nothing but a mode of the other attribute we call extension. If this mode

[34] *Short Treatise*, I, ix.
[35] *Short Treatise*, Second Appendix.

too is destroyed, the human body no longer exists, though the attribute of extension remains immutable.

[3] To understand now what this mode is, which we call soul, how it has its origin from the body, and also how its change depends (only) on the body (which I maintain to be the union of soul and body), we must note:

1. That the most immediate mode of the attribute we call thought has objectively in itself the formal essence of all things, so that if one posited any formal things whose essence did not exist objectively in the above-named attribute, it would not be infinite or supremely perfect in its kind (contrary to P3).[36]

[4] And since Nature or God is one being, of which infinite attributes are said, and which contains in itself all essences of created things, it is necessary that of all this there is produced in thought an infinite idea, which contains in itself objectively the whole of Nature, as it is in itself.

That is why I have also called this idea (in I, ix) a creature created immediately by God, since it has in itself objectively the formal essence of all things, without omission or addition. And this is necessarily only one, taking into consideration that all the essences of the attributes, and the essences of the modes contained in those attributes, are the essence   I/118 of only one infinite being.

[5] 2. It should also be noted that all the remaining modes, such as love, desire, and joy, have their origin in this first immediate mode, so that if it did not precede them, there could be no love, desire, and the like.

[6] From this it may clearly be concluded that the natural love which is in each thing for the preservation of its body can have no other origin than in the idea, or the objective essence of such a body, which is in the thinking attribute.

[7] Furthermore, since for the existence of an idea (or objective essence) nothing is required other than the thinking attribute and the object (or formal essence), it is certain, as we have said, that the idea, or objective essence, is the most immediate mode of the attribute. And consequently there can be, in the thinking attribute, no other mode which would belong to the essence of the soul of each thing, except the idea, which must be of such a thing as really existing, and which must exist in the thinking attribute. For such an idea brings with it the remaining modes of love, desire, and the like.

---

[36] Spinoza refers here to the third proposition in his earliest attempt (in Appendix I of the *Short Treatise*) at a geometric demonstration of his philosophy. That proposition states that "every attribute, or substance, is by its nature infinite, and supremely perfect in its kind."

Now since the idea proceeds from the existence of the object, then if the object changes or is destroyed, the idea itself also changes or is destroyed in the same degree; this being so, it is what is united with the object.

[8] Finally, if we should wish to proceed to ascribe to the essence of the soul that by which it can exist, we would not be able to find anything other than that attribute, and the object of which we have just spoken, and neither of these can belong to the essence of the soul. For the object has nothing of thought, and is really distinct from the soul. And as for the attribute, we have already proven that it cannot belong to the above-mentioned essence. From what we have subsequently said, this should be seen even more clearly; for the attribute, as attribute, is not united with the object, since it neither changes nor is destroyed, though the object changes or is destroyed.

[9] Therefore, the essence of the soul consists only in the being of an idea, or objective essence, in the thinking attribute, arising from the essence of an object which in fact exists in Nature. I say *of an object that really exists*, and so on, without further particulars, in order to include here not only the modes of extension, but also the modes of all the infinite attributes, which have a soul just as much as those of extension do.

[10] To understand this definition in more detail, it will help to consider what I have already said in speaking of the attributes. I have said that the attributes are not distinguished according to their existence, for they themselves are the subjects of their essences, that the essence of each of the modes is contained in the attributes just mentioned; and finally, that all the attributes are attributes of one infinite being.

[11] But it should be noted in addition that these modes, when considered as not really existing, are nevertheless equally contained in their attributes. And because there is no inequality at all in the attributes, nor in the essences of the modes, there can be no particularity in the idea, since it is not in Nature. But whenever any of these modes put on their particular existence, and by that are in some way distinguished from their attributes (because their particular existence, which they have in the attribute, is then the subject of their essence), then a particularity presents itself in the essences of the modes, and consequently in their objective essences, which are necessarily contained in the idea.

[12] This is why we have used these words in the definition, that *the soul is an idea arising from an object which exists in Nature*. And with this we consider that we have sufficiently explained what kind of thing the soul

is in general, understanding by this expression not only the ideas that arise from corporeal modes, but also those that arise from the existence of each mode of the remaining attributes.

[13] But since we do not have, of the remaining attributes, such a knowledge as we have of extension, let us see whether, having regard to the modes of extension, we can discover a more particular definition, which is more suited to express the essence of our soul. For this is our real intention.

[14] Here, then, we shall suppose as a thing proven, that there is no other mode in extension than motion and rest, and that each particular corporeal thing is nothing but a certain proportion of motion and rest, so much so that if there were nothing in extension except motion alone, or nothing except rest alone, there could not be, or be indicated, in the whole of extension, any particular thing. The human body, then, is nothing but a certain proportion of motion and rest.

[15] So this existing proportion's objective essence in the thinking attribute is the soul of the body. Hence when one of these modes (motion or rest) changes, either by increasing or by decreasing, the idea also changes correspondingly. For example, if the rest happens to increase, and the motion to decrease, the pain or sadness we call *cold* is thereby produced. On the other hand, if this [increase] occurs in the motion, then the pain we call *heat* is thereby produced.

[16] And so when the degrees of motion and rest are not equal in all parts of our body, but some have more motion and rest than others, there arises a difference of feeling (e.g., from this comes the different kind of pain we feel when we are struck with a little stick in the eyes or on the hands).

When the external causes which bring changes about differ in themselves, and do not all have the same effects, there arises a difference of feeling in one and the same part (e.g., the difference of feeling from a blow with a piece of wood or iron on the same hand). I/121

And again, if the change which happens in a part is a cause of its returning to its original proportion, from this there arises the joy we call peace, pleasurable activity, and cheerfulness.

[17] Finally, because we have now explained what feeling is, we can easily see how from this there arises a reflexive idea, or knowledge of oneself, experience, and reasoning.

And from all of this (as also because our soul is united with God, and is a part of the infinite idea arising immediately from God) we can see clearly the origin of clear knowledge, and the immortality of the soul. But for the present what we have said will be enough.

E. An Argument for Immortality[37]

I/110   [7] To bring this work to an end, it remains now to indicate briefly what human freedom consists in. To do this, I shall use the following propositions as things which are certain and proven.

> 1. The more essence a thing has, the more it also has of action and the less of passion. For it is certain that the agent acts through what he has, and that the one who is acted on is acted on through what he does not have.

> 2. All passion, whether it is from not being to being, or from being to not being, must proceed from an external agent, and not from an internal one. For no thing, considered in itself, has in itself a cause enabling it to destroy itself (if it exists) or to make itself (if it does not exist).

> 3. Whatever is not produced by external causes can also have nothing in common with them, and consequently will not be able to be changed or transformed by them.

From these last two [propositions], I infer the following fourth proposition.

> 4. No effect of an immanent or internal cause (which is all one, according to me) can possibly perish or change so long as its cause remains. For just as such an effect has not been produced by external causes, so also it cannot be changed [by them] (by the third proposition). And because nothing can be destroyed except through external causes, it is impossible that this effect should be able to perish so long as its cause endures (by the second proposition).

> 5. The freest cause of all, and the one most suited to God, is the immanent. For the effect of this cause depends on it in such a way that without it, [the effect] can neither exist nor be understood;
I/111   nor is [the effect] subjected to any other cause. Moreover, [the effect] is also so united with [the cause] that together they form a whole.

[8] So let us see now what we have to conclude from these propositions. First, then,

---

[37] *Short Treatise*, II, xxvi, §§7–9. This is the second of two arguments for immortality in the *Short Treatise*, the first having been presented in II, xxiii.

1. Since God's essence is infinite, it has an infinite action, and an infinite negation of passion (by the first proposition); consequently, the more things, through their greater essence, are united with God, the more they also have of action, and the less of passion, and the more they are also free of change and corruption.

2. The true intellect can never come to perish, for in itself it can have no cause to make itself perish (by the second proposition). And because it has not proceeded from external causes, but from God, it cannot receive any change from him (by the third proposition). And since God has produced it immediately, and he alone is an internal cause, it follows necessarily that it cannot perish, so long as this, its cause, remains (by the fourth proposition). Now this, its cause, is eternal. Therefore, it too [is eternal].

3. All the effects of the intellect which are united with him are the most excellent, and must be valued above all others. For because they are internal effects, they are the most excellent of all (by the fifth proposition); moreover, they also must be eternal, for their cause is eternal.

4. All the effects which we produce outside ourselves are the more perfect the more they are capable of being united with us to make one and the same nature, for in this way they are nearest to internal effects. For example, if I teach my fellow men to love sensual pleasure, esteem, and greed, then whether I also love these things or not, I am hacked or beaten. This is clear. But [this will] not [be the result] if the only end I strive to attain is to be able to taste union with God, produce true ideas in myself, and make all these things known to my fellow men also. For we can all share equally in this I/112 salvation, as happens when this produces in them the same desire that is in me, bringing it about thereby that their will and mine are one and the same, and producing one and the same nature, agreeing always in all things.

[9] From all that has been said, it can now be very easily conceived what human freedom is. I define it as follows: it is a firm existence, which our intellect acquires through immediate union with God, so that it can produce ideas in itself, and outside itself effects agreeing with its nature, without its effects being subjected, however, to any external causes by which they can be changed or transformed.

At the same time, from what has been said it is also clear which things are in our power and are subjected to no external causes; similarly we have also proven here, and in a different way than before, the eternal and constant duration of the intellect, and finally, which effects we have to value above all others.

F. A Dialogue on God's Causality[38]

I/31

[1] *Erasmus*: I have heard you say, Theophilus, that God is a cause of all things, and moreover, that he can be no other cause than an *immanent* one. If, then, he is an *immanent cause* of all things, how could you call him a remote cause? For that is impossible in an immanent cause.

[2] *Theophilus*: When I said that God is a remote cause, I said that only in respect to those things [which do not depend on him immediately and not those things] which God has produced immediately (without any circumstances, by his existence alone). But I have not at all called him a remote cause absolutely. You could also have inferred this clearly from my words. For I also said that we can, *in some way*, call him a remote cause.

[3] *Erasmus*: Now I understand sufficiently what you want to tell me; but I note also that you said that the effect of an internal cause remains united with its cause in such a way that it makes a whole with it. If that is so, then I think God cannot be an immanent cause. For if he and what he has produced make together a whole, then you ascribe more essence to God at one time than at another. Please, relieve me of this doubt.

[4] *Theophilus*: If you want to escape this confusion, Erasmus, pay close attention to what I am about to tell you. The essence of a thing does not increase through its union with another thing, with which it makes a whole. On the contrary, the first thing remains unchanged.

I/32

[5] I shall give you an example, so that you will understand me better. A sculptor has made various figures of wood, in the likeness of parts of a human body. He takes one of these, which has the shape of a human breast, adds it to another, which has the shape of a human head, and makes of these two a whole which represents the upper part of a human body. Will you say now, on that account, that the essence of the head has increased, because it has been united to the breast? That would be a mistake, for it is the same as it was before.

[6] To make this even clearer, I shall give you another example, namely, an idea I have of a triangle and another, arising from the extension of one of the angles. The angle formed by this extension is necessarily equal to the two opposite internal angles, and so on. I say that these [ideas] have produced a new idea, namely, that the three angles of

---

[38] *Short Treatise*, Second Dialogue.

the triangle are equal to two right angles. This idea is so united to the first, that it can neither be nor be conceived without it.

[7] ... You see now that although this new idea is united to the preceding one, no change takes place on that account in the essence of the preceding one. On the contrary, it remains without the least change. You can also see this in each idea which in itself produces love. This love does not in any way increase the essence of the idea.

[8] But why pile up examples? For you yourself can see this clearly in the matter we are speaking of. I have said distinctly that all the attributes, which depend on no other cause, and to define which no genus is necessary, belong to God's essence. And because created things do not have the power to form an attribute, they do not increase God's essence, no matter how closely they are united to him.

[9] To this we may add that the whole is only a being of reason and differs from the universal only in these respects: that the universal is I/33 made of various disunited individuals, whereas the whole is made of various united individuals, and that the universal includes only parts of the same kind, whereas the whole includes parts of the same kind and of another kind.

[10] *Erasmus*: As far as that question is concerned, you have satisfied me. But you have also said that the effect of an internal cause cannot perish so long as its cause endures. I see, indeed, that this is certainly true. But since it is, how can God be an internal cause of all things, since many things perish?

According to your previous distinction, you will say that God is properly a cause of those effects he has produced immediately, through his attributes alone, without any further circumstances, and that these therefore cannot perish so long as their cause endures; but [you will add] that you do not call God an internal cause of those effects whose existence does not depend immediately on him, but which have come to be from some other thing (except insofar as their causes neither do nor can act without God or outside him); and these, then, can perish, since they have not been produced by God immediately.

[11] But this does not satisfy me. For I see that you conclude that the human intellect is immortal, because it is an effect that God has produced in himself. Now it is impossible that more was needed, to produce such an intellect, than God's attributes alone. For to be a being of such an eminent perfection it must have been created from eternity, like all other things which depend immediately on God. And if I am not mistaken, I have heard you say this yourself. How will you slip out of this without leaving difficulties behind?

[12] *Theophilus*: It is true, Erasmus, that those things which have been

created by him immediately (those which for their existence required nothing but God's attributes) have been created from eternity. But it should be noted that even if it is necessary for the existence of a thing I/34   that a particular modification be present and [so] something outside God's attributes, that still does not prevent God from being able to produce [such] a thing immediately. For of the things required to make things exist, some are required to produce the thing, and others for it to be able to be produced.

For example, if I want to have light in a certain room, I light [a candle] and this, through itself, lights the room—or I open a window [shutter], and though opening it does not itself make light, still it brings it about that the light can come into the room. Similarly, for the motion of a body, another body is required, which must already have that motion which passes from it to the first body.

But to produce an idea of God in us, no other particular thing is required which has what is produced in us; all that is necessary is that there be in Nature a body such that its idea represents God immediately. This too you could have inferred from my words. For I have said that God is known only through himself and not through something else.

[13] But I tell you this: so long as we do not have such a clear idea of God that it so unites us to him as not to let us love anything outside him, we cannot say that we are truly united with God, and so depend immediately on him.

If you still have anything to ask me, leave it for another time. Right now I am required elsewhere. Farewell.

[14] *Erasmus*: For the moment I have nothing. But I shall think about what you have just told me until the next time we meet. I commend you to God.

V. An Early Attempt at Geometrizing Philosophy

A. Spinoza to Oldenburg[39]

Esteemed Sir,

IV/7   . . . I shall try to explain what I think concerning the matters we discussed, though I do not think this will be a means of binding you more closely to me, unless your generosity intervenes. I shall begin, then, by speaking briefly about

[39] Letter 2.

[D1] God, whom I define as a being consisting of infinite attributes, each of which is infinite, *or* supremely perfect in its kind.

Here it should be noted that

[D2] By attribute I understand whatever is conceived through itself and in itself, so that its concept does not involve the concept of another thing.[40]

For example, extension is conceived through itself and in itself, but motion is not. For it is conceived in another and its concept involves extension. That [D1] is a true definition of God is clear from the fact that by God we understand a being supremely perfect and absolutely infinite. Moreover, it is easy to demonstrate from this definition that such a being exists. Since this is not the place for it, I shall omit the demonstration. But what I must show here, to answer satisfactorily your first question [concerning the true distinction between extension and thought] are the following: IV/8

[P1] That two substances cannot exist in nature unless they differ in their whole essence;

[P2] That a substance cannot be produced, but that it is of its essence to exist;

[P3] That every substance must be infinite, *or* supremely perfect in its kind.

Once I have demonstrated these things, then (provided you attend to the definition of God) you will easily be able to see what I am aiming at, so it is not necessary to speak more openly about these matters. But I can think of no better way of demonstrating these things clearly and briefly than to prove them in the geometric manner and subject them to your understanding. So I send them separately with this letter and await your judgment regarding them. . . .[41]
[Rijnsburg, September 1661]

---

[40] Note that this formula will be used to define substance in the *Ethics* (ID3) and that attribute will be defined differently there (ID4). See also Letter 9, in VII.B.

[41] Though the enclosure has been lost, we can reconstruct at least some of its assumptions from subsequent letters. There would have been a further definition:

[D3] By modification, *or* accident, I understand what is in another and is conceived through that in which it is.

And four axioms:

[A1] Substance is by nature prior to its accidents.

[A2] Except for substances and accidents, there is nothing real, *or* outside the intellect.

B. Oldenburg to Spinoza[42]

Excellent Sir, and Dearest Friend,

IV/10   ... I approve very much of your geometric style of proof, but at the same time I blame my own obtuseness that I do not follow so easily the things you teach so exactly. Please, then, let me give you evidence of my slowness by putting the following problems to you, and seeking their solutions.

First, do you understand clearly and without doubt that, merely from the definition you give of God, it is demonstrated that such a being exists? When I reflect that definitions contain only our mind's concepts, that our mind conceives many things which do not exist, and that it is most fruitful in multiplying and increasing things once they have been conceived, I do not yet see how I can infer God's existence from the concept I have of him. To be sure, from the mental collection of all the perfections I find in men, animals, vegetables, minerals, and the like, I can form a conception of some one substance which really possesses all those virtues; indeed my mind is capable of multiplying and increasing them to infinity, so that it can conjure up in itself a most perfect and excellent being. But from this one cannot at all infer the existence of such a being.

Second, are you certain that body is not limited by thought nor thought by body? For the controversy about what thought is, whether it is a corporeal motion or some spiritual act, entirely different from the corporeal, is still unresolved.

IV/11   Third, do you regard the axioms you communicated to me as indemonstrable Principles, known by the light of nature and requiring no proof? Perhaps the first is of that kind, but I do not see how the other three can be so regarded. The second supposes that nothing exists in Nature except substances and accidents, but many maintain that time and place are neither. I am so far from conceiving clearly your third axiom—*Things which have different attributes have nothing in common with one another*—that the whole universe of things seems rather to prove its contrary. For all things known to us both differ from one another in

---

[A3] Things which have different attributes have nothing in common with one another.

[A4] If things have nothing in common with one another, one cannot be the cause of the other.

Apparently in response to Oldenburg's objections, some of the axioms of the enclosure become propositions in the *Ethics*. Axioms 1, 3, and 4 of the enclosure = Propositions 1, 2, and 3 of Part I of the *Ethics*.

[42] Letter 3.

some respects and agree in others. Finally, the fourth axiom—*If things have nothing in common with one another, one cannot be the cause of the other*—is not so evident to my dull intellect that it does not need more light shed on it. Surely God has nothing formally in common with created things, yet nearly all of us regard him as their cause.

Since I do not find these axioms beyond any shadow of a doubt, you will easily guess that the propositions you have built on them cannot but totter. And the more I consider them, the more I am overwhelmed by doubts concerning them. For regarding the first, I consider that two men are two substances, and have the same attribute, since each has the capacity to reason; from that I conclude that there are two substances of the same attribute. Regarding the second, *That a substance cannot be produced, not even by another substance*, I consider that we can hardly grasp how this could be true, since nothing can be its own cause. This proposition sets up every substance as its own cause, and makes them all independent of one another, makes them so many Gods. In this way it denies the first cause of all things.

I readily confess that I cannot grasp this unless you do me the favor of revealing to me somewhat more straightforwardly and fully your opinion concerning this lofty matter and teaching me what is the origin and production of substances, the dependence of things on one another, and their subordination to one another. I entreat you, by the friendship we have entered into, to deal openly and confidently with me in this matter, and I ask you most earnestly to be fully persuaded that whatever things you are pleased to share with me will be safe, and that I will take care that none of them become known to your harm or disadvantage. . . .

Your most devoted,
Henry Oldenburg

London, 27 September 1661

C. Spinoza to Oldenburg[43]

Esteemed Sir,

While I was preparing to go to Amsterdam, to spend a week or two there, I received your very welcome letter and saw your objections to the three propositions I sent you. I shall try to satisfy you only on those points, omitting the rest for lack of time.

To the first, then, I say that it is not from the definition of any thing whatever that the existence of the thing defined follows; it follows only

IV/13

---

[43] Letter 4.

(as I demonstrated in the scholium I attached to the three propositions) from the definition, *or* idea, of some attribute, that is (as I explained clearly in relation to the definition of God), of a thing which is conceived through itself and in itself. In the scholium just mentioned, I have also, unless I am mistaken, stated clearly enough the reason for this difference—especially for a philosopher, who is supposed to know the difference between a fiction and a clear and distinct concept, and the truth of the axiom that every definition, *or* clear and distinct idea, is true. Once these things are noted, I do not see what more is lacking for the solution to the first problem.

So I proceed to the solution of the second, where you seem to concede that if thought does not pertain to the nature of extension, then extension will not be limited by thought, since you raise a doubt only concerning the example. But please note: if someone says that extension is limited not by extension, but by thought, is that not the same as saying that extension is infinite not absolutely, but only so far as it is extension? That is, he does grant me that extension is not infinite absolutely, but only insofar as it is extension, that is, in its own kind.

But, you say, perhaps thought is a corporeal act. So be it (though I do not grant this). Still, you will not deny that extension, insofar as it is extension, is not thought, which is enough to explain my definition and demonstrate my third proposition.

Your third objection against the things I proposed is that the axioms ought not to be counted as common notions. I have no quarrel with that. But you also doubt their truth; indeed you seem to want to show that their contrary is more likely. So please attend to the definitions I gave of substance and of accident, from which all these [axioms] are derived. For by substance I understand what is conceived through itself and in itself, that is, that whose concept does not involve the concept of another thing; but by modification, *or* accident, what is in another and is conceived through what it is in. From this it is clear that:

IV/14

[A1] Substance is by nature prior to its accidents, for without it, they can neither be nor be conceived.

[A2] Except for substances and accidents, nothing exists in reality, *or* outside the intellect,

for whatever there is, is conceived either through itself or through another, and its concept either does or does not involve the concept of another thing,

[A3] Things which have different attributes have nothing in common with one another,

70

for I have explained that an attribute is that whose concept does not involve the concept of another thing.

[A4] If two things have nothing in common with one another, one cannot be the cause of the other,

for since there would be nothing in the effect which it had in common with the cause, whatever the effect had, it would have from nothing.

As for your contention that God has nothing formally in common with created things, and so on, I have maintained the complete opposite of this in my definition. For I have said that God is a being consisting of infinite attributes, of which each is infinite, *or* supremely perfect in its kind. As for your objection to the first proposition, I ask you, my friend, to consider that men are not created, but only generated, and that their bodies already existed before, though formed differently. It may, indeed, be inferred, as I cheerfully acknowledge, that if one part of matter were annihilated, the whole of extension would also vanish at the same time. Moreover, the second proposition does not make many gods, but only one, consisting of infinite attributes, and so on.
[Rijnsburg, October 1661]

VI. Two Criticisms of Descartes

A. On the Cartesian Circle[44]

Finally, to become certain of the things he had called in doubt and to remove all doubt, Descartes proceeds to inquire into the nature of the most perfect being, and whether such a being exists. For when he discovers that there is a most perfect being, by whose power all things are produced and conserved, and with whose nature being a deceiver is incompatible, then that reason for doubting which he had because he was ignorant of his cause will be removed. He will know that a God who is supremely good and veracious did not give him the faculty of distinguishing the true from the false so that he might be deceived. Hence neither mathematical truths nor any of those that seem most evident to him can be at all suspected.   I/145

Next, to remove the remaining causes of doubt, he proceeds to ask how it happens that we sometimes err. When he discovered that this occurs because we use our free will to assent even to things we have perceived only confusedly, he was able to conclude immediately that he could guard against error in the future, provided he gave his assent only   I/146

[44] From the prolegomenon to *Descartes' PRINCIPLES OF PHILOSOPHY.*

to things perceived clearly and distinctly. Each of us can easily accomplish this by himself, since each has the power of restraining the will, and so of bringing it about that it is contained within the limits of the intellect.

But because we have absorbed at an early age many prejudices from which we are not easily freed, he proceeds next to enumerate and examine separately all the simple notions and ideas of which all our thoughts are composed, so that we might be freed from our prejudices, and accept nothing but what we perceive clearly and distinctly. For if he could take note of what was clear and what obscure in each, he would easily be able to distinguish the clear from the obscure and to form clear and distinct thoughts. In this way he would discover easily the real distinction between the soul and the body, what was clear and what obscure in the things we have derived from the senses, and finally, how a dream differs from waking states. Once this was done, he could no longer doubt his waking states nor be deceived by the senses. So he freed himself from all the doubts recounted above.

But before we finish, it seems we must satisfy those who make the following objection. Since God's existence does not become known to us through itself, we seem unable ever to be certain of anything; nor will we ever be able to come to know God's existence. For we have said that everything is uncertain so long as we are ignorant of our origin, and from uncertain premises, nothing certain can be inferred.

To remove this difficulty, Descartes makes the following reply. From the fact that we do not yet know whether the author of our origin had perhaps created us so that we are deceived even in those things that appear most evident to us, we cannot in any way doubt the things that we understand clearly and distinctly either through themselves or through reasoning (so long, at any rate, as we attend to that reasoning). I/147 We can doubt only those things that we have previously demonstrated to be true, and whose memory can recur when we no longer attend to the reasons from which we deduced them and, indeed, have forgotten the reasons. So although God's existence cannot come to be known through itself, but only through something else, we will be able to attain a certain knowledge of his existence so long as we attend very accurately to all the premises from which we have inferred it. See *Principles I,* 13; *Reply to Second Objections,* 3; and Meditation 5, at the end.

But since this answer does not satisfy some people, I shall give another. When we previously discussed the certainty and evidence of our existence, we saw that we inferred it from the fact that, wherever we turned our attention—whether we were considering our own nature, or feigning some cunning deceiver as the author of our nature, or summoning up, outside us, any other reason for doubting whatever—we came upon no reason for doubting that did not by itself convince us of our existence.

So far we have not observed this to happen regarding any other matter. For though, when we attend to the nature of a triangle, we are compelled to infer that its three angles are equal to two right angles, nevertheless we cannot infer the same thing from [the supposition] that perhaps we are deceived by the author of our nature. But from [this supposition] we did most certainly infer our existence. So here we are not compelled, wherever we direct our attention, to infer that the three angles of a triangle are equal to two right angles. On the contrary, we discover a ground for doubting, namely, because we have no idea of God which so affects us that it is impossible for us to think that God is a deceiver. For to someone who does not have a true idea of God (which we now suppose ourselves not to have) it is just as easy to think that his author is a deceiver as to think that he is not a deceiver. Similarly for one who has no idea of a triangle, it is just as easy to think that its three angles are equal to two right angles, as to think that they are not.

So we concede that we cannot be absolutely certain of anything, ex-   I/148
cept our own existence, even though we attend properly to its demonstration, so long as we have no clear and distinct concept of God that makes us affirm that he is supremely veracious, just as the idea we have of a triangle compels us to infer that its three angles are equal to two right angles. But we deny that we cannot, therefore, arrive at knowledge of anything.

For as is evident from everything we have said just now, the crux of the whole matter is that we can form a concept of God which so disposes us that it is not as easy for us to think that he is a deceiver as to think that he is not, but which now compels us to affirm that he is supremely veracious. When we have formed such an idea, that reason for doubting mathematical truths will be removed. Wherever we then direct our attention in order to doubt some one of them, we shall come upon nothing from which we must not instead infer that it is most certain—as happened concerning our existence.

For example, if, after we have discovered the idea of God, we attend to the nature of a triangle, the idea of this will compel us to affirm that its three angles are equal to two right angles; but if we attend to the idea of God, this too will compel us to affirm that he is supremely veracious, and the author and continual conserver of our nature, and therefore that he does not deceive us concerning that truth. Nor will it be less impossible for us to think that he is a deceiver, when we attend to the idea of God (which we now suppose ourselves to have discovered), than it is for us to think that the three angles of a triangle do not equal two right angles, when we attend to the idea of a triangle. And just as we can form such an idea of a triangle, even though we do not know whether the author of our nature deceives us, so also we can make the idea of God clear to ourselves and put it before our eyes, even though we still doubt whether the author of our nature deceives us in all things. And provided we have it, however we have acquired it, it will suffice to remove all doubt, as has just now been shown.

I/149 Therefore, from these premises we reply as follows to the difficulty raised. We can be certain of nothing—not, indeed, so long as we are ignorant of God's existence (for I have not spoken of this)—but as long as we do not have a clear and distinct idea of him.

So if anyone wishes to argue against me, his objection will have to be this: *we can be certain of nothing before we have a clear and distinct idea of God; but we cannot have a clear and distinct idea of God so long as we do not know whether the author of our nature deceives us; therefore, we can be certain of nothing so long as we do not know whether the author of our nature deceives us, and so on.*

To this I reply by conceding the major and denying the minor. For we have a clear and distinct idea of a triangle, although we do not know whether the author of our nature deceives us; and provided we have such an idea (as I have just shown abundantly), we will be able to doubt neither his existence, nor any mathematical truth.

B. On Descartes' Attempt to Prove God's Existence from His Own[45]

To demonstrate [God's existence from his own existence] Descartes
I/161 assumes these two axioms: (1) *What can bring about the greater, or more difficult, can also bring about the lesser*; (2) *It is greater to create, or (by A10) to preserve, a substance than the attributes, or properties, of a substance.* But what he means by this I do not know. What does he call easy, and what difficult? Nothing is said to be easy or difficult absolutely, but only in relation to a cause. So one and the same thing can at the same time be called both easy and difficult in relation to different causes.[46*]

[45] The scholium to P7, Part I, of *Descartes' PRINCIPLES*.

[46] * Take as one example the spider, which easily weaves a web which men could weave only with the greatest difficulty. On the other hand, how many things do men do with the greatest ease which are perhaps impossible for angels? [In a letter to Mesland of 2 May 1644 Descartes replies to a similar objection and concedes that his principle does not hold in the case of "physical and moral causes, which are particular and limited" (such as a man, who can produce another man, but not an ant); but he insists that it must hold in the case of "a universal and unlimited cause" (such as God would be). It seems likely that Spinoza was familiar with this letter; so it is surprising that he ignores Descartes' reply.]

But if he calls difficult those things that can be accomplished [by a cause] with great labor, and easy, those that can be accomplished by the same cause with less labor—as a force which can lift fifty pounds will be able to lift twenty-five twice as easily—then of course, the axiom will not be absolutely true, nor will he be able to demonstrate from it what he wants to. For when he says [AT VII, 168], *if I had the power of preserving myself, I would also have the power of giving myself all the perfections I lack* (because they do not require such a great power), I would concede this to him. The powers I expend in preserving myself could bring about many other things far more easily, if I did not require them for preserving myself. But so long as I use them for preserving myself, I deny that I can expend them to bring about other things, even though they are easier, as is clear in our example.

It does not remove the difficulty if it is said that since I am a thinking thing I would necessarily have to know whether I spend all my powers in preserving myself, and also whether this is the cause of my not giving myself the remaining perfections. The dispute now does not concern this, but only how the necessity of this proposition follows from this axiom. Moreover, if I knew it, I would be greater, and perhaps would require greater powers to preserve myself in that greater perfection than those I have.

And then I do not know whether it is a greater work to create (*or* preserve) a substance than to create (*or* preserve) attributes. To speak more clearly and philosophically, I do not know whether a substance does not require its whole power and essence, by which it perhaps preserves itself, for preserving its attributes.

But let us leave these things to examine further what our most noble author means here, that is, what he understands by easy and difficult. I do not think, nor can I in any way persuade myself, that by difficult he understands what is impossible (so that it cannot in any way be conceived how it happens), and by easy, what implies no contradiction (so that it can easily be conceived how it happens). It is true that he seems at first glance to mean this, when he says in the Third Meditation [AT VII, 48]: *I must not think that perhaps the things I lack are more difficult to acquire than those now in me. On the contrary, it is evident that it was far more difficult for me—that is, a thing, or substance, which thinks—to emerge from nothing than, and so on.* But that would not be consistent with the author's words and would not be worthy of his genius.

For, to pass over the first consideration, there is nothing in common between the possible and the impossible, *or* between the intelligible and the unintelligible, just as there is nothing in common between something and nothing; and power does not agree with impossibilities any

I/162

75

more than creation and generation do with nonexistent things, so they ought not to be compared in any way. Moreover, I can compare things with one another and know the relation between them only if I have a clear and distinct concept of each of them. Hence I deny that it follows that if someone can do the impossible, he should also be able to do what is possible.

What sort of conclusion is this? If someone can make a square circle, he will also be able to make a circle all of whose radii are equal, or, if someone can bring it about that nothing is acted on, and can use it as a material from which to produce something, he will also have the power to make something from some [B: other] thing. As I have said, between these and similar things there is neither agreement, nor proportion, nor comparison, nor anything whatsoever in common. Anyone can see this, if he gives the matter any attention at all. I think Descartes was too intelligent to have meant that.

I/163
But when I consider the second axiom of the two just cited, it seems that by greater and more difficult he means more perfect, and by less and easier, more imperfect. But this is also very obscure. There is the same difficulty here as before. I deny, as before, that he who can do the greater, should be able at the same time and by the same work (as must be supposed in the proposition) to do the lesser.

Again, when he says: *it is greater to create* or *preserve a substance than to create or preserve its attributes,* he can surely not understand by attributes what is contained formally in substance and is distinguished from substance itself only by reason. For then creating a substance is the same as creating its attributes. For the same reason he also cannot understand [by attributes] the properties of a substance which follow necessarily from its essence and definition.

Much less can he understand what he nevertheless seems to mean, namely, the properties and attributes of another substance. So, for example, if I say that I have the power of preserving myself, a finite thinking substance, I cannot on that account say that I also have the power of giving myself the perfections of the infinite substance which differs in its whole essence from my essence. For the power, *or* essence, by which I preserve myself in my being differs entirely from the power, *or* essence, by which the absolutely infinite substance preserves itself, from which its powers and properties are only distinguished by reason.[47*] Hence,

---

[47] * Note that the power by which the substance preserves itself is nothing but its essence, and differs from it only in name. This will be most relevant when we discuss God's power in the Appendix. [Spinoza is apparently referring to a passage later in his work where he identifies life with the force by which things persevere in their being. In the case of things other than God, that force is different from the things themselves, so it is proper to say that they have life. In the case of God, the power by which he perseveres in his being is his essence, so it is better to say that he is life than that he has life. (I/260)]

even though I were to suppose that I preserve myself, if I should wish to conceive that I could give myself the perfections of the absolutely infinite substance, I would be supposing nothing but this—that I can reduce my whole essence to nothing and create afresh an infinite substance. This, of course, would be much greater than only supposing that I can preserve myself, a finite substance.

Since, then, he can understand none of these things by attributes or properties, nothing else remains, except the qualities that the substance itself contains eminently (as, this or that thought in the mind, which I clearly perceive to be lacking in me), but not those another substance contains eminently (as, this or that motion in extension; for such perfections are not perfections for me, a thinking thing, and so are not lacking to me). But then Descartes cannot in any way infer from this axiom the conclusion he wants to demonstrate, that is, that if I preserve myself, I also have the power of giving myself all the perfections that I clearly find to pertain to a supremely perfect Being. I/164

VII. The Study Group has Questions about Definitions

A. Simon de Vries to Spinoza[48]

Most Upright Friend,

... [Y]ou have very often been present in my mind, especially when IV/39 I meditate on your writings and hold them in my hands. But since not everything is clear enough to the members of our group—which is why we have begun meeting again—and so that you will not think I have forgotten you, I have set myself to write this letter.

As for our group, it is arranged in this way: one of us (but each one takes his turn) reads through, explains according to his own conceptions, and then proves everything, following the sequence and order of your propositions. Then if it happens that one cannot satisfy the other, we have thought it worthwhile to make a note of it and to write to you, so that, if possible, it may be made clearer to us, and under your guidance we may be able to defend the truth against those who are superstitiously religious and Christian, and to stand against the attacks of the whole world.

So since, when we first read through and explained the definitions, they did not all seem clear to us, we did not agree about the nature of definition. In your absence we consulted a certain author, a mathematician named Borelli. When he discusses the nature of a definition, an

---

[48] Letter 8.

axiom, and a postulate, he also introduces the opinions of others regarding this matter. His own opinion is as follows:

> Definitions are used in a demonstration as premises. So it is necessary for them to be known evidently, otherwise scientific, *or* very evident, knowledge cannot be acquired from them.

And elsewhere:

> The basis for a construction, or the essential, first and best known property of a subject, must be chosen, not rashly, but with the greatest care. For if the construction or the property named is impossible, then a scientific definition will not result. For example, if someone were to say: "Let two straight lines enclosing a space be called 'figurals,' " this would be a definition of a nonbeing, and would be impossible. So ignorance rather than knowledge would be deduced from it. Next, if the construction or property named is indeed possible and true, but unknown to us, or doubtful, then it will not be a good definition; for conclusions drawn from what is unknown and doubtful will also be uncertain and doubtful. So they will produce suspicion or opinion, but not certain knowledge.

IV/40

Tacquet seems to disagree with this opinion, for as you know, he maintains that one can proceed directly from a false proposition to a true conclusion. But Clavius, whose opinion [Borelli] also introduces, thinks that

> Definitions are technical terms, and it is not necessary to give a reason why a thing is defined in this or that way. It is enough if one never asserts that the thing defined agrees with something unless one has first demonstrated that the definition given agrees with it.

So Borelli maintains that the definition of a subject must consist of a property or construction which is first, essential, best known to us, and true, whereas for Clavius it does not matter whether it is first or best known or true or not, so long as the definition we have given is not asserted to agree with something unless we have first demonstrated that the definition given does agree with that thing.

We prefer Borelli's opinion, but we do not really know, Sir, which of the two you agree with, or whether you agree with neither. Since there are such various disputes about the nature of definition, which is numbered among the principles of demonstration, if the mind is not freed of difficulties regarding this, then it will also be in difficulty regarding those things deduced from it. So if we are not making too much trouble for you, and if you have the time, we would very much like you, Sir, to write to us, giving us your opinion about this matter, and also about what the distinction is between axioms and definitions. Borelli, in fact, admits no true distinction between them, except as regards the name. But I believe you maintain another distinction.

Next, the third definition is not sufficiently clear to us. As an example, IV/41 I reported what you, Sir, said to me at The Hague, that a thing can be considered in two ways, either as it is in itself or as it has a relation to something else. For example, the intellect can be considered either under thought or as consisting of ideas. But we do not see clearly what this distinction would be. For we think that if we conceive thought rightly, we must comprehend it in relation to ideas, since if all ideas were removed from it, we would destroy thought itself. So since the example is not clear enough to us, the thing itself still remains somewhat obscure, and we require further explanation.

Finally, at the beginning of P8S3 you write:

> From these [propositions] it is evident that although two attributes may be conceived to be really distinct (i.e., one may be conceived without the aid of the other), they do not, on that account, consti- tute two beings or two different substances. The reason is that it is of the nature of a substance that all of its attributes (I mean each of them) should be conceived through themselves, since they have [always] been in it together.

In this way you seem, Sir, to suppose that the nature of substance is so constituted that it can have more than one attribute, which you have not yet demonstrated, unless you depend on the fifth definition of an abso- lutely infinite substance, *or* God. Otherwise, if I should say that each substance has only one attribute, and if I had the idea of two attributes, I could rightly conclude that, where there are two different attributes, there are two different substances. We ask you for a clearer explanation of this too. . . .

Your very Devoted
S. J. de Vries

Amsterdam, 24 February 1663

B. Spinoza to De Vries[49]

. . . As for the questions proposed in your group (which is very sensi- IV/42 bly organized), I see that you are in these perplexities because you do not distinguish between different kinds of definition—between one which serves to explain a thing whose essence only is sought, as the only thing there is doubt about, and one which is proposed only to be exam-

---

[49] Letter 9.

ined. For because the former has a determinate object, it ought to be true. But the latter does not require this.

IV/43 For example, if someone asks me for a description of the temple of Solomon, I ought to give him a true description of the temple [NS: as it was] unless I want to talk nonsense to him. But if I have constructed in my mind some temple which I want to build, and if I infer from its description that I must buy land of such a kind and so many thousand stones and other materials, will anyone in his right mind tell me that I have drawn a bad conclusion because I have perhaps used a false definition? Or will anyone require me to prove my definition? To do so would be to tell me that I have not conceived what I have conceived, or to require me to prove that I have conceived what I have conceived. Surely this is trifling.

So a definition either explains a thing as it is [NS: in itself] outside the intellect—and then it ought to be true and to differ from a proposition or axiom only in that a definition is concerned solely with the essences of things or of their affections, whereas an axiom or a proposition extends more widely, to eternal truths as well—or else it explains a thing as we conceive it or can conceive it—and then it also differs from an axiom and a proposition in that it need only be conceived, without any further condition, and need not, like an axiom [NS: and a proposition]

IV/44 be conceived as true. So a bad definition is one that is not conceived.

To help you understand this, I shall take Borelli's example. Suppose someone says, "Let two straight lines enclosing a space be called 'figurals.'" If he understands by a straight line what everyone understands by a curved line, then his definition will be a good one, provided he does not subsequently understand [by it] squares and other figures. . . . But if by a straight line he understands what we commonly understand, the thing is completely inconceivable. So it is no definition. Borelli, whose opinion you are inclined to embrace, confuses all these things completely.

I shall add another example, the one you bring up at the end. If I say that each substance has only one attribute, that is only a proposition and requires a demonstration. But if I say, "By substance I understand what consists of one attribute only," that will be a good definition, provided that afterwards beings consisting of more attributes than one are designated by a word other than substance.

But you say that I have not demonstrated that a substance (*or* being) can have more attributes than one. Perhaps you have neglected to pay

IV/45 attention to my demonstrations. For I have used two: *first*, that nothing is more evident to us than that we conceive each being under some attribute, and that the more reality or being a being has the more attri-

80

butes must be attributed to it; so a being absolutely infinite must be defined, and so on; *second*, and the one I judge best, is that the more attributes I attribute to a being the more I am compelled to attribute existence to it; that is, the more I conceive it as true. It would be quite the contrary if I had feigned a Chimaera, or something like that.

As for your contention that you do not conceive thought except in relation to ideas (because if you remove the ideas, you destroy thought), I believe this happens to you because when you, as a thinking thing, do this, you put aside all your thoughts and concepts. So it is no wonder that when you have done so, nothing afterwards remains for you to think of. But as far as the thing itself is concerned, I think I have demonstrated clearly and evidently enough that the intellect, though infinite, pertains to *Natura naturata*, not to *Natura naturans*.

However, I still do not see what this has to do with understanding D3, nor why it should be a problem. Unless I am mistaken, the definition I gave you was as follows:

> By substance I understand what is in itself and is conceived through   IV/46
> itself, that is, whose concept does not involve the concept of another thing. I understand the same by attribute, except that it is called attribute in relation to the intellect, which attributes such and such a definite nature to substance.

I say that this definition explains clearly enough what I wish to understand by substance, *or* attribute.

Nevertheless, you want me to explain by an example how one and the same thing can be designated by two names (though this is not necessary at all). Not to seem niggardly, I offer two: (i) I say that by Israel I understand the third patriarch; I understand the same by Jacob, the name which was given him because he had seized his brother's heel; (ii) by flat I mean what reflects all rays of light without any change; I understand the same by white, except that it is called white in relation to a man looking at the flat [surface].
[Rijnsburg, March 1663]

C. Spinoza to De Vries Again[50]

Cherished Friend,   IV/47
    You ask me whether we need experience to know whether the definition of any attribute [NS: any thing] is true. To this I reply that we need experience only for those things which cannot be inferred from the def-

---

[50] Letter 10.

inition of the thing, as, for example, the existence of modes (for this cannot be inferred from the definition of the thing); but not for those things whose existence is not distinguished from their essence, and therefore is inferred from their definition. Indeed no experience will ever be able to teach us this, for experience does not teach any essences of things. The most it can do is to determine our mind to think only of certain essences of things. So since the existence of the attributes does not differ from their essence, we will not be able to grasp it by any experience.

You ask, next, whether also things or their affections are eternal truths. I say certainly. If you should ask why I do not call them eternal truths, I answer, to distinguish them (as everyone generally does) from those which do not explain any thing or affection of a thing, as, for example, *nothing comes from nothing*. These and similar propositions, I say, are called absolutely eternal truths, by which they want to signify nothing but that such [propositions] have no place outside the mind, and so on.

[Rijnsburg, March (?) 1663]

VIII. The Worm in the Blood[51]

Spinoza to Henry Oldenburg

IV/170

. . . When you ask me what I think about the question which concerns *how we know how each part of Nature agrees with the whole to which it belongs and how it coheres with the others*, I think you are asking for the reasons by which we are persuaded that each part of Nature agrees with the whole to which it belongs and coheres with the others. For I said in my preceding letter that I do not know absolutely how they really cohere and how each part agrees with its whole. To know this would require knowing the whole of Nature and all its parts. So I shall try to show as briefly as I can the reason which forces me to affirm this. But first I should like to warn that I attribute to Nature neither beauty nor ugliness, neither order nor confusion. For things can only be called beautiful or ugly, orderly or confused, in relation to our imagination.

By the coherence of parts, then, I understand nothing but that the laws *or* nature of the one part so adapt themselves to the laws *or* nature of the other part that they are opposed to each other as little as possible. Concerning whole and parts, I consider things as parts of some whole insofar as the nature of the one so adapts itself to the nature of the other

---

[51] Letter 32.

that so far as possible they are all in harmony with one another. But insofar as they are out of harmony with one another, to that extent each forms an idea distinct from the others in our mind, and therefore it is considered as a whole and not as a part. IV/171

For example, when the motions of the particles of lymph, chyle, and the like, so adapt themselves to one another, in relation to their size and shape, that they are completely in harmony with one another, and they all constitute one fluid together, to that extent only the chyle, lymph, and the like, are considered as parts of the blood. But insofar as we conceive the particles of lymph, by reason of their shape and motion, to differ from the particles of chyle, to that extent we consider them as a whole and not as a part.

Let us conceive now, if you please, that there is a little worm living in the blood which is capable of distinguishing by sight the particles of the blood, of lymph, of chyle, and the like, and capable of observing by reason how each particle, when it encounters another, either bounces back, or communicates a part of its motion, and so on. Indeed, it would live in this blood as we do in this part of the universe, and would consider each particle of the blood as a whole, not as a part. Nor could it know how all the parts of the blood are restrained by the universal nature of the blood, and compelled to adapt themselves to one another, as the universal nature of the blood requires, so that they harmonize with one another in a certain way.

For if we should suppose that there are no causes outside the blood IV/172 which would communicate new motions to the blood, and no space outside the blood, nor any other bodies to which the particles of blood could transfer their motion, it is certain that the blood would always remain in the same state, and its particles would undergo no other variations than those which can be conceived from the given relation of the motion of the blood to those of the lymph, chyle, and the like. Thus the blood would always have to be considered as a whole and not as a part. But because there are a great many other causes which restrain the laws of the nature of the blood in a certain way, and which in turn are restrained by the blood, it happens that other motions and other variations arise in the particles of the blood which follow not simply from the relation of the motion of its parts to one another, but from the relation of the motion of the blood as a whole and of the external causes to one another. In this way the blood has the nature of a part and not of a whole. This is what I say concerning whole and part.

Now all bodies in Nature can and must be conceived as we have here conceived the blood, for all bodies are surrounded by others, and are determined by one another to existing and producing an effect in a cer-

IV/173 tain and determinate way, the same ratio of motion to rest always being preserved in all of them at once, that is, in the whole universe. From this it follows that every body, insofar as it exists modified in a certain way, must be considered as a part of the whole universe, must agree with the whole to which it belongs, and must cohere with the remaining bodies. And since the nature of the universe is not limited, as the nature of the blood is, but is absolutely infinite, its parts are restrained in infinite ways by this nature of the infinite power, and compelled to undergo infinitely many variations.

But in relation to substance I conceive each part to have a closer union with its whole. For as I previously strove to demonstrate in my first letter, which I wrote to you while I was still living in Rijnsburg, since it is of the nature of substance to be infinite, it follows that each part pertains to the nature of corporeal substance, and can neither be nor be conceived without it.

You see, therefore, how and why I think that the human body is a part of Nature. But as far as the human mind is concerned, I think it is a part of Nature too. For I maintain that there is also in Nature an infinite

IV/174 power of thinking, which, insofar as it is infinite, contains in itself objectively the whole of Nature, and whose thoughts proceed in the same way as Nature itself, its object, does.

Next, I maintain that the human mind is this same power, not insofar as it is infinite and perceives the whole of Nature, but insofar as it is finite and perceives only the human body. For this reason I maintain that the human mind is a part of a certain infinite intellect.

But it would take too long here to explain accurately and demonstrate all these things, along with the things which are connected with them. And I do not think you expect this of me at present. Indeed, I wonder whether I have sufficiently grasped your intention, and have not answered a different question than the one you were asking. Please let me know.

Yours with all affection,
B. de Spinoza

Voorburg, 20 November 1665

The Ethics

DEMONSTRATED IN GEOMETRIC ORDER
AND DIVIDED INTO FIVE PARTS,
WHICH TREAT

I. Of God
II. Of the Nature and Origin of the Mind
III. Of the Origin and Nature of the Affects
IV. Of Human Bondage, *or* the Powers of the Affects
V. Of the Power of the Intellect, *or* on Human Freedom

FIRST PART OF THE ETHICS
OF GOD

DEFINITIONS

D1: By cause of itself I understand that whose essence involves existence, *or* that whose nature cannot be conceived except as existing.

D2: That thing is said to be finite in its own kind that can be limited by another of the same nature.

For example, a body is called finite because we always conceive another that is greater. Thus a thought is limited by another thought. But a body is not limited by a thought nor a thought by a body.

D3: By substance I understand what is in itself and is conceived through itself, that is, that whose concept does not require the concept of another thing, from which it must be formed.

D4: By attribute I understand what the intellect perceives of a substance, as constituting its essence.

D5: By mode I understand the affections of a substance, *or* that which is in another through which it is also conceived.

D6: By God I understand a being absolutely infinite, that is, a substance consisting of an infinity of attributes, of which each one expresses an eternal and infinite essence.

85

II/46   Exp.: I say absolutely infinite, not infinite in its own kind; for if something is only infinite in its own kind, we can deny infinite attributes of
it [NS: (i.e., we can conceive infinite attributes which do not pertain to
its nature)]; but if something is absolutely infinite, whatever expresses
essence and involves no negation pertains to its essence.

D7: That thing is called free which exists from the necessity of its nature
alone, and is determined to act by itself alone. But a thing is called
necessary, or rather compelled, which is determined by another to exist
and to produce an effect in a certain and determinate manner.

D8: By eternity I understand existence itself, insofar as it is conceived to
follow necessarily from the definition alone of the eternal thing.

   Exp.: For such existence, like the essence of a thing, is conceived as
an eternal truth, and on that account cannot be explained by duration
or time, even if the duration is conceived to be without beginning or
end.

AXIOMS

A1: Whatever is, is either in itself or in another.

A2: What cannot be conceived through another, must be conceived
through itself.

A3: From a given determinate cause the effect follows necessarily; and
conversely, if there is no determinate cause, it is impossible for an effect
to follow.

A4: The knowledge of an effect depends on, and involves, the knowledge of its cause.

A5: Things that have nothing in common with one another also cannot
be understood through one another, *or* the concept of the one does not
involve the concept of the other.

II/47   A6: A true idea must agree with its object.

A7: If a thing can be conceived as not existing, its essence does not
involve existence.

P1: *A substance is prior in nature to its affections.*
   Dem.: This is evident from D3 and D5.

P2: *Two substances having different attributes have nothing in common with*
one another.
   Dem.: This is also evident from D3. For each must be in itself and be

conceived through itself, *or* the concept of the one does not involve the concept of the other.

P3: *If things have nothing in common with one another, one of them cannot be the cause of the other.*

Dem.: If they have nothing in common with one another, then (by A5) they cannot be understood through one another, and so (by A4) one cannot be the cause of the other, q.e.d.

P4: *Two or more distinct things are distinguished from one another, either by a difference in the attributes of the substances or by a difference in their affections.*

Dem.: Whatever is, is either in itself or in another (by A1), that is (by D3 and D5), outside the intellect there is nothing except substances and their affections. Therefore, there is nothing outside the intellect through which a number of things can be distinguished from one another except substances, *or* what is the same (by D4), their attributes, and their affections, q.e.d.

II/48

P5: *In Nature there cannot be two or more substances of the same nature or attribute.*

Dem.: If there were two or more distinct substances, they would have to be distinguished from one another either by a difference in their attributes, or by a difference in their affections (by P4). If only by a difference in their attributes, then it will be conceded that there is only one of the same attribute. But if by a difference in their affections, then since a substance is prior in nature to its affections (by P1), if the affections are put to one side and [the substance] is considered in itself, that is (by D3 and A6), considered truly, one cannot be conceived to be distinguished from another, that is (by P4), there cannot be many, but only one [of the same nature *or* attribute], q.e.d.

P6: *One substance cannot be produced by another substance.*

Dem.: In Nature there cannot be two substances of the same attribute (by P5), that is (by P2), which have something in common with each other. Therefore (by P3) one cannot be the cause of the other, *or* cannot be produced by the other, q.e.d.

Cor.: From this it follows that a substance cannot be produced by anything else. For in Nature there is nothing except substances and their affections, as is evident from A1, D3, and D5. But it cannot be produced by a substance (by P6). Therefore, substance absolutely cannot be produced by anything else, q.e.d.

Alternatively: This is demonstrated even more easily from the absurdity of its contradictory. For if a substance could be produced by something else, the knowledge of it would have to depend on the knowledge of its cause (by A4). And so (by D3) it would not be a substance.

II/49 P7: *It pertains to the nature of a substance to exist.*

Dem.: A substance cannot be produced by anything else (by P6C); therefore it will be the cause of itself, that is (by D1), its essence necessarily involves existence, *or* it pertains to its nature to exist, q.e.d.

P8: *Every substance is necessarily infinite.*

Dem.: A substance of one attribute does not exist unless it is unique (P5), and it pertains to its nature to exist (P7). Of its nature, therefore, it will exist either as finite or as infinite. But not as finite. For then (by D2) it would have to be limited by something else of the same nature, which would also have to exist necessarily (by P7), and so there would be two substances of the same attribute, which is absurd (by P5). Therefore, it exists as infinite, q.e.d.

Schol. 1: Since being finite is really, in part, a negation, and being infinite is an absolute affirmation of the existence of some nature, it follows from P7 alone that every substance must be infinite. [NS: For if we assumed a finite substance, we would, in part, deny existence to its nature, which (by P7) is absurd.]

Schol. 2: I do not doubt that the demonstration of P7 will be difficult to conceive for all who judge things confusedly, and have not been accustomed to know things through their first causes—because they do not distinguish between the modifications of substances and the substances themselves, nor do they know how things are produced. So it happens that they fictitiously ascribe to substances the beginning which they see that natural things have; for those who do not know the true causes of things confuse everything and without any conflict of mind feign that both trees and men speak, imagine that men are formed both from stones and from seed, and that any form whatever is changed into any other. So also, those who confuse the divine nature with the human easily ascribe human affects to God, particularly so long as they are also ignorant of how those affects are produced in the mind.

II/50 But if men would attend to the nature of substance, they would have no doubt at all of the truth of P7. Indeed, this proposition would be an axiom for everyone, and would be numbered among the common notions. For by substance they would understand what is in itself and is conceived through itself, that is, that the knowledge of which does not require the knowledge of any other thing. But by modifications they would understand what is in another, those things whose concept is formed from the concept of the thing in which they are.

This is how we can have true ideas of modifications which do not exist; for though they do not actually exist outside the intellect, nevertheless their essences are comprehended in another in such a way that they can be conceived through it. But the truth of substances is not outside the intellect unless it is in them themselves, because they are conceived through themselves.

Hence, if someone were to say that he had a clear and distinct, that is, true, idea of a substance, and nevertheless doubted whether such a substance existed, that would indeed be the same as if he were to say that he had a true idea, and nevertheless doubted whether it was false (as is evident to anyone who is sufficiently attentive). Or if someone maintains that a substance is created, he maintains at the same time that a false idea has become true. Of course nothing more absurd can be conceived. So it must be confessed that the existence of a substance, like its essence, is an eternal truth.

And from this we can infer in another way that there is only one [substance] of the same nature, which I have considered it worth the trouble of showing here. But to do this in order, it must be noted,

I. that the true definition of each thing neither involves nor expresses anything except the nature of the thing defined.

From which it follows,

II. that no definition involves or expresses any certain number of individuals,

since it expresses nothing other than the nature of the thing defined. For example, the definition of the triangle expresses nothing but the simple nature of the triangle, but not any certain number of triangles. It is to be noted,

III. that there must be, for each existing thing, a certain cause on account of which it exists.

Finally, it is to be noted,

IV. that this cause, on account of which a thing exists, either must be contained in the very nature and definition of the existing thing (*viz. that it pertains to its nature to exist*) or must be outside it.

From these propositions it follows that if, in Nature, a certain number of individuals exists, there must be a cause why those individuals, and why neither more nor fewer, exist.

For example, if twenty men exist in Nature (*to make the matter clearer,* II/51 *I assume that they exist at the same time, and that no others previously existed*

89

in Nature), it will not be enough (i.e., *to give a reason why twenty men exist*) to show the cause of human nature in general; but it will be necessary in addition to show the cause why not more and not fewer than twenty exist. For (by III) there must necessarily be a cause why each [NS: particular man] exists. But this cause (by II and III) cannot be contained in human nature itself, since the true definition of man does not involve the number 20. So (by IV) the cause why these twenty men exist, and consequently, why each of them exists, must necessarily be outside each of them.

For that reason it is to be inferred absolutely that whatever is of such a nature that there can be many individuals [of that nature] must, to exist, have an external cause to exist. Now since it pertains to the nature of a substance to exist (by what we have already shown in this scholium), its definition must involve necessary existence, and consequently its existence must be inferred from its definition alone. But from its definition (as we have shown from II and III) the existence of a number of substances cannot follow. Therefore it follows necessarily from this, that there exists only one of the same nature, as was proposed.

P9: *The more reality or being each thing has, the more attributes belong to it.*
Dem.: This is evident from D4.

P10: *Each attribute of a substance must be conceived through itself.*
Dem.: For an attribute is what the intellect perceives concerning a substance, as constituting its essence (by D4); so (by D3) it must be conceived through itself, q.e.d.

II/52   Schol.: From these propositions it is evident that although two attributes may be conceived to be really distinct (i.e., one may be conceived without the aid of the other), we still cannot infer from that that they constitute two beings, *or* two different substances. For it is of the nature of a substance that each of its attributes is conceived through itself, since all the attributes it has have always been in it together, and one could not be produced by another, but each expresses the reality, *or* being of substance.

So it is far from absurd to attribute many attributes to one substance. Indeed, nothing in Nature is clearer than that each being must be conceived under some attribute, and the more reality, or being it has, the more it has attributes which express necessity, *or* eternity, and infinity. And consequently there is also nothing clearer than that a being absolutely infinite must be defined (as we taught in D6) as a being that consists of infinite attributes, each of which expresses a certain eternal and infinite essence.

90

But if someone now asks by what sign we shall be able to distinguish the diversity of substances, let him read the following propositions, which show that in Nature there exists only one substance, and that it is absolutely infinite. So that sign would be sought in vain.

P11: *God*, or *a substance consisting of infinite attributes, each of which expresses eternal and infinite essence, necessarily exists.*

Dem.: If you deny this, conceive, if you can, that God does not exist. Therefore (by A7) his essence does not involve existence. But this (by P7) is absurd. Therefore God necessarily exists, q.e.d.

Alternatively: For each thing there must be assigned a cause, *or* reason, both for its existence and for its nonexistence. For example, if a triangle exists, there must be a reason *or* cause why it exists; but if it does not exist, there must also be a reason *or* cause which prevents it from existing, *or* which takes its existence away.

II/53

But this reason, *or* cause, must either be contained in the nature of the thing, or be outside it. For example, the very nature of a square circle indicates the reason why it does not exist, namely, because it involves a contradiction. On the other hand, the reason why a substance exists also follows from its nature alone, because it involves existence (see P7). But the reason why a circle or triangle exists, or why it does not exist, does not follow from the nature of these things, but from the order of the whole of corporeal Nature. For from this [order] it must follow either that the triangle necessarily exists now or that it is impossible for it to exist now. These things are evident through themselves; from them it follows that a thing necessarily exists if there is no reason or cause which prevents it from existing. Therefore, if there can be no reason or cause which prevents God from existing, or which takes his existence away, it must certainly be inferred that he necessarily exists.

But if there were such a reason, *or* cause, it would have to be either in God's very nature or outside it, that is, in another substance of another nature. For if it were of the same nature, that very supposition would concede that God exists. But a substance which was of another nature [NS: than the divine] would have nothing in common with God (by P2), and therefore could neither give him existence nor take it away. Since, then, there can be, outside the divine nature, no reason, *or*, cause which takes away the divine existence, the reason will necessarily have to be in his nature itself, if indeed he does not exist. That is, his nature would involve a contradiction [NS: as in our second example]. But it is absurd to affirm this of a Being absolutely infinite and supremely perfect. Therefore, there is no cause, *or* reason, either in God or outside God, which takes his existence away. And therefore, God necessarily exists, q.e.d.

Alternatively: To be able not to exist is to lack power, and conversely, to be able to exist is to have power (as is known through itself). So, if what now necessarily exists are only finite beings, then finite beings are more powerful than an absolutely infinite Being. But this, as is known through itself, is absurd. So, either nothing exists or an absolutely infinite Being also exists. But we exist, either in ourselves, or in something else, which necessarily exists (see A1 and P7). Therefore an absolutely infinite Being—that is (by D6), God—necessarily exists, q.e.d.

II/54   Schol.: In this last demonstration I wanted to show God's existence a posteriori, so that the demonstration would be perceived more easily—but not because God's existence does not follow a priori from the same foundation. For since being able to exist is power, it follows that the more reality belongs to the nature of a thing, the more powers it has, of itself, to exist. Therefore, an absolutely infinite Being, *or* God, has, of himself, an absolutely infinite power of existing. For that reason, he exists absolutely.

Still, there may be many who will not easily be able to see how evident this demonstration is, because they have been accustomed to contemplate only those things that flow from external causes. And of these, they see that those which quickly come to be, that is, which easily exist, also easily perish. And conversely, they judge that those things to which they conceive more things to pertain are more difficult to do, that is, that they do not exist so easily. But to free them from these prejudices, I have no need to show here in what manner this proposition—*what quickly comes to be, quickly perishes*—is true, nor whether or not all things are equally easy in respect to the whole of Nature. It is sufficient to note only this, that I am not here speaking of things that come to be from external causes, but only of substances that (by P6) can be produced by no external cause.

For things that come to be from external causes—whether they consist of many parts or of few—owe all the perfection or reality they have to the power of the external cause; and therefore their existence arises only from the perfection of their external cause, and not from their own perfection. On the other hand, whatever perfection substance has is not owed to any external cause. So its existence must follow from its nature alone; hence its existence is nothing but its essence.

Perfection, therefore, does not take away the existence of a thing, but on the contrary asserts it. But imperfection takes it away. So there is nothing of whose existence we can be more certain than we are of the existence of an absolutely infinite, *or* perfect, Being—that is, God. For since his essence excludes all imperfection, and involves absolute perfection, by that very fact it takes away every cause of doubting his existence, and gives the greatest certainty concerning it. I believe this will be clear even to those who are only moderately attentive.

P12: *No attribute of a substance can be truly conceived from which it follows* II/55 *that the substance can be divided.*

Dem.: For the parts into which a substance so conceived would be divided either will retain the nature of the substance or will not. If the first [NS: viz. they retain the nature of the substance], then (by P8) each part will have to be infinite, and (by P7) its own cause, and (by P5) each part will have to consist of a different attribute. And so many substances will be able to be formed from one, which is absurd (by P6). Furthermore, the parts (by P2) would have nothing in common with their whole, and the whole (by D4 and P10) could both be and be conceived without its parts, which is absurd, as no one will be able to doubt.

But if the second is asserted, namely, that the parts will not retain the nature of substance, then since the whole substance would be divided into equal parts, it would lose the nature of substance, and would cease to be, which (by P7) is absurd.

P13: *A substance which is absolutely infinite is indivisible.*

Dem.: For if it were divisible, the parts into which it would be divided will either retain the nature of an absolutely infinite substance or they will not. If the first, then there will be a number of substances of the same nature, which (by P5) is absurd. But if the second is asserted, then (as above [NS: P12]), an absolutely infinite substance will be able to cease to be, which (by P11) is also absurd.

Cor.: From these [propositions] it follows that no substance, and consequently no corporeal substance, insofar as it is a substance, is divisible.

Schol.: That substance is indivisible, is understood more simply merely from this, that the nature of substance cannot be conceived unless as infinite, and that by a part of substance nothing can be understood except a finite substance, which (by P8) implies a plain contra- II/56 diction.

P14: *Except God, no substance can be or be conceived.*

Dem.: Since God is an absolutely infinite being, of whom no attribute which expresses an essence of substance can be denied (by D6), and he necessarily exists (by P11), if there were any substance except God, it would have to be explained through some attribute of God, and so two substances of the same attribute would exist, which (by P5) is absurd. And so except God, no substance can be or, consequently, be conceived.

For if it could be conceived, it would have to be conceived as existing. But this (by the first part of this demonstration) is absurd. Therefore, except for God no substance can be or be conceived, q.e.d.

Cor. 1: From this it follows most clearly, first, that God is unique, that is (by D6), that in Nature there is only one substance, and that it is absolutely infinite (as we indicated in P10S).

Cor. 2: It follows, second, that an extended thing and a thinking thing are either attributes of God, or (by A1) affections of God's attributes.

P15: *Whatever is, is in God, and nothing can be or be conceived without God.*

Dem.: Except for God, there neither is, nor can be conceived, any substance (by P14), that is (by D3), thing that is in itself and is conceived through itself. But modes (by D5) can neither be nor be conceived without substance. So they can be in the divine nature alone, and can be conceived through it alone. But except for substances and modes there is nothing (by A1). Therefore, [NS: everything is in God and] nothing can be or be conceived without God, q.e.d.

Schol.: [I.] There are those who feign a God, like man, consisting of a body and a mind, and subject to passions. But how far they wander from the true knowledge of God, is sufficiently established by what has already been demonstrated. Them I dismiss. For everyone who has to any extent contemplated the divine nature denies that God is corporeal. They prove this best from the fact that by body we understand any quantity, with length, breadth, and depth, limited by some certain figure. Nothing more absurd than this can be said of God, namely, of a being absolutely infinite. But meanwhile, by the other arguments by which they strive to demonstrate this same conclusion they clearly show that they entirely remove corporeal, *or* extended, substance itself from the divine nature. And they maintain that it has been created by God. But by what divine power could it be created? They are completely ignorant of that. And this shows clearly that they do not understand what they themselves say. At any rate, I have demonstrated clearly enough—in my judgment, at least—that no substance can be produced or created by another thing (see P6C and P8S2). Next, we have shown (P14) that except for God, no substance can either be or be conceived, and hence [in P14C2] we have concluded that extended substance is one of God's infinite attributes. But to provide a fuller explanation, I shall refute my opponents' arguments, which all reduce to these.

[II.] *First*, they think that corporeal substance, insofar as it is substance, consists of parts. And therefore they deny that it can be infinite, and consequently, that it can pertain to God. They explain this by many examples, of which I shall mention one or two.

II/57

[i] If corporeal substance is infinite, they say, let us conceive it to be divided in two parts. Each part will be either finite or infinite. If the former, then an infinite is composed of two finite parts, which is absurd. If the latter [NS: i.e., if each part is infinite], then there is one infinite twice as large as another, which is also absurd. [ii] Again, if an infinite quantity is measured by parts [each] equal to a foot, it will consist of infinitely many such parts, as it will also, if it is measured by parts [each] equal to an inch. And therefore, one infinite number will be twelve times greater than another [NS: which is no less absurd]. [iii] Finally, if

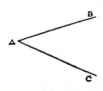

we conceive that from one point of a certain infinite quantity two lines, say AB and AC, are extended to infinity, it is certain that, although in the beginning they are a certain, determinate distance apart, the distance between B and C is continuously increased, and at last, from being determinate, it will become indeterminable. Since these absurdities follow—so they think—from the fact that an infinite quantity is supposed, they infer that corporeal substance must be finite, and consequently cannot pertain to God's essence.

II/58

[III.] Their *second* argument is also drawn from God's supreme perfection. For God, they say, since he is a supremely perfect being, cannot be acted on. But corporeal substance, since it is divisible, can be acted on. It follows, therefore, that it does not pertain to God's essence.

[IV.] These are the arguments which I find Authors using, to try to show that corporeal substance is unworthy of the divine nature, and cannot pertain to it. But anyone who is properly attentive will find that I have already replied to them, since these arguments are founded only on their supposition that corporeal substance is composed of parts, which I have already (P12 and P13C) shown to be absurd. And then anyone who wishes to consider the matter rightly will see that all those absurdities (*if indeed they are all absurd, which I am not now disputing*), from which they wish to infer that extended substance is finite, do not follow at all from the fact that an infinite quantity is supposed, but from the fact that they suppose an infinite quantity to be measurable and composed of finite parts. So from the absurdities which follow from that they can infer only that infinite quantity is not measurable, and that it is not composed of finite parts. This is the same thing we have already demonstrated above (P12, etc.). So the weapon they aim at us, they really turn against themselves. If, therefore, they still wish to infer from this absurdity of theirs that extended substance must be finite, they are indeed doing nothing more than if someone feigned that a circle has the properties of a square, and inferred from that the circle has no center, from which all lines drawn to the circumference are equal. For corporeal substance, which cannot be conceived except as infinite, unique, and indivisible (see P8, 5, and 12), they conceive to be composed of finite parts, to be many, and to be divisible, in order to infer that it is finite.

II/59

So also others, after they feign that a line is composed of points, know how to invent many arguments, by which they show that a line cannot be divided to infinity. And indeed it is no less absurd to assert that corporeal substance is composed of bodies, *or* parts, than that a body is composed of surfaces, the surfaces of lines, and the lines, finally, of points. All those who know that clear reason is infallible must confess this—particularly those who deny that there is a vacuum. For if corporeal substance could be so divided that its parts were really distinct, why, then, could one part not be annihilated, the rest remaining connected with one another as before? And why must they all be so fitted together that there is no vacuum? Truly, of things which are really distinct from one another, one can be, and remain in its condition, without the other. Since, therefore, there is no vacuum in Nature (a subject I discuss elsewhere), but all its parts must so concur that there is no vacuum, it follows also that they cannot be really distinguished, that is, that corporeal substance, insofar as it is a substance, cannot be divided.

[V.] If someone should now ask why we are, by nature, so inclined to divide quantity, I shall answer that we conceive quantity in two ways: abstractly, *or* superficially, as we [NS: commonly] imagine it, or as substance, which is done by the intellect alone [NS: without the help of the imagination]. So if we attend to quantity as it is in the imagination, which we do often and more easily, it will be found to be finite, divisible, and composed of parts; but if we attend to it as it is in the intellect, and conceive it insofar as it is a substance, which happens [NS: seldom and] with great difficulty, then (as we have already sufficiently demonstrated) it will be found to be infinite, unique, and indivisible.

This will be sufficiently plain to everyone who knows how to distinguish between the intellect and the imagination—particularly if it is also noted that matter is everywhere the same, and that parts are distinguished in it only insofar as we conceive matter to be affected in different ways, so that its parts are distinguished only modally, but not really.

II/60

For example, we conceive that water is divided and its parts separated from one another—insofar as it is water, but not insofar as it is corporeal substance. For insofar as it is substance, it is neither separated nor divided. Again, water, insofar as it is water, is generated and corrupted, but insofar as it is substance, it is neither generated nor corrupted.

[VI.] And with this I think I have replied to the second argument also,

96

since it is based on the supposition that matter, insofar as it is substance, is divisible, and composed of parts. Even if this [reply] were not [sufficient], I do not know why [matter] would be unworthy of the divine nature. For (by P14) apart from God there can be no substance by which [the divine nature] would be acted on. All things, I say, are in God, and all things that happen, happen only through the laws of God's infinite nature and follow (as I shall show) from the necessity of his essence. So it cannot be said in any way that God is acted on by another, or that extended substance is unworthy of the divine nature, even if it is supposed to be divisible, so long as it is granted to be eternal and infinite. But enough of this for the present.

P16: *From the necessity of the divine nature there must follow infinitely many things in infinitely many modes, (i.e., everything which can fall under an infinite intellect).*

Dem.: This proposition must be plain to anyone, provided he attends to the fact that the intellect infers from the given definition of any thing a number of properties that really do follow necessarily from it (that is, from the very essence of the thing); and that it infers more properties the more the definition of the thing expresses reality, that is, the more reality the essence of the defined thing involves. But since the divine nature has absolutely infinite attributes (by D6), each of which also expresses an essence infinite in its own kind, from its necessity there must follow infinitely many things in infinite modes (i.e., everything which can fall under an infinite intellect), q.e.d.

Cor. 1: From this it follows that God is the efficient cause of all things which can fall under an infinite intellect.

Cor. 2: It follows, second, that God is a cause through himself and not an accidental cause. II/61

Cor. 3: It follows, third, that God is absolutely the first cause.

P17: *God acts from the laws of his nature alone, and is compelled by no one.*

Dem.: We have just shown (P16) that from the necessity of the divine nature alone, or (what is the same thing) from the laws of his nature alone, absolutely infite things follow, and in P15 we have demonstrated that nothing can be or be conceived without God, but that all things are in God. So there can be nothing outside him by which he is determined or compelled to act. Therefore, God acts from the laws of his nature alone, and is compelled by no one, q.e.d.

Cor. 1: From this it follows, first, that there is no cause, either extrinsically or intrinsically, which prompts God to action, except the perfection of his nature.

Cor. 2: It follows, second, that God alone is a free cause. For God alone exists only from the necessity of his nature (by P11 and P14C1), and acts from the necessity of his nature (by P17). Therefore (by D7) God alone is a free cause, q.e.d.

Schol.: [I.] Others think that God is a free cause because he can (so they think) bring it about that the things which we have said follow from his nature (i.e., which are in his power) do not happen or are not produced by him. But this is the same as if they were to say that God can bring it about that it would not follow from the nature of a triangle that its three angles are equal to two right angles; *or* that from a given cause II/62 the effect would not follow—which is absurd.

Further, I shall show later, without the aid of this proposition, that neither intellect nor will pertain to God's nature. Of course I know there are many who think they can demonstrate that a supreme intellect and a free will pertain to God's nature. For they say they know nothing they can ascribe to God more perfect than what is the highest perfection in us.

Moreover, though they conceive God to actually understand in the highest degree, they still do not believe that he can bring it about that all the things he actually understands exist. For they think that in that way they would destroy God's power. If he had created all the things in his intellect (they say), then he would have been able to create nothing more, which they believe to be incompatible with God's omnipotence. So they prefer to maintain that God is indifferent to all things, not creating anything except what he has decreed to create by some absolute will.

But I think I have shown clearly enough (see P16) that from God's supreme power, *or* infinite nature, infinitely many things in infinitely many modes, that is, all things, have necessarily flowed, or always follow, by the same necessity and in the same way as from the nature of a triangle it follows, from eternity and to eternity, that its three angles are equal to two right angles. So God's omnipotence has been actual from eternity and will remain in the same actuality to eternity. And in this way, at least in my opinion, God's omnipotence is maintained far more perfectly.

Indeed—to speak openly—my opponents seem to deny God's omnipotence. For they are forced to confess that God understands infinitely many creatable things, which nevertheless he will never be able to create. For otherwise, if he created everything he understood [NS: to be creatable] he would (according to them) exhaust his omnipotence and render himself imperfect. Therefore to maintain that God is perfect, they are driven to maintain at the same time that he cannot bring about everything to which his power extends. I do not see what could be feigned which would be more absurd than this or more contrary to God's omnipotence.

[II.] Further—to say something here also about the intellect and will which we commonly attribute to God—if will and intellect do pertain to the eternal essence of God, we must of course understand by each of these attributes something different from what men commonly understand. For the intellect and will which would constitute God's essence would have to differ entirely from our intellect and will, and could not agree with them in anything except the name. They would not agree with one another any more than do the dog that is a heavenly constellation and the dog that is a barking animal. I shall demonstrate this.

II/63

If intellect pertains to the divine nature, it will not be able to be (like our intellect) by nature either posterior to (as most would have it), or simultaneous with, the things understood, since God is prior in causality to all things (by P16C1). On the contrary, the truth and formal essence of things is what it is because it exists objectively in that way in God's intellect. So God's intellect, insofar as it is conceived to constitute God's essence, is really the cause both of the essence and of the existence of things. This seems also to have been noticed by those who asserted that God's intellect, will, and power are one and the same.

Therefore, since God's intellect is the only cause of things (viz. as we have shown, both of their essence and of their existence), he must necessarily differ from them both as to his essence and as to his existence. For what is caused differs from its cause precisely in what it has from the cause [NS: for that reason it is called the effect of such a cause]. For example, a man is the cause of the existence of another man, but not of his essence, for the latter is an eternal truth. Hence, they can agree entirely according to their essence. But in existing they must differ. And for that reason, if the existence of one perishes, the other's existence will not thereby perish. But if the essence of one could be destroyed, and become false, the other's essence would also be destroyed [NS: and become false].

So the thing that is the cause both of the essence and of the existence of some effect, must differ from such an effect, both as to its essence and as to its existence. But God's intellect is the cause both of the essence and of the existence of our intellect. Therefore, God's intellect, insofar as it is conceived to constitute the divine essence, differs from our intellect both as to its essence and as to its existence, and cannot agree with it in anything except in name, as we supposed. The proof proceeds in the same way concerning the will, as anyone can easily see.

P18: *God is the immanent, not the transitive, cause of all things.*

II/64   Dem.: Everything that is, is in God, and must be conceived through God (by P15), and so (by P16C1) God is the cause of [NS: all] things, which are in him. That is the first [thing to be proven]. And then outside God there can be no substance (by P14), that is (by D3), thing which is in itself outside God. That was the second. God, therefore, is the immanent, not the transitive cause of all things, q.e.d.

P19: *God is eternal, or all God's attributes are eternal.*

Dem.: For God (by D6) is substance, which (by P11) necessarily exists, that is (by P7), to whose nature it pertains to exist, or (what is the same) from whose definition it follows that he exists; and therefore (by D8), he is eternal.

Next, by God's attributes are to be understood what (by D4) expresses an essence of the divine substance, that is, what pertains to substance. The attributes themselves, I say, must involve it itself. But eternity pertains to the nature of substance (as I have already demonstrated from P7). Therefore each of the attributes must involve eternity, and so, they are all eternal, q.e.d.

Schol.: This proposition is also as clear as possible from the way I have demonstrated God's existence (P11). For from that demonstration, I say, it is established that God's existence, like his essence, is an eternal truth. And then I have also demonstrated God's eternity in another way (*Descartes' Principles* IP19), and there is no need to repeat it here.

P20: *God's existence and his essence are one and the same.*

Dem.: God (by P19) and all of his attributes are eternal, that is (by D8), each of his attributes expresses existence. Therefore, the same attributes of God which (by D4) explain God's eternal essence at the same time explain his eternal existence, that is, that itself which constitutes

II/65   God's essence at the same time constitutes his existence. So his existence and his essence are one and the same, q.e.d.

Cor. 1: From this it follows, first, that God's existence, like his essence, is an eternal truth.

Cor. 2: It follows, second, that God, *or* all of God's attributes, are immutable. For if they changed as to their existence, they would also (by P20) change as to their essence, that is (as is known through itself), from being true become false, which is absurd.

P21: *All the things which follow from the absolute nature of any of God's attributes have always had to exist and be infinite, or are, through the same attribute, eternal and infinite.*

Dem.: If you deny this, then conceive (if you can) that in some attribute of God there follows from its absolute nature something that is finite and has a determinate existence, *or* duration, for example, God's idea in thought. Now since thought is supposed to be an attribute of God, it is necessarily (by P11) infinite by its nature. But insofar as it has God's idea, [thought] is supposed to be finite. But (by D2) [thought] cannot be conceived to be finite unless it is determined through thought itself. But [thought can] not [be determined] through thought itself, insofar as it constitutes God's idea, for to that extent [thought] is supposed to be finite. Therefore, [thought must be determined] through thought insofar as it does not constitute God's idea, which [thought] nevertheless (by P11) must necessarily exist. Therefore, there is thought which does not constitute God's idea, and on that account God's idea does not follow necessarily from the nature [of this thought] insofar as it is absolute thought (for [thought] is conceived both as constituting God's idea and as not constituting it). [That God's idea does not follow from thought, insofar as it is absolute thought] is contrary to the hypothesis. So if God's idea in thought, or anything else in any attribute of God (for it does not matter what example is taken, since the demonstration is universal), follows from the necessity of the absolute nature of the attribute itself, it must necessarily be infinite. This was the first thing to be proven.

Next, what follows in this way from the necessity of the nature of any attribute cannot have a determinate [NS: existence, or] duration. For if you deny this, then suppose there is, in some attribute of God, a thing which follows from the necessity of the nature of that attribute—for example, God's idea in thought—and suppose that at some time [this idea] did not exist or will not exist. But since thought is supposed to be an attribute of God, it must exist necessarily and be immutable (by P11 and P20C2). So beyond the limits of the duration of God's idea (for it is supposed that at some time [this idea] did not exist or will not exist) thought will have to exist without God's idea. But this is contrary to the hypothesis, for it is supposed that God's idea follows necessarily from the given thought. Therefore, God's idea in thought, or anything else which follows necessarily from the absolute nature of some attribute of God, cannot have a determinate duration, but through the same attribute is eternal. This was the second thing [NS: to be proven]. Note that the same is to be affirmed of any thing which, in some attribute of God, follows necessarily from God's absolute nature.

II/66

P22: *Whatever follows from some attribute of God insofar as it is modified by a modification which, through the same attribute, exists necessarily and is infinite, must also exist necessarily and be infinite.*

Dem.: The demonstration of this proposition proceeds in the same way as the demonstration of the preceding one.

P23: *Every mode which exists necessarily and is infinite has necessarily had to follow either from the absolute nature of some attribute of God, or from some attribute, modified by a modification which exists necessarily and is infinite.*

II/67 Dem.: For a mode is in another, through which it must be conceived (by D5), that is (by P15), it is in God alone, and can be conceived through God alone. So if a mode is conceived to exist necessarily and be infinite, [its necessary existence and infinity] must necessarily be inferred, *or* perceived through some attribute of God, insofar as that attribute is conceived to express infinity and necessity of existence, *or* (what is the same, by D8) eternity, that is (by D6 and P19), insofar as it is considered absolutely. Therefore, the mode, which exists necessarily and is infinite, has had to follow from the absolute nature of some attribute of God—either immediately (see P21) or by some mediating modification, which follows from its absolute nature, that is (by P22), which exists necessarily and is infinite, q.e.d.

P24: *The essence of things produced by God does not involve existence.*

Dem.: This is evident from D1. For that whose nature involves existence (considered in itself), is its own cause, and exists only from the necessity of its nature.

Cor.: From this it follows that God is not only the cause of things' beginning to exist, but also of their persevering in existing, *or* (to use a Scholastic term) God is the cause of the being of things. For—whether the things [NS: produced] exist or not—so long as we attend to their essence, we shall find that it involves neither existence nor duration. So their essence can be the cause neither of their existence nor of their duration, but only God, to whose nature alone it pertains to exist [, can be the cause] (by P14C1).

P25: *God is the efficient cause, not only of the existence of things, but also of their essence.*

Dem.: If you deny this, then God is not the cause of the essence of things; and so (by A4) the essence of things can be conceived without II/68 God. But (by P15) this is absurd. Therefore God is also the cause of the essence of things, q.e.d.

Schol.: This proposition follows more clearly from P16. For from that it follows that from the given divine nature both the essence of things and their existence must necessarily be inferred; and in a word, God must be called the cause of all things in the same sense in which he is called the cause of himself. This will be established still more clearly from the following corollary.

Cor.: Particular things are nothing but affections of God's attributes, *or* modes by which God's attributes are expressed in a certain and determinate way. The demonstration is evident from P15 and D5.

P26: *A thing which has been determined to produce an effect has necessarily been determined in this way by God; and one which has not been determined by God cannot determine itself to produce an effect.*

Dem.: That through which things are said to be determined to produce an effect must be something positive (as is known through itself). And so, God, from the necessity of his nature, is the efficient cause both of its essence and of its existence (by P25 and 16); this was the first thing. And from it the second thing asserted also follows very clearly. For if a thing which has not been determined by God could determine itself, the first part of this [NS: proposition] would be false, which is absurd, as we have shown.

P27: *A thing which has been determined by God to produce an effect, cannot render itself undetermined.*

Dem.: This proposition is evident from A3.

P28: *Every singular thing,* or *any thing which is finite and has a determinate existence, can neither exist nor be determined to produce an effect unless it is determined to exist and produce an effect by another cause, which is also finite and has a determinate existence; and again, this cause also can neither exist nor be determined to produce an effect unless it is determined to exist and produce an effect by another, which is also finite and has a determinate existence, and so on, to infinity.*   II/69

Dem.: Whatever has been determined to exist and produce an effect has been so determined by God (by P26 and P24C). But what is finite and has a determinate existence could not have been produced by the absolute nature of an attribute of God; for whatever follows from the absolute nature of an attribute of God is eternal and infinite (by P21). It had, therefore, to follow either from God or from an attribute of God insofar as it is considered to be affected by some mode. For there is nothing except substance and its modes (by A1, D3, and D5) and modes (by P25C) are nothing but affections of God's attributes. But it also could not follow from God, or from an attribute of God, insofar as it is affected by a modification which is eternal and infinite (by P22). It had, therefore, to follow from, or be determined to exist and produce an effect by God or an attribute of God insofar as it is modified by a modification which is finite and has a determinate existence. This was the first thing to be proven.

And in turn, this cause, *or* this mode (by the same reasoning by which we have already demonstrated the first part of this proposition) had also to be determined by another, which is also finite and has a determinate existence; and again, this last (by the same reasoning) by another, and so always (by the same reasoning) to infinity, q.e.d.

II/70   Schol.: Since certain things had to be produced by God immediately, namely, those which follow necessarily from his absolute nature, and others (which nevertheless can neither be nor be conceived without God) had to be produced by the mediation of these first things, it follows:

I. That God is absolutely the proximate cause of the things produced immediately by him, and not [a proximate cause] in his own kind, as they say. For God's effects can neither be nor be conceived without their cause (by P15 and P24C).

II. That God cannot properly be called the remote cause of singular things, except perhaps so that we may distinguish them from those things that he has produced immediately, or rather, that follow from his absolute nature. For by a remote cause we understand one which is not conjoined in any way with its effect. But all things that are, are in God, and so depend on God that they can neither be nor be conceived without him.

P29: *In nature there is nothing contingent, but all things have been determined from the necessity of the divine nature to exist and produce an effect in a certain way.*

Dem.: Whatever is, is in God (by P15); but God cannot be called a contingent thing. For (by P11) he exists necessarily, not contingently. Next, the modes of the divine nature have also followed from it necessarily and not contingently (by P16)—either insofar as the divine nature is considered absolutely (by P21) or insofar as it is considered to be determined to act in a certain way (by P28). Further, God is the cause of these modes not only insofar as they simply exist (by P24C), but also (by P26) insofar as they are considered to be determined to produce an effect. For if they have not been determined by God, then (by P26) it is impossible, not contingent, that they should determine themselves. Conversely (by P27) if they have been determined by God, it is not

II/71   contingent, but impossible, that they should render themselves undetermined. So all things have been determined from the necessity of the divine nature, not only to exist, but to exist in a certain way, and to produce effects in a certain way. There is nothing contingent, q.e.d.

Schol.: Before I proceed further, I wish to explain here—or rather to advise [the reader]—what we must understand by *Natura naturans* and *Natura naturata*. For from the preceding I think it is already established that by *Natura naturans* we must understand what is in itself and is conceived through itself, *or* such attributes of substance as express an eternal and infinite essence, that is (by P14C1 and P17C2), God, insofar as he is considered as a free cause.

But by *Natura naturata* I understand whatever follows from the necessity of God's nature, *or* from any of God's attributes, that is, all the modes of God's attributes insofar as they are considered as things which are in God, and can neither be nor be conceived without God.

P30: *An actual intellect, whether finite or infinite, must comprehend God's attributes and God's affections, and nothing else.*

Dem.: A true idea must agree with its object (by A6), that is (as is known through itself), what is contained objectively in the intellect must necessarily be in Nature. But in Nature (by P14C1) there is only one substance, namely, God, and there are no affections other than those which are in God (by P15) and which can neither be nor be conceived without God (by P15). Therefore, an actual intellect, whether finite or infinite, must comprehend God's attributes and God's affections, and nothing else, q.e.d.

P31: *The actual intellect, whether finite or infinite, like will, desire, love, and the like, must be referred to* Natura naturata, *not to* Natura naturans.

Dem.: By intellect (as is known through itself) we understand not   II/72
absolute thought, but only a certain mode of thinking, which mode differs from the others, such as desire, love, and the like, and so (by D5) must be conceived through absolute thought, that is (by P15 and D6), it must be so conceived through an attribute of God, which expresses the eternal and infinite essence of thought, that it can neither be nor be conceived without [that attribute]; and so (by P29S), like the other modes of thinking, it must be referred to *Natura naturata*, not to *Natura naturans*, q.e.d.

Schol.: The reason why I speak here of actual intellect is not because I concede that there is any potential intellect, but because, wishing to avoid all confusion, I wanted to speak only of what we perceive as clearly as possible, that is, of the intellection itself. We perceive nothing more clearly than that. For we can understand nothing that does not lead to more perfect knowledge of the intellection.

P32: *The will cannot be called a free cause, but only a necessary one.*

Dem.: The will, like the intellect, is only a certain mode of thinking. And so (by P28) each volition can neither exist nor be determined to produce an effect unless it is determined by another cause, and this cause again by another, and so on, to infinity. Even if the will be supposed to be infinite, it must still be determined to exist and produce an effect by God, not insofar as he is an absolutely infinite substance, but insofar as he has an attribute that expresses the infinite and eternal essence of thought (by P23). So in whatever way it is conceived, whether as finite or as infinite, it requires a cause by which it is determined to exist and produce an effect. And so (by D7) it cannot be called a free cause, but only a necessary or compelled one, q.e.d.

II/73   Cor. 1: From this it follows, first, that God does not produce any effect by freedom of the will.

Cor. 2: It follows, second, that will and intellect are related to God's nature as motion and rest are, and as are absolutely all natural things, which (by P29) must be determined by God to exist and produce an effect in a certain way. For the will, like all other things, requires a cause by which it is determined to exist and produce an effect in a certain way. And although from a given will, *or* intellect infinitely many things may follow, God still cannot be said, on that account, to act from freedom of the will, any more than he can be said to act from freedom of motion and rest on account of those things that follow from motion and rest (for infinitely many things also follow from motion and rest). So will does not pertain to God's nature any more than do the other natural things, but is related to him in the same way as motion and rest, and all the other things which, as we have shown, follow from the necessity of the divine nature and are determined by it to exist and produce an effect in a certain way.

P33: *Things could have been produced by God in no other way, and in no other order than they have been produced.*

Dem.: For all things have necessarily followed from God's given nature (by P16), and have been determined from the necessity of God's nature to exist and produce an effect in a certain way (by P29). Therefore, if things could have been of another nature, or could have been determined to produce an effect in another way, so that the order of Nature was different, then God's nature could also have been other than it is now, and therefore (by P11) that [other nature] would also have had to exist, and consequently, there could have been two or more Gods, which is absurd (by P14C1). So things could have been produced in no other way and no other order, and so on, q.e.d.

II/74   Schol. 1: Since by these propositions I have shown more clearly than the noon light that there is absolutely nothing in things on account of which they can be called contingent, I wish now to explain briefly what we must understand by contingent—but first, what [we must understand] by necessary and impossible.

A thing is called necessary either by reason of its essence or by reason of its cause. For a thing's existence follows necessarily either from its essence and definition or from a given efficient cause. And a thing is also

106

called impossible from these same causes—namely, either because its essence, *or* definition, involves a contradiction, or because there is no external cause which has been determined to produce such a thing.

But a thing is called contingent only because of a defect of our knowledge. For if we do not know that the thing's essence involves a contradiction, or if we do know very well that its essence does not involve a contradiction, and nevertheless can affirm nothing certainly about its existence, because the order of causes is hidden from us, it can never seem to us either necessary or impossible. So we call it contingent or possible.

Schol. 2: From the preceding it clearly follows that things have been produced by God with the highest perfection, since they have followed necessarily from a given most perfect nature. Nor does this convict God of any imperfection, for his perfection compels us to affirm this. Indeed, from the opposite, it would clearly follow (as I have just shown), that God is not supremely perfect; because if things had been produced by God in another way, we would have to attribute to God another nature, different from that which we have been compelled to attribute to him from the consideration of the most perfect being.

However, I have no doubt that many will reject this opinion as absurd, without even being willing to examine it—for no other reason than because they have been accustomed to attribute another freedom to God, far different from that we have taught (D7), namely, an absolute will. But I also have no doubt that, if they are willing to reflect on the matter, and consider properly the chain of our demonstrations, in the end they will utterly reject the freedom they now attribute to God, not only as futile, but as a great obstacle to science. Nor is it necessary for me to repeat here what I said in P17S.   II/75

Nevertheless, to please them, I shall show that even if it is conceded that will pertains to God's essence, it still follows from his perfection that things could have been created by God in no other way or order. It will be easy to show this if we consider, first, what they themselves concede, namely, that it depends on God's decree and will alone that each thing is what it is. For otherwise God would not be the cause of all things. Next, that all God's decrees have been established by God himself from eternity. For otherwise he would be convicted of imperfection and inconstancy. But since, in eternity, there is neither *when*, nor *before*, nor *after*, it follows, from God's perfection alone, that he can never decree anything different, and never could have, *or* that God was not before his decrees, and cannot be without them.

But they will say that even if it were supposed that God had made another nature of things, or that from eternity he had decreed something else concerning Nature and its order, no imperfection in God would follow from that.

Still, if they say this, they will concede at the same time that God can change his decrees. For if God had decreed, concerning Nature and its order, something other than what he did decree, that is, had willed and conceived something else concerning Nature, he would necessarily have had an intellect other than he now has, and a will other than he now has. And if it is permitted to attribute to God another intellect and another will, without any change of his essence and of his perfection, why can he not now change his decrees concerning created things, and nevertheless remain equally perfect? For his intellect and will concerning created things and their order are the same in respect to his essence and his perfection, however his will and intellect may be conceived.

Further, all the philosophers I have seen concede that in God there is no potential intellect, but only an actual one. But since his intellect and his will are not distinguished from his essence, as they all also concede, it follows that if God had another actual intellect, and another will, his II/76 essence would also necessarily be other. And therefore (as I inferred at the beginning) if things had been produced by God otherwise than they now are, God's intellect and his will, that is (as is conceded), his essence, would have to be different [NS: from what it now is]. And this is absurd.

Therefore, since things could have been produced by God in no other way, and no other order, and since it follows from God's supreme perfection that this is true, no truly sound reason can persuade us to believe that God did not will to create all the things which are in his intellect, with that same perfection with which he understands them.

But they will say that there is no perfection or imperfection in things; what is in them, on account of which they are perfect or imperfect, and are called good or bad, depends only on God's will. And so, if God had willed, he could have brought it about that what is now perfection would have been the greatest imperfection, and conversely [NS: that what is now an imperfection in things would have been the most perfect]. How would this be different from saying openly that God, who necessarily understands what he wills, can bring it about by his will that he understands things in another way than he does understand them? As I have just shown, this is a great absurdity.

So I can turn the argument against them in the following way. All things depend on God's power. So in order for things to be able to be different, God's will would necessarily also have to be different. But God's will cannot be different (as we have just shown most evidently from God's perfection). So things also cannot be different.

I confess that this opinion, which subjects all things to a certain indif-

ferent will of God, and makes all things depend on his good pleasure, is
nearer the truth than that of those who maintain that God does all
things for the sake of the good. For they seem to place something outside God, which does not depend on God, to which God attends, as a
model, in what he does, and at which he aims, as at a certain goal. This
is simply to subject God to fate. Nothing more absurd can be maintained about God, whom we have shown to be the first and only free
cause, both of the essence of all things, and of their existence. So I shall
waste no time in refuting this absurdity.

P34: *God's power is his essence itself.*

Dem.: For from the necessity alone of God's essence it follows that   II/77
God is the cause of himself (by P11) and (by P16 and P16C) of all
things. Therefore, God's power, by which he and all things are and act,
is his essence itself, q.e.d.

P35: *Whatever we conceive to be in God's power, necessarily exists.*

Dem.: For whatever is in God's power must (by P34) be so comprehended by his essence that it necessarily follows from it, and therefore
necessarily exists, q.e.d.

P36: *Nothing exists from whose nature some effect does not follow.*

Dem: Whatever exists expresses the nature, *or* essence of God in a
certain and determinate way (by P25C), that is (by P34), whatever exists
expresses in a certain and determinate way the power of God, which is
the cause of all things. So (by P16), from [NS: everything which exists]
some effect must follow, q.e.d.

APPENDIX

With these [demonstrations] I have explained God's nature and properties: that he exists necessarily; that he is unique; that he is and acts from
the necessity alone of his nature; that (and how) he is the free cause of
all things; that all things are in God and so depend on him that without
him they can neither be nor be conceived; and finally, that all things
have been predetermined by God, not from freedom of the will *or* absolute good pleasure, but from God's absolute nature, *or* infinite power.
Further, I have taken care, whenever the occasion arose, to remove prejudices that could prevent my demonstrations from being perceived. But
because many prejudices remain that could, and can, be a great obstacle
to men's understanding the connection of things in the way I have explained it, I considered it worthwhile to submit them here to the scru-   II/78
tiny of reason. All the prejudices I here undertake to expose depend on

this one: that men commonly suppose that all natural things act, as men do, on account of an end; indeed, they maintain as certain that God himself directs all things to some certain end, for they say that God has made all things for man, and man that he might worship God.

So I shall begin by considering this one prejudice, asking *first* [I] why most people are satisfied that it is true, and why all are so inclined by nature to embrace it. *Then* [II] I shall show its falsity, and *finally* [III] how, from this, prejudices have arisen concerning *good* and *evil, merit* and *sin, praise* and *blame, order* and *confusion, beauty* and *ugliness,* and other things of this kind.

[I.] Of course this is not the place to deduce these things from the nature of the human mind. It will be sufficient here if I take as a foundation what everyone must acknowledge: that all men are born ignorant of the causes of things, and that they all want to seek their own advantage, and are conscious of this appetite. From these [assumptions] it follows, *first,* that men think themselves free, because they are conscious of their volitions and their appetite, and do not think, even in their dreams, of the causes by which they are disposed to wanting and willing, because they are ignorant of [those causes]. It follows, *second,* that men act always on account of an end, namely, on account of their advantage, which they want. Hence they seek to know only the final causes of what has been done, and when they have heard them, they are satisfied, because they have no reason to doubt further. But if they cannot hear them from another, nothing remains for them but to turn toward themselves, and reflect on the ends by which they are usually determined to do such things; so they necessarily judge the temperament of the other from their own temperament.

Furthermore, they find—both in themselves and outside themselves—many means that are very helpful in seeking their own advantage, for example, eyes for seeing, teeth for chewing, plants and animals for food, the sun for light, the sea for supporting fish [NS: and so with almost all other things whose natural causes they have no reason to doubt]. Hence, they consider all natural things as means to their own advantage. And knowing that they had found these means, not provided them for themselves, they had reason to believe that there was someone else who had prepared those means for their use. For after they consid-

II/79 ered things as means, they could not believe that the things had made themselves; but from the means they were accustomed to prepare for themselves, they had to infer that there was a ruler, or a number of rulers, of Nature, endowed with human freedom, who had taken care of all things for them, and made all things for their use.

And since they had never heard anything about the temperament of

these rulers, they had to judge it from their own. Hence, they maintained that the gods direct all things for the use of men in order to bind
men to them and be held by men in the highest honor. So it has happened that each of them has thought up from his own temperament
different ways of worshiping God, so that God might love him above all
the rest, and direct the whole of Nature according to the needs of their
blind desire and insatiable greed. Thus this prejudice was changed into
superstition, and struck deep roots in their minds. This was why each of
them strove with great diligence to understand and explain the final
causes of all things.

But while they sought to show that Nature does nothing in vain (i.e.,
nothing not of use to men), they seem to have shown only that Nature
and the gods are as mad as men. See, I ask you, how the matter has
turned out! Among so many conveniences in Nature they had to find
many inconveniences: storms, earthquakes, diseases, and the like.
These, they maintain, happen because the gods [NS: (whom they judge
to be of the same nature as themselves)] are angry on account of wrongs
done to them by men, *or* on account of sins committed in their worship.
And though their daily experience contradicted this, and though infinitely many examples showed that conveniences and inconveniences
happen indiscriminately to the pious and the impious alike, they did not
on that account give up their long-standing prejudice. It was easier for
them to put this among the other unknown things, whose use they were
ignorant of, and so remain in the state of ignorance in which they had
been born, than to destroy that whole construction, and think up a new
one.

So they maintained it as certain that the judgments of the gods far
surpass man's grasp. This alone, of course, would have caused the truth
to be hidden from the human race to eternity, if mathematics, which is
concerned not with ends, but only with the essences and properties of
figures, had not shown men another standard of truth. And besides
mathematics, we can assign other causes also (which it is unnecessary to
enumerate here), which were able to bring it about that men [NS: —but
very few, in relation to the whole human race—] would notice these
common prejudices and be led to the true knowledge of things. II/80

[II.] With this I have sufficiently explained what I promised in the
first place [viz. why men are so inclined to believe that all things act for
an end]. Not many words will be required now to show that Nature has
no end set before it, and that all final causes are nothing but human
fictions. For I believe I have already sufficiently established it, both by
the foundations and causes from which I have shown this prejudice to
have had its origin, and also by P16, P32C1, and C2, and all those

[propositions] by which I have shown that all things proceed by a certain eternal necessity of Nature, and with the greatest perfection.

I shall, however, add this: this doctrine concerning the end turns Nature completely upside down. For what is really a cause, it considers as an effect, and conversely [NS: what is an effect it considers as a cause]. What is by nature prior, it makes posterior. And finally, what is supreme and most perfect, it makes imperfect. For—to pass over the first two, since they are manifest through themselves—as has been established in PP21–23, that effect is most perfect which is produced immediately by God, and the more something requires several intermediate causes to produce it, the more imperfect it is. But if the things which have been produced immediately by God had been made so that God would achieve his end, then the last things, for the sake of which the first would have been made, would be the most excellent of all.

Again, this doctrine takes away God's perfection. For if God acts for the sake of an end, he necessarily wants something which he lacks. And though the theologians and metaphysicians distinguish between an end of need and an end of assimilation, they nevertheless confess that God did all things for his own sake, not for the sake of the things to be created. For before creation they can assign nothing except God for whose sake God would act. And so they are necessarily compelled to confess that God lacked those things for the sake of which he willed to prepare means, and that he desired them. This is clear through itself.

Nor ought we here to pass over the fact that the Followers of this doctrine, who have wanted to show off their cleverness in assigning the ends of things, have introduced—to prove this doctrine of theirs—a new way of arguing: by reducing things, not to the impossible, but to ignorance. This shows that no other way of defending their doctrine was open to them. For example, if a stone has fallen from a roof onto someone's head and killed him, they will show, in the following way, that the stone fell in order to kill the man. For if it did not fall to that end, God willing it, how could so many circumstances have concurred by chance (for often many circumstances do concur at once)? Perhaps you will answer that it happened because the wind was blowing hard and the man was walking that way. But they will persist: why was the wind blowing hard at that time? why was the man walking that way at that same time? If you answer again that the wind arose then because on the preceding day, while the weather was still calm, the sea began to toss, and that the man had been invited by a friend, they will press on—for there is no end to the questions which can be asked: but why was the sea tossing? why was the man invited at just that time? And so they will not stop asking for the causes of causes until you take refuge in the will of God, that is, the sanctuary of ignorance.

Similarly, when they see the structure of the human body, they are struck by a foolish wonder, and because they do not know the causes of so great an art, they infer that it is constructed, not by mechanical, but by divine, or supernatural art, and constituted in such a way that one part does not injure another.

Hence it happens that one who seeks the true causes of miracles, and is eager, like an educated man, to understand natural things, not to wonder at them, like a fool, is generally considered an impious heretic and denounced as such by those whom the people honor as interpreters of Nature and the gods. For they know that if ignorance is taken away, then foolish wonder, the only means they have of arguing and defending their authority, is also taken away. But I leave these things, and pass on to what I have decided to treat here in the *third* place.

[III.] After men persuaded themselves that everything which happens, happens on their account, they had to judge that what is most important in each thing is what is most useful to them, and to rate as most excellent all those things by which they were most pleased. Hence, they had to form these notions, by which they explained natural things: *good, evil, order, confusion, warm, cold, beauty, ugliness*. And because they think themselves free, those notions have arisen: *praise* and *blame*, *sin* and *merit*. The latter I shall explain after I have treated human nature; but the former I shall briefly explain here.

Whatever conduces to health and the worship of God, they have called *good*; but what is contrary to these, *evil*.

And because those who do not understand the nature of things, but only imagine them, affirm nothing concerning things, and take the imagination for the intellect, they firmly believe, in their ignorance of things and of their own nature, that there is an order in things. For when things are so disposed that, when they are presented to us through the senses, we can easily imagine them, and so can easily remember them, we say that they are well-ordered; but if the opposite is true, we say that they are badly ordered, or confused.

II/82

And since those things we can easily imagine are especially pleasing to us, men prefer order to confusion, as if order were anything in Nature more than a relation to our imagination. They also say that God has created all things in order, and so, unknowingly attribute imagination to God—unless, perhaps, they mean that God, to provide for human imagination, has disposed all things so that men can very easily imagine them. Nor will it, perhaps, give them pause that infinitely many things are found which far surpass our imagination, and a great many which confuse it on account of its weakness. But enough of this.

The other notions are also nothing but modes of imagining, by which the imagination is variously affected; and yet the ignorant consider them the chief attributes of things, because, as we have already said, they believe all things have been made for their sake, and call the nature of a thing good or evil, sound or rotten and corrupt, as they are affected by it. For example, if the motion the nerves receive from objects presented through the eyes is conducive to health, the objects by which it is caused are called beautiful; those which cause a contrary motion are called ugly. Those which move the sense through the nose, they call pleasant-smelling or stinking; through the tongue, sweet or bitter, tasty or tasteless; through touch, hard or soft, rough or smooth, and the like; and finally, those which move the ears are said to produce noise, sound, or harmony. Men have been so mad as to believe that God is pleased by harmony. Indeed there are philosophers who have persuaded themselves that the motions of the heavens produce a harmony.

All of these things show sufficiently that each one has judged things according to the disposition of his brain; or rather, has accepted affections of the imagination as things. So it is no wonder (to note this, too, in passing) that we find so many controversies to have arisen among men, and that they have finally given rise to skepticism. For although human bodies agree in many things, they still differ in very many. And for that reason what seems good to one, seems bad to another; what seems ordered to one, seems confused to another; what seems pleasing to one, seems displeasing to another, and so on.

II/83

I pass over the [other notions] here, both because this is not the place to treat them at length, and because everyone has experienced this [variability] sufficiently for himself. That is why we have such sayings as "So many heads, so many attitudes," "everyone finds his own judgment more than enough," and "there are as many differences of brains as of palates." These proverbs show sufficiently that men judge things according to the disposition of their brain, and imagine, rather than understand them. For if men had understood them, the things would at least convince them all, even if they did not attract them all, as the example of mathematics shows.

We see, therefore, that all the notions by which ordinary people are accustomed to explain Nature are only modes of imagining, and do not indicate the nature of anything, only the constitution of the imagination. And because they have names, as if they were [notions] of beings existing outside the imagination, I call them beings, not of reason, but of imagination. So all the arguments in which people try to use such notions against us can easily be warded off.

For many are accustomed to arguing in this way: if all things have followed from the necessity of God's most perfect nature, why are there so many imperfections in Nature? why are things corrupt to the point where they stink? so ugly that they produce nausea? why is there confusion, evil, and sin?

As I have just said, those who argue in this way are easily answered. For the perfection of things is to be judged solely from their nature and power; things are not more or less perfect because they please or offend men's senses, or because they are of use to, or are incompatible with, human nature.

But to those who ask "why God did not create all men so that they would be governed by the command of reason?" I answer only "because he did not lack material to create all things, from the highest degree of perfection to the lowest"; or, to speak more properly, "because the laws of his nature have been so ample that they sufficed for producing all things which can be conceived by an infinite intellect" (as I have demonstrated in P16).

These are the prejudices I undertook to note here. If any of this kind still remain, they can be corrected by anyone with only a little meditation. [NS: And so I find no reason to devote more time to these matters, and so on.]

Second Part of the Ethics
Of the Nature and Origin of the Mind

II/84

I pass now to explaining those things which must necessarily follow from the essence of God, or the infinite and eternal being—not, indeed, all of them, for we have demonstrated (IP16) that infinitely many things must follow from it in infinitely many modes, but only those that can lead us, by the hand, as it were, to the knowledge of the human mind and its highest blessedness.

DEFINITIONS

D1: By body I understand a mode that in a certain and determinate way expresses God's essence insofar as he is considered as an extended thing (see IP25C).

D2: I say that to the essence of any thing belongs that which, being given, the thing is [NS: also] necessarily posited and which, being taken

115

away, the thing is necessarily [NS: also] taken away; or that without which the thing can neither be nor be conceived, and which can neither be nor be conceived without the thing.

D3: By idea I understand a concept of the mind which the mind forms because it is a thinking thing.

II/85   Exp.: *I say concept rather than perception, because the word perception seems to indicate that the mind is acted on by the object. But concept seems to express an action of the mind.*

D4: By adequate idea I understand an idea which, insofar as it is considered in itself, without relation to an object, has all the properties, *or* intrinsic denominations of a true idea.

Exp.: *I say intrinsic to exclude what is extrinsic, namely, the agreement of the idea with its object.*

D5: Duration is an indefinite continuation of existing.

Exp.: *I say indefinite because it cannot be determined at all through the very nature of the existing thing, nor even by the efficient cause, which necessarily posits the existence of the thing, and does not take it away.*

D6: By reality and perfection I understand the same thing.

D7: By singular things I understand things that are finite and have a determinate existence. And if a number of individuals so concur in one action that together they are all the cause of one effect, I consider them all, to that extent, as one singular thing.

AXIOMS

A1: The essence of man does not involve necessary existence, that is, from the order of Nature it can happen equally that this or that man does exist, or that he does not exist.

A2: Man thinks [NS: or, to put it differently, we know that we think].

A3: There are no modes of thinking, such as love, desire, or whatever is
II/86   designated by the word affects of the mind, unless there is in the same individual the idea of the thing loved, desired, and the like. But there can be an idea, even though there is no other mode of thinking.

A4: We feel that a certain body [NS: our body] is affected in many ways.

A5: We neither feel nor perceive any singular things [NS: or anything of *Natura naturata*], except bodies and modes of thinking.
See the postulates after P13.

116

P1: *Thought is an attribute of God, or God is a thinking thing.*

Dem.: Singular thoughts, *or* this or that thought, are modes which express God's nature in a certain and determinate way (by IP25C). Therefore (by ID5) there belongs to God an attribute whose concept all singular thoughts involve, and through which they are also conceived. Therefore, thought is one of God's infinite attributes, which expresses an eternal and infinite essence of God (see ID6), *or* God is a thinking thing, q.e.d.

Schol.: This proposition is also evident from the fact that we can conceive an infinite thinking being. For the more things a thinking being can think, the more reality, *or* perfection, we conceive it to contain. Therefore, a being which can think infinitely many things in infinitely many ways is necessarily infinite in its power of thinking. So since we can conceive an infinite being by attending to thought alone, thought (by ID4 and D6) is necessarily one of God's infinite attributes, as we maintained.

P2: *Extension is an attribute of God, or God is an extended thing.*

Dem: The demonstration of this proceeds in the same way as that of the preceding proposition.   II/87

P3: *In God there is necessarily an idea, both of his essence and of everything which necessarily follows from his essence.*

Dem.: For God (by P1) can think infinitely many things in infinitely many modes, *or* (what is the same, by IP16) can form the idea of his essence and of all the things which necessarily follow from it. But whatever is in God's power necessarily exists (by IP35); therefore, there is necessarily such an idea, and (by IP15) it is only in God, q.e.d.

Schol.: By God's power ordinary people understand God's free will and his right over all things which are, things which on that account are commonly considered to be contingent. For they say that God has the power of destroying all things and reducing them to nothing. Further, they very often compare God's power with the power of kings.

But we have refuted this in IP32C1 and C2, and we have shown in IP16 that God acts with the same necessity by which he understands himself, that is, just as it follows from the necessity of the divine nature (as everyone maintains unanimously) that God understands himself, with the same necessity it also follows that God does infinitely many things in infinitely many modes. And then we have shown in IP34 that God's power is nothing except God's active essence. And so it is as impossible for us to conceive that God does not act as it is to conceive that he does not exist.

Again, if it were agreeable to pursue these matters further, I could also show here that power which ordinary people fictitiously ascribe to God is not only human (which shows that ordinary people conceive God as a man, or as like a man), but also involves lack of power. But I do not wish to speak so often about the same topic. I only ask the reader to reflect repeatedly on what is said concerning this matter in Part I, from P16 to the end. For no one will be able to perceive rightly the things I maintain unless he takes great care not to confuse God's power with the human power or right of kings.

II/88

P4: *God's idea, from which infinitely many things follow in infinitely many modes, must be unique.*

Dem.: An infinite intellect comprehends nothing except God's attributes and his affections (by IP30). But God is unique (by IP14C1). Therefore God's idea, from which infinitely many things follow in infinitely many modes, must be unique, q.e.d.

P5: *The formal being of ideas admits God as a cause only insofar as he is considered as a thinking thing, and not insofar as he is explained by any other attribute. That is, ideas, both of God's attributes and of singular things, admit not the objects themselves, or the things perceived, as their efficient cause, but God himself, insofar as he is a thinking thing.*

Dem.: This is evident from P3. For there we inferred that God can form the idea of his essence, and of all the things that follow necessarily from it, solely from the fact that God is a thinking thing, and not from the fact that he is the object of his own idea. So the formal being of ideas admits God as its cause insofar as he is a thinking thing.

But another way of demonstrating this is the following. The formal being of ideas is a mode of thinking (as is known through itself), that is (by IP25C), a mode which expresses, in a certain way, God's nature insofar as he is a thinking thing. And so (by IP10) it involves the concept of no other attribute of God, and consequently (by IA4) is the effect of no other attribute than thought. And so the formal being of ideas admits God as its cause insofar as he is considered only as a thinking thing, and so on, q.e.d.

II/89

P6: *The modes of each attribute have God for their cause only insofar as he is considered under the attribute of which they are modes, and not insofar as he is considered under any other attribute.*

Dem.: For each attribute is conceived through itself without any other (by IP10). So the modes of each attribute involve the concept of their own attribute, but not of another one; and so (by IA4) they have God for their cause only insofar as he is considered under the attribute of which they are modes, and not insofar as he is considered under any other, q.e.d.

118

Cor.: From this it follows that the formal being of things which are not modes of thinking does not follow from the divine nature because [God] has first known the things; rather the objects of ideas follow and are inferred from their attributes in the same way and by the same necessity as that with which we have shown ideas to follow from the attribute of thought.

P7: *The order and connection of ideas is the same as the order and connection of things.*

Dem.: This is clear from IA4. For the idea of each thing caused depends on the knowledge of the cause of which it is the effect.

Cor.: From this it follows that God's [NS: actual] power of thinking is equal to his actual power of acting. That is, whatever follows formally from God's infinite nature follows objectively in God from his idea in the same order and with the same connection.

Schol.: Before we proceed further, we must recall here what we showed [NS: in the First Part], namely, that whatever can be perceived by an infinite intellect as constituting an essence of substance pertains to one substance only, and consequently that the thinking substance and the extended substance are one and the same substance, which is now comprehended under this attribute, now under that. So also a mode of extension and the idea of that mode are one and the same thing, but expressed in two ways. Some of the Hebrews seem to have seen this, as if through a cloud, when they maintained that God, God's intellect, and the things understood by him are one and the same.

II/90

For example, a circle existing in Nature and the idea of the existing circle, which is also in God, are one and the same thing, which is explained through different attributes. Therefore, whether we conceive Nature under the attribute of extension, or under the attribute of thought, or under any other attribute, we shall find one and the same order, or one and the same connection of causes, that is, that the same things follow one another.

When I said [NS: before] that God is the cause of the idea, say of a circle, only insofar as he is a thinking thing, and [the cause] of the circle, only insofar as he is an extended thing, this was for no other reason than because the formal being of the idea of the circle can be perceived only through another mode of thinking, as its proximate cause, and that mode again through another, and so on, to infinity. Hence, so long as things are considered as modes of thinking, we must explain the order of the whole of Nature, or the connection of causes, through the attribute of thought alone. And insofar as they are considered as modes of extension, the order of the whole of Nature must be explained through

119

the attribute of extension alone. I understand the same concerning the other attributes.

So of things as they are in themselves, God is really the cause insofar as he consists of infinite attributes. For the present, I cannot explain these matters more clearly.

P8: *The ideas of singular things, or of modes, that do not exist must be compre-hended in God's infinite idea in the same way as the formal essences of the singular things, or modes, are contained in God's attributes.*

II/91   Dem.: This proposition is evident from the preceding one, but is understood more clearly from the preceding scholium.

Cor.: From this it follows that so long as singular things do not exist, except insofar as they are comprehended in God's attributes, their ob-jective being, or ideas, do not exist except insofar as God's infinite idea exists. And when singular things are said to exist, not only insofar as they are comprehended in God's attributes, but insofar also as they are said to have duration, their ideas also involve the existence through which they are said to have duration.

Schol.: If anyone wishes me to explain this further by an example, I will, of course, not be able to give one which adequately explains what I speak of here, since it is unique. Still I shall try as far as possible to illustrate the matter: the circle is of such a nature that the rectangles formed from the segments of all the straight lines in-tersecting in it are equal to one another. So in a circle there are contained infinitely many rectangles which are equal to one another. Nevertheless, none of them can be said to exist except insofar as the circle exists, nor also can the idea of any of these rectangles be said to exist except insofar as it is comprehended in the idea of the circle. Now of these infinitely many [rectangles] let two only, namely, [those formed from the segments of lines] D and E, exist. Of course their ideas also exist now, not only insofar as they are only comprehended in the idea of the circle, but also insofar as they involve the existence of those rectangles. By this they are distinguished from the other ideas of the other rectangles.

P9: *The idea of a singular thing which actually exists has God for a cause not insofar as he is infinite, but insofar as he is considered to be affected by*
II/92   *another idea of a singular thing which actually exists; and of this [idea] God is also the cause, insofar as he is affected by another third [NS: idea], and so on, to infinity.*

Dem.: The idea of a singular thing which actually exists is a singular mode of thinking, and distinct from the others (by P8C and S), and so

120

(by P6) has God for a cause only insofar as he is a thinking thing. But not (by IP28) insofar as he is a thing thinking absolutely; rather insofar as he is considered to be affected by another [NS: determinate] mode of thinking. And God is also the cause of this mode, insofar as he is affected by another [NS: determinate mode of thinking], and so on, to infinity. But the order and connection of ideas (by P7) is the same as the order and connection of causes. Therefore, the cause of one singular idea is another idea, *or* God, insofar as he is considered to be affected by another idea; and of this also [God is the cause], insofar as he is affected by another, and so on, to infinity, q.e.d.

Cor.: Whatever happens in the singular object of any idea, there is knowledge of it in God, only insofar as he has the idea of the same object.

Dem.: Whatever happens in the object of any idea, there is an idea of it in God (by P3), not insofar as he is infinite, but insofar as he is considered to be affected by another idea of [NS: an existing] singular thing (by P9); but the order and connection of ideas (by P7) is the same as the order and connection of things; therefore, knowledge of what happens in a singular object will be in God only insofar as he has the idea of the same object, q.e.d.

P10: *The being of substance does not pertain to the essence of man, or substance does not constitute the form of man.*

Dem.: For the being of substance involves necessary existence (by IP7). Therefore, if the being of substance pertained to the essence of man, then substance being given, man would necessarily be given (by D2), and consequently man would exist necessarily, which (by A1) is absurd, q.e.d.

Schol.: This proposition is also demonstrated from IP5, namely, that there are not two substances of the same nature. Since a number of men can exist, what constitutes the form of man is not the being of substance. Further, this proposition is evident from the other properties of substance, namely, that substance is, by its nature, infinite, immutable, indivisible, and so forth, as anyone can easily see.

Cor.: From this it follows that the essence of man is constituted by certain modifications of God's attributes.

Dem.: For the being of substance does not pertain to the essence of man (by P10). Therefore, it is something (by IP15) which is in God, and which can neither be nor be conceived without God, *or* (by IP25C) an affection, *or* mode, which expresses God's nature in a certain and determinate way.

Schol.: Everyone, of course, must concede that nothing can either be

II/93

or be conceived without God. For all confess that God is the only cause of all things, both of their essence and of their existence. That is, God is not only the cause of the coming to be of things, as they say, but also of their being.

But in the meantime many say that anything without which a thing can neither be nor be conceived pertains to the nature of the thing. And so they believe either that the nature of God pertains to the essence of created things, or that created things can be or be conceived without God—or what is more certain, they are not sufficiently consistent.

The cause of this, I believe, was that they did not observe the [proper] order of philosophizing. For they believed that the divine nature, which they should have contemplated before all else (because it is prior both in knowledge and in nature) is last in the order of knowledge, and that the things which are called objects of the senses are prior to all. That is why, when they contemplated natural things, they thought of nothing less than they did of the divine nature; and when afterwards they directed their minds to contemplating the divine nature, they could think of nothing less than of their first fictions, on which they had built the knowledge of natural things, because these could not assist knowledge of the divine nature. So it is no wonder that they have generally contradicted themselves.

II/94

But I pass over this. For my intent here was only to give a reason why I did not say that anything without which a thing can neither be nor be conceived pertains to its essence—namely, because singular things can neither be nor be conceived without God, and nevertheless, God does not pertain to their essence. But I have said that what necessarily constitutes the essence of a thing is that which, if it is given, the thing is posited, and if it is taken away, the thing is taken away, that is, the essence is what the thing can neither be nor be conceived without, and vice versa, what can neither be nor be conceived without the thing.

P11: *The first thing which constitutes the actual being of a human Mind is nothing but the idea of a singular thing which actually exists.*

Dem.: The essence of man (by P10C) is constituted by certain modes of God's attributes, namely (by A2), by modes of thinking, of all of which (by A3) the idea is prior in nature, and when it is given, the other modes (to which the idea is prior in nature) must be in the same individual (by A3). And therefore an idea is the first thing which constitutes the being of a human mind. But not the idea of a thing which does not exist. For then (by P8C) the idea itself could not be said to exist. Therefore, it will be the idea of a thing which actually exists. But not of an infinite thing. For an infinite thing (by IP21 and 22) must always exist necessarily. But (by A1) it is absurd [that this idea should be of a necessarily existing object]. Therefore, the first thing which constitutes the actual being of a human mind is the idea of a singular thing which actually exists, q.e.d.

Cor.: From this it follows that the human mind is a part of the infinite intellect of God. Therefore, when we say that the human mind perceives this or that, we are saying nothing but that God, not insofar as he is infinite, but insofar as he is explained through the nature of the human mind, *or* insofar as he constitutes the essence of the human mind, has this or that idea; and when we say that God has this or that idea, not only insofar as he constitutes the nature of the human mind, but insofar as he also has the idea of another thing together with the human mind, then we say that the human mind perceives the thing only partially, *or* inadequately.

II/95

Schol.: Here, no doubt, my readers will come to a halt, and think of many things which will give them pause. For this reason I ask them to continue on with me slowly, step by step, and to make no judgment on these matters until they have read through them all.

P12: *Whatever happens in the object of the idea constituting the human mind must be perceived by the human mind, or there will necessarily be an idea of that thing in the mind; that is, if the object of the idea constituting a human mind is a body, nothing can happen in that body which is not perceived by the mind.*

Dem.: For whatever happens in the object of any idea, the knowledge of that thing is necessarily in God (by P9C), insofar as he is considered to be affected by the idea of the same object, that is (by P11), insofar as he constitutes the mind of some thing. Therefore, whatever happens in the object of the idea constituting the human mind, the knowledge of it is necessarily in God insofar as he constitutes the nature of the human mind, that is (by P11C), knowledge of this thing will necessarily be in the mind, *or* the mind will perceive it, q.e.d.

Schol.: This proposition is also evident, and more clearly understood from P7S, which you should consult.

P13: *The object of the idea constituting the human mind is the body, or a* II/96 *certain mode of extension which actually exists, and nothing else.*

Dem.: For if the object of the human mind were not the body, the ideas of the affections of the body would not be in God (by P9C) insofar as he constituted our mind, but insofar as he constituted the mind of another thing, that is (by P11C), the ideas of the affections of the body would not be in our mind; but (by A4) we have ideas of the affections of the body. Therefore, the object of the idea which constitutes the human mind is the body, and it (by P11) actually exists.

Next, if the object of the mind were something else also, in addition to the body, then since (by IP36) nothing exists from which there does not follow some effect, there would necessarily (by P12) be an idea in our mind of some effect of it. But (by A5) there is no idea of it. Therefore, the object of our mind is the existing body and nothing else, q.e.d.

Cor.: From this it follows that man consists of a mind and a body, and that the human body exists, as we are aware of it.

Schol.: From these [propositions] we understand not only that the human mind is united to the body, but also what should be understood by the union of mind and body. But no one will be able to understand it adequately, *or* distinctly, unless he first knows adequately the nature of our body. For the things we have shown so far are completely general and do not pertain more to man than to other individuals, all of which, though in different degrees, are nevertheless animate. For of each thing there is necessarily an idea in God, of which God is the cause in the same way as he is of the idea of the human body. And so, whatever we have said of the idea of the human body must also be said of the idea of any thing.

II/97 However, we also cannot deny that ideas differ among themselves, as the objects themselves do, and that one is more excellent than the other, and contains more reality, just as the object of the one is more excellent than the object of the other and contains more reality. And so to determine what is the difference between the human mind and the others, and how it surpasses them, it is necessary for us, as we have said, to know the nature of its object, that is, of the human body. I cannot explain this here, nor is that necessary for the things I wish to demonstrate. Nevertheless, I say this in general, that in proportion as a body is more capable than others of doing many things at once, or being acted on in many ways at once, so its mind is more capable than others of perceiving many things at once. And in proportion as the actions of a body depend more on itself alone, and as other bodies concur with it less in acting, so its mind is more capable of understanding distinctly. And from these [truths] we can know the excellence of one mind over the others, and also see the cause why we have only a completely confused knowledge of our body, and many other things which I shall deduce from them in the following [propositions]. For this reason I have thought it worthwhile to explain and demonstrate these things more accurately. To do this it is necessary to premise a few things concerning the nature of bodies.

124

A1′: All bodies either move or are at rest.

A2′: Each body moves now more slowly, now more quickly.

L1: *Bodies are distinguished from one another by reason of motion and rest, speed and slowness, and not by reason of substance.*

Dem.: I suppose that the first part of this is known through itself. But that bodies are not distinguished by reason of substance is evident both from IP5 and from IP8. But it is more clearly evident from those things which are said in IP15S.

L2: *All bodies agree in certain things.*   II/98

Dem.: For all bodies agree in that they involve the concept of one and the same attribute (by D1), and in that they can move now more slowly, now more quickly, and absolutely, that now they move, now they are at rest.

L3: *A body which moves* or *is at rest must be determined to motion or rest by another body, which has also been determined to motion or rest by another, and that again by another, and so on, to infinity.*

Dem.: Bodies (by D1) are singular things which (by L1) are distinguished from one another by reason of motion and rest; and so (by IP28), each must be determined necessarily to motion or rest by another singular thing, namely (by P6), by another body, which (by A1′) either moves or is at rest. But this body also (by the same reasoning) could not move or be at rest if it had not been determined by another to motion or rest, and this again (by the same reasoning) by another, and so on, to infinity, q.e.d.

Cor.: From this it follows that a body in motion moves until it is determined by another body to rest; and that a body at rest also remains at rest until it is determined to motion by another.

This is also known through itself. For when I suppose that body A, say, is at rest, and do not attend to any other body in motion, I can say nothing about body A except that it is at rest. If afterwards it happens that body A moves, that of course could not have come about from the fact that it was at rest. For from that nothing else could follow but that body A would be at rest.

If, on the other hand, A is supposed to move, then as often as we   II/99
attend only to A, we shall be able to affirm nothing concerning it except that it moves. If afterwards it happens that A is at rest, that of course also could not have come about from the motion it had. For from the motion nothing else could follow but that A would move. Therefore, it happens by a thing which was not in A, namely, by an external cause, by which [NS: the body in motion, A] has been determined to rest.

A1″: All modes by which a body is affected by another body follow both from the nature of the body affected and at the same time from the nature of the affecting body, so that one and the same body may be moved differently according to differences in the nature of the bodies moving it. And conversely, different bodies may be moved differently by one and the same body.

A2″: When a body in motion strikes against another which is at rest and cannot give way, then it is reflected, so that it continues to move, and the angle of the line of the reflected motion with the surface of the body at rest which it struck against will be equal to the angle which the line of the incident motion makes with the same surface.

This will be sufficient concerning the simplest bodies, which are distinguished from one another only by motion and rest, speed and slowness. Now let us move up to composite bodies.

Definition: *When a number of bodies, whether of the same or of different size, are so constrained by other bodies that they lie upon one another, or if they so move, whether with the same degree or different degrees of speed, that they communicate their motions to each other in a certain fixed manner, we shall say that those bodies are united with one another and that they all together compose one body* or *individual, which is distinguished from the others by this union of bodies.*

II/100

A3″: As the parts of an individual, or composite body, lie upon one another over a larger or smaller surface, so they can be forced to change their position with more or less difficulty; and consequently the more or less will be the difficulty of bringing it about that the individual changes its shape. And therefore the bodies whose parts lie upon one another over a large surface, I shall call *hard*; those whose parts lie upon one another over a small surface, I shall call *soft*; and finally those whose parts are in motion, I shall call *fluid*.

L4: *If, of a body, or of an individual, which is composed of a number of bodies, some are removed, and at the same time as many others of the same nature take their place, the [NS: body, or the] individual will retain its nature, as before, without any change of its form.*

Dem.: For (by L1) bodies are not distinguished in respect to substance; what constitutes the form of the individual consists [NS: only] in the union of the bodies (by the preceding definition). But this [NS: union] (by hypothesis) is retained even if a continual change of bodies occurs. Therefore, the individual will retain its nature, as before, both in respect to substance, and in respect to mode, q.e.d.

126

L5: *If the parts composing an individual become greater or less, but in such a proportion that they all keep the same ratio of motion and rest to each other as before, then the individual will likewise retain its nature, as before, without any change of form.*

Dem.: The demonstration of this is the same as that of the preceding lemma.

L6: *If certain bodies composing an individual are compelled to alter the motion they have from one direction to another, but so that they can continue their motions and communicate them to each other in the same ratio as before, the individual will likewise retain its nature, without any change of form.*

II/101

Dem.: This is evident through itself. For it is supposed that it retains everything which, in its definition, we said constitutes its form. [NS: See the definition before L4.]

L7: *Furthermore, the individual so composed retains its nature, whether it, as a whole, moves or is at rest, or whether it moves in this or that direction, so long as each part retains its motion, and communicates it, as before, to the others.*

Dem.: This [NS: also] is evident from the definition preceding L4.

Schol.: By this, then, we see how a composite individual can be affected in many ways, and still preserve its nature. So far we have conceived an individual which is composed only of bodies which are distinguished from one another only by motion and rest, speed and slowness, that is, which is composed of the simplest bodies. But if we should now conceive of another, composed of a number of individuals of a different nature, we shall find that it can be affected in a great many other ways, and still preserve its nature. For since each part of it is composed of a number of bodies, each part will therefore (by L7) be able, without any change of its nature, to move now more slowly, now more quickly, and consequently communicate its motion more quickly or more slowly to the others.

II/102

But if we should further conceive a third kind of individual, composed [NS: of many individuals] of this second kind, we shall find that it can be affected in many other ways, without any change of its form. And if we proceed in this way to infinity, we shall easily conceive that the whole of nature is one individual, whose parts, that is, all bodies, vary in infinite ways, without any change of the whole individual.

If it had been my intention to deal expressly with body, I ought to have explained and demonstrated these things more fully. But I have already said that I intended something else, and brought these things forward only because I can easily deduce from them the things I have decided to demonstrate.

POSTULATES

I. The human body is composed of a great many individuals of different natures, each of which is highly composite.

II. Some of the individuals of which the human body is composed are fluid, some soft, and others, finally, are hard.

III. The individuals composing the human body, and consequently, the human body itself, are affected by external bodies in very many ways.

IV. The human body, to be preserved, requires a great many other bodies, by which it is, as it were, continually regenerated.

II/103   V. When a fluid part of the human body is determined by an external body so that it frequently thrusts against a soft part [of the body], it changes its surface and, as it were, impresses on [the soft part] certain traces of the external body striking against [the fluid part].

VI. The human body can move and dispose external bodies in a great many ways.

P14: *The human mind is capable of perceiving a great many things, and is the more capable, the more its body can be disposed in a great many ways.*

Dem.: For the human body (by Post. 3 and 6) is affected in a great many ways by external bodies, and is disposed to affect external bodies in a great many ways. But the human mind must perceive everything which happens in the human body (by P12). Therefore, the human mind is capable of perceiving a great many things, and is the more capable [, NS: as the human body is more capable], q.e.d.

P15: *The idea that constitutes the formal being* [esse] *of the human mind is not simple, but composed of a great many ideas.*

Dem.: The idea that constitutes the formal being of the human mind is the idea of a body (by P13), which (by Post. 1) is composed of a great many highly composite individuals. But of each individual composing the body, there is necessarily (by P8C) an idea in God. Therefore (by P7), the idea of the human body is composed of these many ideas of the parts composing the body, q.e.d.

P16: *The idea of any mode in which the human body is affected by external bodies must involve the nature of the human body and at the same time the nature of the external body.*

II/104   Dem.: For all the modes in which a body is affected follow from the nature of the affected body, and at the same time from the nature of the affecting body (by A1″ [II/99]). So the idea of them (by IA4) will necessarily involve the nature of each body. And so the idea of each mode in which the human body is affected by an external body involves the nature of the human body and of the external body, q.e.d.

Cor. 1: From this it follows, first, that the human mind perceives the nature of a great many bodies together with the nature of its own body.

Cor. 2: It follows, second, that the ideas which we have of external bodies indicate the condition of our own body more than the nature of the external bodies. I have explained this by many examples in the Appendix of Part I.

P17: *If the human body is affected with a mode that involves the nature of an external body, the human mind will regard the same external body as actually existing, or as present to it, until the body is affected by an affect that excludes the existence or presence of that body.*

Dem.: This is evident. For so long as the human body is so affected, the human mind (by P12) will regard this affection of the body, that is (by P16), it will have the idea of a mode that actually exists, an idea which involves the nature of the external body, that is, an idea which does not exclude, but posits, the existence or presence of the nature of the external body. And so the mind (by P16C1) will regard the external body as actually existing, or as present, until it is affected, and so on, q.e.d.

Cor.: Although the external bodies by which the human body has once been affected neither exist nor are present, the mind will still be able to regard them as if they were present. II/105

Dem.: While external bodies so determine the fluid parts of the human body that they often thrust against the softer parts, they change (by Post. 5) their surfaces with the result (see A2″ after L3) that they are reflected from it in another way than they used to be before, and still later, when the fluid parts, by their spontaneous motion, encounter those new surfaces, they are reflected in the same way as when they were driven against those surfaces by the external bodies. Consequently, while, thus reflected, they continue to move, they will affect the human body with the same mode, concerning which the mind (by P12) will think again, that is (by P17), the mind will again regard the external body as present; this will happen as often as the fluid parts of the human body encounter the same surfaces by their spontaneous motion. So although the external bodies by which the human body has once been affected do not exist, the mind will still regard them as present, as often as this action of the body is repeated, q.e.d.

Schol.: We see, therefore, how it can happen (as it often does) that we regard as present things which do not exist. This can happen from other causes also, but it is sufficient for me here to have shown one through which I can explain it as if I had shown it through its true cause; still, I do not believe that I wander far from the true [cause] since all those postulates which I have assumed contain hardly anything which is not established by experience which we cannot doubt, after we have shown that the human body exists as we are aware of it (see P13C).

Furthermore (from P17C and P16C2), we clearly understand what is the difference between the idea of, say, Peter, which constitutes the essence of Peter's mind, and the idea of Peter which is in another man, say in Paul. For the former directly explains the essence of Peter's body, and does not involve existence, except so long as Peter exists; but the latter indicates the condition of Paul's body more than Peter's nature [NS: see P16C2], and therefore, while that condition of Paul's body lasts, Paul's mind will still regard Peter as present to itself, even though Peter does not exist.

II/106

Next, to retain the customary words, the affections of the human body whose ideas present external bodies as present to us, we shall call images of things, though they do not reproduce the [NS: external] figures of things. And when the mind regards bodies in this way, we shall say that it imagines.

And here, in order to begin to indicate what error is, I should like you to note that the imaginations of the mind, considered in themselves contain no error, *or* that the mind does not err from the fact that it imagines, but only insofar as it is considered to lack an idea which excludes the existence of those things which it imagines to be present to it. For if the mind, while it imagined nonexistent things as present to it, at the same time knew that those things did not exist, it would, of course, attribute this power of imagining to a virtue of its nature, not to a vice—especially if this faculty of imagining depended only on its own nature, that is (by ID7), if the mind's faculty of imagining were free.

P18: *If the human body has once been affected by two or more bodies at the same time, then when the mind subsequently imagines one of them, it will immediately recollect the others also.*

Dem.: The mind (by P17C) imagines a body because the human body is affected and disposed as it was affected when certain of its parts were struck by the external body itself. But (by hypothesis) the body was then so disposed that the mind imagined two [or more] bodies at once; therefore it will now also imagine two [or more] at once, and when the mind imagines one, it will immediately recollect the other also, q.e.d.

Schol.: From this we clearly understand what memory is. For it is nothing other than a certain connection of ideas involving the nature of things which are outside the human body—a connection which is in the

II/107

mind according to the order and connection of the affections of the human body.

I say, *first*, that the connection is only of those ideas which involve the nature of things outside the human body, but not of the ideas which explain the nature of the same things. For they are really (by P16) ideas of affections of the human body which involve both its nature and that of external bodies.

I say, *second*, that this connection happens according to the order and connection of the affections of the human body in order to distinguish it from the connection of ideas which happens according to the order of the intellect, by which the mind perceives things through their first causes, and which is the same in all men.

And from this we clearly understand why the mind, from the thought of one thing, immediately passes to the thought of another, which has no likeness to the first: as, for example, from the thought of the word *pomum* a Roman will immediately pass to the thought of the fruit [viz. an apple], which has no similarity to that articulate sound and nothing in common with it except that the body of the same man has often been affected by these two [NS: at the same time], that is, that the man often heard the word *pomum* while he saw the fruit.

And in this way each of us will pass from one thought to another, as each one's association has ordered the images of things in the body. For example, a soldier, having seen traces of a horse in the sand, will immediately pass from the thought of a horse to the thought of a horseman, and from that to the thought of war, and so on. But a farmer will pass from the thought of a horse to the thought of a plow, and then to that of a field, and so on. And so each one, according as he has been accustomed to join and connect the images of things in this or that way, will pass from one thought to another.

P19: *The human mind does not know the human body itself, nor does it know that it exists, except through ideas of affections by which the body is affected.*

Dem.: For the human mind is the idea itself, *or* knowledge of the human body (by P13), which (by P9) is indeed in God insofar as he is considered to be affected by another idea of a singular thing, or because (by Post. 4) the human body requires a great many bodies by which it is, as it were, continually regenerated; and [NS: because] the order and connection of ideas is (by P7) the same as the order and connection of causes, this idea will be in God insofar as he is considered to be affected by the ideas of a great many singular things. Therefore, God has the idea of the human body, *or* knows the human body, insofar as he is affected by a great many other ideas, and not insofar as he constitutes

II/108

131

the nature of the human mind, that is (by P11C), the human mind does not know the human body.

But the ideas of affections of the body are in God insofar as he constitutes the nature of the human mind, *or* the human mind perceives the same affections (by P12), and consequently (by P16) the human body itself, as actually existing (by P17).

Therefore to that extent only, the human mind perceives the human body itself, q.e.d.

P20: *There is also in God an idea*, or *knowledge, of the human mind, which follows in God in the same way and is related to God in the same way as the idea*, or *knowledge, of the human body*.

Dem.: Thought is an attribute of God (by P1), and so (by P3) there must necessarily be in God an idea both of [NS: thought] and of all of its affections, and consequently (by P11), of the human mind also. Next, this idea, *or* knowledge, of the mind does not follow in God insofar as he is infinite, but insofar as he is affected by another idea of a singular thing (by P9). But the order and connection of ideas is the same as the order and connection of causes (by P7). Therefore, this idea, *or* knowledge, of the mind follows in God and is related to God in the same way as the idea, *or* knowledge, of the body, q.e.d.

II/109   P21: *This idea of the mind is united to the mind in the same way as the mind is united to the body*.

Dem.: We have shown that the mind is united to the body from the fact that the body is the object of the mind (see P12 and 13); and so by the same reasoning the idea of the mind must be united with its own object, that is, with the mind itself, in the same way as the mind is united with the body, q.e.d.

Schol.: This proposition is understood far more clearly from what is said in P7S; for there we have shown that the idea of the body and the body, that is (by P13), the mind and the body, are one and the same individual, which is conceived now under the attribute of thought, now under the attribute of extension. So the idea of the mind and the mind itself are one and the same thing, which is conceived under one and the same attribute, namely, thought. The idea of the mind, I say, and the mind itself follow in God from the same power of thinking and by the same necessity. For the idea of the mind, that is, the idea of the idea, is nothing but the form of the idea insofar as this is considered as a mode of thinking without relation to the object. For as soon as someone knows something, he thereby knows that he knows it, and at the same time knows that he knows that he knows, and so on, to infinity. But more on these matters later.

P22: *The human mind perceives not only the affections of the body, but also the ideas of these affections.*

Dem.: The ideas of the ideas of the affections follow in God in the same way and are related to God in the same way as the ideas themselves of the affections (this is demonstrated in the same way as P20). But the ideas of the affections of the body are in the human mind (by P12), that is (by P11C), in God, insofar as he constitutes the essence of the human mind. Therefore, the ideas of these ideas will be in God insofar as he has the knowledge, *or* idea, of the human mind, that is (by P21), they will be in the human mind itself, which for that reason perceives not only the affections of the body, but also their ideas, q.e.d.

II/110

P23: *The mind does not know itself, except insofar as it perceives the ideas of the affections of the body.*

Dem.: The idea, *or* knowledge, of the mind (by P20) follows in God in the same way, and is related to God in the same way as the idea, *or* knowledge, of the body. But since (by P19) the human mind does not know the human body itself, that is (by P11C), since the knowledge of the human body is not related to God insofar as he constitutes the nature of the human mind, the knowledge of the mind is also not related to God insofar as he constitutes the essence of the human mind. And so (again by P11C) to that extent the human mind does not know itself.

Next, the ideas of the affections by which the body is affected involve the nature of the human body itself (by P16), that is (by P13), agree with the nature of the mind. So knowledge of these ideas will necessarily involve knowledge of the mind. But (by P22) knowledge of these ideas is in the human mind itself. Therefore, the human mind, to that extent only, knows itself, q.e.d.

P24: *The human mind does not involve adequate knowledge of the parts composing the human body.*

Dem.: The parts composing the human body pertain to the essence of the body itself only insofar as they communicate their motions to one another in a certain fixed manner (see the definition after L3C), and not insofar as they can be considered as individuals, without relation to the human body. For (by Post. 1) the parts of the human body are highly composite individuals, whose parts (by L4) can be separated from the human body and communicate their motions (see A1″ after L3) to other bodies in another manner, while the human body completely preserves its nature and form. And so the idea, *or* knowledge, of each part will be in God (by P3), insofar as he is considered to be affected by another idea of a singular thing (by P9), a singular thing which is prior, in the order of Nature, to the part itself (by P7). The same must also be said of each

II/111

part of the individual composing the human body. And so, the knowledge of each part composing the human body is in God insofar as he is affected with a great many ideas of things, and not insofar as he has only the idea of the human body, that is (by P13), the idea which constitutes the nature of the human mind. And so, by (P11C) the human mind does not involve adequate knowledge of the parts composing the human body, q.e.d.

P25: *The idea of any affection of the human body does not involve adequate knowledge of an external body.*

Dem.: We have shown (P16) that the idea of an affection of the human body involves the nature of an external body insofar as the external body determines the human body in a certain fixed way. But insofar as the external body is an Individual which is not related to the human body, the idea, *or* knowledge, of it is in God (by P9) insofar as God is considered to be affected with the idea of another thing which (by P7) is prior in nature to the external body itself. So adequate knowledge of the external body is not in God insofar as he has the idea of an affection of the human body, *or* the idea of an affection of the human body does not involve adequate knowledge of the external body, q.e.d.

II/112   P26: *The human mind does not perceive any external body as actually existing, except through the ideas of the affections of its own body.*

Dem.: If the human body is not affected by an external body in any way, then (by P7) the idea of the human body, that is (by P13) the human mind, is also not affected in any way by the idea of the existence of that body, *or* it does not perceive the existence of that external body in any way. But insofar as the human body is affected by an external body in some way, to that extent [the human mind] (by P16 and P16C1) perceives the external body, q.e.d.

Cor.: Insofar as the human mind imagines an external body, it does not have adequate knowledge of it.

Dem.: When the human mind regards external bodies through ideas of the affections of its own body, then we say that it imagines (see P17S); and the mind cannot in any other way (by P26) imagine external bodies as actually existing. And so (by P25), insofar as the mind imagines external bodies, it does not have adequate knowledge of them, q.e.d.

P27: *The idea of any affection of the human body does not involve adequate knowledge of the human body itself.*

Dem.: Any idea of any affection of the human body involves the nature of the human body insofar as the human body itself is considered to be affected with a certain definite mode (see P16). But insofar as the human body is an individual, which can be affected with many other modes, the idea of this [affection] and so on. (See P25D.)   II/113

P28: *The ideas of the affections of the human body, insofar as they are related only to the human mind, are not clear and distinct, but confused.*

Dem.: For the ideas of the affections of the human body involve the nature of external bodies as much as that of the human body (by P16), and must involve the nature not only of the human body [NS: as a whole], but also of its parts; for the affections are modes (by Post. 3) with which the parts of the human body, and consequently the whole body, are affected. But (by P24 and P25) adequate knowledge of external bodies and of the parts composing the human body is in God, not insofar as he is considered to be affected with the human mind, but insofar as he is considered to be affected with other ideas. Therefore, these ideas of the affections, insofar as they are related only to the human mind, are like conclusions without premises, that is (as is known through itself), they are confused ideas, q.e.d.

Schol.: In the same way we can demonstrate that the idea which constitutes the nature of the human mind is not, considered in itself alone, clear and distinct; we can also demonstrate the same of the idea of the human mind and the ideas of the ideas of the human body's affections [NS: viz. that they are confused], insofar as they are referred to the mind alone. Anyone can easily see this.

P29: *The idea of the idea of any affection of the human body does not involve adequate knowledge of the human mind.*

Dem.: For the idea of an affection of the human body (by P27) does not involve adequate knowledge of the body itself, *or* does not express   II/114 its nature adequately, that is (by P13), does not agree adequately with the nature of the mind; and so (by IA6) the idea of this idea does not express the nature of the human mind adequately, *or* does not involve adequate knowledge of it, q.e.d.

Cor.: From this it follows that so long as the human mind perceives things from the common order of Nature, it does not have an adequate, but only a confused and mutilated knowledge of itself, of its own body, and of external bodies. For the mind does not know itself except insofar as it perceives ideas of the affections of the body (by P23). But it does not perceive its own body (by P19) except through the very ideas themselves of the affections [of the body], and it is also through them alone that it perceives external bodies (by P26). And so, insofar as it has these [ideas], then neither of itself (by P29), nor of its own body (by P27), nor of external bodies (by P25) does it have an adequate knowledge, but only (by P28 and P28S) a mutilated and confused knowledge, q.e.d.

Schol.: I say expressly that the mind has, not an adequate, but only a confused [NS: and mutilated] knowledge, of itself, of its own body, and of external bodies, so long as it perceives things from the common order of Nature, that is, so long as it is determined externally, from fortuitous encounters with things, to regard this or that, and not so long as it is determined internally, from the fact that it regards a number of things at once, to understand their agreements, differences, and oppositions. For so often as it is disposed internally, in this or another way, then it regards things clearly and distinctly, as I shall show below.

P30: *We can have only an entirely inadequate knowledge of the duration of our body.*

II/115

Dem.: Our body's duration depends neither on its essence (by A1), nor even on God's absolute nature (by IP21). But (by IP28) it is determined to exist and produce an effect from such [NS: other] causes as are also determined by others to exist and produce an effect in a certain and determinate manner, and these again by others, and so to infinity. Therefore, the duration of our body depends on the common order of Nature and the constitution of things. But adequate knowledge of how things are constituted is in God, insofar as he has the ideas of all of them, and not insofar as he has only the idea of the human body (by P9C). So the knowledge of the duration of our body is quite inadequate in God, insofar as he is considered to constitute only the nature of the human mind, that is (by P11C), this knowledge is quite inadequate in our mind, q.e.d.

P31: *We can have only an entirely inadequate knowledge of the duration of the singular things which are outside us.*

Dem.: For each singular thing, like the human body, must be determined by another singular thing to exist and produce effects in a certain and determinate way, and this again by another, and so to infinity (by IP28). But since (in P30) we have demonstrated from this common property of singular things that we have only a very inadequate knowledge of the duration of our body, we shall have to draw the same conclusion concerning the duration of singular things [outside us], namely, that we can have only a very inadequate knowledge of their duration, q.e.d.

Cor.: From this it follows that all particular things are contingent and corruptible. For we can have no adequate knowledge of their duration (by P31), and that is what we must understand by the contingency of things and the possibility of their corruption (see IP33S1). For (by

II/116   IP29) beyond that there is no contingency.

P32: *All ideas, insofar as they are related to God, are true.*

Dem.: For all ideas which are in God agree entirely with their objects (by P7C), and so (by IA6) they are all true, q.e.d.

P33: *There is nothing positive in ideas on account of which they are called false.*

Dem.: If you deny this, conceive (if possible) a positive mode of thinking which constitutes the form of error, *or* falsity. This mode of thinking cannot be in God (by P32). But it also can neither be nor be conceived outside God (by IP15). And so there can be nothing positive in ideas on account of which they are called false, q.e.d.

P34: *Every idea which in us is absolute,* or *adequate and perfect, is true.*

Dem.: When we say that there is in us an adequate and perfect idea, we are saying nothing but that (by P11C) there is an adequate and perfect idea in God insofar as he constitutes the essence of our mind, and consequently (by P32) we are saying nothing but that such an idea is true, q.e.d.

P35: *Falsity consists in the privation of knowledge which inadequate,* or *mutilated and confused, ideas involve.*

Dem.: There is nothing positive in ideas which constitutes the form II/117
of falsity (by P33); but falsity cannot consist in an absolute privation (for it is minds, not bodies, which are said to err, or be deceived), nor also in absolute ignorance. For to be ignorant and to err are different. So it consists in the privation of knowledge which inadequate knowledge of things, *or* inadequate and confused ideas, involve, q.e.d.

Schol.: In P17S I explained how error consists in the privation of knowledge. But to explain the matter more fully, I shall give [NS: one or two examples]: men are deceived in that they think themselves free [NS: i.e., they think that, of their own free will, they can either do a thing or forbear doing it], an opinion which consists only in this, that they are conscious of their actions and ignorant of the causes by which they are determined. This, then, is their idea of freedom—that they do not know any cause of their actions. They say, of course, that human actions depend on the will, but these are only words for which they have no idea. For all are ignorant of what the will is, and how it moves the body; those who boast of something else, who feign seats and dwelling places of the soul, usually provoke either ridicule or disgust.

Similarly, when we look at the sun, we imagine it as about two hundred feet away from us, an error which does not consist simply in this imagining, but in the fact that while we imagine it in this way, we are ignorant of its true distance and of the cause of this imagining. For even if we later come to know that it is more than six hundred diameters of the earth away from us, we nevertheless imagine it as near. For we imagine the sun so near not because we do not know its true distance, but because an affection of our body involves the essence of the sun insofar as our body is affected by the sun.

P36: *Inadequate and confused ideas follow with the same necessity as adequate, or clear and distinct ideas.*

II/118   Dem.: All ideas are in God (by IP15); and, insofar as they are related to God, are true (by P32), and (by P7C) adequate. And so there are no inadequate or confused ideas except insofar as they are related to the singular mind of someone (see P24 and P28). And so all ideas—both the adequate and the inadequate—follow with the same necessity (by P6C), q.e.d.

P37: *What is common to all things* (on this see L2, above) *and is equally in the part and in the whole, does not constitute the essence of any singular thing.*

Dem.: If you deny this, conceive (if possible) that it does constitute the essence of some singular thing, say the essence of B. Then (by D2) it can neither be nor be conceived without B. But this is contrary to the hypothesis. Therefore, it does not pertain to the essence of B, nor does it constitute the essence of any other singular thing, q.e.d.

P38: *Those things which are common to all, and which are equally in the part and in the whole, can only be conceived adequately.*

Dem.: Let A be something which is common to all bodies, and which is equally in the part of each body and in the whole. I say that A can only be conceived adequately. For its idea (by P7C) will necessarily be adequate in God, both insofar as he has the idea of the human body and insofar as he has ideas of its affections, which (by P16, P25, and P27) involve in part both the nature of the human body and that of external bodies. That is (by P12 and P13), this idea will necessarily be adequate II/119   in God insofar as he constitutes the human mind, *or* insofar as he has ideas that are in the human mind. The mind, therefore (by P11C), necessarily perceives A adequately, and does so both insofar as it perceives itself and insofar as it perceives its own or any external body. Nor can A be conceived in another way, q.e.d.

Cor.: From this it follows that there are certain ideas, *or* notions, common to all men. For (by L2) all bodies agree in certain things, which (by P38) must be perceived adequately, *or* clearly and distinctly, by all.

P39: *If something is common to, and peculiar to, the human body and certain external bodies by which the human body is usually affected, and is equally in the part and in the whole of each of them, its idea will also be adequate in the mind.*

Dem.: Let A be that which is common to, and peculiar to, the human body and certain external bodies, which is equally in the human body and in the same external bodies, and finally, which is equally in the part of each external body and in the whole. There will be an adequate idea of A in God (by P7C), both insofar as he has the idea of the human body, and insofar as he has ideas of the posited external bodies. Let it be posited now that the human body is affected by an external body through what it has in common with it, that is, by A; the idea of this affection will involve property A (by P16), and so (by P7C) the idea of this affection, insofar as it involves property A, will be adequate in God insofar as he is affected with the idea of the human body, that is (by P13), insofar as he constitutes the nature of the human mind. And so (by P11C), this idea is also adequate in the human mind, q.e.d.

Cor.: From this it follows that the mind is the more capable of perceiving many things adequately as its body has many things in common with other bodies.

II/120

P40: *Whatever ideas follow in the mind from ideas which are adequate in the mind are also adequate.*

Dem.: This is evident. For when we say that an idea in the human mind follows from ideas which are adequate in it, we are saying nothing but that (by P11C) in the divine intellect there is an idea of which God is the cause, not insofar as he is infinite, nor insofar as he is affected with the ideas of a great many singular things, but insofar as he constitutes only the essence of the human mind [NS: and therefore, it must be adequate].

Schol. 1: With this I have explained the cause of those notions which are called *common*, and which are the foundations of our reasoning.

But some axioms, *or* notions, result from other causes which it would be helpful to explain by this method of ours. For from these [explanations] it would be established which notions are more useful than the others, and which are of hardly any use; and then, which are common, which are clear and distinct only to those who have no prejudices, and finally, which are ill-founded. Moreover, we would establish what is the origin of those notions they call *Second*, and consequently of the axioms founded on them, and other things I have thought about, from time to time, concerning these matters. But since I have set these aside for another treatise, and do not wish to give rise to disgust by too long a discussion, I have decided to pass over them here.

But not to omit anything it is necessary to know, I shall briefly add something about the causes from which the terms called *Transcendental* have had their origin—I mean terms like Being, Thing, and Something. These terms arise from the fact that the human body, being limited, is capable of forming distinctly only a certain number of images at the same time (I have explained what an image is in P17S). If that number is exceeded, the images will begin to be confused, and if the number of images the body is capable of forming distinctly in itself at once is greatly exceeded, they will all be completely confused with one another.

Since this is so, it is evident from P17C and P18, that the human mind will be able to imagine distinctly, at the same time, as many bodies as there can be images formed at the same time in its body. But when the images in the body are completely confused, the mind also will imagine all the bodies confusedly, without any distinction, and comprehend them as if under one attribute, namely, under the attribute of Being, Thing, and so forth. This can also be deduced from the fact that images are not always equally vigorous and from other causes like these, which it is not necessary to explain here. For our purpose it is sufficient to consider only one. For they all reduce to this: these terms signify ideas that are confused in the highest degree.

Those notions they call *Universal*, like Man, Horse, Dog, and the like, have arisen from similar causes, namely, because so many images (e.g., of men) are formed at one time in the human body that they surpass the power of imagining—not entirely, of course, but still to the point where the mind can imagine neither slight differences of the singular [men] (such as the color and size of each one, etc.) nor their determinate number, and imagines distinctly only what they all agree in, insofar as they affect the body. For the body has been affected most [NS: forcefully] by [what is common], since each singular has affected it [by this property]. And [NS: the mind] expresses this by the word *man*, and predicates it of infinitely many singulars. For as we have said, it cannot imagine a determinate number of singulars.

But it should be noted that these notions are not formed by all [NS: men] in the same way, but vary from one to another, in accordance with what the body has more often been affected by, and what the mind imagines or recollects more easily. For example, those who have more often regarded men's stature with wonder will understand by the word *man* an animal of erect stature. But those who have been accustomed to consider something else, will form another common image of men—for example, that man is an animal capable of laughter, or a featherless biped, or a rational animal.

And similarly concerning the others—each will form universal images of things according to the disposition of his body. Hence it is not surprising that so many controversies have arisen among the philosophers, who have wished to explain natural things by mere images of things.

Schol. 2: From what has been said above, it is clear that we perceive many things and form universal notions: II/122

I. from singular things which have been represented to us through the senses in a way which is mutilated, confused, and without order for the intellect (see P29C); for that reason I have been accustomed to call such perceptions knowledge from random experience;

II. from signs, for example, from the fact that, having heard or read certain words, we recollect things, and form certain ideas of them, like those through which we imagine the things (P18S); these two ways of regarding things I shall henceforth call knowledge of the first kind, opinion or imagination;

III. finally, from the fact that we have common notions and adequate ideas of the properties of things (see P38C, P39, P39C, and P40). This I shall call reason and the second kind of knowledge.

[IV.] In addition to these two kinds of knowledge, there is (as I shall show in what follows) another, third kind, which we shall call intuitive knowledge. And this kind of knowing proceeds from an adequate idea of the formal essence of certain attributes of God to the adequate knowledge of the [NS: formal] essence of things.

I shall explain all these with one example. Suppose there are three numbers, and the problem is to find a fourth which is to the third as the second is to the first. Merchants do not hesitate to multiply the second by the third, and divide the product by the first, because they have not yet forgotten what they heard from their teacher without any demonstration, or because they have often found this in the simplest numbers, or from the force of the demonstration of P19 in Book VII of Euclid, namely, from the common property of proportionals. But in the simplest numbers none of this is necessary. Given the numbers 1, 2, and 3, no one fails to see that the fourth proportional number is 6—and we see this much more clearly because we infer the fourth number from the ratio which, in one glance, we see the first number to have to the second.

P41: *Knowledge of the first kind is the only cause of falsity, whereas knowledge of the second and of the third kind is necessarily true.*

Dem.: We have said in the preceding scholium that to knowledge of the first kind pertain all those ideas which are inadequate and confused; and so (by P35) this knowledge is the only cause of falsity. Next, we have said that to knowledge of the second and third kinds pertain those which are adequate; and so (by P34) this knowledge is necessarily true. II/123

P42: *Knowledge of the second and third kinds, and not of the first kind, teaches us to distinguish the true from the false.*

Dem.: This proposition is evident through itself. For he who knows how to distinguish between the true and the false must have an adequate idea of the true and of the false, that is (P40S2), must know the true and the false by the second or third kind of knowledge.

P43: *He who has a true idea at the same time knows that he has a true idea, and cannot doubt the truth of the thing.*

Dem.: An idea true in us is that which is adequate in God insofar as he is explained through the nature of the human mind (by P11C). Let us posit, therefore, that there is in God, insofar as he is explained through the nature of the human mind, an adequate idea, A. Of this idea there must necessarily also be in God an idea which is related to God in the same way as idea A (by P20, whose demonstration is universal [NS: and can be applied to all ideas]). But idea A is supposed to be related to God insofar as he is explained through the nature of the human mind; therefore the idea of idea A must also be related to God in the same way, that is (by the same P11C), this adequate idea of idea A will be in the mind itself which has the adequate idea A. And so he who has an adequate idea, *or* (by P34) who knows a thing truly, must at the same time have an adequate idea, *or* true knowledge, of his own knowledge. That is (as is manifest through itself), he must at the same time be certain, q.e.d.

II/124

Schol.: In P21S I have explained what an idea of an idea is. But it should be noted that the preceding proposition is sufficiently manifest through itself. For no one who has a true idea is unaware that a true idea involves the highest certainty. For to have a true idea means nothing other than knowing a thing perfectly, *or* in the best way. And of course no one can doubt this unless he thinks that an idea is something mute, like a picture on a tablet, and not a mode of thinking, namely, the very [act of] understanding. And I ask, who can know that he understands some thing unless he first understands it? That is, who can know that he is certain about some thing unless he is first certain about it? What can there be which is clearer and more certain than a true idea, to serve as a standard of truth? As the light makes both itself and the darkness plain, so truth is the standard both of itself and of the false.

By this I think we have replied to these questions: if a true idea is distinguished from a false one, [NS: not insofar as it is said to be a mode of thinking, but] only insofar as it is said to agree with its object, then a true idea has no more reality or perfection than a false one (since they are distinguished only through the extrinsic denomination [NS: and not through the intrinsic denomination])—and so, does the man who has true ideas [NS: have any more reality or perfection] than he who has only false ideas? Again, why do men have false ideas? And finally, how can someone know certainly that he has ideas which agree with their objects?

To these questions, I say, I think I have already replied. For as far as the difference between a true and a false idea is concerned, it is established from P35 that the true is related to the false as being is to nonbeing. And the causes of falsity I have shown most clearly from P19 to P35S. From this it is also clear what is the difference between the man who has true ideas and the man who has only false ideas. Finally, as to the last, namely, how a man can know that he has an idea which agrees with its object? I have just shown, more than sufficiently, that this arises solely from his having an idea which does agree with its object—or that truth is its own standard. Add to this that our mind, insofar as it perceives things truly, is part of the infinite intellect of God (by P11C); hence, it is as necessary that the mind's clear and distinct ideas are true as that God's ideas are.

II/125

P44: *It is of the nature of reason to regard things as necessary, not as contingent.*

Dem.: It is of the nature of reason to perceive things truly (by P41), namely (by IA6), as they are in themselves, that is (by IP29), not as contingent but as necessary, q.e.d.

Cor. 1: From this it follows that it depends only on the imagination that we regard things as contingent, both in respect to the past and in respect to the future.

Schol.: I shall explain briefly how this happens. We have shown above (by P17 and P17C) that even though things do not exist, the mind still imagines them always as present to itself, unless causes occur which exclude their present existence. Next, we have shown (P18) that if the human body has once been affected by two external bodies at the same time, then afterwards, when the mind imagines one of them, it will immediately recollect the other also, that is, it will regard both as present to itself unless causes occur which exclude their present existence. Moreover, no one doubts but what we also imagine time, namely, from the fact that we imagine some bodies to move more slowly than others, or more quickly, or with the same speed.

Let us suppose, then, a child, who saw Peter for the first time yesterday, in the morning, but saw Paul at noon, and Simon in the evening, and today again saw Peter in the morning. It is clear from P18 that as soon as he sees the morning light, he will immediately imagine the sun taking the same course through the sky as he saw on the preceding day, *or* he will imagine the whole day, and Peter together with the morning, Paul with noon, and Simon with the evening. That is, he will imagine the existence of Paul and of Simon with a relation to future time. On the other hand, if he sees Simon in the evening, he will relate Paul and Peter to the time past, by imagining them together with past time. And he will do this more uniformly, the more often he has seen them in this same order.

II/126

But if it should happen at some time that on some other evening he sees James instead of Simon, then on the following morning he will imagine now Simon, now James, together with the evening time, but not both at once. For it is supposed that he has seen one or the other of them in the evening, but not both at once. His imagination, therefore, will vacillate and he will imagine now this one, now that one, with the future evening time, that is, he will regard neither of them as certainly future, but both of them as contingently future.

And this vacillation of the imagination will be the same if the imagination is of things we regard in the same way with relation to past time or to present time. Consequently we shall imagine things as contingent in relation to present time as well as to past and future time.

Cor 2: It is of the nature of reason to perceive things under a certain species of eternity.

Dem.: It is of the nature of reason to regard things as necessary and not as contingent (by P44). And it perceives this necessity of things truly (by P41), that is (by IA6), as it is in itself. But (by IP16) this necessity of things is the very necessity of God's eternal nature. Therefore, it is of the nature of reason to regard things under this species of eternity.

Add to this that the foundations of reason are notions (by P38) which explain those things which are common to all, and which (by P37) do not explain the essence of any singular thing. On that account, they must be conceived without any relation to time, but under a certain species of eternity, q.e.d.

II/127 P45: *Each idea of each body, or of each singular thing which actually exists, necessarily involves an eternal and infinite essence of God.*

Dem.: The idea of a singular thing which actually exists necessarily involves both the essence of the thing and its existence (by P8C). But singular things (by IP15) cannot be conceived without God—on the contrary, because (by P6) they have God for a cause insofar as he is considered under the attribute of which the things are modes, their ideas must involve the concept of their attribute (by IA4), that is (by ID6), must involve an eternal and infinite essence of God, q.e.d.

144

Schol.: By existence here I do not understand duration, that is, existence insofar as it is conceived abstractly, and as a certain species of quantity. For I am speaking of the very nature of existence, which is attributed to singular things because infinitely many things follow from the eternal necessity of God's nature in infinitely many modes (see IP16). I am speaking, I say, of the very existence of singular things insofar as they are in God. For even if each one is determined by another singular thing to exist in a certain way, still the force by which each one perseveres in existing follows from the eternal necessity of God's nature. Concerning this, see IP24C.

P46: *The knowledge of God's eternal and infinite essence which each idea involves is adequate and perfect.*

Dem.: The demonstration of the preceding proposition is universal, and whether the thing is considered as a part or as a whole, its idea, whether of the whole or of a part (by P45), will involve God's eternal and infinite essence. So what gives knowledge of an eternal and infinite essence of God is common to all, and is equally in the part and in the whole. And so (by P38) this knowledge will be adequate, q.e.d. II/128

P47: *The human mind has an adequate knowledge of God's eternal and infinite essence.*

Dem.: The human mind has ideas (by P22) from which it perceives (by P23) itself, (by P19) its own body, and (by P16C1 and P17) external bodies as actually existing. And so (by P45 and P46) it has an adequate knowledge of God's eternal and infinite essence, q.e.d.

Schol.: From this we see that God's infinite essence and his eternity are known to all. And since all things are in God and are conceived through God, it follows that we can deduce from this knowledge a great many things which we know adequately, and so can form that third kind of knowledge of which we spoke in P40S2 and of whose excellence and utility we shall speak in Part V.

But that men do not have so clear a knowledge of God as they do of the common notions comes from the fact that they cannot imagine God, as they can bodies, and that they have joined the name *God* to the images of things which they are used to seeing. Men can hardly avoid this, because they are continually affected by external bodies.

And indeed, most errors consist only in our not rightly applying names to things. For when someone says that the lines which are drawn from the center of a circle to its circumference are unequal, he surely understands (then at least) by a circle something different from what mathematicians understand. Similarly, when men err in calculating, they have certain numbers in their mind and different ones on the paper. So if you consider what they have in mind, they really do not err, though they seem to err because we think they have in their mind the numbers which are on the paper. If this were not so, we would not believe that they were erring, just as I did not believe that he was erring whom I recently heard cry out that his courtyard had flown into his neighbor's hen [NS: although his words were absurd], because what he had in mind seemed sufficiently clear to me [viz. that his hen had flown into his neighbor's courtyard].

II/129

And most controversies have arisen from this, that men do not rightly explain their own mind, or interpret the mind of the other man badly. For really, when they contradict one another most vehemently, they either have the same thoughts, or they are thinking of different things, so that what they think are errors and absurdities in the other are not.

P48: *In the mind there is no absolute, or free, will, but the mind is determined to will this or that by a cause which is also determined by another, and this again by another, and so to infinity.*

Dem.: The mind is a certain and determinate mode of thinking (by P11), and so (by IP17C2) cannot be a free cause of its own actions, *or* cannot have an absolute faculty of willing and not willing. Rather, it must be determined to willing this or that (by IP28) by a cause which is also determined by another, and this cause again by another, and so on, q.e.d.

Schol.: In this same way it is also demonstrated that there is in the mind no absolute faculty of understanding, desiring, loving, and the like. From this it follows that these and similar faculties are either complete fictions or nothing but metaphysical beings, *or* universals, which we are used to forming from particulars. So intellect and will are to this or that idea, or to this or that volition as 'stone-ness' is to this or that stone, or man to Peter or Paul.

We have explained the cause of men's thinking themselves free in the Appendix of Part I. But before I proceed further, it should be noted here that by will I understand a faculty of affirming and denying, and not desire. I say that I understand the faculty by which the mind affirms or denies something true or something false, and not the desire by which the mind wants a thing or avoids it.

II/130

But after we have demonstrated that these faculties are universal notions which are not distinguished from the singulars from which we form them, we must now investigate whether the volitions themselves are anything beyond the very ideas of things. We must investigate, I say, whether there is any other affirmation or negation in the mind except that which the idea involves, insofar as it is an idea—on this see the following proposition and also D3—so that our thought does not fall into pictures. For by ideas I understand, not the images which are formed at the back of the eye (and, if you like, in the middle of the brain), but concepts of thought [NS: or the objective being of a thing insofar as it consists only in thought].

P49: *In the mind there is no volition, or affirmation and negation, except that which the idea involves insofar as it is an idea.*

Dem.: In the mind (by P48) there is no absolute faculty of willing and not willing, but only singular volitions, namely, this and that affirmation, and this and that negation. Let us conceive, therefore, some singular volition, say a mode of thinking by which the mind affirms that the three angles of a triangle are equal to two right angles.

This affirmation involves the concept, *or* idea, of the triangle, that is, it cannot be conceived without the idea of the triangle. For to say that A must involve the concept of B is the same as to say that A cannot be conceived without B. Further, this affirmation (by A3) also cannot be without the idea of the triangle. Therefore, this affirmation can neither be nor be conceived without the idea of the triangle.

Next, this idea of the triangle must involve this same affirmation, namely, that its three angles equal two right angles. So conversely, this idea of the triangle also can neither be nor be conceived without this affirmation.

So (by D2) this affirmation pertains to the essence of the idea of the triangle and is nothing beyond it. And what we have said concerning this volition (since we have selected it at random), must also be said concerning any volition, namely, that it is nothing apart from the idea, q.e.d.

Cor.: The will and the intellect are one and the same. II/131

Dem.: The will and the intellect are nothing apart from the singular volitions and ideas themselves (by P48 and P48S). But the singular volitions and ideas are one and the same (by P49). Therefore the will and the intellect are one and the same, q.e.d.

Schol.: [I.] By this we have removed what is commonly maintained to be the cause of error. Moreover, we have shown above that falsity consists only in the privation which mutilated and confused ideas involve. So a false idea, insofar as it is false, does not involve certainty. When we say that a man rests in false ideas, and does not doubt them, we do not, on that account, say that he is certain, but only that he does not doubt, or that he rests in false ideas because there are no causes to bring it about that his imagination wavers [NS: or to cause him to doubt them]. On this, see P44S.

Therefore, however stubbornly a man may cling to something false [NS: so that we cannot in any way make him doubt it], we shall still never say that he is certain of it. For by certainty we understand something positive (see P43 and P43S), not the privation of doubt. But by the privation of certainty, we understand falsity.

However, to explain the preceding proposition more fully, there remain certain things I must warn you of. And then I must reply to the objections which can be made against this doctrine of ours. And finally, to remove every uneasiness, I thought it worthwhile to indicate some of the advantages of this doctrine. Some, I say—for the most important ones will be better understood from what we shall say in Part V.

[II.] I begin, therefore, by warning my readers, first, to distinguish accurately between an idea, *or* concept, of the mind, and the images of things which we imagine. And then it is necessary to distinguish between ideas and the words by which we signify things. For because many people either completely confuse these three—ideas, images, and words—or do not distinguish them accurately enough, or carefully enough, they have been completely ignorant of this doctrine concerning the will. But it is quite necessary to know it, both for the sake of speculation and in order to arrange one's life wisely.

II/132

Indeed, those who think that ideas consist in images which are formed in us from encounters with [NS: external] bodies, are convinced that those ideas of things [NS: which can make no trace in our brains, or] of which we can form no similar image [NS: in our brain] are not ideas, but only fictions which we feign from a free choice of the will. They look on ideas, therefore, as mute pictures on a panel, and preoccupied with this prejudice, do not see that an idea, insofar as it is an idea, involves an affirmation or negation.

And then, those who confuse words with the idea, or with the very affirmation which the idea involves, think that they can will something contrary to what they are aware of, when they only affirm or deny with words something contrary to what they are aware of. But these prejudices can easily be put aside by anyone who attends to the nature of thought, which does not at all involve the concept of extension. He will then understand clearly that an idea (since it is a mode of thinking) consists neither in the image of anything, nor in words. For the essence of words and of images is constituted only by corporeal motions, which do not at all involve the concept of thought.

It should suffice to have issued these few words of warning on this matter, so I pass to the objections mentioned above.

[III.A.(i)] The first of these is that they think it clear that the will extends more widely than the intellect, and so is different from the intellect. The reason why they think the will extends more widely than the intellect is that they say they know by experience that they do not require a greater faculty of assenting, *or* affirming, and denying, than we already have, in order to assent to infinitely many other things which we do not perceive—but they do require a greater faculty of understanding. The will, therefore, is distinguished from the intellect because the intellect is finite and the will is infinite.

[III.A.(ii)] Second, it can be objected to us that experience seems to teach nothing more clearly than that we can suspend our judgment so as not to assent to things we perceive. This also seems to be confirmed from the fact that no one is said to be deceived insofar as he perceives something, but only insofar as he assents or dissents. For example, someone who feigns a winged horse does not on that account grant that there is a winged horse, that is, he is not on that account deceived unless at the same time he grants that there is a winged horse. Therefore, experience seems to teach nothing more clearly than that the will, *or* faculty of assenting, is free, and different from the faculty of understanding.

II/133

[III.A.(iii)] Third, it can be objected that one affirmation does not seem to contain more reality than another, that is, we do not seem to require a greater power to affirm that what is true, is true, than to affirm that something false is true. But [NS: with ideas it is different, for] we perceive that one idea has more reality, *or* perfection, than another. As some objects are more excellent than others, so also some ideas of objects are more perfect than others. This also seems to establish a difference between the will and the intellect.

[III.A.(iv)] Fourth, it can be objected that if man does not act from freedom of the will, what will happen if he is in a state of equilibrium, like Buridan's ass? Will he perish of hunger and of thirst? If I concede that he will, I would seem to conceive an ass, or a statue of a man, not a man. But if I deny that he will, then he will determine himself, and consequently have the faculty of going where he wills and doing what he wills.

Perhaps other things in addition to these can be objected. But because I am not bound to force on you what anyone can dream, I shall only take the trouble to reply to these objections—and that as briefly as I can.

[III.B.(i)] To the first I say that I grant that the will extends more widely than the intellect, if by intellect they understand only clear and distinct ideas. But I deny that the will extends more widely than perceptions, *or* the faculty of conceiving. And indeed, I do not see why the faculty of willing should be called infinite, when the faculty of sensing is not. For just as we can affirm infinitely many things by the same faculty of willing (but one after another, for we cannot affirm infinitely many things at once), so also we can sense, *or* perceive, infinitely many bodies by the same faculty of sensing (viz. one after another [NS: and not at once]).

If they say that there are infinitely many things which we cannot perceive, I reply that we cannot reach them by any thought, and consequently, not by any faculty of willing. But, they say, if God willed to bring it about that we should perceive them also, he would have to give us a greater faculty of perceiving, but not a greater faculty of willing than he has given us. This is the same as if they said that, if God should will to bring it about that we understood infinitely many other beings, it would indeed be necessary for him to give us a greater intellect, but not a more universal idea of being, in order for us to embrace the same infinity of beings. For we have shown that the will is a universal being, *or* idea, by which we explain all the singular volitions, that is, it is what is common to them all.

II/134

Therefore, since they believe that this common *or* universal idea of all volitions is a faculty, it is not at all surprising if they say that this faculty extends beyond the limits of the intellect to infinity. For the universal is said equally of one, a great many, or infinitely many individuals.

[III.B(ii)] To the second objection I reply by denying that we have a free power of suspending judgment. For when we say that someone suspends judgment, we are saying nothing but that he sees that he does not perceive the thing adequately. Suspension of judgment, therefore, is really a perception, not [an act of] free will.

To understand this clearly, let us conceive a child imagining a winged horse, and not perceiving anything else. Since this imagination involves the existence of the horse (by P17C), and the child does not perceive anything else which excludes the existence of the horse, he will necessarily regard the horse as present. Nor will he be able to doubt its existence, though he will not be certain of it.

We find this daily in our dreams, and I do not believe there is anyone who thinks that while he is dreaming he has a free power of suspending judgment concerning the things he dreams, and of bringing it about that he does not dream the things he dreams he sees. Nevertheless, it happens that even in dreams we suspend judgment, namely, when we dream that we dream.

Next, I grant that no one is deceived insofar as he perceives, that is, I grant that the imaginations of the mind, considered in themselves, involve no error. But I deny that a man affirms nothing insofar as he perceives. For what is perceiving a winged horse other than affirming wings of the horse? For if the mind perceived nothing else except the winged horse, it would regard it as present to itself, and would not have any cause of doubting its existence, or any faculty of dissenting, unless either the imagination of the winged horse were joined to an idea which excluded the existence of the same horse, or the mind perceived that its idea of a winged horse was inadequate. And then either it will necessarily deny the horse's existence, or it will necessarily doubt it.

[III.B.(iii)] As for the third objection, I think what has been said will be an answer to it too: namely, that the will is something universal, which is predicated of all ideas, and which signifies only what is common to all ideas, namely, the affirmation, whose adequate essence, therefore, insofar as it is thus conceived abstractly, must be in each idea and in this way only must be the same in all, but not insofar as it is considered to constitute the idea's essence; for in that regard the singular affirmations differ from one another as much as the ideas themselves do. For example, the affirmation which the idea of a circle involves differs from that which the idea of a triangle involves as much as the idea of the circle differs from the idea of the triangle. II/135

Next, I deny absolutely that we require an equal power of thinking, to affirm that what is true is true, as to affirm that what is false is true. For if you consider the mind, they are related to one another as being to not-being. For there is nothing positive in ideas which constitutes the form of falsity (see P35, P35S, and P47S). So the thing to note here, above all, is how easily we are deceived when we confuse universals with singulars, and beings of reason and abstractions with real beings.

[III.B. (iv)] Finally, as far as the fourth objection is concerned, I say that I grant entirely that a man placed in such an equilibrium (viz. who perceives nothing but thirst and hunger, and such food and drink as are equally distant from him) will perish of hunger and thirst. If they ask me whether such a man should not be thought an ass, rather than a man, I say that I do not know—just as I also do not know how highly we should esteem one who hangs himself, or children, fools, and madmen, and so on.

[IV.] It remains now to indicate how much knowledge of this doctrine is to our advantage in life. We shall see this easily from the following considerations:

[A.] Insofar as it teaches that we act only from God's command, that we share in the divine nature, and that we do this the more, the more perfect our actions are, and the more and more we understand God. This doctrine, then, in addition to giving us complete peace of mind, also teaches us wherein our greatest happiness, *or* blessedness, consists: namely, in the knowledge of God alone, by which we are led to do only II/136 those things which love and morality advise. From this we clearly understand how far they stray from the true valuation of virtue, who expect to be honored by God with the greatest rewards for their virtue and best actions, as for the greatest bondage—as if virtue itself, and the service of God, were not happiness itself, and the greatest freedom.

[B.] Insofar as it teaches us how we must bear ourselves concerning matters of fortune, *or* things which are not in our power, that is, concerning things which do not follow from our nature—that we must expect and bear calmly both good fortune and bad. For all things follow from God's eternal decree with the same necessity as from the essence of a triangle it follows that its three angles are equal to two right angles.

[C.] This doctrine contributes to social life, insofar as it teaches us to hate no one, to disesteem no one, to mock no one, to be angry at no one, to envy no one; and also insofar as it teaches that each of us should be content with his own things, and should be helpful to his neighbor, not from unmanly compassion, partiality, or superstition, but from the guidance of reason, as the time and occasion demand. I shall show this in the Fourth Part.

[D.] Finally, this doctrine also contributes, to no small extent, to the common society insofar as it teaches how citizens are to be governed and led, not so that they may be slaves, but that they may do freely the things which are best.

And with this I have finished what I had decided to treat in this scholium, and put an end to this our Second Part. In it I think that I have explained the nature and properties of the human mind in sufficient detail, and as clearly as the difficulty of the subject allows, and that I have set out doctrines from which we can infer many excellent things, which are highly useful and necessary to know, as will be established partly in what follows.

THIRD PART OF THE ETHICS
OF THE ORIGIN AND NATURE OF THE AFFECTS

PREFACE

Most of those who have written about the affects, and men's way of living, seem to treat, not of natural things, which follow the common laws of Nature, but of things which are outside Nature. Indeed they seem to conceive man in Nature as a dominion within a dominion. For they believe that man disturbs, rather than follows, the order of Nature, that he has absolute power over his actions, and that he is determined only by himself. And they attribute the cause of human impotence and inconstancy, not to the common power of Nature, but to I know not what vice of human nature, which they therefore bewail, or laugh at, or disdain, or (as usually happens) curse. And he who knows how to censure more eloquently and cunningly the weakness of the human mind is held to be godly.

It is true that there have been some very distinguished men (to whose work and diligence we confess that we owe much), who have written many admirable things about the right way of living, and given men advice full of prudence. But no one, to my knowledge, has determined the nature and powers of the affects, nor what, on the other hand, the mind can do to moderate them. I know, of course, that the celebrated Descartes, although he too believed that the mind has absolute power over its own actions, nevertheless sought to explain   II/138 human affects through their first causes, and at the same time to show the way by which the mind can have absolute dominion over its affects. But in my opinion, he showed nothing but the cleverness of his understanding, as I shall show in the proper place.

For now I wish to return to those who prefer to curse or laugh at the affects and actions of men, rather than understand them. To them it will doubtless seem strange that I should undertake to treat men's vices and absurdities in the geometric style, and that I should wish to demonstrate by certain reasoning things which are contrary to reason, and which they proclaim to be empty, absurd, and horrible.

But my reason is this: nothing happens in Nature which can be attributed to any defect in it, for Nature is always the same, and its virtue and power of acting are everywhere one and the same, that is, the laws and rules of Nature, according to which all things happen, and change from one form to another, are always and everywhere the same. So the way of understanding the nature of anything, of whatever kind, must also be the same, namely, through the universal laws and rules of Nature.

The affects, therefore, of hate, anger, envy, and the like, considered in themselves, follow with the same necessity and force of Nature as the other singular things. And therefore they acknowledge certain causes, through which they are understood, and have certain properties, as worthy of our knowledge as the properties of any other thing, by the mere contemplation of which we are pleased. Therefore, I shall treat the nature and powers of the affects, and the power of the mind over them, by the same method by which, in the preceding parts, I treated God and the mind, and I shall consider human actions and appetites just as if it were a question of lines, planes, and bodies.

DEFINITIONS   II/139

D1: I call that cause adequate whose effect can be clearly and distinctly perceived through it. But I call it partial, *or* inadequate, if its effect cannot be understood through it alone.

D2: I say that we act when something happens, in us or outside us, of which we are the adequate cause, that is (by D1), when something in us or outside us follows from our nature, which can be clearly and distinctly understood through it alone. On the other hand, I say that we are acted on when something happens in us, or something follows from our nature, of which we are only a partial cause.

D3: By affect I understand affections of the body by which the body's power of acting is increased or diminished, aided or restrained, and at the same time, the ideas of these affections.

Therefore, if we can be the adequate cause of any of these affections, I understand by the affect an action; otherwise, a passion.

POSTULATES

Post. 1: The human body can be affected in many ways in which its power of acting is increased or diminished, and also in others which render its power of acting neither greater nor less.

This postulate, or axiom, rests on Post. 1, L5, and L7 (after IIP13).

II/140   Post. 2: The human body can undergo many changes, and nevertheless retain impressions, *or* traces, of the objects (on this see IIPost. 5), and consequently, the same images of things. (For the definition of images, see IIP17S.)

P1: *Our mind does certain things [acts] and undergoes other things, namely, insofar as it has adequate ideas, it necessarily does certain things, and insofar as it has inadequate ideas, it necessarily undergoes other things.*

Dem.: In each human mind some ideas are adequate, but others are mutilated and confused (by IIP40S). But ideas which are adequate in someone's mind are adequate in God insofar as he constitutes the essence of that mind [only] (by IIP11C). And those which are inadequate in the mind are also adequate in God (by the same Cor.), not insofar as he contains only the essence of that mind, but insofar as he also contains in himself, at the same time, the minds of other things. Next, from any given idea some effect must necessarily follow (IP36), of which effect God is the adequate cause (see D1), not insofar as he is infinite, but insofar as he is considered to be affected by that given idea (see IIP9). But if God, insofar as he is affected by an idea which is adequate in someone's mind, is the cause of an effect, that same mind is the effect's adequate cause (by IIP11C). Therefore, our mind (by D2), insofar as it has adequate ideas, necessarily does certain things [acts]. This was the first thing to be proven.

Next, if something necessarily follows from an idea which is adequate in God, not insofar as he has in himself the mind of one man only, but insofar as he has in himself the minds of other things together with the mind of that man, that man's mind (by the same IIP11C) is not its adequate cause, but its partial cause. Hence (by D2), insofar as the mind has inadequate ideas, it necessarily undergoes certain things. This was the second point. Therefore, our mind, and so on, q.e.d.

Cor.: From this it follows that the mind is more liable to passions the more it has inadequate ideas, and conversely, is more active the more it has adequate ideas. II/141

P2: *The body cannot determine the mind to thinking, and the mind cannot determine the body to motion, to rest, or to anything else (if there is anything else).*

Dem.: All modes of thinking have God for a cause, insofar as he is a thinking thing, and not insofar as he is explained by another attribute (by IIP6). So what determines the mind to thinking is a mode of thinking and not of extension, that is (by IID1), it is not the body. This was the first point.

Next, the motion and rest of the body must arise from another body, which has also been determined to motion or rest by another; and absolutely, whatever arises in the body must have arisen from God insofar as he is considered to be affected by some mode of extension, and not insofar as he is considered to be affected by some mode of thinking (also by IIP6), that is, it cannot arise from the mind, which (by IIP11) is a mode of thinking. This was the second point. Therefore, the body cannot determine the mind, and so on, q.e.d.

Schol.: These things are more clearly understood from what is said in IIP7S, namely, that the mind and the body are one and the same thing, which is conceived now under the attribute of thought, now under the attribute of extension. The result is that the order, *or* connection, of things is one, whether Nature is conceived under this attribute or that; hence the order of actions and passions of our body is, by nature, at one with the order of actions and passions of the mind. This is also evident from the way in which we have demonstrated IIP12.

But although these things are such that no reason for doubt remains, still, I hardly believe that men can be induced to consider them fairly unless I confirm them by experience. They are so firmly persuaded that the body now moves, now is at rest, solely from the mind's command, and that it does a great many things which depend only on the mind's will and its art of thinking. II/142

For indeed, no one has yet determined what the body can do, that is, experience has not yet taught anyone what the body can do from the laws of Nature alone, insofar as Nature is only considered to be corporeal, and what the body can do only if it is determined by the mind. For no one has yet come to know the structure of the body so accurately that he could explain all its functions—not to mention that many things are observed in the lower animals which far surpass human ingenuity, and that sleepwalkers do a great many things in their sleep which they would not dare to awake. This shows well enough that the body itself, simply from the laws of its own nature, can do many things which its mind wonders at.

Again, no one knows how, or by what means, the mind moves the body, nor how many degrees of motion it can give the body, nor with what speed it can move it. So it follows that when men say that this or that action of the body arises from the mind, which has dominion over the body, they do not know what they are saying, and they do nothing but confess, in fine-sounding words, that they are ignorant of the true cause of that action, and that they do not wonder at it.

But they will say [i] that—whether or not they know by what means the mind moves the body—they still know by experience that unless the human mind were capable of thinking, the body would be inactive. And then [ii], they know by experience, that it is in the mind's power alone both to speak and to be silent, and to do many other things which they therefore believe depend on the mind's decision.

[i] As far as the first [objection] is concerned, I ask them, does not experience also teach that if, on the other hand, the body is inactive, the mind is at the same time incapable of thinking? For when the body is at rest in sleep, the mind at the same time remains senseless with it, nor does it have the power of thinking, as it does when awake. And then I believe everyone has found by experience that the mind is not always equally capable of thinking of the same object, but that as the body is more susceptible to having the image of this or that object aroused in it, so the mind is more capable of regarding this or that object.

II/143 They will say, of course, that it cannot happen that the causes of buildings, of paintings, and of things of this kind, which are made only by human skill, should be able to be deduced from the laws of Nature alone, insofar as it is considered to be only corporeal; nor would the human body be able to build a temple, if it were not determined and guided by the mind.

But I have already shown that they do not know what the body can do, or what can be deduced from the consideration of its nature alone, and that they know from experience that a great many things happen from the laws of Nature alone which they never would have believed could happen without the direction of the mind—such as the things sleepwalkers do in their sleep, which they wonder at while they are awake.

I add here the very structure of the human body, which, in the ingenuity of its construction, far surpasses anything made by human skill—not to mention that I have shown above that infinitely many things follow from Nature, under whatever attribute it may be considered.

[ii] As for the second [objection], human affairs, of course, would be conducted far more happily if it were equally in man's power to be silent and to speak. But experience teaches all too plainly that men have nothing less in their power than their tongue, and can do nothing less than moderate their appetites.

That is why most men believe that we do freely only those things we have a weak inclination toward (because the appetite for these things can easily be reduced by the memory of another thing which we frequently recollect), but that we do not at all do freely those things we seek by a strong affect, which cannot be calmed by the memory of another thing. But if they had not found by experience that we do many things we afterwards repent, and that often we see the better and follow the worse (viz. when we are torn by contrary affects), nothing would prevent them from believing that we do all things freely.

So the infant believes he freely wants the milk; the angry child that he wants vengeance; and the timid, flight. So the drunk believes it is from a free decision of the mind that he speaks the things he later, when sober, wishes he had not said. So the madman, the chatterbox, the child, and a great many people of this kind believe they speak from a free decision of the mind, when really they cannot contain their impulse to speak.

So experience itself, no less clearly than reason, teaches that men believe themselves free because they are conscious of their own actions, and ignorant of the causes by which they are determined, that the decisions of the mind are nothing but the appetites themselves, which therefore vary as the disposition of the body varies. For each one governs everything from his affect; those who are torn by contrary affects do not know what they want, and those who are not moved by any affect are very easily driven here and there.

All these things, indeed, show clearly that both the decision of the mind and the appetite and the determination of the body by nature exist together—or rather are one and the same thing, which we call a decision when it is considered under, and explained through, the attribute of thought, and which we call a determination when it is considered under the attribute of extension and deduced from the laws of motion and rest. This will be still more clearly evident from what must presently be said.

For there is something else I wish particularly to note here, that we can do nothing from a decision of the mind unless we recollect it. For example, we cannot speak a word unless we recollect it. And it is not in

II/144

the free power of the mind to either recollect a thing or forget it. So this only is believed to be in the power of the mind—that from the mind's decision alone we can either be silent about or speak about a thing we recollect.

But when we dream that we speak, we believe that we speak from a free decision of the mind—and yet we do not speak, or, if we do, it is from a spontaneous motion of the body. And we dream that we conceal certain things from men, and this by the same decision of the mind by which, while we wake, we are silent about the things we know. We dream, finally, that, from a decision of the mind, we do certain things we do not dare to do while we are awake.

So I should very much like to know whether there are in the mind two kinds of decisions—those belonging to our fantasies and those that are free? And if we do not want to go that far in our madness, it must be granted that this decision of the mind which is believed to be free is not distinguished from the imagination itself, *or* the memory, nor is it anything beyond that affirmation which the idea, insofar as it is an idea, necessarily involves (see IIP49). And so these decisions of the mind arise by the same necessity as the ideas of things which actually exist. Those, therefore, who believe that they either speak or are silent, or do anything from a free decision of the mind, dream with open eyes.

P3: *The actions of the mind arise from adequate ideas alone; the passions depend on inadequate ideas alone.*

II/145   Dem.: The first thing which constitutes the essence of the mind is nothing but the idea of an actually existing body (by IIP11 and P13); this idea (by IIP15) is composed of many others, of which some are adequate (IIP38C), and others inadequate (by IIP29C). Therefore, whatever follows from the nature of the mind and has the mind as its proximate cause, through which it must be understood, must necessarily follow from an adequate idea or an inadequate one. But insofar as the mind has inadequate ideas (by P1), it necessarily is acted on. Therefore, the actions of the mind follow from adequate ideas alone; hence, the mind is acted on only because it has inadequate ideas, q.e.d.

Schol.: We see, then, that the passions are not related to the mind except insofar as it has something which involves a negation, *or* insofar as it is considered as a part of Nature which cannot be perceived clearly and distinctly through itself, without the others. In this way I could show that the passions are related to singular things in the same way as to the mind, and cannot be perceived in any other way. But my purpose is only to treat of the human mind.

P4: *No thing can be destroyed except through an external cause.*

Dem.: This proposition is evident through itself. For the definition of any thing affirms, and does not deny, the thing's essence, *or* it posits the thing's essence, and does not take it away. So while we attend only to the thing itself, and not to external causes, we shall not be able to find anything in it which can destroy it, q.e.d.

P5: *Things are of a contrary nature, that is, cannot be in the same subject, insofar as one can destroy the other.*

Dem.: For if they could agree with one another, or be in the same   II/146
subject at once, then there could be something in the same subject which could destroy it, which (by P4) is absurd. Therefore, things and so on, q.e.d.

P6: *Each thing, as far as it can by its own power, strives to persevere in its being.*

Dem.: For singular things are modes by which God's attributes are expressed in a certain and determinate way (by IP25C), that is (by IP34), things that express, in a certain and determinate way, God's power, by which God is and acts. And no thing has anything in itself by which it can be destroyed, *or* which takes its existence away (by P4). On the contrary, it is opposed to everything which can take its existence away (by P5). Therefore, as far as it can, and it lies in itself, it strives to persevere in its being, q.e.d.

P7: *The striving by which each thing strives to persevere in its being is nothing but the actual essence of the thing.*

Dem.: From the given essence of each thing some things necessarily follow (by IP36), and things are able [to produce] nothing but what follows necessarily from their determinate nature (by IP29). So the power of each thing, *or* the striving by which it (either alone or with others) does anything, or strives to do anything—that is (by P6), the power, *or* striving, by which it strives to persevere in its being, is nothing but the given, *or* actual, essence of the thing itself, q.e.d.

P8: *The striving by which each thing strives to persevere in its being involves*   II/147
no finite time, but an indefinite time.

Dem.: For if [the striving by which a thing strives to persevere in its being] involved a limited time, which determined the thing's duration, then it would follow just from that very power by which the thing exists that it could not exist after that limited time, but that it would have to be destroyed. But (by P4) this is absurd. Therefore, the striving by which a thing exists involves no definite time. On the contrary, since (by P4) it will always continue to exist by the same power by which it now exists, unless it is destroyed by an external cause, this striving involves indefinite time, q.e.d.

P9: *Both insofar as the mind has clear and distinct ideas, and insofar as it has confused ideas, it strives, for an indefinite duration, to persevere in its being and it is conscious of this striving it has.*

Dem.: The essence of the mind is constituted by adequate and by inadequate ideas (as we have shown in P3). So (by P7) it strives to persevere in its being both insofar as it has inadequate ideas and insofar as it has adequate ideas; and it does this (by P8) for an indefinite duration. But since the mind (by IIP23) is necessarily conscious of itself through ideas of the body's affections, the mind (by P7) is conscious of its striving, q.e.d.

Schol.: When this striving is related only to the mind, it is called will; but when it is related to the mind and body together, it is called appetite. This appetite, therefore, is nothing but the very essence of man, from whose nature there necessarily follow those things that promote his preservation. And so man is determined to do those things.

II/148   Between appetite and desire there is no difference, except that desire is generally related to men insofar as they are conscious of their appetite. So *desire* can be defined as *Appetite together with consciousness of the appetite.*

From all this, then, it is clear that we neither strive for, nor will, neither want, nor desire anything because we judge it to be good; on the contrary, we judge something to be good because we strive for it, will it, want it, and desire it.

P10: *An idea that excludes the existence of our body cannot be in our mind, but is contrary to it.*

Dem.: Whatever can destroy our body cannot be in it (by P5), and so the idea of this thing cannot be in God insofar as he has the idea of our body (by IIP9C), that is (by IIP11 and P13), the idea of this thing cannot be in our mind. On the contrary, since (by IIP11 and P13) the first thing that constitutes the essence of the mind is the idea of an actually existing body, the first and principal [tendency] of the striving of our mind (by P7) is to affirm the existence of our body. And so an idea that denies the existence of our body is contrary to our mind, and so on, q.e.d.

P11: *The idea of any thing that increases or diminishes, aids or restrains, our body's power of acting, increases or diminishes, aids or restrains, our mind's power of thinking.*

Dem.: This proposition is evident from IIP7, or also from IIP14.

Schol.: We see, then, that the mind can undergo great changes, and pass now to a greater, now to a lesser perfection. These passions, indeed, explain to us the affects of joy and sadness. By *joy*, therefore, I shall understand in what follows that *passion by which the mind passes to a greater perfection*. And by *sadness*, that *passion by which it passes to a lesser perfection*. The *affect of joy which is related to the mind and body at once* I call *pleasure* or *cheerfulness*, and that of *sadness*, *pain* or *melancholy*.

But it should be noted [NS: here] that pleasure and pain are ascribed to a man when one part of him is affected more than the rest, whereas cheerfulness and melancholy are ascribed to him when all are equally affected.

Next, I have explained in P9S what desire is, and apart from these three I do not acknowledge any other primary affect. For I shall show in what follows that the rest arise from these three. But before I proceed further, I should like to explain P10 more fully here, so that it may be more clearly understood how one idea is contrary to another.

In IIP17S we have shown that the idea which constitutes the essence of the mind involves the existence of the body so long as the body itself exists. Next from what we have shown in IIP8C and its scholium, it follows that the present existence of our mind depends only on this, that the mind involves the actual existence of the body. Finally, we have shown that the power of the mind by which it imagines things and recollects them also depends on this (see IIP17, P18, P18S), that it involves the actual existence of the body.

From these things it follows that the present existence of the mind and its power of imagining are taken away as soon as the mind ceases to affirm the present existence of the body. But the cause of the mind's ceasing to affirm this existence of the body cannot be the mind itself (by P4), nor also that the body ceases to exist. For (by IIP6) the cause of the mind's affirming the body's existence is not that the body has begun to exist. So by the same reasoning, it does not cease to affirm the body's existence because the body ceases to exist, but (by IIP8) this [sc. ceasing to affirm the body's existence] arises from another idea which excludes the present existence of our body, and consequently of our mind, and which is thus contrary to the idea that constitutes our mind's essence.

P12: *The mind as far as it can, strives to imagine those things that increase or*   II/150
aid the body's power of acting.

Dem.: So long as the human body is affected with a mode that involves the nature of an external body, the human mind will regard the same body as present (by IIP17) and consequently (by IIP7) so long as the human mind regards some external body as present, that is (by IIP17S), imagines it, the human body is affected with a mode that involves the nature of that external body. Hence, so long as the mind imagines those things that increase or aid our body's power of acting, the body is affected with modes that increase or aid its power of acting (see Post. 1), and consequently (by P11) the mind's power of thinking is increased or aided. Therefore (by P6 or P9), the mind, as far as it can, strives to imagine those things, q.e.d.

P13: *When the mind imagines those things that diminish or restrain the body's power of acting, it strives, as far as it can, to recollect things which exclude their existence.*

Dem.: So long as the mind imagines anything of this kind, the power both of mind and of body is diminished or restrained (as we have demonstrated in P12); nevertheless, the mind will continue to imagine this thing until it imagines something else that excludes the thing's present existence (by IIP17), that is (as we have just shown), the power both of mind and of body is diminished or restrained until the mind imagines something else that excludes the existence of this thing; so the mind (by P9), as far as it can, will strive to imagine or recollect that other thing, q.e.d.

II/151   Cor.: From this it follows that the mind avoids imagining those things that diminish or restrain its or the body's power.

Schol.: From this we understand clearly what love and hate are. *Love is* nothing but *joy with the accompanying idea of an external cause*, and *hate* is nothing but *sadness with the accompanying idea of an external cause*. We see, then, that one who loves necessarily strives to have present and preserve the thing he loves; and on the other hand, one who hates strives to remove and destroy the thing he hates. But all of these things will be discussed more fully in what follows.

P14: *If the mind has once been affected by two affects at once, then afterwards, when it is affected by one of them, it will also be affected by the other.*

Dem.: If the human body has once been affected by two bodies at once, then afterwards, when the mind imagines one of them, it will immediately recollect the other also (by IIP18). But the imaginations of the mind indicate the affects of our body more than the nature of external bodies (by IIP16C2). Therefore, if the body, and consequently the mind (see D3), has once been affected by two affects [NS: at once], then afterwards, when it is affected by one of them, it will also be affected by the other, q.e.d.

P15: *Any thing can be the accidental cause of joy, sadness, or desire.*

Dem.: Suppose the mind is affected by two affects at once, one of which neither increases nor diminishes its power of acting, while the other either increases it or diminishes it (see Post. 1). From P14 it is clear that when the mind is afterwards affected with the former affect as by its true cause, which (by hypothesis) through itself neither increases nor diminishes its power of thinking, it will immediately be affected with the latter also, which increases or diminishes its power of thinking, that is (by P11S), with joy, or sadness. And so the former thing will be the cause of joy or sadness—not through itself, but accidentally. And in the same way it can easily be shown that that thing can be the accidental cause of desire, q.e.d.

II/152

Cor.: From this alone—that we have regarded a thing with an affect of joy or sadness, of which it is not itself the efficient cause, we can love it or hate it.

Dem.: For from this alone it comes about (by P14) that when the mind afterwards imagines this thing, it is affected with an affect of joy or sadness, that is (by P11S), that the power both of the mind and of the body is increased or diminished. And consequently (by P12), the mind desires to imagine the thing or (by P13C) avoids it, that is (by P13S), it loves it or hates it, q.e.d.

Schol.: From this we understand how it can happen that we love or hate some things without any cause known to us, but only (as they say) from sympathy or antipathy. And to this must be related also those objects that affect us with joy or sadness only because they have some likeness to objects that usually affect us with these affects, as I shall show in P16. I know, of course, that the authors who first introduced the words sympathy and antipathy intended to signify by them certain occult qualities of things. Nevertheless, I believe we may be permitted to understand by them also qualities that are known or manifest.

P16: *From the mere fact that we imagine a thing to have some likeness to an object which usually affects the mind with joy or sadness, we love it or hate it, even though that in which the thing is like the object is not the efficient cause of these affects.*

II/153

Dem.: What is like the object, we have (by hypothesis) regarded in the object itself with an affect of joy or sadness. And so (by P14), when the mind is affected by its image, it will immediately be affected also with this or that affect. Consequently the thing we perceive to have this same [quality] will (by P15) be the accidental cause of joy or sadness; and so (by P15C) although that in which it is like the object is not the efficient cause of these affects, we shall still love it or hate it, q.e.d.

P17: *If we imagine that a thing which usually affects us with an affect of sadness is like another which usually affects us with an equally great affect of joy, we shall hate it and at the same time love it.*

Dem.: For (by hypothesis) this thing is through itself the cause of sadness, and (by P13S) insofar as we imagine it with this affect, we hate it. And moreover, insofar as it has some likeness to the other thing, which usually affects us with an equally great affect of joy, we shall love it with an equally great striving of joy (by P16). And so we shall both hate it and at the same time love it, q.e.d.

Schol.: This *constitution of the mind which arises from two contrary affects* is called *vacillation of mind*, which is therefore related to the affect as doubt is to the imagination (see IIP44S); nor do vacillation of mind and doubt differ from one another except in degree.

II/154 But it should be noted that in the preceding proposition I have deduced these vacillations of mind from causes which are the cause through themselves of one affect and the accidental cause of the other. I have done this because in this way they could more easily be deduced from what has gone before, not because I deny that vacillations of mind for the most part arise from an object which is the efficient cause of each affect. For the human body (by IIPost. 1) is composed of a great many individuals of different natures, and so (by IIA1″ [at II/99]), it can be affected in a great many different ways by one and the same body. And on the other hand, because one and the same thing can be affected in many ways, it will also be able to affect one and the same part of the body in many different ways. From this we can easily conceive that one and the same object can be the cause of many and contrary affects.

P18: *Man is affected with the same affect of joy or sadness from the image of a past or future thing as from the image of a present thing.*

Dem.: So long as a man is affected by the image of a thing, he will regard the thing as present, even if it does not exist (by IIP17 and P17C); he imagines it as past or future only insofar as its image is joined to the image of a past or future time (see IIP44S). So the image of a thing, considered only in itself, is the same, whether it is related to time past or future, or to the present, that is (by IIP16C2), the constitution of the body, *or* affect, is the same, whether the image is of a thing past or future, or of a present thing. And so, the affect of joy or sadness is the same, whether the image is of a thing past or future, or of a present thing, q.e.d.

Schol. 1: I call a thing past or future here, insofar as we have been affected by it, or will be affected by it. For example, insofar as we have seen it or will see it, insofar as it has refreshed us or will refresh us, has injured us or will injure us. For insofar as we imagine it in this way, we affirm its existence, that is, the body is not affected by any affect that excludes the thing's existence. And so (by IIP17) the body is affected with the image of the thing in the same way as if the thing itself were present. However, because it generally happens that those who have experienced many things vacillate so long as they regard a thing as future or past, and most often doubt the thing's outcome (see IIP44S), the affects which arise from similar images of things are not so constant, but are generally disturbed by the images of other things, until men become more certain of the thing's outcome.

II/155

Schol. 2: From what has just been said, we understand what hope and fear, confidence and despair, gladness and remorse are. For *hope* is nothing but *an inconstant joy which has arisen from the image of a future or past thing whose outcome we doubt; fear*, on the other hand, is *an inconstant sadness, which has also arisen from the image of a doubtful thing.* Next, if the doubt involved in these affects is removed, hope becomes *confidence*, and fear, *despair*—namely, *a joy or sadness which has arisen from the image of a thing we feared or hoped for.* Finally, *gladness is a joy which has arisen from the image of a past thing whose outcome we doubted,* while *remorse is a sadness which is opposite to gladness.*

P19: *He who imagines that what he loves is destroyed will be saddened; but he who imagines it to be preserved, will rejoice.*

Dem.: Insofar as it can, the mind strives to imagine those things which increase or aid the body's power of acting (by P12), that is (by P13S), those it loves. But the imagination is aided by what posits the existence of a thing, and on the other hand, is restrained by what excludes the existence of a thing (by IIP17). Therefore, the images of things that posit the existence of a thing loved aid the mind's striving to imagine the thing loved, that is (by P11S), affect the mind with joy. On the other hand, those which exclude the existence of a thing loved, restrain the same striving of the mind, that is (by P11S), affect the mind with sadness. Therefore, he who imagines that what he loves is destroyed will be saddened, and so on, q.e.d.

P20: *He who imagines that what he hates is destroyed will rejoice.*

II/156

Dem.: The mind (by P13) strives to imagine those things that exclude the existence of things by which the body's power of acting is diminished or restrained, that is (by P13S), strives to imagine those things which exclude the existence of things it hates. So the image of a thing which excludes the existence of what the mind hates aids this striving of the mind, that is (by P11S), affects the mind with joy. Therefore, he who imagines that what he hates is destroyed will rejoice, q.e.d.

P21: *He who imagines what he loves to be affected with joy or sadness will also be affected with joy or sadness; and each of those affects will be greater or lesser in the lover as they are greater or lesser in the thing loved.*

Dem.: The images of things (as we have demonstrated in P19) which posit the existence of a thing loved aid the striving by which the mind strives to imagine the thing loved. But joy posits the existence of the joyous thing, and posits more existence, the greater the affect of joy is. For (by P11S) it is a transition to a greater perfection. Therefore, the image in the lover of the loved thing's joy aids his mind's striving, that is (by P11S), affects the lover with joy, and the more so, the greater this affect was in the thing loved. This was the first thing to be proved.

Next, insofar as a thing is affected with sadness, it is destroyed, and the more so, the greater the sadness with which it is affected (by P11S). So (by P19) he who imagines what he loves to be affected with sadness, will also be affected with sadness, and the more so, the greater this affect was in the thing loved, q.e.d.

II/157   P22: *If we imagine someone to affect with joy a thing we love, we shall be affected with love toward him. If, on the other hand, we imagine him to affect the same thing with sadness, we shall also be affected with hate toward him.*

Dem.: He who affects a thing we love with joy or sadness affects us also with joy or sadness, if we imagine that the thing loved is affected by that joy or sadness (by P21). But this joy or sadness is supposed to be accompanied in us by the idea of an external cause. Therefore (by P13S), if we imagine that someone affects with joy or sadness a thing we love, we shall be affected with love or hate toward him, q.e.d.

Schol.: P21 explains to us what *pity* is, which we can define as *sadness which has arisen from injury to another*. By what name we should call the joy which arises from another's good I do not know. Next, *love toward him who has done good to another* we shall call *favor*, and *hatred toward him who has done evil to another* we shall call *indignation*.

Finally, it should be noted that we do not pity only a thing we have loved (as we have shown in P21), but also one toward which we have previously had no affect, provided that we judge it to be like us (as I shall show below). And so also we favor him who has benefited someone like us, and are indignant at him who has injured one like us.

P23: *He who imagines what he hates to be affected with sadness will rejoice; if, on the other hand, he should imagine it to be affected with joy, he will be saddened. And both these affects will be the greater or lesser, as its contrary is greater or lesser in what he hates.*

II/158   Dem.: Insofar as a hateful thing is affected with sadness, it is destroyed, and the more so, the greater the sadness by which it is affected (by P11S). Therefore (by P20), he who imagines a thing he hates to be affected with sadness will on the contrary be affected with joy, and the more so, the greater the sadness with which he imagines the hateful thing to have been affected. This was the first point.

166

Next, joy posits the existence of the joyous thing (by P11S), and the more so, the greater the joy is conceived to be. [Therefore] if someone imagines him whom he hates to be affected with joy, this imagination (by P13) will restrain his striving, that is (by P11S), he who hates will be affected with sadness, and so on, q.e.d.

Schol.: This joy can hardly be enduring and without any conflict of mind. For (as I shall show immediately in P27) insofar as one imagines a thing like oneself to be affected with an affect of sadness, one must be saddened. And the opposite, if one imagines the same thing to be affected with joy. But here we attend only to hate.

P24: *If we imagine someone to affect with joy a thing we hate, we shall be affected with hate toward him also. On the other hand, if we imagine him to affect the same thing with sadness, we shall be affected with love toward him.*

Dem.: This proposition is demonstrated in the same way as P22.

Schol.: These and similar affects of hate are related to *envy* which, therefore, is nothing but *hate, insofar as it is considered so to dispose a man that he is glad at another's ill fortune and saddened by his good fortune.*

P25: *We strive to affirm, concerning ourselves and what we love, whatever we*   II/159
imagine to affect with joy ourselves or what we love. On the other hand, we strive to deny whatever we imagine affects with sadness ourselves or what we love.

Dem.: Whatever we imagine to affect what we love with joy or sadness, affects us with joy or sadness (by P21). But the mind (by P12) strives as far as it can to imagine those things which affect us with joy, that is (by IIP17 and P17C), to regard them as present; and on the other hand (by P13) it strives to exclude the existence of those things which affect us with sadness. Therefore, we strive to affirm, concerning ourselves and what we love, whatever we imagine to affect with joy ourselves or what we love, and conversely, q.e.d.

P26: *We strive to affirm, concerning what we hate, whatever we imagine to affect it with sadness, and on the other hand, to deny whatever we imagine to affect it with joy.*

Dem.: This proposition follows from P23, as P25 follows from P21.

Schol.: From these propositions we see that it easily happens that a man thinks more highly of himself and what he loves than is just, and on the other hand, thinks less highly than is just of what he hates. When this imagination concerns the man himself who thinks more highly of himself than is just, it is called pride, and is a species of madness, because the man dreams, with open eyes, that he can do all those things which he achieves only in his imagination, and which he therefore regards as real and triumphs in, so long as he cannot imagine those things which exclude the existence [of these achievements] and determine his power of acting.

II/160

Pride, therefore, is joy born of the fact that a man thinks more highly of himself than is just. And the *joy born of the fact that a man thinks more highly of another than is just* is called *overestimation*, while *that which stems from thinking less highly of another than is just* is called *scorn*.

P27: *If we imagine a thing like us, toward which we have had no affect, to be affected with some affect, we are thereby affected with a like affect.*

Dem.: The images of things are affections of the human body whose ideas represent external bodies as present to us (by IIP17S), that is (by IIP16), whose ideas involve the nature of our body and at the same time the present nature of the external body. So if the nature of the external body is like the nature of our body, then the idea of the external body we imagine will involve an affection of our body like the affection of the external body. Consequently, if we imagine someone like us to be affected with some affect, this imagination will express an affection of our body like this affect. And so, from the fact that we imagine a thing like us to be affected with an affect, we are affected with a like affect. But if we hate a thing like us, then (by P23) we shall be affected with an affect contrary to its affect, not like it, q.e.d.

Schol.: This imitation of the affects, when it is related to sadness is called *pity* (on which, see P22S); but related to desire it is called *emulation*, which, therefore, *is* nothing but *the desire for a thing which is generated in us from the fact that we imagine others like us to have the same desire.*

Cor. 1: If we imagine that someone toward whom we have had no affect affects a thing like us with joy, we shall be affected with love toward him. On the other hand, if we imagine him to affect it with sadness, we shall be affected with hate toward him.

II/161

Dem.: This is demonstrated from P27 in the same way P22 is demonstrated from P21.

Cor. 2: We cannot hate a thing we pity from the fact that its suffering affects us with sadness.

Dem.: For if we could hate it because of that, then (by P23) we would rejoice in its sadness, which is contrary to the hypothesis.

Cor. 3: As far as we can, we strive to free a thing we pity from its suffering.

Dem.: Whatever affects with sadness what we pity, affects us also with a like sadness (by P27). And so (by P13) we shall strive to think of whatever can take away the thing's existence, *or* destroy the thing, that is (by P9S), we shall want to destroy it, *or* shall be determined to destroy it. And so we strive to free the thing we pity from its suffering, q.e.d.

Schol.: This will, *or* appetite to do good, born of our pity for the thing on which we wish to confer a benefit, is called *benevolence*, which *is* therefore nothing but a *desire born of pity*. As for love and hate toward him who has done well or ill to a thing we imagine to be like us, see P22S.

P28: *We strive to further the occurrence of whatever we imagine will lead to joy, and to avert or destroy what we imagine is contrary to it,* or *will lead to sadness.*

Dem.: We strive to imagine, as far as we can, what we imagine will lead to joy (by P12), that is (by IIP17), we strive, as far as we can, to regard it as present, *or* as actually existing. But the mind's striving, *or* power of thinking, is equal to and at one in nature with the body's striving, *or* power of acting (as clearly follows from IIP7C and P11C). Therefore, we strive absolutely, *or* (what, by P9S, is the same) want and intend that it should exist. This was the first point.

Next, if we imagine that what we believe to be the cause of sadness, that is (by P13S), what we hate, is destroyed, we shall rejoice (by P20), and so (by the first part of this [NS: proposition]) we shall strive to destroy it, *or* (by P13) to avert it from ourselves, so that we shall not regard it as present. This was the second point. Therefore, [we strive to further the occurrence of] whatever we imagine will lead to joy, and so on, q.e.d.

P29: *We shall strive to do also whatever we imagine men to look on with joy, and on the other hand, we shall be averse to doing what we imagine men are averse to.*

Dem.: From the fact that we imagine men to love or hate something, we shall love or hate it (by P27), that is (by P13S), we shall thereby rejoice in or be saddened by the thing's presence. And so (by P28) we shall strive to do whatever we imagine men to love, or to look on with joy, and so on, q.e.d.

Schol.: *This striving to do something (and also to omit doing something) solely to please men* is called *ambition*, especially when we strive so eagerly to please the people that we do or omit certain things to our own injury, or another's. In other cases, it is usually called *human kindness*. Next, *the joy with which we imagine the action of another by which he has striven to please us* I call *praise*. On the other hand, *the sadness with which we are averse to his action* I call *blame*.

II/162

II/163

P30: *If someone has done something which he imagines affects others with joy, he will be affected with joy accompanied by the idea of himself as cause, or he will regard himself with joy. If, on the other hand, he has done something which he imagines affects others with sadness, he will regard himself with sadness.*

Dem.: He who imagines that he affects others with joy or sadness will thereby (by P27) be affected with joy or sadness. But since man (by IIP19 and P23) is conscious of himself through the affections by which he is determined to act, then he who has done something which he imagines affects others with joy will be affected with joy, together with a consciousness of himself as the cause, *or*, he will regard himself with joy, and the converse, q.e.d.

Schol.: Since love (by P13S) is joy, accompanied by the idea of an external cause, and hate is sadness, accompanied also by the idea of an external cause, this joy and sadness are species of love and hate. But because love and hate are related to external objects, we shall signify these affects by other names. *Joy accompanied by the idea of an internal cause*, we shall call *love of esteem*, and *the sadness contrary to it, shame*—I mean *when the joy or sadness arises from the fact that the man believes that he is praised or blamed*. Otherwise, I shall call *joy accompanied by the idea of an internal cause, self-esteem*, and *the sadness contrary to it, repentance*.

Next, because (by IIP17C) it can happen that the joy with which someone imagines that he affects others is only imaginary, and (by P25) everyone strives to imagine concerning himself whatever he imagines affects himself with joy, it can easily happen that one who exults at being esteemed is proud and imagines himself to be pleasing to all, when he is burdensome to all.

II/164

P31: *If we imagine that someone loves, desires, or hates something we ourselves love, desire, or hate, we shall thereby love, desire, or hate it with greater constancy. But if we imagine that he is averse to what we love, or the opposite [NS: that he loves what we hate], then we shall undergo vacillation of mind.*

Dem.: Simply because we imagine that someone loves something, we thereby love the same thing (by P27). But we suppose that we already love it without this [cause of love]; so there is added to the love a new cause, by which it is further encouraged. As a result, we shall love what we love with greater constancy.

Next, from the fact that we imagine someone to be averse to something, we shall be averse to it (by P27). But if we suppose that at the same time we love it, then at the same time we shall both love and be averse to the same thing, *or* (see P17S) we shall undergo vacillation of mind, q.e.d.

Cor.: From this and from P28 it follows that each of us strives, so far as he can, that everyone should love what he loves, and hate what he hates. Hence that passage of the poet:

> Speremus pariter, pariter metuamus amantes;
> Ferreus est, si quis, quod sinit alter, amat.[1]

Schol.: This striving to bring it about that everyone should approve his love and hate is really ambition (see P29S). And so we see that each of us, by his nature, wants the others to live according to his temperament; when all alike want this, they are alike an obstacle to one another, and when all wish to be praised, *or* loved, by all, they hate one another.

P32: *If we imagine that someone enjoys some thing that only one can possess, we shall strive to bring it about that he does not possess it.*

II/165

Dem.: From the mere fact that we imagine someone to enjoy something (by P27 and P27C1), we shall love that thing and desire to enjoy it. But (by hypothesis) we imagine his enjoyment of this thing as an obstacle to our joy. Therefore (by P28), we shall strive that he not possess it, q.e.d.

Schol.: We see, therefore, that for the most part human nature is so constituted that men pity the unfortunate and envy the fortunate, and (by P32) [envy them] with greater hate the more they love the thing they imagine the other to possess. We see, then, that from the same property of human nature from which it follows that men are compassionate, it also follows that the same men are envious and ambitious.

Finally, if we wish to consult experience, we shall find that it teaches all these things, especially if we attend to the first years of our lives. For we find from experience that children, because their bodies are continually, as it were, in a state of equilibrium, laugh or cry simply because they see others laugh or cry. Moreover, whatever they see others do, they immediately desire to imitate it. And finally, they desire for themselves all those things by which they imagine others are pleased—because, as we have said, the images of things are the very affections of the human body, *or* modes by which the human body is affected by external causes, and disposed to do this or that.

P33: *When we love a thing like ourselves, we strive, as far as we can, to bring it about that it loves us in return.*

---

[1] The lines are from Ovid's *Amores* II, xix, 4–5. It appears from the context that Spinoza understands them as follows: "As lovers, let us hope together and fear together; he has a heart of steel, who loves what another man leaves alone." It is not clear, however, that that would be a correct translation in the Ovidian context. Cf. Guy Lee's translation of the *Amores* (London: John Murray, 1968).

Dem.: As far as we can, we strive to imagine, above all others, the thing we love (by P12). Therefore, if a thing is like us, we shall strive to affect it with joy above all others (by P29), *or* we shall strive, as far as we can, to bring it about that the thing we love is affected with joy, accompanied by the idea of ourselves [as cause], that is (by P13S), that it loves us in return, q.e.d.

II/166

P34: *The greater the affect with which we imagine a thing we love to be affected toward us, the more we shall exult at being esteemed.*

Dem.: We strive (by P33), as far as we can, that a thing we love should love us in return, that is (by P13S), that a thing we love should be affected with joy, accompanied by the idea of ourselves [as cause]. So the greater the joy with which we imagine a thing we love to be affected on our account, the more this striving is aided, that is (by P11 and P11S), the greater the joy with which we are affected. But since we rejoice because we have affected another, like us, with joy, then we regard ourselves with joy (by P30). Therefore, the greater the affect with which we imagine a thing we love to be affected toward us, the greater the joy with which we shall regard ourselves, *or* (by P30S) the more we shall exult at being esteemed, q.e.d.

P35: *If someone imagines that a thing he loves is united with another by as close, or by a closer, bond of friendship than that with which he himself, alone, possessed the thing, he will be affected with hate toward the thing he loves, and will envy the other.*

Dem.: The greater the love with which someone imagines a thing he loves to be affected toward him, the more he will exult at being esteemed (by P34), that is (by P30S), the more he will rejoice. And so (by P28) he will strive, as far as he can, to imagine the thing he loves to be bound to him as closely as possible. This striving, *or* appetite, is encouraged if he imagines another to desire the same thing he does (by P31). But this striving, *or* appetite, is supposed to be restrained by the image of the thing he loves, accompanied by the image of him with whom the thing he loves is united. So (by P11S) he will thereby be affected with sadness, accompanied by the idea of the thing he loves as a cause, together with the image of the other; that is (by P13S), he will be affected with hate toward the thing he loves, and, at the same time, toward the other (by P15C), whom he will envy because of the pleasure the other takes in the thing he loves (by P23), q.e.d.

II/167

Schol.: This hatred toward a thing we love, combined with envy, is called *jealousy*, which is therefore nothing but *a vacillation of mind born of love and hatred together, accompanied by the idea of another who is envied.* Moreover, this hatred toward the thing he loves will be greater in proportion to the joy with which the jealous man was usually affected from the love returned to him by the thing he loves, and also in proportion to the affect with which he was affected toward him with whom he imagines the thing he loves to unite itself. For if he hated him, he will thereby hate the thing he loves (by P24), because he imagines that what he loves affects with joy what he hates, and also (by P15C) because he is forced to join the image of the thing he loves to the image of him he hates.

This latter reason is found, for the most part, in love toward a woman. For he who imagines that a woman he loves prostitutes herself to another not only will be saddened, because his own appetite is restrained, but also will be repelled by her, because he is forced to join the image of the thing he loves to the shameful parts and excretions of the other. To this, finally, is added the fact that she no longer receives the jealous man with the same countenance as she used to offer him. From this cause, too, the lover is saddened, as I shall show.

P36: *He who recollects a thing by which he was once pleased desires to possess it in the same circumstances as when he first was pleased by it.*

Dem.: Whatever a man sees together with a thing that pleased him (by P15) will be the accidental cause of joy. And so (by P28) he will desire to possess it all, together with the thing that pleased him, *or* he will desire to possess the thing with all the same circumstances as when he first was pleased by it, q.e.d.

II/168

Cor.: Therefore, if the lover has found that one of those circumstances is lacking, he will be saddened.

Dem.: For insofar as he finds that a circumstance is lacking, he imagines something which excludes the existence of this thing. But since, from love, he desires this thing, *or* circumstance (by P36), then insofar as he imagines it to be lacking, he will be saddened, q.e.d.

Schol.: This sadness, insofar as it concerns the absence of what we love, is called longing.

P37: *The desire which arises from sadness or joy, and from hatred or love, is greater, the greater the affect is.*

Dem.: Sadness diminishes or restrains a man's power of acting (by P11S), that is (by P7), diminishes or restrains the striving by which a man strives to persevere in his being; so it is contrary to this striving (by P5), and all a man affected by sadness strives for is to remove sadness. But (by the definition of sadness) the greater the sadness, the greater is the part of the man's power of acting to which it is necessarily opposed. Therefore, the greater the sadness, the greater the power of acting with which the man will strive to remove the sadness, that is (by P9S), the greater the desire, *or* appetite, with which he will strive to remove the sadness.

Next, since joy (by the same P11S) increases or aids man's power of acting, it is easily demonstrated in the same way that the man affected with joy desires nothing but to preserve it, and does so with the greater desire, as the joy is greater.

II/169

Finally, since hate and love are themselves affects of sadness or of joy, it follows in the same way that the striving, appetite, or desire which arises from hate or love will be greater as the hate and love are greater, q.e.d.

P38: *If someone begins to hate a thing he has loved, so that the love is com-pletely destroyed, then (from an equal cause) he will have a greater hate for it than if he had never loved it, and this hate will be the greater as the love before was greater.*

Dem.: For if someone begins to hate a thing he loves, more of his appetites will be restrained than if he had not loved it. For love is a joy (by P13S), which the man, as far as he can (by P28), strives to preserve; and (by the same scholium) he does this by regarding the thing he loves as present, and by affecting it, as far as he can, with joy (by P21). This striving (by P37) is greater as the love is greater, as is the striving to bring it about that the thing he loves loves him in return (see P33). But these strivings are restrained by hatred toward the thing he loves (by P13C and P23); therefore, the lover (by P11S) will be affected with sadness from this cause also, and the more so as his love was greater. That is, apart from the sadness which was the cause of the hate, another arises from the fact that he loved the thing. And consequently he will regard the thing he loved with a greater affect of sadness, that is (by P13S), he will have a greater hatred for it than if he had not loved it. And this hate will be the greater as the love was greater, q.e.d.

P39: *He who hates someone will strive to do evil to him, unless he fears that a greater evil to himself will arise from this; and on the other hand, he who loves someone will strive to benefit him by the same law.*

II/170

Dem.: To hate someone (by P13S) is to imagine him as the cause of [NS: one's] sadness; and so (by P28), he who hates someone will strive to remove or destroy him. But if from that he fears something sad-der, *or* (what is the same) a greater evil to himself, and believes that he can avoid this sadness by not doing to the one he hates the evil he was contemplating, he will desire to abstain from doing evil (by the same P28)—and that (by P37) with a greater striving than that by which he was bound to do evil. So this greater striving will prevail, as we maintained.

The second part of this demonstration proceeds in the same way. Therefore, he who hates someone, and so on, q.e.d.

Schol.: By good here I understand every kind of joy, and whatever leads to it, and especially what satisfies any kind of longing, whatever that may be. And by evil [I understand here] every kind of sadness, and especially what frustrates longing. For we have shown above (in P9S) that we desire nothing because we judge it to be good, but on the contrary, we call it good because we desire it. Consequently, what we are averse to we call evil.

So each one, from his own affect, judges, *or* evaluates, what is good and what is bad, what is better and what is worse, and finally, what is best and what is worst. So the greedy man judges an abundance of money best, and poverty worst. The ambitious man desires nothing so much as esteem and dreads nothing so much as shame. To the envious nothing is more agreeable than another's unhappiness, and nothing more burdensome than another's happiness. And so, each one, from his own affect, judges a thing good or bad, useful or useless.

Further, this affect, by which a man is so disposed that he does not will what he wills, and wills what he does not will, is called *timidity*, which is therefore nothing but *fear insofar as a man is disposed by it to avoid an evil he judges to be future by encountering a lesser evil* (see P28). But if *the evil he is timid toward is shame*, then the timidity is called *a sense of shame*. Finally, if *the desire to avoid a future evil is restrained by timidity regarding another evil, so that he does not know what he would rather do*, then the fear is called *consternation*, particularly if each evil he fears is of the greatest. II/171

P40: *He who imagines he is hated by someone, and believes he has given the other no cause for hate, will hate the other in return.*

Dem.: He who imagines someone to be affected with hate will thereby also be affected with hate (by P27), that is (by P13S), with sadness accompanied by the idea of an external cause. But (by hypothesis) he imagines no cause of this sadness except the one who hates him. So from imagining himself to be hated by someone, he will be affected with sadness, accompanied by the idea of the one who hates him [as a cause of the sadness] *or* (by the same scholium) he will hate the other, q.e.d.

Schol. If he imagines he has given just cause for this hatred, he will be affected with shame (by P30 and P30S). But this rarely happens (by P25). Moreover, this reciprocity of hatred can also arise from the fact that hatred is followed by a striving to do evil to him who is hated (by P39). He, therefore, who imagines that someone hates him will imagine the other to be the cause of an evil, *or* sadness. And so, he will be affected with sadness, *or* fear, accompanied by the idea of the one who hates him, as a cause. That is, he will be affected with hate in return, as above.

Cor. 1: He who imagines one he loves to be affected with hate toward him will be tormented by love and hate together. For insofar as he imagines that [the one he loves] hates him, he is determined to hate [that person] in return (by P40). But (by hypothesis) he nevertheless loves him. So he will be tormented by love and hate together.

II/172   Cor. 2: If someone imagines that someone else, toward whom he has previously had no affect, has, out of hatred, done him some evil, he will immediately strive to return the same evil.

Dem.: He who imagines someone to be affected with hate toward him, will hate him in return (by P40), and (by P26) will strive to think of everything which can affect [that person] with sadness, and be eager to bring it to him (by P39). But (by hypothesis) the first thing he imagines of this kind is the evil done him. So he will immediately strive to do the same to [that person], q.e.d.

Schol.: *The striving to do evil to him we hate* is called *anger*; and *the striving to return an evil done us* is called *vengeance*.

P41: *If someone imagines that someone loves him, and does not believe he has given any cause for this, he will love [that person] in return.*

Dem.: This proposition is demonstrated in the same way as the preceding one. See also its scholium.

Schol.: But if he believes that he has given just cause for this love, he will exult at being esteemed (by P30 and P30S). This, indeed, happens rather frequently (by P25) and is the opposite of what we said happens when someone imagines that someone hates him (see P40S).

Next, this *reciprocal love, and consequent* (by P39) *striving to benefit one who loves us, and strives* (by the same P39) *to benefit us*, is called *thankfulness, or gratitude*. And so it is evident that men are far more ready for vengeance than for returning benefits.

II/173   Cor.: He who imagines he is loved by one he hates will be torn by hate and love together. This is demonstrated in the same way as P40C1.

Schol.: But if the hate has prevailed, he will strive to do evil to the one who loves him. This affect is called *cruelty*, especially if it is believed that the one who loves has given no ordinary cause for hatred.

P42: *He who has benefited someone—whether moved to do so by love or by the hope of esteem—will be saddened if he sees his benefit accepted in an ungrateful spirit.*

Dem.: He who loves a thing like himself strives, as far as he can, to be loved by it in return (by P33). So he who has benefited someone from love does this from a longing by which he is bound that he may be loved in return—that is (by P34), from the hope of Esteem *or* (by P30S) Joy;

so (by P12) he will strive, as far as he can, to imagine this cause of Esteem, *or* to regard it as actually existing. But (by hypothesis) he imagines something else that excludes the existence of this cause. So (by P19) he will be saddened by this.

P43: *Hate is increased by being returned, but can be destroyed by love.*

Dem.: He who imagines one he hates to be affected with hate toward him will feel a new hate (by P40), while the first (by hypothesis) continues. If, on the other hand, he imagines that the one he hates is affected with love toward him, then insofar as he imagines this, he regards himself with joy (by P30) and will strive to please the one he hates (by P29), that is (by P41), he strives not to hate him and not to affect him with sadness. This striving (by P37) will be greater or lesser in proportion to the affect from which it arises. So if it is greater than that which arises from hate, and by which he strives to affect the thing he hates with sadness (by P26), then it will prevail over it and efface the hate from his mind, q.e.d.

II/174

P44: *Hate completely conquered by love passes into love, and the love is therefore greater than if hate had not preceded it.*

Dem.: The proof of this proceeds in the same way as that of P38. For he who begins to love a thing he has hated, *or* used to regard with sadness, rejoices because he loves, and to this joy which love involves (see its definition in P13S) there is also added a joy arising from this—the striving to remove the sadness hate involves (as we have shown in P37) is strengthened in every respect, and accompanied by the idea of the one he hated, [who is regarded] as a cause [of joy].

Schol.: Although this is so, still, no one will strive to hate a thing, or to be affected with sadness, in order to have this greater joy, that is, no one will desire to suffer injury in the hope of recovering, or long to be sick in the hope of getting better. For each one will strive always to preserve his being, and to put aside sadness as far as he can. But if, on the contrary, one could conceive that a man could desire to hate someone, in order afterwards to have the greater love for him, then he would always desire to hate him. For as the hate was greater, so the love would be greater, and so he would always desire his hate to become greater and greater. And by the same cause, a man would strive to become more and more ill, so that afterwards he might have the greater joy from restoring his health; and so he would always strive to become ill, which (by P6) is absurd.

P45: *If someone imagines that someone like himself is affected with hate toward a thing like himself which he loves, he will hate that [person].*

II/175

Dem.: For the thing he loves hates in return the one who hates it (by

P40), and so the lover, who imagines that someone hates the thing he loves, thereby imagines the thing he loves to be affected with hate, that is (by P13S), with sadness. And consequently (by P21), he is saddened, and his sadness is accompanied by the idea of the one who hates the thing he loves—[this other being regarded] as the cause [of the sadness]. That is (by P13S), he will hate him, q.e.d.

P46: *If someone has been affected with joy or sadness by someone of a class, or nation, different from his own, and this joy or sadness is accompanied by the idea of that person as its cause, under the universal name of the class or nation, he will love or hate, not only that person, but everyone of the same class or nation.*

Dem.: The demonstration of this matter is evident from P16.

P47: *The joy which arises from our imagining that a thing we hate is destroyed, or affected with some other evil, does not occur without some sadness of mind.*

Dem.: This is evident from P27. For insofar as we imagine a thing like us to be affected with sadness, we are saddened.

Schol.: This proposition can also be demonstrated from IIP17C. For II/176 as often as we recollect a thing—even though it does not actually exist—we still regard it as present, and the body is affected in the same way [NS: as if it were present]. So insofar as the memory of the thing is strong, the man is determined to regard it with sadness. While the image of the thing still remains, this determination is, indeed, restrained by the memory of those things that exclude its existence; but it is not taken away. And so the man rejoices only insofar as this determination is restrained.

So it happens that this joy, which arises from the misfortune occurring to the thing we hate, is repeated as often as we recollect the thing. For as we have said, when the image of this thing is aroused, because it involves the existence of the thing, it determines the man to regard the thing with the same sadness as he used to before, when it existed. But because he has joined to the image of this thing other images which exclude its existence, this determination to sadness is immediately restrained, and the man rejoices anew. This happens as often as the repetition occurs.

This is also the cause of men's rejoicing when they recall some evil now past, and why they enjoy telling of dangers from which they have been freed. For when they imagine a danger, they regard it as future, and are determined to fear it. This determination is restrained anew by the idea of freedom, which they have joined to the idea of the danger, when they have been freed from it. This renders them safe again, and so they rejoice again.

178

P48: *Love or hate—say, of Peter—is destroyed if the sadness the hate involves, or the joy the love involves, is attached to the idea of another cause, and each is diminished to the extent that we imagine that Peter was not its only cause.*

Dem.: This is evident simply from the definitions of love and hate—see P13S. For this joy is called love of Peter, or this sadness, hatred of Peter, only because Peter is considered to be the cause of the one affect or the other. If this is taken away—either wholly or in part—the affect toward Peter is also diminished, either wholly or in part, q.e.d.

II/177

P49: *Given an equal cause of love, love toward a thing will be greater if we imagine the thing to be free than if we imagine it to be necessary. And similarly for hate.*

Dem.: A thing we imagine to be free must be perceived through itself, without others (by ID7). So if we imagine it to be the cause of joy or sadness, we shall thereby love or hate it (by P13S), and shall do so with the greatest love or hate that can arise from the given affect (by P48). But if we should imagine as necessary the thing which is the cause of this affect, then (by the same ID7) we shall imagine it to be the cause of the affect, not alone, but with others. And so (by P48) our love or hate toward it will be less, q.e.d.

Schol.: From this it follows that because men consider themselves to be free, they have a greater love or hate toward one another than toward other things. To this is added the imitation of the affects, on which see PP27, 34, 40, and 43.

P50: *Anything whatever can be the accidental cause of hope or fear.*

Dem.: This proposition is demonstrated in the same way as P15. Consult it together with P18S2.

Schol.: Things which are accidental causes of hope or fear are called good or bad omens. And insofar as these same omens are causes of hope or fear, they are causes of joy or sadness (by the definitions of hope and fear; see P18S2); consequently (by P15C), we love them or hate them, and strive (by P28) either to use them as means to the things we hope for, or to remove them as obstacles or causes of fear.

II/178

Furthermore, as follows from P25, we are so constituted by nature that we easily believe the things we hope for, but believe only with difficulty those we fear, and that we regard them more or less highly than is just. This is the source of the superstitions by which men are everywhere troubled.

For the rest, I do not think it worth the trouble to show here the vacillations of mind which stem from hope and fear since it follows simply from the definition of these affects that there is no hope without fear, and no fear without hope (as we shall explain more fully in its place). Moreover, insofar as we hope for or fear something, we love it or hate it; so whatever we have said of love and hate, anyone can easily apply to hope and fear.

P51: *Different men can be affected differently by one and the same object; and one and the same man can be affected differently at different times by one and the same object.*

Dem.: The human body (by IIPost. 3) is affected in a great many ways by external bodies. Therefore, two men can be differently affected at the same time, and so (by IIA1″ [II/99]) they can be affected differently by one and the same object.

Next (by the same Post.) the human body can be affected now in this way, now in another. Consequently (by the same axiom) it can be affected differently at different times by one and the same object, q.e.d.

Schol.: We see, then, that it can happen that what the one loves, the other hates, what the one fears, the other does not, and that one and the same man may now love what before he hated, and now dare what before he was too timid for.

II/179   Next, because each one judges from his own affect what is good and what is bad, what is better and what worse (see P39S) it follows that men can vary as much in judgment as in affect. The result is that when we compare one with another, we distinguish them only by a difference of affects, and call some intrepid, others timid, and others, finally, by another name.

For example, I shall call him *intrepid* who disdains an evil I usually fear. Moreover, if I attend to the fact that his desire to do evil to one he hates, and good to one he loves, is not restrained by timidity regarding an evil by which I am usually restrained, I shall call him *daring*. Someone will seem *timid* to me if he is afraid of an evil I usually disdain. If, moreover, I attend to the fact that his desire [to do evil to those he hates and good to those he loves] is restrained by timidity regarding an evil which cannot restrain me, I shall call him *cowardly*. In this way will everyone judge.

Finally, because of this inconstancy of man's nature and judgment, and also because he often judges things only from an affect, because the things which he believes will make for joy or sadness, and which he therefore strives to promote or prevent (by P28), are often only imaginary not to mention the other conclusions we have reached in Part II about the uncertainty of things we easily conceive that a man can often be the cause both of his own sadness and his own joy, *or* that he is affected both with joy and with sadness, accompanied by the idea of himself as their cause. So we easily understand what repentance and self-esteem are: *repentance is sadness accompanied by the idea of oneself as cause*, and *self-esteem is joy accompanied by the idea of oneself as cause*. Be-cause men believe themselves free, these affects are very violent (see P49).

P52: *If we have previously seen an object together with others, or we imagine it has nothing but what is common to many things, we shall not consider it so long as one which we imagine to have something singular.*

Dem.: As soon as we imagine an object we have seen with others, we shall immediately recollect the others (by IIP18 and P18S), and so from considering one we immediately pass to considering another. And the reasoning is the same concerning the object we imagine to have nothing but what is common to many things. For imagining that is supposing that we consider nothing in it but what we have seen before with others. II/180

But when we suppose that we imagine in an object something singu-lar, which we have never seen before, we are only saying that when the mind considers that object, it has nothing in itself which it is led to consider from considering that. And so it is determined to consider only that. Therefore, if we have seen, and so on, q.e.d.

Schol.: This affection of the mind, *or this imagination of a singular thing, insofar as it is alone in the mind*, is called *wonder*. But *if it is aroused by an object we fear*, it is called *consternation*, because wonder at an evil keeps a man so suspended in considering it that he cannot think of other things by which he could avoid that evil. But *if what we wonder at is a man's prudence, diligence, or something else of that kind, because we consider him as far surpassing us in this*, then the wonder is called *veneration*. Oth-erwise, *if what we wonder at is the man's anger, envy, and the like*, the wonder is called *dread*.

Next, if we wonder at the prudence, diligence, and the like, of a man we love, the love will thereby (by P12) be greater and this *love joined to wonder*, or *veneration*, we call *devotion*. In this way we can also conceive hate, hope, confidence, and other affects to be joined to wonder, and so we can deduce more affects than those which are usually indicated by the accepted words. So it is clear that the names of the affects are found more from the ordinary usage [of words] than from an accurate knowl-edge [of the affects].

To wonder is opposed *disdain*, the cause of which, however, is gener-ally this: because we see that someone wonders at, loves, or fears some-thing, or something appears at first glance like things we admire, love, fear, and so on (by P15, P15C, and P27), we are determined to wonder at, love, fear, and so on, the same thing; but if, from the thing's pres-ence, or from considering it more accurately, we are forced to deny it whatever can be the cause of wonder, love, fear, and the like, then the mind remains determined by the thing's presence to think more of the II/181 things which are not in the object than of those which are (though the object's presence usually determines [the mind] to think chiefly of what is in the object).

Next, as devotion stems from wonder at a thing we love, so *mockery* stems from *disdain for a thing we hate or fear*, and *contempt* from *disdain for folly*, as veneration stems from wonder at prudence. Finally, we can conceive love, hope, love of esteem, and other affects joined to disdain, and from that we can deduce in addition other affects, which we also do not usually distinguish from the others by any single term.

P53: *When the mind considers itself and its power of acting, it rejoices, and does so the more, the more distinctly it imagines itself and its power of acting.*

Dem.: A man does not know himself except through affections of his body and their ideas (by IIP19 and P23). So when it happens that the mind can consider itself, it is thereby supposed to pass to a greater perfection, that is (by P11S), to be affected with joy, and with greater joy the more distinctly it can imagine its power of acting, q.e.d.

Cor.: This joy is more and more encouraged the more the man imagines himself to be praised by others. For the more he imagines himself II/182 to be praised by others, the greater the joy with which he imagines himself to affect others, a joy accompanied by the idea of himself (by P29S). And so (by P27) he himself is affected with a greater joy, accompanied by the idea of himself, q.e.d.

P54: *The mind strives to imagine only those things which posit its power of acting.*

Dem.: The mind's striving, *or* power, is its very essence (by P7); but the mind's essence (as is known through itself) affirms only what the mind is and can do, not what it is not and cannot do. So it strives to imagine only what affirms, *or* posits, its power of acting, q.e.d.

P55: *When the mind imagines its own lack of power, it is saddened by it.*

Dem.: The mind's essence affirms only what the mind is and can do, *or* it is of the nature of the mind to imagine only those things which posit its power of acting (by P54). So when we say that the mind, in considering itself, imagines its lack of power, we are saying nothing but that the mind's striving to imagine something which posits its power of acting is restrained, *or* (by P11S) that it is saddened, q.e.d.

Cor.: This sadness is more and more encouraged if we imagine ourselves to be blamed by others. This is demonstrated in the same way as P53C.

Schol.: This *sadness, accompanied by the idea of our own weakness* is called II/183 *humility*. But *joy arising from considering ourselves*, is called *self-love* or *self-esteem*. And since this is renewed as often as a man considers his virtues, *or* his power of acting, it also happens that everyone is anxious to tell his own deeds, and show off his powers, both of body and of mind and that men, for this reason, are troublesome to one another.

From this it follows, again, that men are by nature envious (see P24S and P32S), *or* are glad of their equals' weakness and saddened by their equals' virtue. For whenever anyone imagines his own actions, he is affected with joy (by P53), and with a greater joy, the more his actions express perfection, and the more distinctly he imagines them, that is (by IIP40S1), the more he can distinguish them from others, and consider them as singular things. So everyone will have the greatest gladness from considering himself, when he considers something in himself which he denies concerning others.

But if he relates what he affirms of himself to the universal idea of man or animal, he will not be so greatly gladdened. And on the other hand, if he imagines that his own actions are weaker, compared to others' actions, he will be saddened (by P28), and will strive to put aside this sadness, either by wrongly interpreting his equals' actions or by magnifying his own as much as he can. It is clear, therefore, that men are naturally inclined to hate and envy.

Education itself adds to natural inclination. For parents generally spur their children on to virtue only by the incentive of honor and envy.

But perhaps this doubt remains: that not infrequently we admire and venerate men's virtues. To remove this scruple, I shall add the following corollary.

Cor.: No one envies another's virtue unless he is an equal.

Dem.: Envy is hatred itself (see P24S), *or* (by P13S) a sadness, that is (by P11S), an affection by which a man's power of acting, *or* striving, is restrained. But a man (by P9S) neither strives to do, nor desires, anything unless it can follow from his given nature. So no man desires that there be predicated of him any power of acting, *or* (what is the same) II/184 virtue, which is peculiar to another's nature and alien to his own. Hence, his desire cannot be restrained, that is (by P11S), he cannot be saddened because he considers a virtue in someone unlike himself. Consequently he also cannot envy him. But he can, indeed, envy his equal, who is supposed to be of the same nature as he, q.e.d.

Schol.: So when we said above (in P52S) that we venerate a man because we wonder at his prudence, strength of character, and so on, that happens (as is evident from the proposition itself) because we imagine these virtues to be peculiarly in him, and not as common to our nature. Therefore, we shall not envy him these virtues any more than we envy trees their height, or lions their strength.

P56: *There are as many species of joy, sadness, and desire, and consequently of each affect composed of these (like vacillation of mind) or derived from them (like love, hate, hope, fear, etc.), as there are species of objects by which we are affected.*

Dem.: Joy and sadness, and consequently the affects composed of them or derived from them, are passions (by P11S). But we are necessarily acted on (by P1) insofar as we have inadequate ideas, and only insofar as we have them (by P3) are we acted on, that is (see IIP40S), necessarily we are acted on only insofar as we imagine, *or* (see IIP17 and P17S) insofar as we are affected with an affect which involves both the nature of our body and the nature of an external body. Therefore, the nature of each passion must necessarily be so explained that the nature of the object by which we are affected is expressed.

II/185 For example, the joy arising from A involves the nature of object A, that arising from object B involves the nature of object B, and so these two affects of joy are by nature different, because they arise from causes of a different nature. So also the affect of sadness arising from one object is different in nature from the sadness stemming from another cause. The same must also be understood of love, hate, hope, fear, vacillation of mind, and so on.

Therefore, there are as many species of joy, sadness, love, hate, and the like, as there are species of objects by which we are affected.

But desire is the very essence, *or* nature, of each [man] insofar as it is conceived to be determined, by whatever constitution he has, to do something (see P9S). Therefore, as each [man] is affected by external causes with this or that species of joy, sadness, love, hate, and so on, that is, as his nature is constituted in one way or the other, so his desires vary and the nature of one desire must differ from the nature of the other as much as the affects from which each arises differ from one another.

Therefore, there are as many species of desire as there are species of joy, sadness, love, and the like, and consequently (through what has already been shown) as there are species of objects by which we are affected, q.e.d.

Schol.: Noteworthy among these species of affects, which (by P56) must be very many, are gluttony, drunkenness, lust, greed, and ambition, which are only notions of love or desire which explain the nature of each of these affects through the objects to which they are related. For by gluttony, drunkenness, lust, greed, and ambition we understand nothing but an immoderate love or desire for eating, drinking, sexual union, wealth, and esteem.

Moreover, these affects, insofar as we distinguish them from the others only through the object to which they are related, do not have opposites. For moderation, which we usually oppose to gluttony, sobriety which we usually oppose to drunkenness, and chastity, which we usually oppose to lust, are not affects *or* passions, but indicate the power of the mind, a power which moderates these affects.

I cannot explain the other species of affects here, for there are as many as there are species of objects. But even if I could, it is not necessary. For our purpose, which is to determine the powers of the affects and the power of the mind over the affects, it is enough to have a general definition of each affect. It is enough, I say, for us to understand the common properties of the affects and of the mind, so that we can determine what sort of power, and how great a power, the mind has to moderate and restrain the affects. So though there is a great difference between this or that affect of love, hate or desire for example, between the love of one's children and the love of one's wife, it is still not necessary for us to know these differences, nor to investigate the nature and origin of the affects further.

P57: *Each affect of each individual differs from the affect of another as much as the essence of the one from the essence of the other.*

Dem.: This proposition is evident from IIA1″ [II/99]. But nevertheless we shall demonstrate it from the definitions of the three primitive affects.

All the affects are related to desire, joy, or sadness, as the definitions we have given of them show. But desire is the very nature, *or* essence, of each [individual] (see the definition of desire in P9S). Therefore, the desire of each individual differs from the desire of another as much as the nature, *or* essence, of the one differs from the essence of the other.

Next, joy and sadness are passions by which each one's power, *or* striving to persevere in his being, is increased or diminished, aided or restrained (by P11 and P11S). But by the striving to persevere in one's being, insofar as it is related to the mind and body together, we understand appetite and desire (see P9S). So joy and sadness are the desire, *or* appetite, itself insofar as it is increased or diminished, aided or restrained, by external causes. That is (by the same scholium), it is the very nature of each [individual]. And so, the joy or sadness of each [individual] also differs from the joy or sadness of another as much as the nature, *or* essence, of the one differs from the essence of the other. Consequently, each affect of each individual differs from the affect of another as much, and so on, q.e.d.

Schol.: From this it follows that the affects of the animals which are called irrational (for after we know the origin of the mind, we cannot in

II/186

II/187

any way doubt that the lower animals feel things) differ from men's affects as much as their nature differs from human nature. Both the horse and the man are driven by a lust to procreate; but the one is driven by an equine lust, the other by a human lust. So also the lusts and appetites of insects, fish, and birds must vary. Therefore, though each individual lives content with his own nature, by which he is constituted, and is glad of it, nevertheless that life with which each one is content, and that gladness, are nothing but the idea, *or* soul, of the individual. And so the gladness of the one differs in nature from the gladness of the other as much as the essence of the one differs from the essence of the other.

Finally, from P57 it follows that there is no small difference between the gladness by which a drunk is led and the gladness a philosopher possesses. I wished to mention this in passing.

This will be enough concerning the affects which are related to man insofar as he is acted on. It remains to add a few words about those which are related to him insofar as he acts.

P58: *Apart from the joy and desire which are passions, there are other affects of joy and desire which are related to us insofar as we act.*

Dem.: When the mind conceives itself and its power of acting, it rejoices (by P53). But the mind necessarily considers itself when it conceives a true, *or* adequate, idea (by IIP43). But the mind conceives some II/188 adequate ideas (by IIP40S2). Therefore, it also rejoices insofar as it conceives adequate ideas, that is (by P1), insofar as it acts.

Next, the mind strives to persevere in its being, both insofar as it has clear and distinct ideas and insofar as it has confused ideas (by P9). But by striving we understand [NS: here] desire (by P9S). Therefore, desire also is related to us insofar as we understand, *or* (by P1) insofar as we act, q.e.d.

P59: *Among all the affects which are related to the mind insofar as it acts, there are none which are not related to joy or desire.*

Dem.: All the affects are related to desire, joy, or sadness, as the definitions we have given of them show. But by sadness we understand the fact that the mind's power of acting is diminished or restrained (by P11 and P11S). And so insofar as the mind is saddened, its power of understanding, that is (by P1), of acting, is diminished or restrained. Hence no affects of sadness can be related to the mind insofar as it acts, but only affects of joy and desire, which (by P58) are also so far related to the mind, q.e.d.

Schol.: *All actions that follow from affects related to the mind insofar as it understands* I relate to *strength of character*, which I divide into tenacity and nobility. For by *tenacity* I understand *the desire by which each one strives, solely from the dictate of reason, to preserve his being.* By *nobility* I understand *the desire by which each one strives, solely from the dictate of reason, to aid other men and join them to him in friendship.*

Those actions, therefore, which aim only at the agent's advantage, I relate to tenacity, and those which aim at another's advantage, I relate to nobility. So moderation, sobriety, presence of mind in danger, and so forth, are species of tenacity, whereas courtesy, mercy, and so forth, are species of nobility.

And with this I think I have explained and shown through their first causes the main affects and vacillations of mind which arise from the composition of the three primitive affects, namely, desire, joy, and sadness. From what has been said it is clear that we are driven about in many ways by external causes, and that, like waves on the sea, driven by contrary winds, we toss about, not knowing our outcome and fate.

II/189

But I said that I have shown only the main [NS: affects], not all the conflicts of mind there can be. For by proceeding in the same way as above, we can easily show that love is joined to repentance, contempt, shame, and so on. Indeed, from what has already been said I believe it is clear to anyone that the various affects can be compounded with one another in so many ways, and that so many variations can arise from this composition that they cannot be defined by any number. But it is sufficient for my purpose to enumerate only the main affects. [To consider] those I have omitted would be more curious than useful.

Nevertheless, this remains to be noted about love: very often it happens that while we are enjoying a thing we wanted, the body acquires from this enjoyment a new constitution, by which it is differently determined, and other images of things are aroused in it; and at the same time the mind begins to imagine other things and desire other things.

For example, when we imagine something which usually pleases us by its taste, we desire to enjoy it—that is, to consume it. But while we thus enjoy it, the stomach is filled, and the body constituted differently. So if (while the body is now differently disposed) the presence of the food or drink encourages the image of it, and consequently also the striving, *or* desire to consume it, then that new constitution will be opposed to this desire, *or* striving. Hence, the presence of the food or drink we used to want will be hateful. This is what we call *disgust* and *weariness.*

As for the external affections of the body, which are observed in the affects—such as trembling, paleness, sobbing, laughter, and the like—I have neglected them, because they are related to the body only, without any relation to the mind. Finally, there are certain things to be noted about the definitions of the affects. I shall therefore repeat them here in order, interposing the observations required on each one.

I. Desire is man's very essence, insofar as it is conceived to be determined, from any given affection of it, to do something.

Exp.: We said above, in P9S, that desire is appetite together with the consciousness of it. And appetite is the very essence of man, insofar as it is determined to do what promotes his preservation.

But in the same scholium I also warned that I really recognize no difference between human appetite and desire. For whether a man is conscious of his appetite or not, the appetite still remains one and the same. And so—not to seem to commit a tautology—I did not wish to explain desire by appetite, but was anxious to so define it that I would comprehend together all the strivings of human nature that we signify by the name of appetite, will, desire, or impulse. For I could have said that desire is man's very essence, insofar as it is conceived to be determined to do something. But from this definition (by IIP23) it would not follow that the mind could be conscious of its desire, *or* appetite. Therefore, in order to involve the cause of this consciousness, it was necessary (by the same proposition) to add: *insofar as it is conceived, from some given affection of it, to be determined*, and so on. For by an affection of the human essence we understand any constitution of that essence, whether it is innate [NS: or has come from outside], whether it is conceived through the attribute of thought alone, or through the attribute of extension alone, or is referred to both at once.

Here, therefore, by the word *desire* I understand any of a man's strivings, impulses, appetites, and volitions, which vary as the man's constitution varies, and which are not infrequently so opposed to one another that the man is pulled in different directions and knows not where to turn.

II/191

II. Joy is a man's passage from a lesser to a greater perfection.

III. Sadness is a man's passage from a greater to a lesser perfection.

Exp.: I say a passage. For joy is not perfection itself. If a man were born with the perfection to which he passes, he would possess it without an affect of joy.

This is clearer from the affect of sadness, which is the opposite of joy. For no one can deny that sadness consists in a passage to a lesser perfection, not in the lesser perfection itself, since a man cannot be saddened insofar as he participates in some perfection. Nor can we say that sadness consists in the privation of a greater perfection. For a privation is nothing, whereas the affect of sadness is an act, which can therefore be no other act than that of passing to a lesser perfection, that is, an act by which man's power of acting is diminished or restrained (see P11S).

As for the definitions of cheerfulness, pleasure, melancholy, and pain, I omit them, because they are chiefly related to the body, and are only species of joy or sadness.

IV. Wonder is an imagination of a thing in which the mind remains fixed because this singular imagination has no connection with the others. (See P52 and P52S.)

Exp.: In IIP18S we showed the cause why the mind, from considering one thing, immediately passes to the thought of another—because the images of these things are connected with one another, and so ordered that one follows the other. This, of course, cannot be conceived when the image of the thing is new. Rather the mind will be detained in regarding the same thing until it is determined by other causes to think of other things.

So the imagination of a new thing, considered in itself, is of the same nature as the other [imaginations], and for this reason I do not number wonder among the affects. Nor do I see why I should, since this distraction of the mind does not arise from any positive cause which distracts the mind from other things, but only from the fact that there is no cause determining the mind to pass from regarding one thing to thinking of others. II/192

So as I pointed out in P11S, I recognize only three primitive, *or* primary, affects: joy, sadness, and desire. I have spoken of wonder only because it has become customary for some to indicate the affects derived from these three by other names when they are related to objects we wonder at. For the same reason I shall also add the definition of disdain to these.

V. Disdain is an imagination of a thing which touches the mind so little that the thing's presence moves the mind to imagining more what is not in it than what is. (See P52S).

I omit, here, the definitions of veneration and contempt because no affects that I know of derive their names from them.

VI. Love is a joy, accompanied by the idea of an external cause.

Exp.: This definition explains the essence of love clearly enough. But the definition of those authors who define *love* as *a will of the lover to join himself to the thing loved* expresses a property of love, not its essence. And because these authors did not see clearly enough the essence of love, they could not have any clear concept of this property. Hence everyone has judged their definition quite obscure.

But it should be noted that when I say it is a property in the lover, that he wills to join himself to the thing loved, I do not understand by will a consent, or a deliberation of the mind, *or* free decision (for we have demonstrated that this is a fiction in IIP48). Nor do I understand a desire of joining oneself to the thing loved when it is absent or continu- II/193

189

ing in its presence when it is present. For love can be conceived without either of these desires. Rather, by will I understand a satisfaction in the lover on account of the presence of the thing loved, by which the lover's joy is strengthened or at least encouraged.

VII. Hate is a sadness, accompanied by the idea of an external cause.

Exp.: The things to be noted here will be perceived easily from what has been said in the explanation of the preceding definition. (See also P13S.)

VIII. Inclination is a joy accompanied by the idea of a thing which is the accidental cause of joy.

IX. Aversion is a sadness accompanied by the idea of something which is the accidental cause of sadness. (On this see P15S.)

X. Devotion is a love of one whom we wonder at.

Exp.: That wonder arises from the newness of the thing we have shown in P52. So if it happens that we often imagine what we wonder at, we shall cease to wonder at it. And so we see that the affect of devotion easily changes into simple love.

XI. Mockery is a joy born of the fact that we imagine something we disdain in a thing we hate.

Exp.: Insofar as we disdain a thing we hate, we deny existence to it (see P52S), and so far we rejoice (by P20). But since we suppose that man nevertheless hates what he mocks, it follows that this joy is not enduring. (See P47S.)

II/194   XII. Hope is an inconstant joy, born of the idea of a future or past thing whose outcome we to some extent doubt.

XIII. Fear is an inconstant sadness, born of the idea of a future or past thing whose outcome we to some extent doubt. (See P18S2.)

Exp.: From these definitions it follows that there is neither hope without fear, nor fear without hope. For he who is suspended in hope and doubts a thing's outcome is supposed to imagine something which excludes the existence of the future thing. And so to that extent he is saddened (by P19), and consequently, while he is suspended in hope, he fears that the thing [he imagines] will happen.

Conversely, he who is in fear, that is, who doubts the outcome of a thing he hates, also imagines something which excludes the existence of that thing. And so (by P20) he rejoices, and hence, to that extent has hope that the thing will not take place.

XIV. Confidence is a joy born of the idea of a future or past thing, concerning which the cause of doubting has been removed.

XV. Despair is a sadness born of the idea of a future or past thing concerning which the cause of doubting has been removed.

Exp.: Confidence, therefore, is born of hope and despair of fear, when the cause of doubt concerning the thing's outcome is removed. This happens because man imagines that the past or future thing is there, and regards it as present, or because he imagines other things, excluding the existence of the things which put him in doubt. For though we can never be certain of the outcome of singular things (by IIP31C), it can still happen that we do not doubt their outcome. As we have shown (see IIP49S), it is one thing not to doubt a thing, and another to be certain of it. And so it can happen that we are affected, from the image of a past or future thing, with the same affect of joy or sadness as from the image of a present thing (as we have demonstrated in P18; II/195 see also its [first] scholium).

XVI. Gladness is a joy, accompanied by the idea of a past thing which has turned out better than we had hoped.

XVII. Remorse is a sadness, accompanied by the idea of a past thing which has turned out worse than we had hoped.

XVIII. Pity is a sadness, accompanied by the idea of an evil which has happened to another whom we imagine to be like us. (See P22S and P27S.)

Exp.: There seems to be no difference between pity and compassion, except perhaps that pity concerns the singular affect, whereas compassion concerns the habitual disposition of this affect.

XIX. Favor is a love toward someone who has benefited another.

XX. Indignation is a hate toward someone who has done evil to another.

Exp.: I know that in their common usage these words mean something else. But my purpose is to explain the nature of things, not the meaning of words. I intend to indicate these things by words whose usual meaning is not entirely opposed to the meaning with which I wish to use them. One warning of this should suffice. As for the cause of these affects, see P27C1 and P22S.

XXI. Overestimation is thinking more highly of someone than is just, out of love.

XXII. Scorn is thinking less highly of someone than is just, out of hate.

Exp.: Overestimation, therefore, is an effect, *or* property, of love, and II/196 scorn an effect of hate. And so *overestimation* can also be defined as *love insofar as it so affects a man that he thinks more highly than is just of the thing loved.* On the other hand, scorn can be defined as *hate insofar as it so affects a man that he thinks less highly than is just of the one he hates.* (See P26S.)

XXIII. Envy is hate insofar as it so affects a man that he is saddened by another's happiness and, conversely, glad at his ill fortune.

Exp.: To envy one commonly opposes compassion, which can therefore (in spite of the meaning of the word) be defined as follows.

XXIV. Compassion is love, insofar as it so affects a man that he is glad at another's good fortune, and saddened by his ill fortune.

Exp.: As far as envy is concerned, see P24S and P32S. These are the affects of joy and sadness which are accompanied by the idea of an external thing as cause, either through itself or accidentally. I pass now to the others, which are accompanied by the idea of an internal thing as cause.

XXV. Self-esteem is a joy born of the fact that a man considers himself and his own power of acting.

XXVI. Humility is a sadness born of the fact that a man considers his own lack of power, or weakness.

II/197 Exp.: Self-esteem is opposed to humility, insofar as we understand by it a joy born of the fact that we consider our power of acting. But insofar as we also understand by it a joy, accompanied by the idea of some deed which we believe we have done from a free decision of the mind, it is opposed to repentance, which we define as follows.

XXVII. Repentance is a sadness accompanied by the idea of some deed we believe ourselves to have done from a free decision of the mind.

Exp.: We have shown the causes of these affects in P51S, P53, P54, P55, and P55S. On the free decision of the mind, see IIP35S.

But we ought also to note here that it is no wonder sadness follows absolutely all those acts which from custom are called *wrong*, and joy, those which are called *right*. For from what has been said above we easily understand that this depends chiefly on education. Parents—by blaming the former acts, and often scolding their children on account of them, and on the other hand, by recommending and praising the latter acts—have brought it about that emotions of sadness were joined to the one kind of act, and those of joy to the other.

Experience itself also confirms this. For not everyone has the same custom and religion. On the contrary, what among some is holy, among others is unholy; and what among some is honorable, among others is dishonorable. Hence, according as each one has been educated, so he either repents of a deed or exults at being esteemed for it.

XXVIII. Pride is thinking more highly of oneself than is just, out of love of oneself.

Exp.: The difference, therefore, between pride and overestimation is that the latter is related to an external object, whereas pride is related to the man himself, who thinks more highly of himself than is just. Further, as overestimation is an effect or property of love, so *pride* is an effect or property of self-love. Therefore, it can also be defined as *love of oneself*, or *self-esteem, insofar as it so affects a man that he thinks more highly of himself than is just.* (See P26S.)

There is no opposite of this affect. For no one, out of hate, thinks less highly of himself than is just. Indeed, no one thinks less highly of himself than is just, insofar as he imagines that he cannot do this or that. For whatever man imagines he cannot do, he necessarily imagines; and he is so disposed by this imagination that he really cannot do what he imagines he cannot do. For so long as he imagines that he cannot do this or that, he is not determined to do it, and consequently it is impossible for him to do it.

But if we attend to those things which depend only on opinion, we shall be able to conceive it possible that a man thinks less highly of himself than is just. For it can happen that, while someone sad considers his weakness, he imagines himself to be disdained by everyone—even while the others think of nothing less than to disdain him. Moreover, it can happen that a man thinks less highly of himself than is just, if in the present he denies something of himself in relation to a future time of which he is uncertain—for example, if he denies that he can conceive of anything certain, or that he can desire or do anything but what is wrong or dishonorable. Again, we can say that someone thinks less highly of himself than is just, when we see that, from too great a fear of shame, he does not dare things which others equal to him dare.

So we can oppose this affect—which I shall call despondency—to pride. For as pride is born of self-esteem, so despondency is born of humility. We can therefore define it as follows.

XXIX. Despondency is thinking less highly of oneself than is just, out of sadness.

Exp.: We are, nevertheless, often accustomed to oppose humility to pride. But then we attend more to the effects than to the nature of the two. For we usually call him proud who exults too much at being esteemed (see P30S), who tells of nothing but his own virtues and the vices of others, who wishes to be given precedence over all others, and finally who proceeds with the gravity and attire usually adopted by others who are placed far above him.

On the other hand, we call him humble who quite often blushes, who confesses his own vices and tells the virtues of others, who yields to all, and finally, who walks with head bowed, and neglects to adorn himself.

These affects—humility and despondency—are very rare. For human nature, considered in itself, strains against them, as far as it can (see P13 and P54). So those who are believed to be most despondent and humble are usually most ambitious and envious.

XXX. Love of esteem is a joy accompanied by the idea of some action of ours which we imagine that others praise.

XXXI. Shame is a sadness, accompanied by the idea of some action [NS: of ours] which we imagine that others blame.

Exp.: On these, see P30S. But the difference between shame and a sense of shame should be noted here. For shame is a sadness which follows a deed one is ashamed of; whereas a sense of shame is a fear of, *or* timidity regarding, shame, by which man is restrained from doing something dishonorable. To a sense of shame is usually opposed shamelessness, but the latter is really not an affect, as I shall show in the proper place. But as I have already pointed out, the names of the affects are guided more by usage than by nature.

And with this I have finished what I had set out to explain concerning the affects of joy and sadness. So I proceed to those I relate to desire.

XXXII. Longing is a desire, *or* appetite, to possess something which is encouraged by the memory of that thing, and at the same time restrained by the memory of other things which exclude the existence of the thing wanted.

Exp.: When we recollect a thing (as we have often said before), we are thereby disposed to regard it with the same affect as if it were present. But while we are awake, this disposition, *or* striving, is generally restrained by images of things which exclude the existence of what we recollect. So when we remember a thing which affects us with some II/200 kind of joy, we thereby strive to regard it as present with the same affect of joy—a striving which, of course, is immediately restrained by the memory of things which exclude its existence.

Longing, therefore, is really a sadness which is opposed to that joy which arises from the absence of a thing we hate (see P47S). But because the word *longing* seems to concern desire, I relate this affect to the affects of desire.

XXXIII. Emulation is a desire for a thing which is generated in us because we imagine that others have the same desire.

Exp.: If someone flees because he sees others flee, or is timid because he sees others timid, or, because he sees that someone else has burned his hand, withdraws his own hand and moves his body as if his hand were burned, we shall say that he imitates the other's affect, but not that he emulates it—not because we know that emulation has one cause and imitation another, but because it has come about by usage that we call emulous only one who imitates what we judge to be honorable, useful, or pleasant.

As for the cause of emulation, see P27 and P27S. And on why envy is generally joined to this affect, see P32 and P32S.

XXXIV. Thankfulness, *or* gratitude, is a desire, *or* eagerness of love, by which we strive to benefit one who has benefited us from a like affect of love. (See P39 and P41S.)

XXXV. Benevolence is a desire to benefit one whom we pity. (See P27S.)

XXXVI. Anger is a desire by which we are spurred, from hate, to do evil to one we hate. (See P39.)

XXXVII. Vengeance is a desire by which, from reciprocal hate, we are roused to do evil to one who, from a like affect, has injured us. (See P40C2 and P40C2S.)

II/201

XXXVIII. Cruelty, *or* severity, is a desire by which someone is roused to do evil to one whom we love or pity.

Exp.: To cruelty is opposed mercy, which is not a passion, but a power of the mind, by which a man governs anger and vengeance.

XXXIX. Timidity is a desire to avoid a greater evil, which we fear, by a lesser one. (See P39S.)

XL. Daring is a desire by which someone is spurred to do something dangerous which his equals fear to take on themselves.

XLI. Cowardice is ascribed to one whose desire is restrained by timidity regarding a danger which his equals dare to take on themselves.

Exp.: Cowardice, therefore, is nothing but fear of some evil, which most people do not usually fear. So I do not relate it to affects of desire. Nevertheless I wished to explain it here, because insofar as we attend to the desire, it is really opposed to daring.

XLII. Consternation is attributed to one whose desire to avoid an evil is restrained by wonder at the evil he fears.

Exp.: Consternation, therefore, is a species of cowardice. But because consternation arises from a double timidity, it can be more conveniently defined as *a fear which keeps a man senseless or vacillating so that he cannot avert the evil*. I say *senseless* insofar as we understand that his desire to avert the evil is restrained by wonder, and *vacillating* insofar as we conceive that that desire is restrained by timidity regarding another evil, which torments him equally, so that he does not know which of the two to avert. On these see P39S and P52S. As for cowardice and daring, see P51S.

II/202

XLIII. Human kindness, *or* courtesy, is a desire to do what pleases men and not do what displeases them.

XLIV. Ambition is an excessive desire for esteem.

Exp.: Ambition is a desire by which all the affects are encouraged and strengthened (by P27 and P31); so this affect can hardly be overcome. For as long as a man is bound by any desire, he must at the same time be bound by this one. As Cicero says, *Every man is led by love of esteem, and the more so, the better he is. Even the philosophers who write books on how esteem is to be disdained put their names to these works.*

XLV. Gluttony is an immoderate desire for and love of eating.

XLVI. Drunkenness is an immoderate desire for and love of drinking.

XLVII. Greed is an immoderate desire for and love of wealth.

XLVIII. Lust is also a desire for and love of joining one body to another.

Exp.: Whether this desire for sexual union is moderate or not, it is usually called lust.

Moreover, these five affects (as I pointed out in P56S) have no opposites. For courtesy is a species of ambition (see P29S), and I have already pointed out also that moderation, sobriety, and chastity indicate the power of the mind, and not a passion. And even if it can happen that a greedy, ambitious, or timid man abstains from too much food, drink, and sexual union, still, greed, ambition, and timidity are not opposites of gluttony, drunkenness, or lust.

For the greedy man generally longs to gorge himself on another's food and drink. And the ambitious will not be moderate in anything, provided he can hope he will not be discovered; if he lives among the drunken and the lustful, then because he is ambitious, he will be the more inclined to these vices. Finally, the timid man does what he does not wish to do. For though he may hurl his wealth into the sea to avoid death, he still remains greedy. And if the lustful man is sad because he cannot indulge his inclinations, he does not on that account cease to be lustful.

Absolutely, these affects do not so much concern the acts of eating, drinking, and so forth, as the appetite itself and the love. Therefore, nothing can be opposed to these affects except nobility and tenacity, which will be discussed later on.

I pass over in silence the definitions of jealousy and the other vacillations of mind, both because they arise from the composition of affects we have already defined, and because most of them do not have names. This shows that it is sufficient for practical purposes to know them only in general. Furthermore, from the definitions of the affects which we have explained it is clear that they all arise from desire, joy, or sadness— *or* rather, that they are nothing but these three, each one generally being called by a different name on account of its varying relations and extrinsic denominations. If we wish now to attend to these primitive affects, and to what was said above about the nature of the mind, we shall be able to define the affects, insofar as they are related only to the mind, as follows.

GENERAL DEFINITION OF THE AFFECTS

An affect which is called a passion of the mind is a confused idea, by which the mind affirms of its body, or of some part of it, a greater or lesser force of existing than before, which, when it is given, determines the mind to think of this rather than that.

Exp.: I say, first, that an affect, *or* passion of the mind, is a *confused idea.*   II/204
For we have shown (P3) that the mind is acted on only insofar as it has
inadequate, *or* confused, ideas.

Next, I say *by which the mind affirms of its body or of some part of it a*
greater or lesser force of existing than before. For all the ideas we have of
bodies indicate the actual constitution of our own body (by IIP16C2)
more than the nature of the external body. But this [idea], which constitutes the form of the affect, must indicate or express a constitution of
the body (or of some part of it), which the body (or some part of it) has
because its power of acting, *or* force of existing, is increased or diminished, aided or restrained.

But it should be noted that, when I say *a greater or lesser force of existing*
than before, I do not understand that the mind compares its body's present constitution with a past constitution, but that the idea which constitutes the form of the affect affirms of the body something which really
involves more or less of reality than before.

And because the essence of the mind consists in this (by IIP11 and
P13), that it affirms the actual existence of its body, and we understand
by perfection the very essence of the thing, it follows that the mind
passes to a greater or lesser perfection when it happens that it affirms of
its body (or of some part of the body) something which involves more
or less reality than before. So when I said above that the mind's power
of thinking is increased or diminished, I meant nothing but that the
mind has formed of its body (or of some part of it) an idea which expresses more or less reality than it had affirmed of the body. For the
excellence of ideas and the [mind's] actual power of thinking are measured by the excellence of the object.

Finally, I added *which determines the mind to think of this rather than*
that in order to express also, in addition to the nature of joy and sadness
(which the first part of the definition explains), the nature of desire.

FOURTH PART OF THE ETHICS   II/205
OF HUMAN BONDAGE, *OR* THE POWERS
OF THE AFFECTS

PREFACE

Man's lack of power to moderate and restrain the affects I call bondage.
For the man who is subject to affects is under the control, not of himself, but of fortune, in whose power he so greatly is that often, though
he sees the better for himself, he is still forced to follow the worse. In
this part, I have undertaken to demonstrate the cause of this, and what

there is of good and evil in the affects. But before I begin, I choose to say a few words first on perfection and imperfection, good and evil.

If someone has decided to make something, and has finished it, then he will call his thing perfect—and so will anyone who rightly knows, or thinks he knows, the mind and purpose of the author of the work. For example, if someone sees a work (which I suppose to be not yet completed), and knows that the purpose of the author of that work is to build a house, he will say that it is imperfect. On the other hand, he will call it perfect as soon as he sees that the work has been carried through to the end which its author had decided to give it. But if someone sees a work whose like he has never seen, and does not know the mind of its maker, he will, of course, not be able to know whether that work is II/206 perfect or imperfect. And this seems to have been the first meaning of these words.

But after men began to form universal ideas, and devise models of houses, buildings, towers, and the like, and to prefer some models of things to others, it came about that each one called perfect what he saw agreed with the universal idea he had formed of this kind of thing, and imperfect, what he saw agreed less with the model he had conceived, even though its maker thought he had entirely finished it.

Nor does there seem to be any other reason why men also commonly call perfect or imperfect natural things, which have not been made by human hand. For they are accustomed to form universal ideas of natural things as much as they do of artificial ones. They regard these universal ideas as models of things, and believe that Nature (which they think does nothing except for the sake of some end) looks to them, and sets them before itself as models. So when they see something happen in Nature which does not agree with the model they have conceived of this kind of thing, they believe that Nature itself has failed or sinned, and left the thing imperfect.

We see, therefore, that men are accustomed to call natural things perfect or imperfect more from prejudice than from true knowledge of those things. For we have shown in the Appendix of Part I, that Nature does nothing on account of an end. That eternal and infinite being we call God, *or* Nature, acts from the same necessity from which he exists. For we have shown (IP16) that the necessity of nature from which he acts is the same as that from which he exists. The reason, therefore, *or* II/207 cause, why God, *or* Nature, acts, and the reason why he exists, are one and the same. As he exists for the sake of no end, he also acts for the sake of no end. Rather, as he has no principle or end of existing, so he also has none of acting. What is called a final cause is nothing but a human appetite insofar as it is considered as a principle, *or* primary cause, of some thing.

For example, when we say that habitation was the final cause of this or that house, surely we understand nothing but that a man, because he imagined the conveniences of domestic life, had an appetite to build a house. So habitation, insofar as it is considered as a final cause, is nothing more than this singular appetite. It is really an efficient cause, which is considered as a first cause, because men are commonly ignorant of the causes of their appetites. For as I have often said before, they are conscious of their actions and appetites, but not aware of the causes by which they are determined to want something.

As for what they commonly say—that Nature sometimes fails or sins, and produces imperfect things—I number this among the fictions I treated in the Appendix of Part I.

Perfection and imperfection, therefore, are only modes of thinking, that is, notions we are accustomed to feign because we compare individuals of the same species or genus to one another. This is why I said above (IID6) that by reality and perfection I understand the same thing. For we are accustomed to refer all individuals in Nature to one genus, which is called the most general, that is, to the notion of being, which pertains absolutely to all individuals in Nature. So insofar as we refer all individuals in Nature to this genus, compare them to one another, and find that some have more being, or reality, than others, we say that some are more perfect than others. And insofar as we attribute something to them which involves negation, like a limit, an end, lack of power, and so on, we call them imperfect, because they do not affect our mind as much as those we call perfect, and not because something is lacking in them which is theirs, or because Nature has sinned. For nothing belongs to the nature of anything except what follows from the necessity of the nature of the efficient cause. And whatever follows from the necessity of the nature of the efficient cause happens necessarily.

II/208

As far as good and evil are concerned, they also indicate nothing positive in things, considered in themselves, nor are they anything other than modes of thinking, or notions we form because we compare things to one another. For one and the same thing can, at the same time, be good, and bad, and also indifferent. For example, music is good for one who is melancholy, bad for one who is mourning, and neither good nor bad to one who is deaf.

But though this is so, still we must retain these words. For because we desire to form an idea of man, as a model of human nature which we may look to, it will be useful to us to retain these same words with the meaning I have indicated. In what follows, therefore, I shall understand by good what we know certainly is a means by which we may approach nearer and nearer to the model of human nature we set before ourselves. By evil, what we certainly know prevents us from becoming like that model. Next, we shall say that men are more perfect or imperfect, insofar as they approach more or less near to this model.

For the main thing to note is that when I say that someone passes from a lesser to a greater perfection, and the opposite, I do not understand that he is changed from one essence, or form, to another. For example, a horse is destroyed as much if it is changed into a man as if it is changed into an insect. Rather, we conceive that his power of acting, insofar as it is understood through his nature, is increased or diminished.

II/209 Finally, by perfection in general I shall, as I have said, understand reality, that is, the essence of each thing insofar as it exists and produces an effect, having no regard to its duration. For no singular thing can be called more perfect for having persevered in existing for a longer time. Indeed, the duration of things cannot be determined from their essence, since the essence of things involves no certain and determinate time of existing. But any thing whatever, whether it is more perfect or less, will always be able to persevere in existing by the same force by which it begins to exist; so they are all equal in this regard.

DEFINITIONS

D1: By good I shall understand what we certainly know to be useful to us.

D2: By evil, however, I shall understand what we certainly know prevents us from being masters of some good.

Exp.: On these definitions, see the preceding preface [208/18–22].

D3: I call singular things contingent insofar as we find nothing, while we attend only to their essence, which necessarily posits their existence or which necessarily excludes it.

D4: I call the same singular things possible, insofar as, while we attend to the causes from which they must be produced, we do not know whether those causes are determined to produce them.

In IP33S1 I drew no distinction between the possible and the contingent, because there was no need there to distinguish them accurately.

D5: By opposite affects I shall understand, in what follows, those which
II/210 pull a man differently, although they are of the same genus—such as gluttony and greed, which are species of love, and are opposite, not by nature, but accidentally.

D6: I have explained in IIIP18S1 and S2 what I shall understand by an affect toward a future thing, a present one, and a past.

But here it should be noted in addition that just as we can distinctly imagine distance of place only up to a certain limit, so also we can distinctly imagine distance of time only up to a certain limit. That is, we usually imagine all those objects which are more than two hundred feet away from us, or whose distance from the place where we are surpasses what we can distinctly imagine, to be equally far from us; we therefore usually imagine them as if they were in the same plane; in the same way, we imagine to be equally far from the present all those objects whose time of existing we imagine to be separated from the present by an interval longer than that we are used to imagining distinctly; so we relate them, as it were, to one moment of time.

D7: By the end for the sake of which we do something I understand appetite.

D8: By virtue and power I understand the same thing, that is (by IIIP7), virtue, insofar as it is related to man, is the very essence, or nature, of man, insofar as he has the power of bringing about certain things, which can be understood through the laws of his nature alone.

AXIOM

[A1:] There is no singular thing in Nature than which there is not another more powerful and stronger. Whatever one is given, there is another more powerful by which the first can be destroyed.

P1: *Nothing positive which a false idea has is removed by the presence of the* II/211
true insofar as it is true.
  Dem.: Falsity consists only in the privation of knowledge which inadequate ideas involve (by IIP35), and they do not have anything positive on account of which they are called false (by IIP33). On the contrary, insofar as they are related to God, they are true (by IIP32). So if what a false idea has which is positive were removed by the presence of the true insofar as it is true, then a true idea would be removed by itself, which (by IIIP4) is absurd. Therefore, nothing positive which a false idea has, and so on, q.e.d.
  Schol.: This proposition is understood more clearly from IIP16C2. For an imagination is an idea which indicates the present constitution of the human body more than the nature of an external body—not distinctly, of course, but confusedly. This is how it happens that the mind is said to err.
  For example, when we look at the sun, we imagine it to be about two hundred feet away from us. In this we are deceived so long as we are ignorant of its true distance; but when its distance is known, the error is

removed, not the imagination, that is, the idea of the sun, which explains its nature only so far as the body is affected by it. And so, although we come to know the true distance, we shall nevertheless imagine it as near us. For as we said in IIP35S, we do not imagine the sun to be so near because we are ignorant of its true distance, but because the mind conceives the sun's size insofar as the body is affected by the sun. Thus, when the rays of the sun, falling on the surface of the water, are reflected to our eyes, we imagine it as if it were in the water, even if we know its true place.

And so it is with the other imaginations by which the mind is deceived, whether they indicate the natural constitution of the body, or II/212 that its power of acting is increased or diminished: they are not contrary to the true, and do not disappear on its presence. It happens, of course, when we wrongly fear some evil, that the fear disappears on our hearing news of the truth. But on the other hand, it also happens, when we fear an evil which is certain to come, that the fear vanishes on our hearing false news. So imaginations do not disappear through the presence of the true insofar as it is true, but because there occur others, stronger than them, which exclude the present existence of the things we imagine, as we showed in IIP17.

P2: *We are acted on, insofar as we are a part of Nature, which cannot be conceived through itself, without the others.*

Dem.: We say that we are acted on when something arises in us of which we are only the partial cause (by IIID2), that is (by IIID1), something which cannot be deduced from the laws of our nature alone. Therefore, we are acted on insofar as we are a part of Nature, which cannot be conceived through itself without the others, q.e.d.

P3: *The force by which a man perseveres in existing is limited, and infinitely surpassed by the power of external causes.*

Dem.: This is evident from A1. For given a man, there is something else, say A, more powerful. And given A, there is something else again, say B, more powerful than A, and so on, to infinity. Therefore, the power of man is limited by the power of another thing and infinitely surpassed by the power of external causes, q.e.d.

P4: *It is impossible that a man should not be a part of Nature, and that he should be able to undergo no changes except those which can be understood through his own nature alone, and of which he is the adequate cause.*

II/213 Dem.: [i] The power by which singular things (and consequently, [any] man) preserve their being is the power itself of God, *or* Nature (by IP24C), not insofar as it is infinite, but insofar as it can be explained through the man's actual essence (by IIIP7). The man's power, therefore, insofar as it is explained through his actual essence, is part of God *or* Nature's infinite power, that is (by IP34), of its essence. This was the first point.

[ii] Next, if it were possible that a man could undergo no changes except those which can be understood through the man's nature alone, it would follow (by IIIP4 and P6) that he could not perish, but that necessarily he would always exist. And this would have to follow from a cause whose power would be either finite or infinite, namely, either from the power of the man alone, who would be able to avert from himself other changes which could arise from external causes, or from the infinite power of Nature, by which all singular things would be directed so that the man could undergo no other changes except those which assist his preservation. But the first is absurd (by P3, whose demonstration is universal and can be applied to all singular things).

Therefore, if it were possible for a man to undergo no changes except those which could be understood through the man's nature alone, so that (as we have already shown) he would necessarily always exist, this would have to follow from God's infinite power; and consequently (by IP16) the order of the whole of Nature, insofar as it is conceived under the attributes of extension and thought, would have to be deduced from the necessity of the divine nature, insofar as it is considered to be affected with the idea of some man. And so (by IP21) it would follow that the man would be infinite. But this (by part [i] of this demonstration) is absurd.

Therefore, it is impossible that a man should undergo no other changes except those of which he himself is the adequate cause, q.e.d.

Cor.: From this it follows that man is necessarily always subject to passions, that he follows and obeys the common order of Nature, and accommodates himself to it as much as the nature of things requires.

P5: *The force and growth of any passion, and its perseverance in existing, are* II/214
not defined by the power by which we strive to persevere in existing, but by the
power of an external cause compared with our own.

Dem.: The essence of a passion cannot be explained through our essence alone (by IIID1 and D2), that is (by IIIP7), the power of a passion cannot be defined by the power by which we strive to persevere in our being; but (as has been shown in IIP16) it must necessarily be defined by the power of an external cause compared with our own, q.e.d.

P6: *The force of any passion, or affect, can surpass the other actions, or power, of a man, so that the affect stubbornly clings to the man.*

Dem.: The force and growth of any passion, and its perseverance in existing, are defined by the power of an external cause compared with our own (by P5). And so (by P3) it can surpass the power of a man, and so on, q.e.d.

P7: *An affect cannot be restrained or taken away except by an affect opposite to, and stronger than, the affect to be restrained.*

Dem.: An affect, insofar as it is related to the mind, is an idea by which the mind affirms of its body a greater or lesser force of existing than before (by the general Definition of the Affects [II/203/29–33]). When, therefore, the mind is troubled by some affect, the body is at the same time affected with an affection by which its power of acting is increased or diminished.

II/215   Next, this affection of the body (by P5) receives from its cause its force for persevering in its being, which, therefore, can neither be restrained nor removed, except by a corporeal cause (by IIP6) which affects the body with an affection opposite to it (by IIIP5), and stronger than it (by A1).

And so (by IIP12), the mind will be affected with the idea of an affection stronger than, and opposite to, the first affection, that is (by the general definition of the affects), the mind will be affected with an affect stronger than, and opposite to, the first affect, which will exclude or take away the existence of the first affect.

Therefore, an affect can neither be taken away nor restrained except through an opposite and stronger affect, q.e.d.

Cor.: An affect, insofar as it is related to the mind, can neither be restrained nor taken away except by the idea of an opposite affection of the body stronger than the affection by which we are acted on. For an affect by which we are acted on can neither be restrained nor taken away except by an affect stronger than it and contrary to it (by P7), that is (by the general definition of the affects), except by an idea of an affection of the body stronger than and contrary to the affection by which we are acted on.

P8: *The knowledge of good and evil is nothing but an affect of joy or sadness, insofar as we are conscious of it.*

Dem.: We call good, or evil, what is useful to, or harmful to, preserving our being (by D1 and D2), that is (by IIIP7), what increases or diminishes, aids or restrains, our power of acting. Therefore (by the definitions of joy and sadness in IIIP11S), insofar as we perceive that a thing affects us with joy or sadness, we call it good or evil. And so knowledge of good and evil is nothing but an idea of joy or sadness which follows necessarily from the affect of joy or sadness itself (by IIP22).

But this idea is united to the affect in the same way as the mind is united to the body (by IIP21), that is (as I have shown in IIP21S), this idea is not really distinguished from the affect itself, *or* (by the general definition of the affects) from the idea of the body's affection; it is only conceptually distinguished from it. Therefore, this knowledge of good and evil is nothing but the affect itself, insofar as we are conscious of it, q.e.d.

II/216

P9: *An affect whose cause we imagine to be with us in the present is stronger than if we did not imagine it to be with us.*

Dem.: An imagination is an idea by which the mind considers a thing as present (see its definition in IIP17S), which nevertheless indicates the constitution of the human body more than the nature of the external thing (by IIP16C2). An affect, therefore (by the general definition of the affects), is an imagination, insofar as [the affect] indicates the constitution of the body. But an imagination (by IIP17) is more intense so long as we imagine nothing which excludes the present existence of the external thing. Hence, an affect whose cause we imagine to be with us in the present is more intense, *or* stronger, than if we did not imagine it to be with us, q.e.d.

Schol.: I said above (in IIIP18) that when we imagine a future or past thing, we are affected with the same affect as if we were imagining something present; but I expressly warned then that this is true insofar as we attend to the thing's image only. For it is of the same nature whether we have imagined the thing as present or not. But I did not deny that it is made weaker when we consider as present to us other things, which exclude the present existence of the future thing. I neglected to point this out then, because I had decided to treat the powers of the affects in this Part.

Cor.: Other things equal, the image of a future or past thing (i.e., of a thing we consider in relation to a future or past time, the present being excluded) is weaker than the image of a present thing; and consequently, an affect toward a future or past thing is milder, other things equal, than an affect toward a present thing.

II/217

P10: *We are affected more intensely toward a future thing which we imagine will quickly be present, than if we imagined the time when it will exist to be further from the present. We are also affected more intensely by the memory of a thing we imagine to be not long past, than if we imagined it to be long past.*

Dem.: Insofar as we imagine that a thing will quickly be present, or is not long past, we thereby imagine something which excludes the presence of the thing less than if we imagined that the time when it will exist were further from the present, or that it were far in the past (as is known through itself). And so (by P9), to that extent we will be affected more intensely toward it, q.e.d.

Schol.: From what we noted at D6, it follows that we are still affected equally mildly toward objects separated from the present by an interval of time longer than that we can determine by imagining, even though we may understand that they are separated from one another by a long interval of time.

P11: *An affect toward a thing we imagine as necessary is more intense, other things equal, than one toward a thing we imagine as possible or contingent, or not necessary.*

II/218

Dem.: Insofar as we imagine a thing to be necessary, we affirm its existence. On the other hand, we deny its existence insofar as we imagine it not to be necessary (by IP33S1), and therefore (by P9), an affect toward a necessary thing is more intense, other things equal, than toward one not necessary, q.e.d.

P12: *An affect toward a thing which we know does not exist in the present, and which we imagine as possible, is more intense, other things equal, than one toward a contingent thing.*

Dem.: Insofar as we imagine a thing as contingent, we are not affected by any image of another thing which posits the thing's existence (by D3); but on the other hand (according to the hypothesis), we imagine certain things which exclude its present existence. But insofar as we imagine a thing in the future to be possible, we imagine certain things which posit its existence (by D4), that is (by IIIP18), which encourage hope or fear. And so an affect toward a possible thing is more violent [, other things equal, than one toward a contingent thing], q.e.d.

Cor.: An affect toward a thing which we know does not exist in the present, and which we imagine as contingent, is much milder than if we imagined the thing as with us in the present.

Dem.: An affect toward a thing which we imagine to exist in the present is more intense than if we imagined it as future (by P9C), and [an affect toward a thing we imagine to exist in the future is] much more violent if we imagine the future time to be not far from the present (by P10). Therefore, an affect toward a thing which we imagine will exist at a time far from the present is much milder than if we imagined it as present. And nevertheless (by P12), it is more intense than if we imagined that thing as contingent. And so an affect toward a contingent thing will be much milder than if we imagined the thing to be with us in the present, q.e.d.

P13: *An affect toward a contingent thing which we know does not exist in the present is milder, other things equal, than an affect toward a past thing.*

Dem.: Insofar as we imagine a thing as contingent, we are not affected by any image of another thing which posits the thing's existence (by D3). But on the other hand (according to the hypothesis), we imagine certain things which exclude its present existence. Now insofar as we imagine a thing in relation to past time, we are supposed to imagine something which brings it back to our memory, *or* that arouses the image of the thing (see IIP18 and P18S), and therefore brings it about that we consider it as if it were present (by IIP17C). And so (by P9) an affect toward a contingent thing which we know does not exist in the present will be milder, other things equal, than an affect toward a past thing, q.e.d.

P14: *No affect can be restrained by the true knowledge of good and evil insofar as it is true, but only insofar as it is considered as an affect.*

Dem.: An affect is an idea by which the mind affirms of its body a greater or lesser force of existing than before (by the general Definition of the Affects). So (by P1), it has nothing positive which could be removed by the presence of the true. Consequently the true knowledge of good and evil, insofar as it is true, cannot restrain any affect.

But insofar as it is an affect (see P8), if it is stronger than the affect to be restrained, to that extent only (by P7) can it restrain the affect, q.e.d.

P15: *A desire which arises from a true knowledge of good and evil can be extinguished or restrained by many other desires which arise from affects by which we are tormented.*

Dem.: From a true knowledge of good and evil, insofar as this is an affect (by P8), there necessarily arises a desire (by Def. Aff. I), which is the greater as the affect from which it arises is greater (by IIIP37). But because this desire arises (by hypothesis) from the fact that we understand something truly, it follows in us insofar as we act (by IIIP3). And so it must be understood through our essence alone (by IIID2), and consequently (by IIIP7), its force and growth can be defined only by human power alone.

Next, desires which arise from affects by which we are torn are also greater as these affects are more violent. And so their force and growth (by P5) must be defined by the power of external causes, which, if it were compared with ours, would indefinitely surpass our power (by P3). Hence, desires which arise from such affects can be more violent than the desire which arises from a true knowledge of good and evil, and can therefore (by P7) restrain or extinguish it, q.e.d.

P16: *A desire which arises from a true knowledge of good and evil, insofar as this knowledge concerns the future, can be quite easily restrained or extinguished by a desire for the pleasures of the moment.*

Dem.: An affect toward a thing we imagine as future is milder than one toward a present thing (by P9C). But a desire which arises from a true knowledge of good and evil, even if this knowledge concerns things which are good now, can be restrained or extinguished by some rash desire (by P15, whose demonstration is universal). Therefore, a desire which arises from the same knowledge, insofar as this concerns a future thing, can be quite easily restrained or extinguished, and so on, q.e.d.

II/221

P17: *A desire which arises from a true knowledge of good and evil, insofar as this concerns contingent things, can be restrained much more easily still by a desire for things which are present.*

Dem.: This proposition is demonstrated in the same way as the preceding one, from P12C.

Schol.: With this I believe I have shown the cause why men are moved more by opinion than by true reason, and why the true knowledge of good and evil arouses disturbances of the mind, and often yields to lust of every kind. Hence that verse of the Poet:

> . . . video meliora, proboque,
> deteriora sequor. . . .[2]

Ecclesiastes also seems to have had the same thing in mind when he said: "He who increases knowledge increases sorrow."[3]

I do not say these things in order to infer that it is better to be ignorant than to know, or that there is no difference between the fool and the man who understands when it comes to moderating the affects. My reason, rather, is that it is necessary to come to know both our nature's power and its lack of power, so that we can determine what reason can do in moderating the affects, and what it cannot do. I said that in this part I would treat only of man's lack of power. For I have decided to treat reason's power over the affects separately.

P18: *A desire which arises from joy is stronger, other things equal, than one which arises from sadness.*

II/222

Dem.: Desire is the very essence of man (by Def. Aff. I), that is (by IIIP7), a striving by which a man strives to persevere in his being. So a desire which arises from joy is aided or increased by the affect of joy itself (by the Def. of joy in IIIP11S), whereas one which arises from

---

[2] Ovid, *Metamorphoses* VII, 20–21: "I see and approve the better, but follow the worse." Medea is torn between reason's demand that she obey her father and her passion for Jason.
[3] *Ecclesiastes* 1:18.

sadness is diminished or restrained by the affect of sadness (by the same Schol.). And so the force of a desire which arises from joy must be defined both by human power and the power of the external cause, whereas the force of a desire which arises from sadness must be defined by human power alone. The former, therefore, is stronger than the latter, q.e.d.

Schol.: With these few words I have explained the causes of man's lack of power and inconstancy, and why men do not observe the precepts of reason. Now it remains for me to show what reason prescribes to us, which affects agree with the rules of human reason, and which, on the other hand, are contrary to those rules. But before I begin to demonstrate these things in our cumbersome geometric order, I should like first to show briefly here the dictates of reason themselves, so that everyone may more easily perceive what I think.

Since reason demands nothing contrary to Nature, it demands that everyone love himself, seek his own advantage, what is really useful to him, want what will really lead a man to greater perfection, and absolutely, that everyone should strive to preserve his own being as far as he can. This, indeed, is as necessarily true as that the whole is greater than its part (see IIIP4).

Further, since virtue (by D8) is nothing but acting from the laws of one's own nature, and no one strives to preserve his being (by IIIP7) except from the laws of his own nature, it follows:

(i) that the foundation of virtue is this very striving to preserve one's own being, and that happiness consists in a man's being able to preserve his being;

(ii) that we ought to want virtue for its own sake, and that there is not anything preferable to it, or more useful to us, for the sake of which we ought to want it; and finally (iii) that those who kill themselves are weakminded and completely conquered by external causes contrary to their nature.

Again, from IIPost. 4 [II/102/29–31] it follows that we can never bring it about that we require nothing outside ourselves to preserve our being, nor that we live without having dealings with things outside us. II/223 Moreover, if we consider our mind, our intellect would of course be more imperfect if the mind were alone and did not understand anything except itself. There are, therefore, many things outside us which are useful to us, and on that account to be sought.

Of these, we can think of none more excellent than those which agree entirely with our nature. For if, for example, two individuals of entirely the same nature are joined to one another, they compose an individual twice as powerful as each one. To man, then, there is nothing more useful than man. Man, I say, can wish for nothing more helpful to the preservation of his being than that all should so agree in all things that the minds and bodies of all would compose, as it were, one mind and one body; that all should strive together, as far as they can, to preserve their being; and that all, together, should seek for themselves the common advantage of all.

From this it follows that men who are governed by reason—that is, men who, from the guidance of reason, seek their own advantage—want nothing for themselves which they do not desire for other men. Hence, they are just, honest, and honorable.

These are those dictates of reason which I promised to present briefly here before I began to demonstrate them in a more cumbersome order. I have done this to win, if possible, the attention of those who believe that this principle—that everyone is bound to seek his own advantage—is the foundation, not of virtue and morality, but of immorality. Now that I have shown briefly that the contrary is true, I proceed to demonstrate this in the same way I have followed up to this point.

P19: *From the laws of his own nature, everyone necessarily wants, or is repelled by, what he judges to be good or evil.*

Dem.: Knowledge of good and evil (by P8) is itself an affect of joy or sadness, insofar as we are conscious of it. And therefore (by IIIP28), everyone necessarily wants what he judges to be good, and conversely, is repelled by what he judges to be evil. But this appetite is nothing but the very essence, *or* nature, of man (by the definition of appetite; see IIIP9S and Def. Aff. I). Therefore, everyone, from the laws of his own nature, necessarily, wants or is repelled by, and so on, q.e.d.

II/224

P20: *The more each one strives, and is able, to seek his own advantage, that is, to preserve his being, the more he is endowed with virtue; conversely, insofar as each one neglects his own advantage, that is, neglects to preserve his being, he lacks power.*

Dem.: Virtue is human power itself, which is defined by man's essence alone (by D8), that is (by IIIP7), solely by the striving by which man strives to persevere in his being. So the more each one strives, and is able, to preserve his being, the more he is endowed with virtue. And consequently (by IIIP4 and P6), insofar as someone neglects to preserve his being, he lacks power, q.e.d.

Schol: No one, therefore, unless he is defeated by causes external, and contrary, to his nature, neglects to seek his own advantage, *or* to preserve his being. No one, I say, avoids food or kills himself from the necessity of his own nature. Those who do such things are compelled by external causes, which can happen in many ways. Someone may kill himself because he is compelled by another, who twists his right hand (which happened to hold a sword) and forces him to direct the sword against his heart; or because he is forced by the command of a tyrant (as Seneca was) to open his veins, that is, he desires to avoid a greater evil by [submitting to] a lesser; or finally because hidden external causes so dispose his imagination, and so affect his body, that it takes on another nature, contrary to the former, a nature of which there cannot be an idea in the mind (by IIIP10). But that a man should, from the necessity of his own nature, strive not to exist, or to be changed into another form, is as impossible as that something should come from nothing. Anyone who gives this a little thought will see it.

II/225

P21: *No one can desire to be blessed, to act well and to live well, unless at the same time he desires to be, to act, and to live, that is, to actually exist.*

Dem.: The demonstration of this proposition, *or* rather the thing itself, is evident through itself, and also from the definition of desire. For the desire (by Def. Aff. I) to live blessedly, *or* well, to act, and so on, is the very essence of man, that is (by IIIP7), the striving by which each one strives to preserve his being. Therefore, no one can desire, and so on, q.e.d.

P22: *No virtue can be conceived prior to this [virtue] (viz. the striving to preserve oneself).*

Dem.: The striving to preserve itself is the very essence of a thing (by IIIP7). Therefore, if some virtue could be conceived prior to this [virtue], namely, to this striving, the very essence of the thing would be conceived prior to itself (by D8), which is absurd (as is known through itself). Therefore, no virtue, and so on, q.e.d.

Cor.: The striving to preserve oneself is the first and only foundation of virtue. For no other principle can be conceived prior to this one (by P22) and no virtue can be conceived without it (by P21).

P23: *A man cannot be said absolutely to act from virtue insofar as he is determined to do something because he has inadequate ideas, but only insofar as he is determined because he understands.*

Dem.: Insofar as a man is determined to act from the fact that he has inadequate ideas, he is acted on (by IIIP1), that is (by IIID1 and D2), he does something which cannot be perceived through his essence alone, that is (by D8), which does not follow from his virtue. But insofar as he is determined to do something from the fact that he understands, he acts (by IIIP1), that is (by IIID2), does something which is perceived through his essence alone, *or* (by D8) which follows adequately from his virtue, q.e.d.

II/226

P24: *Acting absolutely from virtue is nothing else in us but acting, living, and preserving our being (these three signify the same thing) by the guidance of reason, from the foundation of seeking one's own advantage.*

Dem.: Acting absolutely from virtue is nothing but acting from the laws of our own nature (by D8). But we act only insofar as we understand (by IIIP3). Therefore, acting from virtue is nothing else in us but acting, living, and preserving one's being by the guidance of reason, and doing this (by P22C) from the foundation of seeking one's own advantage, q.e.d.

P25: *No one strives to preserve his being for the sake of anything else.*

Dem.: The striving by which each thing strives to persevere in its being is defined by the thing's essence alone (by IIIP7). If this [essence] alone is given, then it follows necessarily that each one strives to preserve his being—but this does not follow necessarily from the essence of any other thing (by IIIP6).

II/227   This proposition, moreover, is evident from P22C. For if a man strove to preserve his being for the sake of something else, then that thing would be the first foundation of virtue (as is known through itself). But (by P22C) this is absurd. Therefore, no one strives, and so on, q.e.d.

P26: *What we strive for from reason is nothing but understanding; nor does the mind, insofar as it uses reason, judge anything else useful to itself except what leads to understanding.*

Dem.: The striving to preserve itself is nothing but the essence of the thing itself (by IIIP7), which, insofar as it exists as it does, is conceived to have a force for persevering in existing (by IIIP6) and for doing those things which necessarily follow from its given nature (see the definition of appetite in IIIP9S). But the essence of reason is nothing but our mind, insofar as it understands clearly and distinctly (see the definition of this in IIP40S2). Therefore (by IIP40) whatever we strive for from reason is nothing but understanding.

Next, since this striving of the mind, by which the mind, insofar as it reasons, strives to preserve its being, is nothing but understanding (by the first part of this demonstration), this striving for understanding (by P22C) is the first and only foundation of virtue, nor do we strive to understand things for the sake of some end (by P25). On the contrary, the mind, insofar as it reasons, cannot conceive anything to be good for itself except what leads to understanding (by D1), q.e.d.

P27: *We know nothing to be certainly good or evil, except what really leads to understanding or what can prevent us from understanding.*

Dem.: Insofar as the mind reasons, it wants nothing other than to understand, nor does it judge anything else to be useful to itself except what leads to understanding (by P26). But the mind (by IIP41, P43, and P43S) has certainty of things only insofar as it has adequate ideas, *or* (what is the same thing, by IIP40S) insofar as it reasons. Therefore, we know nothing to be certainly good except what really leads to understanding, and conversely, know nothing to be certainly evil except what can prevent us from understanding, q.e.d.

II/228

P28: *Knowledge of God is the mind's greatest good; its greatest virtue is to know God.*

Dem.: The greatest thing the mind can understand is God, that is (by ID6), a being absolutely infinite, without which (by IP15) nothing can either be or be conceived. And so (by P26 and P27), the mind's greatest advantage, *or* (by D1) good, is knowledge of God.

Next, only insofar as the mind understands (by IIIP1 and P3), does it act, and can it be said absolutely to act from virtue (by P23). The absolute virtue of the mind, then, is understanding. But the greatest thing the mind can understand is God (as we have already demonstrated). Therefore, the greatest virtue of the mind is to understand, *or* know, God, q.e.d.

P29: *Any singular thing whose nature is entirely different from ours can neither aid nor restrain our power of acting, and absolutely, no thing can be either good or evil for us, unless it has something in common with us.*

Dem.: The power of each singular thing, and consequently (by IIP10C), man's power, by which he exists and produces an effect, is not determined except by another singular thing (by IP28), whose nature must be understood (by IIP6) through the same attribute through which human nature is conceived. Our power of acting, therefore, however it is conceived, can be determined, and hence aided or restrained, by the power of another singular thing which has something in common with us, and not by the power of a thing whose nature is completely different from ours.

II/229

And because we call good or evil what is the cause of joy or sadness (by P8), that is (by IIIP11S), what increases or diminishes, aids or restrains, our power of acting, a thing whose nature is completely different from ours can be neither good nor evil for us, q.e.d.

P30: *No thing can be evil through what it has in common with our nature; but insofar as it is evil for us, it is contrary to us.*

Dem.: We call evil what is the cause of sadness (by P8), that is (by the definition of sadness, see IIIP11S), what diminishes or restrains our power of acting. So if a thing were evil for us through what it has in common with us, then the thing could diminish or restrain what it has in common with us. But (by IIIP4) this is absurd. Therefore, no thing can be evil for us through what it has in common with us. On the contrary, insofar as it is evil, that is (as we have already shown), insofar as it can diminish or restrain our power of acting, it is contrary to us (by IIIP5), q.e.d.

P31: *Insofar as a thing agrees with our nature, it is necessarily good.*

Dem.: Insofar as a thing agrees with our nature, it cannot be evil (by
II/230 P30). So it must either be good or indifferent. If the latter is posited, namely, that it is neither good nor evil, then (by A3) nothing will follow from its nature which aids the preservation of our nature, that is (by hypothesis), which aids the preservation of the nature of the thing itself. But this is absurd (by IIIP6). Hence, insofar as it agrees with our nature, it must be good, q.e.d.

Cor.: From this it follows that the more a thing agrees with our nature, the more useful, *or* better, it is for us, and conversely, the more a thing is useful to us, the more it agrees with our nature.

For insofar as it does not agree with our nature, it will necessarily be different from it or contrary to it. If it is different from it, then (by P29) it can be neither good nor evil. And if it is contrary, then it will also be contrary to that which agrees with our nature, that is (by P31), contrary to the good, *or* evil. Nothing, therefore, can be good except insofar as it agrees with our nature. So the more a thing agrees with our nature, the more useful it is, and conversely, q.e.d.

P32: *Insofar as men are subject to passions, they cannot be said to agree in nature.*

Dem.: Things which are said to agree in nature are understood to agree in power (by IIIP7), but not in lack of power, *or* negation, and consequently (see IIIP3S) not in passion either. So insofar as men are subject to passions, they cannot be said to agree in nature, q.e.d.

Schol.: This matter is also evident through itself. If someone says that black and white agree only in this, that neither is red, he affirms absolutely that black and white agree in nothing. Similarly, if someone says that a stone and a man agree only in this, that each is finite, lacks
II/231 power, does not exist from the necessity of its nature, or, finally, is indefinitely surpassed by the power of external causes, he affirms completely that a stone and a man do not agree in anything. For things which agree only in a negation, *or* in what they do not have, really agree in nothing.

P33: *Men can disagree in nature insofar as they are torn by affects which are passions; and to that extent also one and the same man is changeable and inconstant.*

Dem.: The nature, *or* essence, of the affects cannot be explained through our essence, *or* nature, alone (by IIID1 and D2), but must be defined by the power, that is (by IIIP7), by the nature of external causes compared with our own. That is why there are as many species of each affect as there are species of objects by which we are affected (see IIIP56); that is why men are affected differently by one and the same object (see IIIP51), and to that extent, disagree in nature. And finally, that is also why one and the same man (again, by IIIP51) is affected differently toward the same object, and to that extent is changeable, and so on, q.e.d.

P34: *Insofar as men are torn by affects which are passions, they can be contrary to one another.*

Dem.: A man—Peter, say—can be a cause of Paul's being saddened, because he has something like a thing Paul hates (by IIIP16), or because Peter alone possesses something which Paul also loves (see IIIP32 and P32S), or on account of other causes (for the main causes, see IIIP55S). And so it will happen, as a result (by Def. Aff. VII), that Paul hates Peter. Hence, it will easily happen (by IIIP40 and P40S) that Peter hates Paul II/232 in return, and so (by IIIP39) that they strive to harm one another; that is (by P30), that they are contrary to one another. But an affect of sadness is always a passion (by IIIP59). Therefore, men, insofar as they are torn by affects which are passions, can be contrary to one another, q.e.d.

Schol.: I have said that Paul hates Peter because he imagines that Peter possesses what Paul himself also loves. At first glance it seems to follow from this that these two are injurious to one another because they love the same thing, and hence, because they agree in nature. If this were true, then P30 and P31 would be false.

But if we are willing to examine the matter fairly, we shall see that all these propositions are completely consistent. For these two are not troublesome to one another insofar as they agree in nature, that is, insofar as each loves the same thing, but insofar as they disagree with one another. For insofar as each loves the same thing, each one's love is thereby encouraged (by IIIP31). That is (by Def. Aff. VI), each one's joy is thereby encouraged. So it is far from true that they are troublesome to one another insofar as they love the same thing and agree in nature.

Instead, as I have said, the cause of [their enmity] is nothing but the fact that (as we suppose) they disagree in nature. For we suppose that

Peter has the idea of a thing he loves which is already possessed, whereas Paul has the idea of a thing he loves which is lost. That is why the one is affected with joy and the other with sadness, and to that extent they are contrary to one another.

In this way we can easily show that the other causes of hate depend only on the fact that men disagree in nature, not on that in which they agree.

P35: *Only insofar as men live according to the guidance of reason, must they always agree in nature.*

Dem.: Insofar as men are torn by affects which are passions, they can be different in nature (by P33), and contrary to one another (by P34). But insofar as men live according to the guidance of reason, they are said only to act (by IIIP3). Hence, whatever follows from human nature, insofar as it is defined by reason, must be understood through human nature alone (by IIID2), as through its proximate cause. But because each one, from the laws of his own nature, wants what he judges to be good, and strives to avert what he judges to be evil (by P19), and moreover, because what we judge to be good or evil when we follow the dictate of reason must be good or evil (by IIP41), it follows that insofar as men live according to the guidance of reason, they must do only those things which are good for human nature, and hence, for each man, that is (by P31C), those things which agree with the nature of each man. Hence, insofar as men live according to the guidance of reason, they must always agree among themselves, q.e.d.

Cor. 1: There is no singular thing in Nature which is more useful to man than a man who lives according to the guidance of reason.

For what is most useful to man is what most agrees with his nature (by P31C), that is (as is known through itself), man. But a man acts entirely from the laws of his own nature when he lives according to the guidance of reason (by IIID2), and only to that extent must he always agree with the nature of the other man (by P35). Therefore, among singular things there is nothing more useful to man than a man, and so on, q.e.d.

Cor. 2.: When each man most seeks his own advantage for himself, then men are most useful to one another.

For the more each one seeks his own advantage, and strives to preserve himself, the more he is endowed with virtue (by P20), *or* what is the same (by D8), the greater is his power of acting according to the laws of his own nature, that is (by IIIP3), of living from the guidance of reason. But men most agree in nature, when they live according to the guidance of reason (by P35). Therefore (by P35C1), men will be most useful to one another, when each one most seeks his own advantage, q.e.d.

Schol.: What we have just shown is also confirmed by daily experi- II/234 ence, which provides so much and such clear evidence that this saying is in almost everyone's mouth: man is a God to man.

Still, it rarely happens that men live according to the guidance of reason. Instead, their lives are so constituted that they are usually envious and burdensome to one another. They can hardly, however, live a solitary life; hence, that definition which makes man a social animal has been quite pleasing to most. And surely we do derive, from the society of our fellow men, many more advantages than disadvantages.

So let the satirists laugh as much as they like at human affairs, let the theologians curse them, let melancholics praise as much as they can a life that is uncultivated and wild, let them disdain men and admire the lower animals. Men still find from experience that by helping one another they can provide themselves much more easily with the things they require, and that only by joining forces can they avoid the dangers which threaten on all sides—not to mention that it is much preferable and more worthy of our knowledge to consider the deeds of men, rather than those of the lower animals. But I shall treat this topic more fully elsewhere.

P36: *The greatest good of those who seek virtue is common to all, and can be enjoyed by all equally.*

Dem.: To act from virtue is to act according to the guidance of reason (by P24), and whatever we strive for from reason is understanding (by P26). Hence (by P28), the greatest good of those who seek virtue is to know God, that is (by IIP47 and P47S), a good that is common to all men, and can be possessed equally by all men insofar as they are of the same nature, q.e.d.

Schol.: But suppose someone should ask: what if the greatest good of those who seek virtue were not common to all? Would it not follow II/235 from that, as above (see P34), that men who live according to the guidance of reason, that is (by P35), men, insofar as they agree in nature, would be contrary to one another?

To this the answer is that it is not by accident that man's greatest good is common to all; rather, it arises from the very nature of reason, because it is deduced from the very essence of man, insofar as [that essence] is defined by reason, and because man could neither be nor be conceived if he did not have the power to enjoy this greatest good. For it pertains to the essence of the human mind (by IIP47) to have an adequate knowledge of God's eternal and infinite essence.

P37: *The good which everyone who seeks virtue wants for himself, he also desires for other men; and this desire is greater as his knowledge of God is greater.*

Dem.: Insofar as men live according to the guidance of reason, they are most useful to man (by P35C1); hence (by P19), according to the guidance of reason, we necessarily strive to bring it about that men live according to the guidance of reason. Now, the good which everyone who lives according to the dictate of reason (i.e., by P24, who seeks virtue) wants for himself is understanding (by P26). Therefore, the good which everyone who seeks virtue wants for himself, he also desires for other men.

Next, desire, insofar as it is related to the mind, is the very essence of the mind (by Def. Aff. I). Now the essence of the mind consists in knowledge (by IIP11), which involves knowledge of God (by IIP47). Without this [knowledge the mind] can neither be nor be conceived (by IP15). Hence, as the mind's essence involves a greater knowledge of God, so will the desire also be greater by which one who seeks virtue desires for another the good he wants for himself, q.e.d.

Alternative Dem.: The good which man wants for himself and loves, II/236 he will love more constantly if he sees that others love it (by IIIP31). So (by IIIP31C), he will strive to have the others love the same thing. And because this good is common to all (by P36), and all can enjoy it, he will therefore (by the same reason) strive that all may enjoy it. And this striving will be the greater, the more he enjoys this good (by IIIP37), q.e.d.

Schol. 1: He who strives, only because of an affect, that others should love what he loves, and live according to his temperament, acts only from impulse and is hateful—especially to those to whom other things are pleasing, and who also, therefore, strive eagerly, from the same impulse, to have other men live according to their own temperament. And since the greatest good men seek from an affect is often such that only one can possess it fully, those who love are not of one mind in their love—while they rejoice to sing the praises of the thing they love, they fear to be believed. But he who strives from reason to guide others acts not by impulse, but kindly, generously, and with the greatest steadfastness of mind.

Again, whatever we desire and do of which we are the cause insofar as we have the idea of God, *or* insofar as we know God, I relate to religion. The desire to do good generated in us by our living according to the guidance of reason, I call morality. The desire by which a man who lives according to the guidance of reason is bound to join others to himself in friendship, I call being honorable, and I call that honorable which men who live according to the guidance of reason praise; on the other hand, what is contrary to the formation of friendship, I call dishonorable.

In addition to this, I have also shown what the foundations of the state are.

Furthermore, from what has been said above, one can easily perceive the difference between true virtue and lack of power; true virtue is nothing but living according to the guidance of reason, and so lack of power consists only in this, that a man allows himself to be guided by things outside him, and to be determined by them to do what the common constitution of external things demands, not what his own nature, considered in itself, demands.

These are the things I promised, in P18S, to demonstrate. From them it is clear that the law against killing animals is based more on empty superstition and unmanly compassion than sound reason. The rational principle of seeking our own advantage teaches us to establish a bond with men, but not with the lower animals, or with things whose nature is different from human nature. We have the same right against them that they have against us. Indeed, because the right of each one is defined by his virtue, *or* power, men have a far greater right against the lower animals than they have against men. Not that I deny that the lower animals have sensations. But I do deny that we are therefore not permitted to consider our own advantage, use them at our pleasure, and treat them as is most convenient for us. For they do not agree in nature with us, and their affects are different in nature from human affects (see IIIP57S). II/237

It remains now for me to explain what is just and what unjust, what sin is, and finally, what merit is. These matters will be taken up in the following scholium.

Schol. 2: In the Appendix of Part I, I promised to explain what praise and blame, merit and sin, and justice and injustice are. As far as praise and blame are concerned, I have explained them in IIIP29S. This will be the place to speak of the others. But first a few words must be said about man's natural state and his civil state.

Everyone exists by the highest right of Nature, and consequently everyone, by the highest right of Nature, does those things which follow from the necessity of his own nature. So everyone, by the highest right of Nature, judges what is good and what is evil, considers his own advantage according to his own temperament (see P19 and P20), avenges himself (see IIIP40C2), and strives to preserve what he loves and destroy what he hates (see IIIP28).

If men lived according to the guidance of reason, everyone would possess this right of his (by P35C1) without any injury to anyone else.

But because they are subject to the affects (by P4C), which far surpass man's power, *or* virtue (by P6), they are often drawn in different directions (by P33) and are contrary to one another (by P34), while they require one another's aid (by P35S).

In order, therefore, that men may be able to live harmoniously and be of assistance to one another, it is necessary for them to give up their natural right and to make one another confident that they will do noth-

II/238   ing which could harm others. How it can happen that men who are necessarily subject to affects (by P4C), inconstant and changeable (by P33) should be able to make one another confident and have trust in one another, is clear from P7 and IIIP39. No affect can be restrained except by an affect stronger than and contrary to the affect to be restrained, and everyone refrains from doing harm out of timidity regarding a greater harm.

By this law, therefore, society can be maintained, provided it appropriates to itself the right everyone has of avenging himself, and of judging concerning good and evil. In this way society has the power to prescribe a common rule of life, to make laws, and to maintain them— not by reason, which cannot restrain the affects (by P17S), but by threats. This society, maintained by laws and the power it has of preserving itself, is called a state, and those who are defended by its law, citizens.

From this we easily understand that there is nothing in the state of nature which, by the agreement of all, is good or evil; for everyone who is in the state of nature considers only his own advantage, and decides what is good and what is evil from his own temperament, and only insofar as he takes account of his own advantage. He is not bound by any law to submit to anyone except himself. So in the state of nature no sin can be conceived.

But in the civil state, of course, it is decided by common agreement what is good or what is evil. And everyone is bound to submit to the state. Sin, therefore, is nothing but disobedience, which for that reason can be punished only by the law of the state. On the other hand, obedience is considered a merit in a citizen, because on that account he is judged worthy of enjoying the advantages of the state.

Again, in the state of nature there is no one who by common consent is Master of anything, nor is there anything in Nature which can be said to be this man's and not that man's. Instead, all things belong to all. So in the state of nature, there cannot be conceived any will to give to each his own, or to take away from someone what is his. That is, in the state of nature nothing is done which can be called just or unjust.

But in the civil state, of course, where it is decided by common consent what belongs to this man, and what to that [, things are done which can be called just or unjust].

From this it is clear that just and unjust, sin and merit, are extrinsic notions, not attributes which explain the nature of the mind. But enough of this.

P38: *Whatever so disposes the human body that it can be affected in a great many ways, or renders it capable of affecting external bodies in a great many ways, is useful to man; the more it renders the body capable of being affected in a great many ways, or of affecting other bodies, the more useful it is; on the other hand, what renders the body less capable of these things is harmful.*

Dem.: The more the body is rendered capable of these things, the more the mind is rendered capable of perceiving (by IIP14). And so what disposes the body in this way, and renders it capable of these things, is necessarily good, *or* useful (by P26 and P27), and the more useful the more capable of these things it renders the body. On the other hand (by the converse of IIP14, and by P26 and P27), it is harmful if it renders the body less capable of these things, q.e.d.

P39: *Those things are good which bring about the preservation of the proportion of motion and rest the human body's parts have to one another; on the other hand, those things are evil which bring it about that the parts of the human body have a different proportion of motion and rest to one another.*

Dem.: To be preserved, the human body requires a great many other bodies (by IIPost. 4). But what constitutes the form of the human body consists in this, that its parts communicate their motions to one another in a certain fixed proportion (by the definition [at II/99–100]). Therefore, things which bring it about that the parts of the human body preserve the same proportion of motion and rest to one another, preserve the human body's form. Hence, they bring it about that the human body can be affected in many ways, and that it can affect external bodies in many ways (by IIPost. 3 and Post. 6). So they are good (by P38).

Next, things which bring it about that the human body's parts acquire a different proportion of motion and rest to one another bring it about (by the same definition [at II/99–100]) that the human body takes on another form, that is (as is known through itself, and as I pointed out at the end of the preface of this part), that the human body is destroyed, and hence rendered completely incapable of being affected in many ways. So (by P38), they are evil, q.e.d.

Schol.: In Part V I shall explain how much these things can be harmful to or beneficial to the mind. But here it should be noted that I understand the body to die when its parts are so disposed that they acquire a different proportion of motion and rest to one another. For I dare not deny that—even though the circulation of the blood is maintained, as well as the other [signs] on account of which the body is thought to be alive—the human body can nevertheless be changed into another nature entirely different from its own. For no reason compels me to maintain that the body does not die unless it is changed into a corpse.

And, indeed, experience seems to urge a different conclusion. Sometimes a man undergoes such changes that I should hardly have said he was the same man. I have heard stories, for example, of a spanish poet who suffered an illness; though he recovered, he was left so oblivious to his past life that he did not believe the tales and tragedies he had written were his own. He could surely have been taken for a grown-up infant if he had also forgotten his native language.

If this seems incredible, what shall we say of infants? A man of advanced years believes their nature to be so different from his own that he could not be persuaded that he was ever an infant, if he did not make this conjecture concerning himself from [NS: the example of] others. But rather than provide the superstitious with material for raising new questions, I prefer to leave this discussion unfinished.

II/241   P40: *Things which are of assistance to the common society of men,* or *which bring it about that men live harmoniously, are useful; those, on the other hand, are evil which bring discord to the state.*

Dem.: For things which bring it about that men live harmoniously, at the same time bring it about that they live according to the guidance of reason (by P35). And so (by P26 and P27) they are good.

And on the other hand (by the same reasoning), those are evil which arouse discord, q.e.d.

P41: *Joy is not directly evil, but good; sadness, on the other hand, is directly evil.*

Dem.: Joy (by IIIP11 and P11S) is an affect by which the body's power of acting is increased or aided. Sadness, on the other hand, is an affect by which the body's power of acting is diminished or restrained. And so (by P38) joy is directly good, and so on, q.e.d.

P42: *Cheerfulness cannot be excessive, but is always good; melancholy, on the other hand, is always evil.*

Dem.: Cheerfulness (see its Def. in IIIP11S) is a joy which, insofar as it is related to the body, consists in this, that all parts of the body are equally affected. That is (by IIIP11), the body's power of acting is increased or aided, so that all of its parts maintain the same proportion of motion and rest to one another. And so (by P39), cheerfulness is always good, and cannot be excessive.

But melancholy (see its Def., also in IIIP11S) is a sadness, which,   II/242
insofar as it is related to the body, consists in this, that the body's power
of acting is absolutely diminished or restrained. And so (by P38) it is
always evil, q.e.d.

P43: *Pleasure can be excessive and evil, whereas pain can be good insofar as the*
pleasure, or joy, is evil.

Dem.: Pleasure is a joy which, insofar as it is related to the body,
consists in this, that one (or several) of its parts are affected more than
the others (see its Def. in IIIP11S). The power of this affect can be so
great that it surpasses the other actions of the body (by P6), remains
stubbornly fixed in the body, and so prevents the body from being capable of being affected in a great many other ways. Hence (by P38), it can
be evil.

Pain, on the other hand, which is a sadness, cannot be good, considered in itself alone (by P41). But because its force and growth are defined by the power of an external cause compared with our power (by
P5), we can conceive infinite degrees and modes of the powers of this
affect (by P3). And so we can conceive it to be such that it can restrain
pleasure, so that it is not excessive, and thereby prevent the body from
being rendered less capable (by the first part of this proposition). To
that extent, therefore, it will be good, q.e.d.

P44: *Love and desire can be excessive.*

Dem.: Love is joy, accompanied by the idea of an external cause (by
Def. Aff. VI). Pleasure, therefore (by IIIP11S), accompanied by the idea
of an external cause, is love. And so, love (by P43) can be excessive.

Again, desire is greater as the affect from which it arises is greater (by   II/243
IIIP37). Hence, as an affect (by P6) can surpass the rest of man's actions,
so also the desire which arises from that affect can surpass the rest of his
desires. It can therefore be excessive in the same way we have shown
pleasure can be (in P43), q.e.d.

Schol.: Cheerfulness, which I have said is good, is more easily conceived than observed. For the affects by which we are daily torn are
generally related to a part of the body which is affected more than the
others. Generally, then, the affects are excessive, and occupy the mind
in the consideration of only one object so much that it cannot think of
others. And though men are liable to a great many affects, so that one
rarely finds them to be always agitated by one and the same affect, still
there are those in whom one affect is stubbornly fixed. For we sometimes see that men are so affected by one object that, although it is not
present, they still believe they have it with them.

When this happens to a man who is not asleep, we say that he is mad or insane. Nor are they thought to be less mad who burn with love, and dream, both night and day, only of a lover or a courtesan. For they usually provoke laughter. But when a greedy man thinks of nothing else but profit, or money, and an ambitious man of esteem, they are not thought to be mad, because they are usually troublesome and are considered worthy of hate. But greed, ambition, and lust really are species of madness, even though they are not numbered among the diseases.

P45: *Hate can never be good.*

Dem.: We strive to destroy the man we hate (by IIIP39), that is (by P37), we strive for something which is evil. Therefore, and so on, q.e.d.

II/244   Schol.: Note that here and in what follows I understand by hate only hate toward men.

Cor. 1: Envy, mockery, disdain, anger, vengeance, and the rest of the affects which are related to hate or arise from it, are evil. This too is evident from P37 and IIIP39.

Cor. 2: Whatever we want because we have been affected with hate is dishonorable; and [if we live] in a state, it is unjust. This too is evident from IIIP39, and from the definitions of dishonorable and unjust (see P37S).

Schol.: I recognize a great difference between mockery (which, in Cor. 1, I said was evil) and laughter. For laughter and joking are pure joy. And so, provided they are not excessive, they are good through themselves (by P41). Nothing forbids our pleasure except a savage and sad superstition. For why is it more proper to relieve our hunger and thirst than to rid ourselves of melancholy?

My account of the matter, the view I have arrived at, is this: no deity, nor anyone else, unless he is envious, takes pleasure in my lack of power and my misfortune; nor does he ascribe to virtue our tears, sighs, fear, and other things of that kind, which are signs of a weak mind. On the contrary, the greater the joy with which we are affected, the greater the perfection to which we pass, that is, the more we must participate in the divine nature. To use things, therefore, and take pleasure in them as far as possible—not, of course, to the point where we are disgusted with them, for there is no pleasure in that—this is the part of a wise man.

It is the part of a wise man, I say, to refresh and restore himself in moderation with pleasant food and drink, with scents, with the beauty of green plants, with decoration, music, sports, the theater, and other things of this kind, which anyone can use without injury to another. For the human body is composed of a great many parts of different natures, which constantly require new and varied nourishment, so that the whole body may be equally capable of all the things which can follow from its nature, and hence, so that the mind also may be equally capable of understanding many things at once.

This plan of living, then, agrees best both with our principles and with common practice. So, if any other way of living [is to be commended], this one is best, and to be commended in every way. Nor is it necessary for me to treat these matters more clearly or more fully.

P46: *He who lives according to the guidance of reason strives, as far as he can, to repay the other's hate, anger, and disdain toward him, with love,* or *nobility.*

Dem.: All affects of hate are evil (by P45C1). So he who lives according to the guidance of reason will strive, as far as he can, to bring it about that he is not troubled with affects of hate (by P19), and consequently (by P37), will strive that the other also should not undergo those affects. Now hate is increased by being returned, and on the other hand, can be destroyed by love (by IIIP43), so that the hate passes into love (by IIIP44). Therefore, one who lives according to the guidance of reason will strive to repay the other's hate, and so on, with love, and so on, with nobility (see its Def. in IIIP59S), q.e.d.

Schol.: He who wishes to avenge wrongs by hating in return surely lives miserably. On the other hand, one who is eager to overcome hate by love, strives joyously and confidently, resists many men as easily as one, and requires the least help from fortune. Those whom he conquers yield joyously, not from a lack of strength, but from an increase in their powers. All these things follow so clearly simply from the definitions of love and of intellect, that there is no need to demonstrate them separately.

P47: *Affects of hope and fear cannot be good of themselves.*

Dem.: There are no affects of hope or fear without sadness. For fear is a sadness (by Def. Aff. XIII), and there is no hope without fear (see the explanation following Def. Aff. XII and XIII). Therefore (by P41) these affects cannot be good of themselves, but only insofar as they can restrain an excess of joy (by P43), q.e.d.

Schol.: We may add to this that these affects show a defect of knowledge and a lack of power in the mind. For this reason also confidence and despair, gladness and remorse are signs of a mind lacking in power. For though confidence and gladness are affects of joy, they still presuppose that a sadness has preceded them, namely, hope and fear. Therefore, the more we strive to live according to the guidance of reason, the more we strive to depend less on hope, to free ourselves from fear, to

II/245

II/246

conquer fortune as much as we can, and to direct our actions by the certain counsel of reason.

P48: *Affects of overestimation and scorn are always evil.*

Dem.: These affects are contrary to reason (by Def. Aff. XXI and XXII). So (by P26 and P27) they are evil, q.e.d.

P49: *Overestimation easily makes the man who is overestimated proud.*

Dem.: If we see that someone, out of love, thinks more highly of us than is just, we shall easily exult at being esteemed (by IIIP41S), *or* be affected with joy (by Def. Aff. XXX), and we shall easily believe the good we hear predicated of us (by IIIP25). And so, out of love of ourselves, we shall think more highly of ourselves than is just, that is (by Def. Aff. XXVIII), we shall easily become proud, q.e.d.

II/247 P50: *Pity, in a man who lives according to the guidance of reason, is evil of itself and useless.*

Dem.: For pity (by Def. Aff. XVIII) is a sadness, and therefore (by P41), of itself, evil.

Moreover, the good which follows from it, namely, that we strive to free the man we pity from his suffering (by IIIP27C3), we desire to do from the dictate of reason alone (by P37), and we can only do from the dictate of reason alone something which we know certainly to be good (by P27).

Hence, pity, in a man who lives according to the guidance of reason, is both evil of itself and useless, q.e.d.

Cor.: From this it follows that a man who lives according to the dictate of reason, strives, as far as he can, not to be touched by pity.

Schol.: He who rightly knows that all things follow from the necessity of the divine nature, and happen according to the eternal laws and rules of Nature, will surely find nothing worthy of hate, mockery, or disdain, nor anyone whom he will pity. Instead he will strive, as far as human virtue allows, to act well, as they say, and rejoice.

To this we may add that he who is easily touched by the affect of pity, and moved by another's suffering or tears, often does something he later repents—both because, from an affect, we do nothing which we certainly know to be good, and because we are easily deceived by false tears.

Here I am speaking expressly of a man who lives according to the guidance of reason. For one who is moved to aid others neither by reason nor by pity is rightly called inhuman. For (by IIIP27) he seems to be unlike a man.

P51: *Favor is not contrary to reason, but can agree with it and arise from it.*   II/248

Dem.: For favor is a love toward him who has benefited another (by Def. Aff. XIX), and so can be related to the mind insofar as it is said to act (by IIIP59), that is (by IIIP3), insofar as it understands. Therefore, it agrees with reason, and so on, q.e.d.

Alternate Dem.: He who lives according to the guidance of reason, desires for the other, too, the good he wants for himself (by P37). So because he sees someone benefiting another, his own striving to do good is aided, that is (by IIIP11S), he will rejoice. And this joy (by hypothesis) will be accompanied by the idea of him who has benefited another. He will, therefore (by Def. Aff. XIX), favor him, q.e.d.

Schol.: Indignation, as we define it (see Def. Aff. XX), is necessarily evil (by P45). But it should be noted that when the supreme power, bound by its desire to preserve peace, punishes a citizen who has wronged another, I do not say that it is indignant toward the citizen. For it punishes him, not because it has been aroused by hate to destroy him, but because it is moved by duty.

P52: *Self-esteem can arise from reason, and only that self-esteem which does arise from reason is the greatest there can be.*

Dem.: Self-esteem is a joy born of the fact that man considers himself and his power of acting (by Def. Aff. XXV). But man's true power of acting, *or* virtue, is reason itself (by IIIP3), which man considers clearly and distinctly (by IIP40 and P43). Therefore, self-esteem arises from   II/249
reason.

Next, while a man considers himself, he perceives nothing clearly and distinctly, *or* adequately, except those things which follow from his power of acting (by IIID2), that is (by IIIP3), which follow from his power of understanding. And so the greatest self-esteem there can be arises only from this reflection, q.e.d.

Schol.: Self-esteem is really the highest thing we can hope for. For (as we have shown in P25) no one strives to preserve his being for the sake of any end. And because this self-esteem is more and more encouraged and strengthened by praise (by IIIP53C), and on the other hand, more and more upset by blame (by IIIP55C), we are guided most by love of esteem and can hardly bear a life in disgrace.

P53: *Humility is not a virtue,* or *does not arise from reason.*

Dem.: Humility is a sadness which arises from the fact that a man considers his own lack of power (by Def. Aff. XXVI). Moreover, insofar as a man knows himself by true reason, it is supposed that he understands his own essence, that is (by IIIP7), his own power. So if a man, in

227

considering himself, perceives some lack of power of his, this is not because he understands himself, but because his power of acting is restrained (as we have shown in IIIP55). But if we suppose that the man conceives his lack of power because he understands something more powerful than himself, by the knowledge of which he determines his power of acting, then we conceive nothing but that the man understands himself distinctly *or* (by P26) that his power of acting is aided. So humility, *or* the sadness which arises from the fact that a man reflects on his own lack of power, does not arise from a true reflection, *or* reason, and is a passion, not a virtue, q.e.d.

II/250 P54: *Repentance is not a virtue, or does not arise from reason; instead, he who repents what he has done is twice wretched, or lacking in power.*

Dem.: The first part of this is demonstrated as P53 was. The second is evident simply from the definition of this affect (see Def. Aff. XXVII). For first he suffers himself to be conquered by an evil desire, and then by sadness.

Schol.: Because men rarely live from the dictate of reason, these two affects, humility and repentance, and in addition, hope and fear, bring more advantage than disadvantage. So since men must sin, they ought rather to sin in that direction. If weak-minded men were all equally proud, ashamed of nothing, and afraid of nothing, how could they be united or restrained by any bonds?

The mob is terrifying, if unafraid. So it is no wonder that the prophets, who considered the common advantage, not that of the few, commended humility, repentance, and reverence so greatly. Really, those who are subject to these affects can be guided far more easily than others, so that in the end they may live from the guidance of reason, that is, may be free and enjoy the life of the blessed.

P55: *Either very great pride or very great despondency is very great ignorance of oneself.*

Dem.: This is evident from Defs. Aff. XXVIII and XXIX.

P56: *Either very great pride or very great despondency indicates very great weakness of mind.*

II/251 Dem.: The first foundation of virtue is preserving one's being (by P22C) and doing this from the guidance of reason (by P24). Therefore, he who is ignorant of himself is ignorant of the foundation of all the virtues, and consequently, ignorant of all the virtues. Next, acting from virtue is nothing but acting from the guidance of reason (by P24), and he who acts from the guidance of reason must know that he acts from the guidance of reason (by IIP43). Therefore, he who is ignorant of himself, and consequently (as we have just now shown) of all the virtues, does not act from virtue at all, that is (as is evident from D8), is extremely weak-minded. And so (by P55) either very great pride or very great despondency indicate very great weakness of mind, q.e.d.

Cor.: From this it follows very clearly that the proud and the despondent are highly liable to affects.

Schol.: Nevertheless, despondency can be corrected more easily than pride, since pride is an affect of joy, whereas despondency is an affect of sadness. And so (by P18), pride is stronger than despondency.

P57: *The proud man loves the presence of parasites, or flatterers, but hates the presence of the noble.*

Dem.: Pride is a joy born of the fact that man thinks more highly of himself than is just (see Defs. Aff. XXVIII and VI). The proud man will strive as far as he can to encourage this opinion (see IIIP13S). And so the proud will love the presence of parasites or flatterers (I have omitted the definitions of these because they are too well known) and will flee the presence of the noble, who think of them as is appropriate, q.e.d.

Schol.: It would take too long to enumerate all the evils of pride here, since the proud are subject to all the affects (though they are least subject to affects of love and compassion). But we ought not to pass over in silence here the fact that he also is called proud who thinks less highly of others than is just. So in this sense pride should be defined as a joy born of a man's false opinion that he is above others. And the despondency contrary to this pride would need to be defined as a sadness born of a man's false opinion that he is below others.

But this being posited, we easily conceive that the proud man must be envious (see IIIP55S) and hate those most who are most praised for their virtues, that his hatred of them is not easily conquered by love or benefits (see IIIP41S), and that he takes pleasure only in the presence of those who humor his weakness of mind and make a madman of a fool.

Although despondency is contrary to pride, the despondent man is still very near the proud one. For since his sadness arises from the fact that he judges his own lack of power from the power, *or* virtue, of others, his sadness will be relieved, that is, he will rejoice, if his imagination is occupied in considering the vices of others. Hence the proverb: *misery loves company*.

On the other hand, the more he believes himself to be below others, the more he will be saddened. That is why no one is more prone to envy than the despondent man is, and why they strive especially to observe men's deeds, more for the sake of finding fault than to improve them, and why, finally, they praise only despondency, and exult over it—but in such a way that they still seem despondent.

These things follow from this affect as necessarily as it follows from the nature of a triangle that its three angles are equal to two right angles. I have already said that I call these, and like affects, evil insofar as I attend only to human advantage. But the laws of Nature concern the common order of Nature, of which man is a part. I wished to remind my readers of this here, in passing, in case anyone thought my purpose was only to tell about men's vices and their absurd deeds, and not to demonstrate the nature and properties of things. For as I said in the Preface of
II/253   Part III, I consider men's affects and properties just like other natural things. And of course human affects, if they do not indicate man's power, at least indicate the power and skill of Nature, no less than many other things we wonder at and take pleasure in contemplating. But I continue to note, concerning the affects, those things which bring advantage to men, and those which bring them harm.

P58: *Love of esteem is not contrary to reason, but can arise from it.*

Dem.: This is evident from Def. Aff. XXX, and from the definition of what is honorable (see P37S1).

Schol.: The love of esteem which is called empty is a self-esteem that is encouraged only by the opinion of the multitude. When that ceases, the self-esteem ceases, that is (by P52S), the highest good that each one loves. That is why he who exults at being esteemed by the multitude is made anxious daily, strives, acts, and schemes, in order to preserve his reputation. For the multitude is fickle and inconstant; unless one's reputation is guarded, it is quickly destroyed. Indeed, because everyone desires to secure the applause of the multitude, each one willingly puts down the reputation of the other. And since the struggle is over a good thought to be the highest, this gives rise to a monstrous lust of each to crush the other in any way possible. The one who at last emerges as victor exults more in having harmed the other than in having benefited himself. This love of esteem, *or* self-esteem, then, is really empty, because it is nothing.

The things which must be noted about shame are easily inferred from what we said about compassion and repentance. I add only this, that like pity, shame, though not a virtue, is still good insofar as it indicates, in the man who blushes with shame, a desire to live honorably. In the same way pain is said to be good insofar as it indicates that the injured part is not yet decayed. So though a man who is ashamed of some deed is really
II/254   sad, he is still more perfect than one who is shameless, who has no desire to live honorably.

These are the things I undertook to note concerning the affects of joy and sadness. As far as desires are concerned, they, of course, are good or evil insofar as they arise from good or evil affects. But all of them, really, insofar as they are generated in us from affects which are passions, are blind (as may easily be inferred from what we said in P44S), and would be of no use if men could easily be led to live according to the dictate of reason alone. I shall now show this concisely.

P59: *To every action to which we are determined from an affect which is a passion, we can be determined by reason, without that affect.*

Dem.: Acting from reason is nothing but doing those things which follow from the necessity of our nature, considered in itself alone (by IIIP3 and D2). But sadness is evil insofar as it decreases or restrains this power of acting (by P41). Therefore, from this affect we cannot be determined to any action which we could not do if we were led by reason.

Furthermore, joy is bad [only] insofar as it prevents man from being capable of acting (by P41 and P43), and so to that extent also, we cannot be determined to any action which we could not do if we were guided by reason.

Finally, insofar as joy is good, it agrees with reason (for it consists in this, that a man's power of acting is increased or aided), and is not a passion except insofar as the man's power of acting is not increased to the point where he conceives himself and his actions adequately. So if a man affected with Joy were led to such a great perfection that he conceived himself and his actions adequately, he would be capable—indeed more capable—of the same actions to which he is now determined from affects which are passions.

But all affects are related to joy, sadness, or desire (see the explanation of Def. Aff. IV), and desire (by Def. Aff. I) is nothing but the striving to act itself. Therefore, to every action to which we are determined from an affect which is a passion, we can be led by reason alone, without the affect, q.e.d.

II/255

Alternate Dem.: Any action is called evil insofar as it arises from the fact that we have been affected with hate or with some evil affect (see P45C1). But no action, considered in itself, is good or evil (as we have shown in the Preface of this Part); instead, one and the same action is now good, now evil. Therefore, to the same action which is now evil, *or* which arises from some evil affect, we can (by P19) be led by reason, q.e.d.

Schol.: These things are more clearly explained by an example. The act of beating, insofar as it is considered physically, and insofar as we attend only to the fact that the man raises his arm, closes his fist, and moves his whole arm forcefully up and down, is a virtue, which is conceived from the structure of the human body. Therefore, if a man moved by anger or hate is determined to close his fist or move his arm, that (as we have shown in Part II) happens because one and the same action can be joined to any images of things whatever. And so we can be determined to one and the same action both from those images of things which we conceive confusedly and [from those images of things?] we conceive clearly and distinctly.

It is evident, therefore, that every desire which arises from an affect which is a passion would be of no use if men could be guided by reason. Let us see now why we call a desire blind which arises from an affect which is a passion.

P60: *A desire arising from either a joy or a sadness related to one, or several, but not to all parts of the body, has no regard for the advantage of the whole man.*

II/256

Dem.: Suppose, for example, that part A of the body is so strengthened by the force of some external cause that it prevails over the others (by P6). This part will not, on that account, strive to lose its powers so that the other parts of the body may fulfill their function. For [if it did], it would have to have a force, *or* power, of losing its own powers, which (by IIIP6) is absurd. Therefore, that part will strive, and consequently (by IIIP7 and P12), the mind also will strive, to preserve that state. And so the desire which arises from such an affect of joy does not have regard to the whole.

If, on the other hand, it is supposed that part A is restrained so that the others prevail, it is demonstrated in the same way that the desire which arises from sadness also does not have regard to the whole, q.e.d.

Schol.: Therefore, since joy is generally (by P44S) related to one part of the body, for the most part we desire to preserve our being without regard to our health as a whole. To this we may add that the desires by which we are most bound (by P9C) have regard only to the present and not to the future.

P61: *A desire which arises from reason cannot be excessive.*

Dem.: Desire, considered absolutely, is the very essence of man (by Def. Aff. I), insofar as it is conceived to be determined in any way to doing something. And so a desire which arises from reason, that is (by IIIP3), which is generated in us insofar as we act is the very essence, *or* nature, of man, insofar as it is conceived to be determined to doing those things which are conceived adequately through man's essence alone (by IIID2). So if this desire could be excessive, then human nature, considered in itself alone, could exceed itself, *or* could do more than it can. This is a manifest contradiction. Therefore, this desire cannot be excessive, q.e.d.

P62: *Insofar as the mind conceives things from the dictate of reason, it is affected equally, whether the idea is of a future or past thing, or of a present one.*   II/257

Dem.: Whatever the mind conceives under the guidance of reason, it conceives under the same species of eternity, *or* necessity (by IIP44C2) and is affected with the same certainty (by IIP43 and P43S). So whether the idea is of a future or a past thing, or of a present one, the mind conceives the thing with the same necessity and is affected with the same certainty. And whether the idea is of a future or a past thing or of a present one, it will nevertheless be equally true (by IIP41), that is (by IID4), it will nevertheless always have the same properties of an adequate idea. And so, insofar as the mind conceives things from the dictate of reason, it is affected in the same way, whether the idea is of a future or a past thing, or of a present one, q.e.d.

Schol.: If we could have adequate knowledge of the duration of things, and determine by reason their times of existing, we would regard future things with the same affect as present ones, and the mind would want the good it conceived as future just as it wants the good it conceives as present. Hence, it would necessarily neglect a lesser present good for a greater future one, and what would be good in the present, but the cause of some future ill, it would not want at all, as we shall soon demonstrate.

But we can have only a quite inadequate knowledge of the duration of things (by IIP31), and we determine their times of existing only by the imagination (by IIP44S), which is not equally affected by the image of a present thing and the image of a future one. That is why the true knowledge we have of good and evil is only abstract, *or* universal, and the judgment we make concerning the order of things and the connection of causes, so that we may be able to determine what in the present is good or evil for us, is imaginary, rather than real. And so it is no wonder if the desire which arises from a knowledge of good and evil,   II/258
insofar as this looks to the future, can be rather easily restrained by a desire for the pleasures of the moment. On this, see P16.

P63: *He who is guided by fear, and does good to avoid evil, is not guided by reason.*

Dem.: The only affects which are related to the mind insofar as it acts, that is (by IIIP3), which are related to reason, are affects of joy and desire (by IIIP59). And so (by Def. Aff. XIII) one who is guided by fear, and does good from timidity regarding an evil, is not guided by reason, q.e.d.

Schol.: The superstitious know how to reproach people for their vices better than they know how to teach them virtues, and they strive, not to guide men by reason, but to restrain them by fear, so that they flee the evil rather than love virtues. Such people aim only to make others as wretched as they themselves are, so it is no wonder that they are generally burdensome and hateful to men.

Cor.: By a desire arising from reason, we directly follow the good, and indirectly flee the evil.

Dem.: For a desire which arises from reason can arise solely from an affect of joy which is not a passion (by IIIP59), that is, from a joy which cannot be excessive (by P61). But it cannot arise from sadness, and therefore this desire (by P8) arises from knowledge of the good, not knowledge of the evil. And so from the guidance of reason we want the good directly, and to that extent only, we flee the evil, q.e.d.

Schol.: This corollary may be illustrated by the example of the sick and the healthy. The sick man, from timidity regarding death, eats what he is repelled by, whereas the healthy man enjoys his food, and in this way enjoys life better than if he feared death, and directly desired to avoid it. Similarly, a judge who condemns a guilty man to death—not from hate or anger, and the like, but only from a love of the general welfare—is guided only by reason.

II/259

P64: *Knowledge of evil is an inadequate knowledge.*

Dem.: Knowledge of evil (by P8) is sadness itself, insofar as we are conscious of it. But sadness is a passage to a lesser perfection (by Def. Aff. III), which therefore cannot be understood through man's essence itself (by IIIP6 and P7). Hence (by IIID2), it is a passion, which (by IIIP3) depends on inadequate ideas. Therefore (by IIP29), knowledge of this, namely, knowledge of evil, is inadequate, q.e.d.

Cor.: From this it follows that if the human mind had only adequate ideas, it would form no notion of evil.

P65: *From the guidance of reason, we shall follow the greater of two goods or the lesser of two evils.*

Dem.: A good which prevents us from enjoying a greater good is really an evil. For good and evil (as we have shown in the Preface of this Part) are said of things insofar as we compare them to one another. By the same reasoning, a lesser evil is really a good, so (by P63C) from the guidance of reason we want, *or* follow, only the greater good and the lesser evil, q.e.d.

Cor.: From the guidance of reason, we shall follow a lesser evil as a greater good, and pass over a lesser good which is the cause of a greater evil. For the evil which is here called lesser is really good, and the good which is here called lesser, on the other hand, is evil. So (by P63C) we want the [lesser evil] and pass over the [lesser good], q.e.d. II/260

P66: *From the guidance of reason we want a greater future good in preference to a lesser present one, and a lesser present evil in preference to a greater future one.*

Dem.: If the mind could have an adequate knowledge of a future thing, it would be affected toward it with the same affect as it is toward a present one (by P62). So insofar as we attend to reason itself, as in this proposition we suppose ourselves to do, the thing will be the same, whether the greater good or evil is supposed to be future or present. And therefore (by P65), we want the greater future good in preference to the lesser present one, and so on, q.e.d.

Cor.: From the guidance of reason, we shall want a lesser present evil which is the cause of a greater future good, and pass over a lesser present good which is the cause of a greater future evil. This corollary stands to P66 as P65C does to P65.

Schol.: If these things are compared with those we have shown in this Part up to P18, concerning the powers of the affects, we shall easily see what the difference is between a man who is led only by an affect, *or* by opinion, and one who is led by reason. For the former, whether he will or not, does those things he is most ignorant of, whereas the latter complies with no one's wishes but his own, and does only those things he knows to be the most important in life, and therefore desires very greatly. Hence, I call the former a slave, but the latter, a free man.

I wish now to note a few more things concerning the free man's temperament and manner of living.

P67: *A free man thinks of nothing less than of death, and his wisdom is a meditation on life, not on death.* II/261

Dem.: A free man, that is, one who lives according to the dictate of reason alone, is not led by fear (by P63), but desires the good directly (by P63C), that is (by P24), acts, lives, and preserves his being from the foundation of seeking his own advantage. And so he thinks of nothing less than of death. Instead his wisdom is a meditation on life, q.e.d.

P68: *If men were born free, they would form no concept of good and evil so long as they remained free.*

Dem.: I call him free who is led by reason alone. Therefore, he who is born free, and remains free, has only adequate ideas, and so has no concept of evil (by P64C). And since good and evil are correlates, he also has no concept of good, q.e.d.

Schol.: It is evident from P4 that the hypothesis of this proposition is false, and cannot be conceived unless we attend only to human nature, *or* rather to God, not insofar as he is infinite, but insofar only as he is the cause of man's existence.

This and the other things I have now demonstrated seem to have been indicated by Moses in that story of the first man. For in it the only power of God conceived is that by which he created man, that is, the power by which he consulted only man's advantage. And so we are told that God prohibited a free man from eating of the tree of knowledge of good and evil, and that as soon as he should eat of it, he would imme-

II/262 diately fear death, rather than desiring to live; and then, that, the man having found a wife who agreed completely with his nature, he knew that there could be nothing in Nature more useful to him than she was; but that after he believed the lower animals to be like himself, he immediately began to imitate their affects (see IIIP27) and to lose his freedom; and that afterwards this freedom was recovered by the patriarchs, guided by the Spirit of Christ, that is, by the idea of God, on which alone it depends that man should be free, and desire for other men the good he desires for himself (as we have demonstrated above, by P37).

P69: *The virtue of a free man is seen to be as great in avoiding dangers as in overcoming them.*

Dem.: An affect can be neither restrained nor removed except by an affect contrary to and stronger than the affect to be restrained (by P7). But blind daring and fear are affects which can be conceived to be equally great (by P3 and P5). Therefore, an equally great virtue of the mind, *or* strength of character (for the definition of this, see IIIP59S) is required to restrain daring as to restrain fear, that is (by Defs. Aff. XL and XLI), a free man avoids dangers by the same virtue of the mind by which he tries to overcome them, q.e.d.

Cor.: In a free man, a timely flight is considered to show as much tenacity as fighting; or a free man chooses flight with the same tenacity, *or* presence of mind, as he chooses a contest.

Schol.: I have explained in IIIP59S what tenacity is, or what I understand by it. And by danger I understand whatever can be the cause of some evil, such as sadness, hate, discord, and the like.

P70: *A free man who lives among the ignorant strives, as far as he can, to avoid their favors.*

II/263 Dem.: Everyone judges according to his own temperament what is good (see IIIP39). Someone who is ignorant, therefore, and who has conferred a favor on someone else, will value it according to his own temperament, and will be saddened if he sees it valued less by him to whom it was given (by IIIP42). But a free man strives to join other men to him in friendship (by P37), not to repay men with benefits which are equivalent in their eyes, but to lead himself and the others by the free judgment of reason, and to do only those things which he himself knows to be most excellent. Therefore, a free man will strive, as far as he can, to avoid the favors of the ignorant, so as not to be hated by them, and at the same time to yield only to reason, not to their appetite, q.e.d.

Schol.: I say *as far as he can*. For though men may be ignorant, they are still men, who in situations of need can bring human aid. And there is no better aid than that. So it often happens that it is necessary to accept favors from them, and hence to return thanks to them according to their temperament [i.e., in a way they will appreciate].

To this we may add that we must be careful in declining favors, so that we do not seem to disdain them, or out of greed to be afraid of repayment. For in that way, in the very act of avoiding their hate, we would incur it. So in declining favors we must take account both of what is useful and of what is honorable.

P71: *Only free men are very thankful to one another.*

Dem.: Only free men are very useful to one another, are joined to one another by the closest bond of friendship (by P35 and P35C1), and strive to benefit one another with equal eagerness for love (by P37). So (by Def. Aff. XXXIV) only free men are very thankful to one another, q.e.d.

Schol.: The thankfulness which men are led by blind desire to display toward one another is for the most part a business transaction *or* an entrapment, rather than thankfulness. II/264

Again, ingratitude is not an affect. Nevertheless, ingratitude is dishonorable because it generally indicates that the man is affected with too much hate, anger, pride, greed, and so on. For one who, out of foolishness, does not know how to reckon one gift against another, is not ungrateful; much less one who is not moved by the gifts of a courtesan to assist her lust, nor by those of a thief to conceal his thefts, nor by those of anyone else like that. On the contrary, he shows firmness of mind who does not allow any gifts to corrupt him, to his or to the general ruin.

P72: *A free man always acts honestly, not deceptively.*

Dem.: If a free man, insofar as he is free, did anything by deception, he would do it from the dictate of reason (for so far only do we call him free). And so it would be a virtue to act deceptively (by P24), and hence (by the same Prop.), everyone would be better advised to act deceptively to preserve his being. That is (as is known through itself), men would be better advised to agree only in words, and be contrary to one another in fact. But this is absurd (by P31C). Therefore, a free man and so on, q.e.d.

Schol.: Suppose someone now asks: What if a man could save himself from the present danger of death by treachery? Would not the principle of preserving his own being recommend, without qualification, that he be treacherous?

The reply to this is the same. If reason should recommend that, it would recommend it to all men. And so reason would recommend, without qualification, that men should make agreements to join forces and to have common laws only by deception—that is, that really they should have no common laws. This is absurd.

P73: *A man who is guided by reason is more free in a state, where he lives according to a common decision, than in solitude, where he obeys only himself.*

II/265   Dem.: A man who is guided by reason is not led to obey by fear (by P63), but insofar as he strives to preserve his being from the dictate of reason, that is (by P66S), insofar as he strives to live freely, desires to maintain the principle of common life and common advantage (by P37). Consequently (as we have shown in P37S2), he desires to live according to the common decision of the state. Therefore, a man who is guided by reason desires, in order to live more freely, to keep the common laws of the state, q.e.d.

Schol.: These and similar things which we have shown concerning the true freedom of man are related to strength of character, that is (by IIIP59S), to tenacity and nobility. I do not consider it worthwhile to demonstrate separately here all the properties of strength of character, much less that a man strong in character hates no one, is angry with no one, envies no one, is indignant with no one, scorns no one, and is not at all proud. For these and all things which relate to true life and religion are easily proven from P37 and P46, namely, that hate is to be conquered by returning love, and that everyone who is led by reason desires for others also the good he wants for himself.

To this we may add what we have noted in P50S and in other places: a man strong in character considers this most of all, that all things follow from the necessity of the divine nature, and hence, that whatever he thinks is troublesome and evil, and moreover, whatever seems immoral, dreadful, unjust, and dishonorable, arises from the fact that he conceives the things themselves in a way which is disordered, mutilated, and confused. For this reason, he strives most of all to conceive things as they are in themselves, and to remove the obstacles to true knowledge, like hate, anger, envy, mockery, pride, and the rest of the things we have noted in the preceding pages.

And so, as we have said [II/47/21], he strives, as far as he can, to act well and rejoice. In the following part, I shall demonstrate how far human virtue can go in the attainment of these things, and what it is capable of.

APPENDIX

The things I have taught in this part concerning the right way of living have not been so arranged that they could be seen at a glance. Instead, I have demonstrated them at one place or another, as I could more easily deduce one from another. So I have undertaken to collect them here and bring them under main headings.

I. All our strivings, *or* desires, follow from the necessity of our nature in such a way that they can be understood either through it alone, as through their proximate cause, or insofar as we are a part of Nature, which cannot be conceived adequately through itself without other individuals.

II. The desires which follow from our nature in such a way that they can be understood through it alone are those which are related to the mind insofar as it is conceived to consist of adequate ideas. The remaining desires are not related to the mind except insofar as it conceives things inadequately, and their force and growth must be defined not by human power, but by the power of things which are outside us. The former, therefore, are rightly called actions, while the latter are rightly called passions. For the former always indicate our power, whereas the latter indicate our lack of power and mutilated knowledge.

III. Our actions—that is, those desires which are defined by man's power, *or* reason—are always good; but the other [desires] can be both good and evil.

IV. In life, therefore, it is especially useful to perfect, as far as we can, our intellect, *or* reason. In this one thing consists man's highest happiness, *or* blessedness. Indeed, blessedness is nothing but that satisfaction of mind which stems from the intuitive knowledge of God. But perfecting the intellect is nothing but understanding God, his attributes, and his actions, which follow from the necessity of his nature. So the ultimate end of the man who is led by reason, that is, his highest desire, by which he strives to moderate all the others, is that by which he is led to conceive adequately both himself and all things which can fall under his understanding.

V. No life, then, is rational without understanding, and things are good only insofar as they aid man to enjoy the life of the mind, which is defined by understanding. On the other hand, those which prevent man from being able to perfect his reason and enjoy the rational life, those only we say are evil.

VI. But because all those things of which man is the efficient cause must be good, nothing evil can happen to a man except by external causes, namely, insofar as he is a part of the whole of Nature, whose laws human nature is compelled to obey, and to which it is forced to accommodate itself in ways nearly infinite.

II/268 VII. It is impossible for man not to be a part of Nature and not to follow the common order of Nature. But if he lives among such individuals as agree with his nature, his power of acting will thereby be aided and encouraged. On the other hand, if he is among men who do not agree at all with his nature, he will hardly be able to accommodate himself to them without greatly changing himself.

VIII. It is permissible for us to avert, in the way which seems safest, whatever there is in Nature which we judge to be evil, *or* able to prevent us from being able to exist and enjoy a rational life. On the other hand, we may take for our own use, and use in any way, whatever there is which we judge to be good, *or* useful for preserving our being and enjoying a rational life. And absolutely, it is permissible for everyone to do, by the highest right of Nature, what he judges will contribute to his advantage.

IX. Nothing can agree more with the nature of any thing than other individuals of the same species. And so (by VII) nothing is more useful to man in preserving his being and enjoying a rational life than a man who is guided by reason. Again, because, among singular things, we know nothing more excellent than a man who is guided by reason, we II/269 can show best how much our skill and understanding are worth by educating men so that at last they live according to the command of their own reason.

X. Insofar as men are moved against one another by envy or some [NS: other] affect of hate, they are contrary to one another, and consequently are the more to be feared, as they can do more than other individuals in Nature.

XI. Minds, however, are conquered not by arms, but by love and nobility.

XII. It is especially useful to men to form associations, to bind themselves by those bonds most apt to make one people of them, and absolutely, to do those things which serve to strengthen friendships.

XIII. But skill and alertness are required for this. For men vary—there being few who live according to the rule of reason—and yet generally they are envious, and more inclined to vengeance than to compassion. So it requires a singular power of mind to bear with each one according to his understanding, and to restrain oneself from imitating their affects.

But those who know how to find fault with men, to castigate vices rather than teach virtues, and to break men's minds rather than strengthen them—they are burdensome both to themselves and to others. That is why many, from too great an impatience of mind, and a false zeal for religion, have preferred to live among the lower animals rather II/270 than among men. They are like boys or young men who cannot bear calmly the scolding of their parents, and take refuge in the army. They choose the inconveniences of war and the discipline of an absolute commander in preference to the conveniences of home and the admonitions of a father; and while they take vengeance on their parents, they allow all sorts of burdens to be placed on them.

XIV. Though men, therefore, generally direct everything according to their own lust, nevertheless, more advantages than disadvantages follow from their forming a common society. So it is better to bear men's wrongs calmly, and apply one's zeal to those things which help to bring men together in harmony and friendship.

XV. The things which beget harmony are those which are related to justice, fairness, and being honorable. For men find it difficult to bear, not only what *is* unjust and unfair, but also what *is thought* dishonorable, *or* that someone rejects the accepted practices of the state. But especially necessary to bring people together in love, are the things which concern religion and morality. On this, see P37S1 and S2, P46S, and P73S.

XVI. Harmony is also commonly born of fear, but then it is without trust. Add to this that fear arises from weakness of mind, and therefore II/271 does not pertain to the exercise of reason. Nor does pity, though it seems to present the appearance of morality.

XVII. Men are also won over by generosity, especially those who do not have the means of acquiring the things they require to sustain life. But to bring aid to everyone in need far surpasses the powers and advantage of a private person. For his riches are quite unequal to the task. Moreover the capacity of one man is too limited for him to be able to unite all men to him in friendship. So the care of the poor falls upon society as a whole, and concerns only the general advantage.

XVIII. In accepting favors and returning thanks an altogether different care must be taken. See P70S and P71S.

XIX. A purely sensual love, moreover, that is, a Lust to procreate which arises from external appearance, and absolutely, all love which has a cause other than freedom of mind, easily passes into hate—unless (which is worse) it is a species of madness. And then it is encouraged more by discord than by harmony. See IIIP31.

XX. As for marriage, it certainly agrees with reason, if the desire for physical union is not generated only by external appearance but also by a love of begetting children and educating them wisely, and moreover, if the love of each, of both the man and the woman, is caused not by external appearance only, but mainly by freedom of mind.

XXI. Flattery also gives rise to harmony, but by the foul crime of bondage, or by treachery. No one is more taken in by flattery than the proud, who wish to be first and are not.

XXII. In despondency, there is a false appearance of morality and religion. And though despondency is the opposite of pride, still the despondent man is very near the proud. See P57S.

XXIII. Shame, moreover, contributes to harmony only in those things which cannot be hidden. Again, because shame itself is a species of sadness, it does not belong to the exercise of reason.

XXIV. The other affects of sadness toward men are directly opposed to justice, fairness, being honorable, morality, and religion. And though indignation seems to present an appearance of fairness, nevertheless, when each one is allowed to pass judgment on another's deeds, and to enforce either his own or another's right, we live without a law.

XXV. Courtesy, that is, the desire to please men which is determined by reason, is related to morality (as we said in P37S1). But if it arises from an affect, it is ambition, *or* a desire by which men generally arouse discord and seditions, from a false appearance of morality. For one who desires to aid others by advice or by action, so that they may enjoy the highest good together, will aim chiefly at arousing their love for him, but not at leading them into admiration so that his teaching will be called after his name. Nor will he give any cause for envy. Again, in common conversations he will beware of relating men's vices, and will take care to speak only sparingly of a man's lack of power, but generously of the man's virtue, *or* power, and how it can be perfected, so that men, moved not by fear or aversion, but only by an affect of Joy, may strive to live as far as they can according to the rule of reason.

XXVI. Apart from men we know no singular thing in Nature whose mind we can enjoy, and which we can join to ourselves in friendship, or some kind of association. And so whatever there is in Nature apart from men, the principle of seeking our own advantage does not demand that we preserve it. Instead, it teaches us to preserve or destroy it according to its use, or to adapt it to our use in any way whatever.

XXVII. The principal advantage we derive from things outside us— apart from the experience and knowledge we acquire from observing

II/272

II/273

them and changing them from one form into another—lies in the preservation of our body. That is why those things are most useful to us II/274 which can feed and maintain it, so that all its parts can perform their function properly. For the more the body is capable of affecting, and being affected by, external bodies in a great many ways, the more the mind is capable of thinking (see P38 and P39).

But there seem to be very few things of this kind in Nature. So to nourish the body in the way required, it is necessary to use many different kinds of food. Indeed, the human body is composed of a great many parts of different natures, which require continuous and varied food so that the whole body may be equally capable of doing everything which can follow from its nature, and consequently, so that the mind may also be equally capable of conceiving many things.

XXVIII. Now to achieve these things the powers of each man would hardly be sufficient if men did not help one another. But money has provided a convenient instrument for acquiring all these aids. That is why its image usually occupies the mind of the multitude more than anything else. For they can imagine hardly any species of joy without the accompanying idea of money as its cause.

XXIX. But this is a vice only in those who seek money neither from need nor on account of necessities, but because they have learned the art of making money and pride themselves on it very much. As for the body, they feed it according to custom, but sparingly, because they believe they lose as much of their goods as they devote to the preservation II/275 of their body. Those, however, who know the true use of money, and set bounds to their wealth according to need, live contentedly with little.

XXX. Since those things are good which assist the parts of the body to perform their function, and joy consists in the fact that man's power, insofar as he consists of mind and body, is aided or increased, all things which bring joy are good. Nevertheless, since things do not act in order to affect us with joy, and their power of acting is not regulated by our advantage, and finally, since joy is generally related particularly to one part of the body, most affects of joy are excessive (unless reason and alertness are present). Hence, the desires generated by them are also excessive. To this we may add that when we follow our affects, we value most the pleasures of the moment, and cannot appraise future things with an equal affect of mind. See P44S and P60S.

XXXI. Superstition, on the other hand, seems to maintain that the good is what brings sadness, and the evil, what brings joy. But as we have already said (see P45S), no one, unless he is envious, takes pleasure in my lack of power and misfortune. For as we are affected with a greater joy, we pass to a greater perfection, and consequently participate more

II/276 in the divine nature. Nor can joy which is governed by the true principle of our advantage ever be evil. On the other hand, he who is led by fear, and does the good only to avoid evil, is not governed by reason.

XXXII. But human power is very limited and infinitely surpassed by the power of external causes. So we do not have an absolute power to adapt things outside us to our use. Nevertheless, we shall bear calmly those things which happen to us contrary to what the principle of our advantage demands, if we are conscious that we have done our duty, that the power we have could not have extended itself to the point where we could have avoided those things, and that we are a part of the whole of Nature, whose order we follow. If we understand this clearly and distinctly, that part of us which is defined by understanding, that is, the better part of us, will be entirely satisfied with this, and will strive to persevere in that satisfaction. For insofar as we understand, we can want nothing except what is necessary, nor absolutely be satisfied with anything except what is true. Hence, insofar as we understand these things rightly, the striving of the better part of us agrees with the order of the whole of Nature.

II/277

FIFTH PART OF THE ETHICS
OF THE POWER OF THE INTELLECT, *OR* ON HUMAN FREEDOM

PREFACE

I pass, finally, to the remaining part of the Ethics, *which concerns the means, or way, leading to freedom. Here, then, I shall treat of the power of reason, showing what it can do against the affects, and what freedom of mind, or blessedness, is. From this we shall see how much more the wise man can do than the ignorant. But it does not pertain to this investigation to show how the intellect must be perfected, or in what way the body must be cared for, so that it can perform its function properly. The former is the concern of logic, and the latter of medicine.*

Here, then, as I have said, I shall treat only of the power of the mind, or of reason, and shall show, above all, how great its dominion over the affects is, and what kind of dominion it has for restraining and moderating them. For we have already demonstrated above that it does not have an absolute dominion over them. Nevertheless, the Stoics thought that they depend entirely on our will, and that we can command them absolutely. But experience cries out against this, and has forced them, in spite of their principles, to confess that much practice and application are required to restrain and moderate them. If I remember rightly, someone tried to show this by the example of two dogs, one

II/278 *a house dog, the other a hunting dog. For by practice he was finally able to bring it about that the house dog was accustomed to hunt, and the hunting dog to refrain from chasing hares.*

Descartes was rather inclined to this opinion. For he maintained that the soul, or mind, was especially united to a certain part of the brain, called the pineal gland, by whose aid the mind is aware of all the motions aroused in the body and of external objects, and which the mind can move in various ways simply by willing. He contended that this gland was suspended in the middle of the brain in such a way that it could be moved by the least motion of the animal spirits. He maintained further that this gland is suspended in the middle of the brain in as many varying ways as there are varying ways that the animal spirits strike against it, and moreover, that as many varying traces are impressed upon it as there are varying external objects which drive the animal spirits against it. That is why, if the soul's will afterwards moves the gland so that it is suspended as it once was by the motion of the animal spirits, the gland will drive and determine the animal spirits in the same way as when they were driven back before by a similar placement of the gland.

Furthermore, he maintained that each will of the mind is united by nature to a certain fixed motion of this gland. For example, if someone has a will to look at a distant object, this will brings it about that the pupil is dilated. But if he thinks only of the pupil which is to be dilated, nothing will be accomplished by having a will for this, because Nature has not joined the motion of the gland which serves to drive the animal spirits against the optic nerve in a way suitable for dilating or contracting the pupil with the will to dilate or contract it. Instead, it has joined that motion with the will to look at distant or near objects.

Finally, he maintained that even though each motion of this gland seems to have been connected by nature from the beginning of our life with a particular II/279 *one of our thoughts, they can still be joined by habit to others. He tries to prove this in* The Passions of the Soul I, 50. *From these claims, he infers that there is no soul so weak that it cannot—when it is well directed—acquire an absolute power over its passions. For as he defines them, these are*

perceptions, or feelings, or emotions of the soul, which are particularly related to the soul, and which [NB] are produced, preserved, and strengthened by some motion of the spirits (see *The Passions of the Soul I, 27*).

But since to any will we can join any motion of the gland (and consequently any motion of the spirits), and since the determination of the will depends only on our power, we shall acquire an absolute dominion over our passions, if we determine our will by firm and certain judgments according to which we will to direct the actions of our life, and if we join to these judgments the motions of the passions we will to have.

Such is the opinion of that most distinguished man—as far as I can gather it from his words. I would hardly have believed it had been propounded by so great a man, had it not been so subtle. Indeed, I cannot wonder enough that a philosopher of his caliber—one who had firmly decided to deduce nothing except from principles known through themselves, and to affirm nothing which he did not perceive clearly and distinctly, one who had so often censured the Scholastics for wishing to explain obscure things by occult qualities—that such a philosopher should assume a hypothesis more occult than any occult quality.

What, I ask, does he understand by the union of mind and body? What clear and distinct concept does he have of a thought so closely united to some little portion of quantity? Indeed, I wish he had explained this union by its proximate

II/280   *cause. But he had conceived the mind to be so distinct from the body that he could not assign any singular cause, either of this union or of the mind itself. Instead, it was necessary for him to have recourse to the cause of the whole Universe, that is, to God.*

Again, I should like very much to know how many degrees of motion the mind can give to that pineal gland, and how great a force is required to hold it in suspense. For I do not know whether this gland is driven about more slowly by the mind than by the animal spirits, or more quickly; nor do I know whether the motions of the passions which we have joined closely to firm judgments can be separated from them again by corporeal causes. If so, it would follow that although the mind had firmly resolved to face dangers, and had joined the motions of daring to this decision, nevertheless, once the danger had been seen, the gland might be so suspended that the mind could think only of flight. And of course, since there is no common measure between the will and motion, there is also no comparison between the power, or forces, of the mind and those of the body. Consequently, the forces of the body cannot in any way be determined by those of the mind. To this we may add that this gland is not found to be so placed in the middle of the brain that it can be driven about so easily and in so many ways, and that not all the nerves extend to the cavities of the brain. Finally, I pass over all those things he claimed about the will and its freedom, since I have already shown, more than adequately, that they are false.

Therefore, because the power of the mind is defined only by understanding, as I have shown above, we shall determine, by the mind's knowledge alone, the remedies for the affects. I believe everyone in fact knows them by experience, though they neither observe them accurately, nor see them distinctly. From that we shall deduce all those things which concern the mind's blessedness.

II/281   AXIOMS

A1: If two contrary actions are aroused in the same subject, a change will have to occur, either in both of them, or in one only, until they cease to be contrary.

A2: The power of an effect is defined by the power of its cause, insofar as its essence is explained or defined by the essence of its cause.

This axiom is evident from IIIP7.

P1: *In just the same way as thoughts and ideas of things are ordered and connected in the mind, so the affections of the body, or images of things are ordered and connected in the body.*

Dem.: The order and connection of ideas is the same as the order and connection of things (by IIP7), and vice versa, the order and connection of things is the same as the order and connection of ideas (by IIP6C and P7). So just as the order and connection of ideas happens in the mind according to the order and connection of affections of the body (by IIP18), so vice versa (by IIIP2), the order and connection of affections of the body happens as thoughts and ideas of things are ordered and connected in the mind, q.e.d.

P2: *If we separate emotions, or affects, from the thought of an external cause, and join them to other thoughts, then the love, or hate, toward the external cause is destroyed, as are the vacillations of mind arising from these affects.*

Dem.: For what constitutes the form of love, or hate, is joy, or sad- II/282 ness, accompanied by the idea of an external cause (by Defs. Aff. VI, VII). So if this is taken away, the form of love or hate is taken away at the same time. Hence, these affects, and those arising from them, are destroyed, q.e.d.

P3: *An affect which is a passion ceases to be a passion as soon as we form a clear and distinct idea of it.*

Dem.: An affect which is a passion is a confused idea (by Gen. Def. Aff.). Therefore, if we should form a clear and distinct idea of the affect itself, this idea will only be distinguished by reason from the affect itself, insofar as it is related only to the mind (by IIP21 and P21S). Therefore (by IIIP3), the affect will cease to be a passion, q.e.d.

Cor.: The more an affect is known to us, then, the more it is in our power, and the less the mind is acted on by it.

P4: *There is no affection of the body of which we cannot form a clear and distinct concept.*

Dem.: Those things which are common to all can only be conceived adequately (by IIP38), and so (by IIP12 and L2 [II/98]) there is no affection of the body of which we cannot form some clear and distinct concept, q.e.d.

Cor.: From this it follows that there is no affect of which we cannot form some clear and distinct concept. For an affect is an idea of an II/283 affection of the body (by Gen. Def. Aff.), which therefore (by P4) must involve some clear and distinct concept.

Schol.: There is nothing from which some effect does not follow (by IP36), and we understand clearly and distinctly whatever follows from an idea which is adequate in us (by IIP40); hence, each of us has—in part, at least, if not absolutely—the power to understand himself and his affects, and consequently, the power to bring it about that he is less acted on by them.

We must, therefore, take special care to know each affect clearly and distinctly (as far as this is possible), so that in this way the mind may be determined from an affect to thinking those things which it perceives clearly and distinctly, and with which it is fully satisfied, and so that the affect itself may be separated from the thought of an external cause and joined to true thoughts. The result will be not only that love, hate, and the like, are destroyed (by P2), but also that the appetites, *or* desires, which usually arise from such an affect, cannot be excessive (by IVP61).

For it must particularly be noted that the appetite by which a man is said to act, and that by which he is said to be acted on, are one and the same. For example, we have shown that human nature is so constituted that each of us wants the others to live according to his temperament (see IIIP31S). And indeed, in a man who is not led by reason this appetite is the passion called ambition, which does not differ much from pride. On the other hand, in a man who lives according to the dictate of reason it is the action, *or* virtue, called morality (see IVP37S1 and P37 Alternate Dem.).

In this way, all the appetites, *or* desires, are passions only insofar as they arise from inadequate ideas, and are counted as virtues when they are aroused or generated by adequate ideas. For all the desires by which we are determined to do something can arise as much from adequate ideas as from inadequate ones (by IVP59). And—to return to the point from which I have digressed—we can devise no other remedy for the affects which depends on our power and is more excellent than this, which consists in a true knowledge of them. For the mind has no other power than that of thinking and forming adequate ideas, as we have shown (by IIIP3) above.

II/284

P5: *The greatest affect of all, other things equal, is one toward a thing we imagine simply, and neither as necessary, nor as possible, nor as contingent.*

Dem.: An affect toward a thing we imagine to be free is greater than that toward a thing we imagine to be necessary (by IIIP49), and consequently is still greater than that toward a thing we imagine as possible or contingent (by IVP11). But imagining a thing as free can be nothing but simply imagining it while we are ignorant of the causes by which it has been determined to act (by what we have shown in IIP35S). Therefore, an affect toward a thing we imagine simply is, other things equal, greater than that toward a thing we imagine as necessary, possible, or contingent. Hence, it is the greatest of all, q.e.d.

P6: *Insofar as the mind understands all things as necessary, it has a greater power over the affects, or is less acted on by them.*

Dem.: The mind understands all things to be necessary (by IP29), and to be determined by an infinite connection of causes to exist and produce effects (by IP28). And so (by P5) to that extent [the mind] brings it about that it is less acted on by the affects springing from these things, and (by IIIP48) is less affected toward them, q.e.d.

Schol.: The more this knowledge that things are necessary is concerned with singular things, which we imagine more distinctly and vividly, the greater is this power of the mind over the affects, as experience itself also testifies. For we see that sadness over some good which has perished is lessened as soon as the man who has lost it realizes that this good could not, in any way, have been kept. Similarly, we see that no one pities infants because of their inability to speak, to walk, or to reason, or because they live so many years, as it were, unconscious of themselves. But if most people were born grown up, and only one or two were born infants, then everyone would pity the infants, because they would regard infancy itself, not as a natural and necessary thing, but as a vice of nature, *or* a sin. We could point out many other things along this line.

P7: *Affects arising from or aroused by reason are, if we take account of time, more powerful than those related to singular things we regard as absent.*

Dem.: We regard a thing as absent, not because of the affect by which we imagine it, but because the body is affected by another affect which excludes the thing's existence (by IIP17). So an affect related to a thing we regard as absent is not of such a nature that it surpasses men's other actions and power (see IVP6); on the contrary, its nature is such that it can, in some measure, be restrained by those affections which exclude the existence of its external cause (by IVP9). But an affect arising from reason is necessarily related to the common properties of things (see the Def. of reason in IIP40S2), which we always regard as present (for there can be nothing which excludes their present existence) and which we always imagine in the same way (by IIP38). So such an affect will always remain the same, and hence (by A1), the affects which are contrary to it and are not encouraged by their external causes will have to accommodate themselves to it more and more, until they are no longer contrary to it. To that extent, an affect arising from reason is more powerful, q.e.d.

II/285

II/286

P8: *The more an affect arises from a number of causes concurring together, the greater it is.*

Dem.: A number of causes together can do more than if they were fewer (by IIIP7). And so (by IVP5), the more an affect is aroused by a number of causes together, the stronger it is, q.e.d.

Schol.: This proposition is also evident from A2.

P9: *If an affect is related to more and different causes which the mind considers together with the affect itself, it is less harmful, we are less acted on by it, and we are affected less toward each cause, than is the case with another, equally great affect, which is related only to one cause, or to fewer causes.*

Dem.: An affect is only evil, *or* harmful, insofar as it prevents the mind from being able to think (by IVP26 and P27). And so that affect which determines the mind to consider many objects together is less harmful than another, equally great affect which engages the mind solely in considering one, or a few objects, so that it cannot think of others. This was the first point.

Next, because the mind's essence, that is, power (by IIIP7), consists only in thought (by IIP11), the mind is less acted on by an affect which determines it to consider many things together than by an equally great affect which keeps the mind engaged solely in considering one or a few objects. This was the second point.

II/287   Finally (by IIIP48), insofar as this affect is related to many external causes, it is also less toward each one, q.e.d.

P10: *So long as we are not torn by affects contrary to our nature, we have the power of ordering and connecting the affections of the body according to the order of the intellect.*

Dem.: Affects which are contrary to our nature, that is (by IVP30), which are evil, are evil insofar as they prevent the mind from understanding (by IVP27). Therefore, so long as we are not torn by affects contrary to our nature, the power of the mind by which it strives to understand things (by IVP26) is not hindered. So long, then, the mind has the power of forming clear and distinct ideas, and of deducing some from others (see IIP40S2 and P47S). And hence, so long do we have (by P1) the power of ordering and connecting the affections of the body according to the order of the intellect, q.e.d.

Schol.: By this power of rightly ordering and connecting the affections of the body, we can bring it about that we are not easily affected with evil affects. For (by P7) a greater force is required for restraining affects ordered and connected according to the order of the intellect than for restraining those which are uncertain and random. The best thing, then, that we can do, so long as we do not have perfect knowledge of our affects, is to conceive a correct principle of living, *or* sure maxims of life, to commit them to memory, and to apply them constantly to the particular cases frequently encountered in life. In this way our imagination will be extensively affected by them, and we shall always have them ready.

For example, we have laid it down as a maxim of life (see IVP46 and P46S) that hate is to be conquered by love, *or* nobility, not by repaying it with hate in return. But in order that we may always have this rule of reason ready when it is needed, we ought to think about and meditate frequently on the common wrongs of men, and how they may be warded off best by nobility. For if we join the image of a wrong to the imagination of this maxim, it will always be ready for us (by IIP18) when a wrong is done to us. If we have ready also the principle of our own true advantage, and also of the good which follows from mutual friendship and common society, and keep in mind, moreover, that the highest satisfaction of mind stems from the right principle of living (by IVP52), and that men, like other things, act from the necessity of nature, then the wrong, *or* the hate usually arising from it, will occupy a very small part of the imagination, and will easily be overcome.

II/288

Or if the anger which usually arises from the greatest wrongs is not so easily overcome, it will still be overcome, though not without some vacillation. And it will be overcome in far less time than if we had not considered these things beforehand in this way (as is evident from P6, P7, and P8).

To put aside fear, we must think in the same way of tenacity: that is, we must recount and frequently imagine the common dangers of life, and how they can be best avoided and overcome by presence of mind and strength of character.

But it should be noted that in ordering our thoughts and images, we must always (by IVP63C and IIIP59) attend to those things which are good in each thing so that in this way we are always determined to acting from an affect of joy. For example, if someone sees that he pursues esteem too much, he should think of its correct use, the end for which it ought be pursued, and the means by which it can be acquired, not of its misuse and emptiness, and men's inconstancy, or other things of this kind, which only someone sick of mind thinks of. For those who are most ambitious are most upset by such thoughts when they despair of attaining the honor they strive for; while they spew forth their anger, they wish to seem wise. So it is certain that they most desire esteem who cry out most against its misuse, and the emptiness of the world.

Nor is this peculiar to the ambitious—it is common to everyone whose luck is bad and whose mind is weak. For the poor man, when he is also greedy, will not stop talking about the misuse of money and the vices of the rich. In doing this he only distresses himself, and shows others that he cannot bear calmly either his own poverty, or the wealth of others.

So also, one who has been badly received by a lover thinks of nothing but the inconstancy and deceptiveness of women, and their other, often sung vices. All of these he immediately forgets as soon as his lover receives him again.

One, therefore, who is anxious to moderate his affects and appetites from the love of freedom alone will strive, as far as he can, to come to know the virtues and their causes, and to fill his mind with the gladness which arises from the true knowledge of them, but not at all to consider men's vices, or to disparage men, or to enjoy a false appearance of freedom. And he who will observe these [rules] carefully—for they are not difficult—and practice them, will soon be able to direct most of his actions according to the command of reason.

P11: *As an image is related to more things, the more frequent it is, or the more often it flourishes, and the more it engages the mind.*

Dem.: For as an image, *or* affect, is related to more things, there are more causes by which it can be aroused and encouraged, all of which the mind (by hypothesis) considers together as a result of the affect itself. And so the affect is the more frequent, *or* flourishes more often, and (by P8) engages the mind more, q.e.d.

P12: *The images of things are more easily joined to images related to things we understand clearly and distinctly than to other images.*

Dem.: Things we understand clearly and distinctly are either common properties of things or deduced from them (see the Def. of reason in IIP40S2), and consequently (by P11) are aroused in us more often. And so it can more easily happen that we consider other things together with them rather than with [things we do not understand clearly and distinctly]. Hence (by IIP18), [images of things] are more easily joined with [things we understand clearly and distinctly] than with others, q.e.d.

P13: *The more an image is joined with other images, the more often it flourishes.*

Dem.: For the more an image is joined with other images, the more causes there are (by IIP18) by which it can be aroused, q.e.d.

P14: *The mind can bring it about that all the body's affections, or images of things, are related to the idea of God.*

Dem.: There is no affection of the body of which the mind cannot

252

form some clear and distinct concept (by P4). And so it can bring it about (by IP15) that they are related to the idea of God, q.e.d.

P15: *He who understands himself and his affects clearly and distinctly loves God, and does so the more, the more he understands himself and his affects.*

Dem.: He who understands himself and his affects clearly and distinctly rejoices (by IIIP53), and this joy is accompanied by the idea of God (by P14). Hence (by Def. Aff. VI), he loves God, and (by the same reasoning) does so the more, the more he understands himself and his affects, q.e.d.

P16: *This love toward God must engage the mind most.*

Dem.: For this love is joined to all the affections of the body (by P14), which all encourage it (by P15). And so (by P11), it must engage the mind most, q.e.d.

II/291

P17: *God is without passions, and is not affected with any affect of joy or sadness.*

Dem.: All ideas, insofar as they are related to God, are true (by IIP32), that is (by IID4), adequate. And so (by Gen. Def. Aff.), God is without passions.

Next, God can pass neither to a greater nor a lesser perfection (by IP20C2); hence (by Defs. Aff. II, III) he is not affected with any affect of joy or sadness, q.e.d.

Cor.: Strictly speaking, God loves no one, and hates no one. For God (by P17) is not affected with any affect of joy or sadness. Consequently (by Defs. Aff. VI, VII), he also loves no one and hates no one.

P18: *No one can hate God.*

Dem.: The idea of God which is in us is adequate and perfect (by IIP46, P47). So insofar as we consider God, we act (by IIIP3). Consequently (by IIIP59), there can be no sadness accompanied by the idea of God, that is (by Def. Aff. VII), no one can hate God, q.e.d.

Cor.: Love toward God cannot be turned into hate.

Schol.: But, it can be objected, while we understand God to be the cause of all things, we thereby consider God to be the cause of sadness. To this I reply that insofar as we understand the causes of sadness, it ceases (by P3) to be a passion, that is (by IIIP59), to that extent it ceases to be sadness. And so, insofar as we understand God to be the cause of sadness, we rejoice.

II/292

P19: *He who loves God cannot strive that God should love him in return.*

Dem.: If a man were to strive for this, he would desire (by P17C) that God, whom he loves, not be God. Consequently (by IIIP19), he would desire to be saddened, which is absurd (by IIIP28). Therefore, he who loves God, and so on, q.e.d.

P20: *This love toward God cannot be tainted by an affect of envy or jealousy: instead, the more men we imagine to be joined to God by the same bond of love, the more it is encouraged.*

Dem.: This love toward God is the highest good which we can want from the dictate of reason (by IVP28), and is common to all men (by IVP36); we desire that all should enjoy it (by IVP37). And so (by Def. Aff. XXIII), it cannot be stained by an affect of envy, nor (by P18 and the Def. of jealousy, see IIIP35S) by an affect of jealousy. On the contrary (by IIIP31), the more men we imagine to enjoy it, the more it must be encouraged, q.e.d.

Schol.: Similarly we can show that there is no affect which is directly contrary to this love and by which it can be destroyed. So we can conclude that this love is the most constant of all the affects, and insofar as it is related to the body, cannot be destroyed, unless it is destroyed with the body itself. What the nature of this love is insofar as it is related only to the mind, we shall see later.

And with this, I have covered all the remedies for the affects, *or* all that the mind, considered only in itself, can do against the affects. From this it is clear that the power of the mind over the affects consists:

I. In the knowledge itself of the affects (see P4S);

II. In the fact that it separates the affects from the thought of an external cause, which we imagine confusedly (see P2 and P4S);

III. In the time by which the affections related to things we understand surpass those related to things we conceive confusedly, *or* in a mutilated way (see P7);

IV. In the multiplicity of causes by which affections related to common properties or to God are encouraged (see P9 and P11);

V. Finally, in the order by which the mind can order its affects and connect them to one another (see P10, and in addition, P12, P13, and P14).

But to understand better this power of the mind over the affects, the most important thing to note is that we call affects great when we compare the affect of one man with that of another, and see that the same affect troubles one more than the other, or when we compare the affects of one and the same man with each other, and find that he is affected, *or* moved, more by one affect than by another. For (by IVP5) the force of each affect is defined by the power of the external cause

II/293

compared with our own. But the power of the mind is defined by knowledge alone, whereas lack of power, *or* passion, is judged solely by the privation of knowledge, that is, by that through which ideas are called inadequate.

From this it follows that that mind is most acted on, of which inadequate ideas constitute the greatest part, so that it is distinguished more by what it undergoes than by what it does. On the other hand, that mind acts most, of which adequate ideas constitute the greatest part, so that though it may have as many inadequate ideas as the other, it is still distinguished more by those which are attributed to human virtue than by those which betray man's lack of power.

Next, it should be noted that sickness of the mind and misfortunes take their origin especially from too much love toward a thing which is liable to many variations and which we can never fully possess. For no one is disturbed or anxious concerning anything unless he loves it, nor do wrongs, suspicions, and enmities arise except from love for a thing which no one can really fully possess. II/294

From what we have said, we easily conceive what clear and distinct knowledge—and especially that third kind of knowledge (see IIP47S), whose foundation is the knowledge of God itself—can accomplish against the affects. Insofar as the affects are passions, if clear and distinct knowledge does not absolutely remove them (see P3 and P4S), at least it brings it about that they constitute the smallest part of the mind (see P14). And then it begets a love toward a thing immutable and eternal (see P15), which we really fully possess (see IIP45), and which therefore cannot be tainted by any of the vices which are in ordinary love, but can always be greater and greater (by P15), and occupy the greatest part of the mind (by P16), and affect it extensively.

With this I have completed everything which concerns this present life. Anyone who attends to what we have said in this scholium, and at the same time, to the definitions of the mind and its affects, and finally to IIIP1 and P3, will easily be able to see what I said at the beginning of this scholium, namely, that in these few words I have covered all the remedies for the affects. So it is time now to pass to those things which pertain to the mind's duration without relation to the body.

P21: *The mind can neither imagine anything, nor recollect past things, except while the body endures.*

Dem.: The mind neither expresses the actual existence of its body, nor conceives the body's affections as actual, except while the body endures (by IIP8C); consequently (by IIP26), it conceives no body as actually existing except while its body endures. Therefore, it can neither imagine anything (see the Def. of imagination in IIP17S) nor recollect past things (see the Def. of Memory in IIP18S) except while the body endures, q.e.d.

P22: *Nevertheless, in God there is necessarily an idea that expresses the essence of this or that human body, under a species of eternity.*

Dem.: God is the cause, not only of the existence of this or that human body, but also of its essence (by IP25), which therefore must be conceived through the very essence of God (by IA4), by a certain eternal necessity (by IP16), and this concept must be in God (by IIP3), q.e.d.

P23: *The human mind cannot be absolutely destroyed with the body, but something of it remains which is eternal.*

Dem.: In God there is necessarily a concept, *or* idea, which expresses the essence of the human body (by P22), an idea, therefore, which is necessarily something that pertains to the essence of the human mind (by IIP13). But we do not attribute to the human mind any duration that can be defined by time, except insofar as it expresses the actual existence of the body, which is explained by duration, and can be defined by time, that is (by IIP8C), we do not attribute duration to it except while the body endures. However, since what is conceived, with a certain eternal necessity, through God's essence itself (by P22) is nevertheless something, this something that pertains to the essence of the mind will necessarily be eternal, q.e.d.

Schol.: As we have said, this idea, which expresses the essence of the body under a species of eternity, is a certain mode of thinking, which pertains to the essence of the mind, and which is necessarily eternal. II/296 And though it is impossible that we should recollect that we existed before the body—since there cannot be any traces of this in the body, and eternity can neither be defined by time nor have any relation to time—still, we feel and know by experience that we are eternal. For the mind feels those things that it conceives in understanding no less than those it has in the memory. For the eyes of the mind, by which it sees and observes things, are the demonstrations themselves.

Therefore, though we do not recollect that we existed before the body, we nevertheless feel that our mind, insofar as it involves the essence of the body under a species of eternity, is eternal, and that this existence it has cannot be defined by time *or* explained through duration. Our mind, therefore, can be said to endure, and its existence can be defined by a certain time, only insofar as it involves the actual existence of the body, and to that extent only does it have the power of determining the existence of things by time, and of conceiving them under duration.

P24: *The more we understand singular things, the more we understand God.*
 Dem.: This is evident from IP25C.

P25: *The greatest striving of the mind, and its greatest virtue is understanding things by the third kind of knowledge.*
 Dem.: The third kind of knowledge proceeds from an adequate idea of certain attributes of God to an adequate knowledge of the essence of things (see its Def. in IIP40S2), and the more we understand things in this way, the more we understand God (by P24). Therefore (by IVP28), the greatest virtue of the mind, that is (by IVD8), the mind's power, *or* nature, *or* (by IIIP7) its greatest striving, is to understand things by the third kind of knowledge, q.e.d.

P26: *The more the mind is capable of understanding things by the third kind of knowledge, the more it desires to understand them by this kind of knowledge.* II/297
 Dem.: This is evident. For insofar as we conceive the mind to be capable of understanding things by this kind of knowledge, we conceive it as determined to understand things by the same kind of knowledge. Consequently (by Def. Aff. I), the more the mind is capable of this, the more it desires it, q.e.d.

P27: *The greatest satisfaction of mind there can be arises from this third kind of knowledge.*
 Dem.: The greatest virtue of the mind is to know God (by IVP28), *or* to understand things by the third kind of knowledge (by P25). Indeed, this virtue is the greater, the more the mind knows things by this kind of knowledge (by P24). So he who knows things by this kind of knowledge passes to the greatest human perfection, and consequently (by Def. Aff. II), is affected with the greatest Joy, accompanied (by IIP43) by the idea of himself and his virtue. Therefore (by Def. Aff. XXV), the greatest satisfaction there can be arises from this kind of knowledge, q.e.d.

P28: *The striving, or desire, to know things by the third kind of knowledge cannot arise from the first kind of knowledge, but can indeed arise from the second.*
 Dem.: This proposition is evident through itself. For whatever we understand clearly and distinctly, we understand either through itself, II/298 or through something else which is conceived through itself; that is, the ideas which are clear and distinct in us, *or* which are related to the third kind of knowledge (see IIP40S2), cannot follow from mutilated and confused ideas, which (by IIP40S2) are related to the first kind of knowledge; but they can follow from adequate ideas, *or* (by IIP40S2) from the second and third kind of knowledge. Therefore (by Def.

Aff. I), the desire to know things by the third kind of knowledge cannot arise from the first kind of knowledge, but can from the second, q.e.d.

P29: *Whatever the mind understands under a species of eternity, it understands not from the fact that it conceives the body's present actual existence, but from the fact that it conceives the body's essence under a species of eternity.*

Dem.: Insofar as the mind conceives the present existence of its body, it conceives duration, which can be determined by time, and to that extent only it has the power of conceiving things in relation to time (by P21 and IIP26). But eternity cannot be explained by duration (by ID8 and its explanation). Therefore, to that extent the mind does not have the power of conceiving things under a species of eternity.

But because it is of the nature of reason to conceive things under a species of eternity (by IIP44C2), and it also pertains to the nature of the mind to conceive the body's essence under a species of eternity (by P23), and beyond these two, nothing else pertains to the mind's essence (by IIP13), this power of conceiving things under a species of eternity pertains to the mind only insofar as it conceives the body's essence under a species of eternity, q.e.d.

Schol.: We conceive things as actual in two ways: either insofar as we conceive them to exist in relation to a certain time and place, or insofar as we conceive them to be contained in God and to follow from the necessity of the divine nature. But the things we conceive in this second way as true, *or* real, we conceive under a species of eternity, and their ideas involve the eternal and infinite essence of God (as we have shown in IIP45 and P45S).

II/299

P30: *Insofar as our mind knows itself and the body under a species of eternity, it necessarily has knowledge of God, and knows that it is in God and is conceived through God.*

Dem.: Eternity is the very essence of God insofar as this involves necessary existence (by ID8). To conceive things under a species of eternity, therefore, is to conceive things insofar as they are conceived through God's essence, as real beings, *or* insofar as through God's essence they involve existence. Hence, insofar as our mind conceives itself and the body under a species of eternity, it necessarily has knowledge of God, and knows, and so on, q.e.d.

P31: *The third kind of knowledge depends on the mind, as on a formal cause, insofar as the mind itself is eternal.*

Dem.: The mind conceives nothing under a species of eternity except insofar as it conceives its body's essence under a species of eternity (by P29), that is, (by P21 and P23), except insofar as it is eternal. So (by P30) insofar as it is eternal, it has knowledge of God, knowledge which is necessarily adequate (by IIP46). And therefore, the mind, insofar as it is eternal, is capable of knowing all those things which can follow from this given knowledge of God (by IIP40), that is, of knowing things by the third kind of knowledge (see the Def. of this in IIP40S2); therefore, the mind, insofar as it is eternal, is the adequate, *or* formal, cause of the third kind of knowledge (by IIID1), q.e.d.

Schol.: Therefore, the more each of us is able to achieve in this kind II/300 of knowledge, the more he is conscious of himself and of God, that is, the more perfect and blessed he is. This will be even clearer from what follows.

But here it should be noted that although we are already certain that the mind is eternal, insofar as it conceives things under a species of eternity, nevertheless, for an easier explanation and better understanding of the things we wish to show, we shall consider it as if it were now beginning to be, and were now beginning to understand things under a species of eternity, as we have done up to this point. We may do this without danger of error, provided we are careful to draw our conclusions only from evident premises.

P32: *Whatever we understand by the third kind of knowledge we take pleasure in, and our pleasure is accompanied by the idea of God as a cause.*

Dem.: From this kind of knowledge there arises the greatest satisfaction of mind there can be (by P27), that is (by Def. Aff. XXV), joy; this joy is accompanied by the idea of oneself, and consequently (by P30) it is also accompanied by the idea of God, as its cause, q.e.d.

Cor.: From the third kind of knowledge, there necessarily arises an intellectual love of God. For from this kind of knowledge there arises (by P32) joy, accompanied by the idea of God as its cause, that is (by Def. Aff. VI), love of God, not insofar as we imagine him as present (by P29), but insofar as we understand God to be eternal. And this is what I call intellectual love of God.

P33: *The intellectual love of God, which arises from the third kind of knowledge, is eternal.*

Dem.: For the third kind of knowledge (by P31 and by IA3) is eternal. II/301
And so (by IA3), the love that arises from it must also be eternal, q.e.d.

Schol.: Although this love toward God has had no beginning (by P33), it still has all the perfections of love, just as if it had come to be (as we have feigned in P32C). There is no difference here, except that the mind has had eternally the same perfections which, in our fiction, now come to it, and that it is accompanied by the idea of God as an eternal cause. If joy, then, consists in the passage to a greater perfection, blessedness must surely consist in the fact that the mind is endowed with perfection itself.

P34: *Only while the body endures is the mind subject to affects which are related to the passions.*

Dem.: An imagination is an idea by which the mind considers a thing as present (see its Def. in IIP17S), which nevertheless indicates the present constitution of the human body more than the nature of the external thing (by IIP16C2). An affect, then, (by the Gen. Def. Aff.) is an imagination, insofar as it indicates the present constitution of the body. So (by P21) only while the body endures is the mind subject to affects which are related to passions, q.e.d.

Cor.: From this it follows that no love except intellectual love is eternal.

II/302 Schol.: If we attend to the common opinion of men, we shall see that they are indeed conscious of the eternity of their mind, but that they confuse it with duration, and attribute it to the imagination, *or* memory, which they believe remains after death.

P35: *God loves himself with an infinite intellectual love.*

Dem.: God is absolutely infinite (by ID6), that is (by IID6), the nature of God enjoys infinite perfection, accompanied (by IIP3) by the idea of himself, that is (by IP11 and D1), by the idea of his cause. And this is what we said (P32C) intellectual love is.

P36: *The mind's intellectual love of God is the very love of God by which God loves himself, not insofar as he is infinite, but insofar as he can be explained by the human mind's essence, considered under a species of eternity; that is, the mind's intellectual love of God is part of the infinite love by which God loves himself.*

Dem.: This love the mind has must be related to its actions (by P32C and IIIP3); it is, then, an action by which the mind contemplates itself, with the accompanying idea of God as its cause (by P32 and P32C), that is (by IP25C and IIP11C), an action by which God, insofar as he can be explained through the human mind, contemplates himself, with the accompanying idea of himself [as the cause]; so (by P35), this love the mind has is part of the infinite love by which God loves himself, q.e.d.

Cor.: From this it follows that insofar as God loves himself, he loves men, and consequently that God's love of men and the mind's intellectual love of God are one and the same.

II/303 Schol.: From this we clearly understand wherein our salvation, *or* blessedness, *or* freedom, consists, namely, in a constant and eternal love of God, *or* in God's love for men. And this love, *or* blessedness, is called glory in the Sacred Scriptures—not without reason. For whether this love is related to God or to the mind, it can rightly be called satisfaction of mind, which is really not distinguished from glory (by Defs. Aff. XXV and XXX). For insofar as it is related to God (by P35), it is joy (if I may still be permitted to use this term), accompanied by the idea of himself [as its cause]. And similarly insofar as it is related to the mind (by P27).

Again, because the essence of our mind consists only in knowledge, of which God is the beginning and foundation (by IP15 and IIP47S), it is clear to us how our mind, with respect both to essence and existence, follows from the divine nature, and continually depends on God.

I thought this worth the trouble of noting here, in order to show by this example how much the knowledge of singular things I have called intuitive, or knowledge of the third kind (see IIP40S2), can accomplish, and how much more powerful it is than the universal knowledge I have called knowledge of the second kind. For although I have shown generally in Part I that all things (and consequently the human mind also) depend on God both for their essence and their existence, nevertheless, that demonstration, though legitimate and put beyond all chance of doubt, still does not affect our mind as much as when this is inferred from the very essence of any singular thing which we say depends on God.

P37: *There is nothing in Nature which is contrary to this intellectual love, or which can take it away.*

Dem.: This intellectual love follows necessarily from the nature of the mind insofar as it is considered as an eternal truth, through God's nature (by P33 and P29). So if there were something contrary to this love, it would be contrary to the true; consequently, what could remove this love would bring it about that what is true would be false. This (as is known through itself) is absurd. Therefore, there is nothing in Nature, and so on, q.e.d.

II/304

Schol.: IVA1 concerns singular things insofar as they are considered in relation to a certain time and place. I believe no one doubts this.

P38: *The more the mind understands things by the second and third kind of knowledge, the less it is acted on by affects which are evil, and the less it fears death.*

Dem.: The mind's essence consists in knowledge (by IIP11); therefore, the more the mind knows things by the second and third kind of knowledge, the greater the part of it that remains (by P23 and P29), and consequently (by P37), the greater the part of it that is not touched by affects which are contrary to our nature, that is, which (by IVP30) are evil. Therefore, the more the mind understands things by the second and third kind of knowledge, the greater the part of it that remains unharmed, and hence, the less it is acted on by affects, and so on, q.e.d.

Schol.: From this we understand what I touched on in IVP39S, and what I promised to explain in this part, namely, that death is less harmful to us, the greater the mind's clear and distinct knowledge, and hence, the more the mind loves God.

Next, because (by P27) the highest satisfaction there can be arises from the third kind of knowledge, it follows from this that the human mind can be of such a nature that the part of the mind which we have shown perishes with the body (see P21) is of no moment in relation to what remains. But I shall soon treat this more fully.

P39: *He who has a body capable of a great many things has a mind whose greatest part is eternal.*

II/305   Dem.: He who has a body capable of doing a great many things is least troubled by evil affects (by IVP38), that is (by IVP30), by affects contrary to our nature. So (by P10) he has a power of ordering and connecting the affections of his body according to the order of the intellect, and consequently (by P14), of bringing it about that all the affections of the body are related to the idea of God. The result (by P15) is that it is affected with a love of God, which (by P16) must occupy, *or* constitute the greatest part of the mind. Therefore (by P33), he has a mind whose greatest part is eternal, q.e.d.

Schol.: Because human bodies are capable of a great many things, there is no doubt but what they can be of such a nature that they are related to minds which have a great knowledge of themselves and of God, and of which the greatest, *or* chief, part is eternal. So they hardly fear death.

But for a clearer understanding of these things, we must note here that we live in continuous change, and that as we change for the better or worse, we are called happy or unhappy. For he who has passed from being an infant or child to being a corpse is called unhappy. On the other hand, if we pass the whole length of our life with a sound mind in a sound body, that is considered happiness. And really, he who, like an infant or child, has a body capable of very few things, and very heavily dependent on external causes, has a mind which considered solely in itself is conscious of almost nothing of itself, or of God, or of things. On the other hand, he who has a body capable of a great many things, has a mind which considered only in itself is very much conscious of itself, and of God, and of things.

In this life, then, we strive especially that the infant's body may change (as much as its nature allows and assists) into another, capable of a great many things and related to a mind very much conscious of itself, of God, and of things. We strive, that is, that whatever is related to its memory or imagination is of hardly any moment in relation to the intellect (as I have already said in P38S).

P40: *The more perfection each thing has, the more it acts and the less it is acted*   II/306
on; and conversely, the more it acts, the more perfect it is.

Dem.: The more each thing is perfect, the more reality it has (by IID6), and consequently (by IIIP3 and P3S), the more it acts and the less it is acted on. This demonstration indeed proceeds in the same way in reverse, from which it follows that the more a thing acts, the more perfect it is, q.e.d.

Cor.: From this it follows that the part of the mind that remains, however great it is, is more perfect than the rest.

For the eternal part of the mind (by P23 and P29) is the intellect, through which alone we are said to act (by IIIP3). But what we have shown to perish is the imagination (by P21), through which alone we are said to be acted on (by IIIP3 and the Gen. Def. Aff.). So (by P40), the intellect, however extensive it is, is more perfect than the imagination, q.e.d.

Schol.: These are the things I have decided to show concerning the mind, insofar as it is considered without relation to the body's existence. From them—and at the same time from IP21 and other things—it is clear that our mind, insofar as it understands, is an eternal mode of thinking, which is determined by another eternal mode of thinking, and this again by another, and so on, to infinity; so that together, they all constitute God's eternal and infinite intellect.

P41: *Even if we did not know that our mind is eternal, we would still regard as of the first importance morality, religion, and absolutely all the things we have shown (in Part IV) to be related to tenacity and nobility.*

Dem.: The first and only foundation of virtue, *or* of the method of living rightly (by IVP22C and P24) is the seeking of our own advantage. But to determine what reason prescribes as useful, we took no account of the eternity of the mind, which we only came to know in the Fifth Part. Therefore, though we did not know then that the mind is eternal,   II/307 we still regarded as of the first importance the things we showed to be related to tenacity and nobility. And so, even if we also did not know this now, we would still regard as of the first importance the same rules of reason, q.e.d.

Schol.: The usual conviction of the multitude seems to be different. For most people apparently believe that they are free to the extent that they are permitted to yield to their lust, and that they give up their right to the extent that they are bound to live according to the rule of the divine law. Morality, then, and religion, and absolutely everything related to strength of character, they believe to be burdens, which they hope to put down after death, when they also hope to receive a reward for their bondage, that is, for their morality and religion. They are induced to live according to the rule of the divine law (as far as their weakness and lack of character allows) not only by this hope, but also, and especially, by the fear that they may be punished horribly after death. If men did not have this hope and fear, but believed instead that minds die with the body, and that the wretched, exhausted with the burden of morality, cannot look forward to a life to come, they would return to their natural disposition, and would prefer to govern all their actions according to lust, and to obey fortune rather than themselves.

These opinions seem no less absurd to me than if someone, because he does not believe he can nourish his body with good food to eternity, should prefer to fill himself with poisons and other deadly things, or because he sees that the mind is not eternal, *or* immortal, should prefer to be mindless, and to live without reason. These [common beliefs] are so absurd they are hardly worth mentioning.

P42: *Blessedness is not the reward of virtue, but virtue itself; nor do we enjoy it because we restrain our lusts; on the contrary, because we enjoy it, we are able to restrain them.*

Dem.: Blessedness consists in love of God (by P36 and P36S), a love which arises from the third kind of knowledge (by P32C). So this love (by IIIP59 and P3) must be related to the mind insofar as it acts. Therefore (by IVD8), it is virtue itself. This was the first point.

Next, the more the mind enjoys this divine love, *or* blessedness, the more it understands (by P32), that is (by P3C), the greater the power it has over the affects, and (by P38) the less it is acted on by evil affects. So because the mind enjoys this divine love *or* blessedness, it has the power of restraining lusts. And because human power to restrain the affects consists only in the intellect, no one enjoys blessedness because he has restrained the affects. Instead, the power to restrain lusts arises from blessedness itself, q.e.d.

Schol.: With this I have finished all the things I wished to show concerning the mind's power over the affects and its freedom. From what has been shown, it is clear how much the wise man is capable of, and how much more powerful he is than one who is ignorant and is driven only by lust. For not only is the ignorant man troubled in many ways by external causes, and unable ever to possess true peace of mind, but he

II/308

264

also lives as if he knew neither himself, nor God, nor things; and as soon as he ceases to be acted on, he ceases to be. On the other hand, the wise man, insofar as he is considered as such, is hardly troubled in spirit, but being, by a certain eternal necessity, conscious of himself, and of God, and of things, he never ceases to be, but always possesses true peace of mind.

If the way I have shown to lead to these things now seems very hard, still, it can be found. And of course, what is found so rarely must be hard. For if salvation were at hand, and could be found without great effort, how could nearly everyone neglect it? But all things excellent are as difficult as they are rare.

Objections and Replies

FROM THE CORRESPONDENCE BETWEEN
SPINOZA AND TSCHIRNHAUS

I. Tschirnhaus on Freedom[1]

. . . Both Descartes, who argues for free will, and you, who argue against it, seem to me to be speaking the truth, as each of you conceives of freedom. For Descartes calls that free which is not compelled by any cause, whereas you call that free which is not determined by any cause to something. So I acknowledge, with you, that in everything we are determined by a definite cause to something, and so that we have no free will, but on the other hand I also think, with Descartes, that in certain matters (as I shall immediately explain) we are not in any way compelled, as so have free will. I shall take an example from what I am presently doing.

There are three things to consider in this matter: (1) Whether we have, absolutely, some power over things outside us? To this I say "no." For example, it is not absolutely in my power that I now write this letter, since I certainly would have written earlier if I had not been prevented either by the absence, or by the presence of friends. (2) Whether we have, absolutely, power over the motions of the body, which follow, when the will determines them to some motion? This I answer with a qualified "yes," namely, provided we are living in a sound body. For if I am healthy, then I can apply myself to writing or not. (3) Whether, when I am permitted to exercise my reason, I can use it completely freely, that is, absolutely? To this I say "yes." For who could deny (without contradicting his own consciousness) that in my thoughts I can think either that I want to write or that I do not. As far also as the act of writing is concerned (this concerns the second question), I have indeed the capacity either to write or not to write because external causes permit this. I acknowledge, indeed, with you, that there are causes which determine me to this, that I am now writing, namely, because you first

wrote to me and in doing so asked me to reply as soon as I could, and because there is now an opportunity, which I would not willingly lose. But I also affirm as certain, on the evidence of consciousness and with

---

[1] From Letter 57, Tschirnhaus to Spinoza, 8 October 1674.

Descartes, that things of that kind do not thereby compel me, and that notwithstanding these reasons, I really can omit this [act of writing]. It seems impossible to deny this.

Also, if we were compelled by external things, who could acquire the habit of virtue? Indeed on this assumption every wicked act would be excusable. But does not it often happen that we are determined to something by external things and yet we resist it, with an unyielding and constant spirit?

II. Freedom and Necessity[2]

. . . I pass to that definition of freedom which he says is mine. But I do not know where he got it from. I say that a thing is free if it exists and acts from the necessity of its own nature alone, and compelled if it is determined by something else to exist and produce effects in a certain and determinate way. For example, even though God exists necessarily, still he exists freely, because he exists from the necessity of his own nature alone. So God also understands himself, and absolutely all things, freely, because it follows from the necessity of his nature alone that he understands all things. You see then that I place freedom not in a free decree, but in free necessity. IV/265

But let us descend to created things, which are all determined by external causes to exist and to produce effect in a certain and determinate way. To clearly understand this, let us conceive something very simple—say, a stone which receives a certain quantity of motion from an external cause which sets it in motion. Afterward the stone will necessarily continue to move, even though the thrust of the external cause ceases, because it has this quantity of motion. Therefore, this permanence of the stone in motion is compelled, not because it is necessary, but because it must be defined by the thrust of the external cause. What is to be understood here concerning the stone should be understood concerning any singular thing whatever, no matter how composite it is, and capable of doing a great many things: that each thing is necessarily determined by some external cause to exist and produce effects in a certain and determinate way. IV/266

Next, conceive now, if you will, that while the stone continues to move, it thinks, and knows that as far as it can, it strives to continue to move. Of course since the stone is conscious only of its striving, and not

---

[2] From Letter 58, Spinoza to Schuller for Tschirnhaus. Sentences in italics seem to be quotations from a letter from Tschirnhaus to Schuller.

at all indifferent, it will believe itself to be free, and to persevere in motion for no other cause than because it wills to. And this is that famous human freedom which everyone brags of having, and which consists only in this: that men are conscious of their appetite and ignorant of the causes by which they are determined.

So the infant believes that he freely wants the milk; the angry boy that he wants vengeance; and the timid, flight. Again, the drunk believes it is from a free decision of the mind that he says those things which afterward, when sober, he wishes he had not said. Similarly, the madman, the chatterbox, and a great many people of this kind believe that they act from a free decision of the mind, and not that they are carried away by impulse. Because this prejudice is innate in all men, they are not easily freed from it. For though experience teaches abundantly that there is nothing less in man's power than to restrain his appetites, and that often, when men are torn by contrary affects, they see the better and follow the worse, they still believe themselves to be free, because they want certain things only slightly, so that their appetite for these things can easily be restricted by the memory of another thing which they recall more frequently.

With this, if I am not mistaken, I have explained sufficiently what my opinion is concerning free and compelled necessity, and concerning that fictitious human freedom. From this it is easy to reply to your friend's objections. For when Descartes says that he is free who is compelled by no external cause, if he understands by a man who is compelled one who acts unwillingly, then I grant that in certain things we are not at all compelled, and in this respect we have free will. But if by compelled he understands one who acts necessarily, though not unwillingly, then (as I have explained above) I deny that we are free in anything.

But your friend affirms, for his part, that *we can use the exercise of our reason completely freely, that is, absolutely.* He persists in this opinion with great—not to say too much—confidence. *For who,* he says, *would deny, except by contradicting his own consciousness, that I can think, in my thoughts, that I will to write, and that I do not will to write.* I should very much like to know what sort of consciousness he is speaking about, beyond that which I have explained above in the example of the stone. For my part, unless I contradict my consciousness, that is, contradict reason and experience, and unless I encourage prejudices and ignorance, I deny that I can think, by any absolute power of thinking, that I do will to write and that I do not will to write. But I appeal to his consciousness, for doubtless he has experienced that in dreams he does not have the power of

IV/267

thinking that he wills to write and does not will to write. Nor when he dreams that he wills to write does he have the power of not dreaming that he wills to write. Nor do I believe that he has learned anything less from experience than that the mind is not always equally capable of thinking of the same object, but that, as the body is more capable of having the image of this or that object stirred up in it, so the mind is more capable of contemplating this or that object.

When he adds, moreover, that the causes of his having applied his mind to writing have indeed prompted him to write, but have not compelled him to, all that signifies (if you wish to examine the matter fairly) is that his mind was then so constituted that causes which could not have caused him to go in that direction at another time (e.g., when he was torn by some great affect) could at that time easily do this. That is, that the causes which could not compel him at another time have now compelled him, not to write unwillingly, but to necessarily have a desire to write.

As for what he has maintained next—*that if we were compelled by external causes, no one could acquire the habit of virtue*—I do not know who has told him that it cannot happen from a fatal necessity, but only from a free decision of the mind, that we should have a strong and constant disposition.

And as for what he adds finally—*that if this is assumed, all wicked conduct would be excusable*—what of it? For evil men are no less to be feared, nor are they any less destructive, when they are necessarily evil. . . . Finally, I should like your friend, who raises these objections to me, to tell me how he conceives the human virtue which arises from the free decree of the mind to coexist with God's preordination. If he confesses, along with Descartes,[3] that he does not know how to reconcile these things, then he is trying to hurl at me the spear by which he himself is already pierced through. . . . IV/268

III. Tschirnhaus on Problems about the Attributes and Infinite Modes[4]

. . . First, would you be willing, Sir, to convince us by some direct demonstration, and not by a reduction to impossibility, that we cannot know more attributes of God than thought and extension? Moreover, does it follow from that that creatures which consist of other attributes cannot IV/275

[3] Cf. Descartes, *Principles* I, 39–41.
[4] From Letter 63, from Schuller to Spinoza on behalf of Tschirnhaus, 25 July 1675.

conceive extension, so that there would seem to be constituted as many worlds as there are attributes of God? For example, our world of extension, so to speak, exists with a certain abundance. So also, with the same abundance, would there exist worlds which consist of other attributes. And as we perceive nothing besides extension except thought, so the creatures of those worlds would have to perceive nothing but the attribute of their own world and thought.

Second, since God's intellect differs from our intellect both in essence and in existence, it will have nothing in common with our intellect, and therefore, by IP3, God's intellect cannot be the cause of our intellect.

Third, in P10S you say that nothing in Nature is clearer than that each being must be conceived under some attribute (which I see very well), and that the more reality or being it has, the more attributes belong to it. From this it would seem to follow that there are beings which have three, four, and so on, attributes. Nevertheless, one could infer from the things which have been demonstrated that each being consists of only two attributes, of some definite attribute of God and the idea of that attribute.

IV/276
Fourth, I would like examples of those things which are produced immediately by God, and those which are produced by the mediation of some infinite modification. Thought and extension seem to me to be examples of the first kind; examples of the second kind seem to be, in thought, intellect, and in extension, motion, and so on.

These are the doubts which our Tschirnhaus and I would like you to clear up, if your spare time permits. . . .

IV. On Knowledge of Other Attributes and Examples of Infinite Modes[5]

IV/277
. . . To your first doubt I say that the human mind can only achieve knowledge of those things which the idea of an actually existing body involves, or what can be inferred from this idea itself. For the power of each thing is defined solely by its essence (by E IIIP7). But (by IIP13) the essence of the mind consists only in this, that it is the idea of a body which actually exists. And therefore, the mind's power of understanding extends only to those things which this idea of the body contains in itself, or which follow from it. But this idea of the body neither involves nor expresses any other attributes of God than extension and thought.

[5] From Letter 64, Spinoza to Schuller for him and Tschirnhaus, 29 July 1675.

For (by IIP6) its object, namely, the body, has God for a cause insofar as he is considered under the attribute of extension, and not insofar as he is considered under any other attribute. And so (by IA6) this idea of the body involves knowledge of God only insofar as he is considered under the attribute of extension.

Next, this idea, insofar as it is a mode of thinking, also (by IIP6 again) has God for a cause insofar as he is a thinking thing, and not insofar as he is considered under any other attribute. Therefore, (by IA6 again) the idea of this idea involves knowledge of God insofar as he is considered under thought, but not insofar as he is considered under another attribute.

It is evident, then, that the human mind, *or* the idea of the human body, neither involves nor expresses any other attributes of God besides these two. From these two attributes, moreover, or from their affections, no other attribute of God (by IP10) can be inferred or conceived. And so I infer that the human mind cannot achieve knowledge of any other attribute of God beyond these, as was proposed. IV/278

You ask in addition, whether as a result there are not as many worlds constituted as there are attributes? On this, see E IIP7S.

Moreover, this proposition could be demonstrated more easily by reducing the thing to an absurdity. Indeed, I usually prefer that kind of demonstration when the proposition is negative, because it agrees better with the nature of such propositions. But because you ask only for a positive demonstration, I pass to the second thing, which is, whether one thing can be produced by another from which it differs, both with respect to essence and with respect to existence. For things which differ in this way from one another seem to have nothing in common. But since all singular things, except those which are produced by their likes, differ from their causes, both with respect to essence and with respect to existence, I do not see any reason for doubting here. Moreover, I believe I have already explained sufficiently (in E IP25C and S) in what sense I understand that God is the efficient cause both of the essence and of the existence of things.

We form the axiom of IP10S (as I indicated at the end of that scholium) from the idea which we have of an absolutely infinite being, and not from the fact that there are, or could be, beings which have three, four, and so on, attributes.

Finally, the examples [of infinite modes] which you ask for: examples of the first kind [i.e., of things produced immediately by God] are, in thought, absolutely infinite intellect, and in extension, motion and rest; an example of the second kind [i.e., of those produced by the mediation of some infinite modification] is the face of the whole universe, which [face], although it varies in infinite ways, nevertheless always remains the same. On this, see L7S before IIP14 [II/101–102]. . . .

V. Tschirnhaus on Knowledge of Other Attributes[6]

IV/279 I ask you for a demonstration of what you say: namely, that the soul cannot perceive more attributes of God than extension and thought. Although I see this evidently, still it seems to me that the contrary can be deduced from E IIP7S. Perhaps this is only because I do not perceive the meaning of this scholium accurately enough. I have decided, therefore, to explain how I deduce these things, begging you urgently, Sir, to be willing to come to my aid with your accustomed kindness, wherever I do not follow your meaning rightly.

Here is how things stand. Although I gather from that scholium that the world is absolutely unique, still it is no less clear also from that scholium that it is expressed in infinite ways. And therefore each singular thing is expressed in infinite ways. From this it seems to follow that that modification which constitutes my mind and that modification which expresses my body, although it is one and the same modification, is nevertheless expressed in infinite ways, in one way through thought, in another through extension, in a third through an attribute of God unknown to me, and so on to infinity, since there are infinitely many attributes of God, and the order and connection of the modifications seem to be the same in all.

From this, now, the question arises why the mind, which represents a certain modification, and which same modification is expressed not only in extension, but also in infinite other ways, why, I ask, does the mind perceive only that modification expressed through extension, that is, the human body, and no other expression through other attributes? . . .

VI. Each Thing Is Expressed by Many Minds[7]

IV/280 To reply to your objection, I say that although each thing is expressed in infinite ways in the infinite intellect of God, nevertheless those infinite ideas by which it is expressed cannot constitute one and the same mind of a singular thing, but infinitely many minds, since each of these

---

[6] From Letter 65, Tschirnhaus to Spinoza, 12 August 1675.
[7] Letter 66, Spinoza to Tschirnhaus, 18 August 1675.

infinite ideas has no connection with any other, as I have explained in the same scholium, that to E IIP7, and as is evident from IP10. If you will attend a bit to these things, you will see that no difficulty remains.

VII. Tschirnhaus Presses His Objection[8]

Regarding the objection [he] most recently made [in Letter 65], he replies that those few words I had written at your request [relaying the contents of Letter 66] have opened your meaning to him more intimately, and that he had already harbored the same thoughts (since [your words in the *Ethics*] chiefly admit of explanation in these two ways). But two reasons led him to follow the train of thought which was contained in the objection recently made.

IV/302

First, that otherwise PP5 and 7 of Book II seem to him to be opposed. In the first of these it is maintained that objects are the efficient cause of ideas, which nevertheless seems to be overturned by the demonstration of the latter, because of the citation of IA4, or (as I rather persuade myself) I do not apply this axiom rightly, according to the intention of the author, which, of course, I would be very glad to learn from him, if his affairs permit it.

The second reason which prevented me from following the explanation given was that in this way the attribute of thought is held to extend itself much more widely than the other attributes. But since each of the attributes constitutes the essence of God, I certainly do not see how the one is not contrary to the other.

In any case, let me add this: if I may judge other understandings from my own, IIPP7 and 8 will be very difficult to understand, for no other reason than that it has pleased the author (no doubt because they seemed so evident to him) to provide them with such short demonstrations and not to explain them with more words. . . .

VIII. Spinoza Replies Again[9]

. . . I do not see what [Tschirnhaus] finds in IA4 which seems to contradict IIP5. For in this proposition it is affirmed that the essence of each idea has God for a cause insofar as he is considered as a thinking thing; but in that axiom it is affirmed that the knowledge *or* idea of an effect depends on the knowledge *or* idea of its cause.

IV/305

To confess the truth, I do not sufficiently follow the meaning of your

[8] From Letter 70, from Schuller to Spinoza, on behalf of Tschirnhaus, 14 November 1675.

[9] From Letter 72, Spinoza to Schuller for Tschirnhaus, 18 November 1675.

letter in this matter, and I believe that there is a slip of the pen, due to haste, either in your letter or in his copy [of the *Ethics*]. For you write that in P5 it is affirmed that objects are the efficient cause of ideas, whereas this is expressly denied in the same proposition. And it is from this, I now think, that all the confusion arises. So it would be pointless for me now to undertake to write about this more fully. I ought to wait until you explain his mind more clearly to me and I know whether he has a copy which is adequately corrected. . . .

IX. TSCHIRNHAUS ON DEDUCING THE EXISTENCE OF BODIES[10]

IV/331 . . . it is only with great difficulty that I can conceive how the existence of bodies, which have motions and shapes, is demonstrated a priori. For in extension, considering the thing absolutely, no such thing occurs. . . .

X. ON THE USELESSNESS OF DESCARTES' PRINCIPLES OF NATURAL THINGS[11]

IV/332 . . . from extension, it, that is, as a mass at rest, it is not only difficult to demonstrate the existence of bodies, as you say, but quite impossible. For matter at rest, insofar as it is in itself, will persevere in its rest, and will not be set in motion unless by a more powerful external cause. For this reason I did not hesitate, previously, to affirm that Descartes' principles of natural things are useless, not to say absurd.

XI. TSCHIRNHAUS PRESSES THE OBJECTION[12]

IV/333 I would like you to oblige me in this matter by indicating how, according to your meditations, the variety of things can be shown a priori from the concept of extension. For you recall Descartes' opinion: he maintained that he could not deduce it from extension in any other way than by supposing that this was brought about in extension by a motion started by God. In my opinion, therefore, he does not deduce the existence of bodies from a matter which is at rest, unless, perhaps, you would consider the supposition of God as a mover to be nothing. For you do not show how [the existence of bodies] must necessarily follow a priori from God's essence, something which Descartes believed surpassed man's grasp.

---

[10] From Letter 80, Tschirnhaus to Spinoza, 2 May 1676.
[11] From Letter 81, Spinoza to Tschirnhaus, 5 May 1676.
[12] From Letter 82, Tschirnhaus to Spinoza, 23 June 1676.

So I ask this of you, well knowing that you have other thoughts—unless perhaps there is some other valid reason why you have so far not wished to make this plain. And if this [concealment] had not been necessary, which I do not doubt, you would not indicate such a thing so obscurely. But be assured that whether you indicate something to me openly or whether you conceal it, my feeling toward you will always remain unchanged.

Nevertheless, the reasons why I would particularly desire an explanation of this are these: I have always observed in mathematics that we can deduce only one property from any thing considered in itself, that is, from the definition of any thing; but if we want to deduce more properties, it is necessary for us to relate the thing defined to others; then, indeed, from the conjunction of the definitions of these things, new properties result.

For example, if I consider only the circumference of a circle, I will not be able to infer anything except that it is everywhere like itself, *or* uniform, by which property, indeed, it differs essentially from all other IV/334
curves. Nor will I ever be able to deduce any other properties. But if I relate it to other things, such as the radii drawn from the center, or two lines intersecting [within the circle], or also to other lines, I shall certainly be able to deduce more properties from this.

In some way, in fact, this seems to be contrary to E IP16, nearly the most important proposition in Book I of your Treatise. In this proposition, it is assumed as known that from the given definition of any thing many properties can be deduced. This seems to me impossible, if we do not relate the thing defined to other things. And it has the further result that I cannot see how, from any attribute considered by itself, for example, from infinite extension, the variety of bodies can arise. Or if you think that this too cannot be inferred from one considered by itself, but can be inferred from all of them taken together, I should like you to explain how this would be conceived. . . .

XII. Spinoza's Last Reply[13]

You ask whether the variety of things can be demonstrated a priori from IV/334
the concept of extension alone. I believe I have already shown sufficiently clearly that this is impossible, and that therefore Descartes defines matter badly by extension, but that it must necessarily be defined by an attribute which expresses eternal and infinite essence. But perhaps I will treat these matters more clearly with you some other time, if life

---

[13] From Letter 83, Spinoza to Tschirnhaus, 15 July 1676.

lasts. For up till now I have not been able to set out anything concerning them in an orderly way.

IV/335   But as for what you add—that from the definition of any thing, considered in itself, we can only deduce one property—perhaps this is correct for very simple things, or beings of reason (under which I include shapes also), but not for real beings. For from the mere fact that I define God to be a being to whose essence existence pertains, I infer many of his properties: that he exists necessarily, that he is unique, immutable, infinite, and so on. In this way, I might bring up many other examples, but for the present I will omit them. . . .

INDEX

NOTE: This index † is intended to provide a basic guide to the key concepts of Spinoza's philosophy, as represented by the works selected for this volume. The construction of an index for a set of translations presents formidable problems, arising mainly from the frequent lack of a one-to-one correspondence between the terms of the original text and those of the translation (but compounded in the case of Spinoza by the fact that, whereas the original text is usually in Latin, sometimes it is in Dutch). I have discussed and attempted to deal with those problems in the glossary-index of volume 1 of the *Collected Works of Spinoza* (Princeton University Press, 1985), but cannot undertake anything so complex here. Students who may want to undertake a more comprehensive investigation of Spinoza's terminology, can consult the glossary-index of that volume. ‡

Page numbers marked with an asterisk contain definitions.

†I am very much indebted to my wife Ruth for her work on the construction of this index, as well as for her help with the proofreading of the text.

‡The electronic version of that volume is available now with a very fast and powerful search program from InteLex Corp., P.O. Box 1827, Clayton, Georgia, 30525-1827. (This provides, in effect, a complete concordance to the text.)